The New Appalachian Trail

The New Appalachian Trail

EDWARD B. GARVEY

Illustrations by
Sharon H. Garvey

MENASHA RIDGE PRESS
Birmingham, Alabama

Copyright © 1997 by Edward B. Garvey
Printed in the United States of America
Published by Menasha Ridge Press
Distributed by the Globe Pequot Press
First Edition, Sixth Printing, 2005

Text and Cover Design by Grant Tatum
Cover Photo of Ed Garvey in the Bigelow Mountain Range by Sharon H. Garvey
Back Cover Photo by Chuck Logan
Interior photos © 1997 by Ed Garvey except pages 2 and 3 courtesy of Steven M. Krech, Boy Scout Troup 118; pages 12 and 15 by Harold Arnovitz; pages 88, 105, 130, 131, 154, 188, 249, 259, and 264 (top) by Sharon H. Garvey; page 129 by Eddie Watson; page 147 courtesy of Mike Callahan; page 163 courtesy of Chris Gibson; pages 178 and 183 courtesy of the Appalachian Trail Conference; page 185 courtesy of Dan Bruce; page 190 courtesy of Appalachian Outfitters; page 192 by Tex Griffith; and page 221 by Linda White.
Illustrations © 1997 by Sharon Garvey except page vi by Juliet Menéndez

Library of Congress Cataloging-in-Publication Data
Garvey, Edward B.
    The new Appalachian Trail / by Edward B. Garvey;
    illustrations by Sharon H. Garvey.
        p.   cm.
    ISBN 0-89732-209-6
    1. Hiking—Appalachian Trail. 2. Appalachian Trail—Description and travel.
    I. Title.
GV199.42.A68G37   1997
796.51'0974—dc21
                                        97-10897
                                        CIP

Menasha Ridge Press
P.O. Box 43673
Birmingham, AL 35243
www.menasharidge.com

Table of Contents

Dedication vi
Acknowledgments vii
Foreword ix
1 The Trail and I 1
2 An Appalachian Hiker–At Age 75 9
3 Finding and Hiking The Trail 176
4 Food 193
5 Evaluating Equipment 217
6 The Pack 222
7 Sleeping 232
8 Clothing 237
9 Footwear 244
10 Not Necessary but Nice 258
11 Trail Etiquette 261
12 Trail Acquisition and Management 268
13 Miscellany and Concluding Thoughts 284
A Appendix: Appalachian Trail Maintaining Clubs 299
B Appendix: Honorary Members of the ATC 301
C Appendix: Recorded Appalachian Trail Hikers 304
Appalachian Trail Conference Membership Enrollment Form 310

Dedication

This book is dedicated to the memory of Edward Hanlon, my long-time hiking companion and very close friend, who died suddenly of a heart attack September 18, 1996.

Juliet Menendez

Acknowledgments

Many people and organizations have assisted me in this adventure—some while I was hiking the Trail, others by providing a specific piece of information needed for the preparation of this book. The names of many already appear within the pages of this book. In making these acknowledgments, I know full well that I will fail to remember the names of some worthy individuals, and for this I apologize.

My thanks to: Arthur and Myrtis Benoit; Charlie Huppuch; members of the Benton MacKaye Trail Association and the Georgia Appalachian Trail Club for the wonderful send-off in north Georgia, April, 1990; George and Sandra Owen; Chuck Logan; Tillie Wood and Dorothy Mauldin; Dorothy and Jeff Hansen; Marty Dominy and Dave Sherman for providing refreshments for 800 miles of the hike; Dr. and Mrs. Fletcher Raiford; Sam Waddle; Byrl McKinney; Charlie Trivett; Ed Hanlon; Pete Hudson; Mark Elliott and Sandra Bernoi; Warren Doyle; Dick Cates; Ken Miller; Carl McMurray and family; Barbara Tolbert; Russel Norton; Bill Miller; Ed Seibert; Judy Jenner; Levi Long and wife Jan; The Brits—Tim Osman and Melanie Dean; Homer and Therese Witcher; John and Pam Carr; Jeff Kingsbury; Chuck Young; Dick Kelly; J.P. McMullin; Mrs. Ruth Duff; Jack and Dorothy Carlic; Andy Reece; Gary Eanes; Rusty Nesbitt; Tom Bellamy; Tom Freling; Erick Mathias; Larry Linebrink; Bill Wade, Superintendent of Shenandoah National Park; Jerry and Joan Hyndman, Frank Harrison; Peyton Robertson; Ron Tipton; Emerson Bowman, for providing off-trail transportation in Maryland; Ken Osterman, for providing transportation, lodging, and food at his summer home in Maryland; Frank O. Moore; Dave Parsons, caretaker of the Leroy Smith Shelter in Pennsylvania; Rex Looney, trail maintainer; Hugh O'Hara and Jim Longo, who provided me with a small tape recorder; Mrs. Frances DuBois, volunteer at the Boiling Springs, Pennsylvania

ATC office; Jack Scanlon, U.S. State Department employee; John Garman, owner and manager of a rooming house in Boiling Springs, Pennsylvania; Frank Spirek and Dianne Ensminger, thru-hikers and fellow "guests" at the Doyle Hotel in Duncannon, Pennsylvania; Eddie Watson, AT hiker who drove my van to Maine and accompanied me on the climb up Katahdin; Mark Di Miceli, who provided first aid and bandaged my eye in Maine; Chris Monroe and Chris Gibson; Charlie Sweet; Larry Young and Bowdoin Neally at Antlers Camp, for providing a meal and information; Jeff Walker; Roseanne Tallentire, who provided me with some much needed food in Maine; Steven Krech, for furnishing pictures of my Boy Scout days in the twenties and thirties; *The Dakota County Tribune;* Lila Johns of Appalachian Outfitters, for providing information and cost figures for backpacking equipment; Don King; Jean Cashin, Laurie Potteiger, and the staff at the Appalachian Trail Conference headquarters in Harpers Ferry, West Virginia.

Foreword

This is the third book I have written on hiking the Trail from one end to the other. The first, published in 1971, described my 1970 hike from Georgia to Maine. The second book, published in 1978, was an update of the first. This third book describes what was intended to be another Georgia-to-Maine hike at age seventy-five.

Much as I have enjoyed backpacking, I had no burning desire to participate in another end-to-end hike of the Trail in a single year. Between the 1970 and 1990 hikes, I hiked extensively on the Trail, sometimes on seven- to ten-day trips, many times for a shorter duration. And, through an odd quirk of fate, I found myself on numerous hiking trips in Yugoslavia and even one in eastern Siberia. The decision to do another thru-hike started at the 1983 general membership meeting of the Appalachian Trail Conference in New Paltz, New York.

David Sherman, of the National Park Service, and Ronald Tipton, of The Wilderness Society, had been discussing the exciting progress being made by the U.S. Forest Service and the National Park Service in acquiring the Trail right-of-way from Georgia to Maine. At the speed land was being acquired, they felt that by 1990, the entire Trail right-of-way would have been secured and the maintaining clubs would have completed the relocations and marking. David and Ronald felt it would then be a great time to hike the "new Appalachian Trail." They had discussed the idea with three-time thru-hiker Albie Pokrob, who agreed to do it one more time. They asked if I would join them.

Actually, the hike they proposed was not entirely new to me. On several occasions, when I visited the National Park Service Appalachian Trail Project office in Harpers Ferry, then Project Manager David Richie would inform me of the progress being made on the land acquisition work. He would conclude by saying only somewhat in jest, "Ed, when this land is all acquired, you are going to have to hike the Appalachian Trail one more time and then write another book on it." So, when presented with a specific proposal and date, I readily consented. It would mean that I would have three younger and stronger men to assist in the project, and I would welcome the companionship. So it was that, on April 14, 1990, I found myself at the southern terminus of the Trail on Springer Mountain in north Georgia, surrounded by more than thirty members of the Benton MacKaye Trail Association (BMTA) and the Georgia Appalachian Trail Club (GATC); I was about to set forth on my second attempt to thru-hike the Appalachian Trail. Ironically, because of job and family commitments, the other three men were forced to forego the hike.

I wish to express my thanks to Judy Jenner, editor of the *Appalachian Trailway News,* and to David M. Sherman for reviewing my manuscript and offering helpful suggestions; and my special thanks to my daughter, Sharon, without whose help this book would never have been published.

Edward B. Garvey
1997

1

The Trail and I

This is a story of the Appalachian Trail, the famous footpath that stretches more than 2,000 miles along the crest of the Appalachian Mountains from Maine to Georgia. Specifically, it is the story of my own hike along this exciting trail during the period between April 14, 1990, and September 5, 1990.

As I stood there that spring day at the southern terminus of the Trail, about to begin the long hike north to Maine, I found myself surrounded by friends and well wishers. I contemplated the 2,000 mile hike ahead of me, just as I had twenty years before, and wondered if I would really make it to Katahdin way up north in Maine . . . and I wondered what adventures would come my way during the months on the Trail. The events of my life certainly had prepared me for this final long-distance hike at the age of 75.

In 1926, in the little town of Farmington in southern Minnesota, two events took place that certainly had some bearing on my later hiking activities. The first was the high school principal's announcement that a Boy Scout troop was about to be formed. This coincided with my birthday, November 13, when I turned 12—then the minimum age for becoming a Scout. I became a charter member of that Boy Scout troop. One of those who assisted the high school principal in forming the troop was a 17-year-old high school junior named Kenneth E. Parr. Remarkably, on October 7, 1970, when I completed my 2,000-mile-long hike at Katahdin and hiked back to the base camp at Katahdin Stream Campground, on hand to meet me was this same Kenneth E. Parr, then 60 years of age, who, with his wife Ingrid, had motored over from Vermont to congratulate me. But let's get back to 1926.

As I moved through the Scouting ranks—Second Class, First Class, and on toward Eagle—I found that many of the requirements emphasized hiking, camping, and outdoor cooking. The skills thus acquired in those years of Scouting were later to stand me in good stead. I drifted away from Scouting and

Ed as a young Boy Scout in Farmington, Minnesota.

Boy Scouts Ed Garvey and Fred Grunewald at Square Lake Boy Scout Camp, Stillwater, Minnesota, 1932.

hiking for about a 15-year period and did not again become involved until 1952. My wife and I and three children had moved to Falls Church, Virginia, in 1949. In 1951, I learned of the Appalachian Trail and the Potomac Appalachian Trail Club (PATC). The PATC maintained some 300 miles of hiking trails in Pennsylvania, Maryland, and Virginia, as well as some 19 trailside shelters and 13 locked cabins. They also issued high-quality maps of the hiking trails, primarily the Appalachian Trail, in those states. I promptly purchased a complete set of the 14 maps available at that time.

By this time my oldest son, Dennis, had joined a Boy Scout troop in Falls Church. In 1952, I was prevailed upon to accompany the troop for three or four days to the Herbert Hoover Boy Scout Camp in nearby Shenandoah National Park. In order to give the Scoutmaster a breather, I volunteered to take 13 of the boys on an overnight hike to one of the nearby trailside shelters on the Appalachian Trail. We spent the night at the Lewis Falls Shelter, sharing it with its lone occupant, Francis A. Smith, M.D., of Buffalo, New York. Smith, although a lifelong resident of Buffalo, had joined the Washington, D.C.–based PATC in 1950. As we sat around the campfire that July night, we listened on Smith's radio to the proceedings of the Republican National Convention, which was in the process of nominating Dwight D. Eisenhower as the Republican presidential candidate. I also listened to Smith as he urged me to join the PATC.

I joined PATC in October 1952. One of the first publications I received, the January–March 1953 issue of the *PATC Bulletin,* contained an article describing the 2,000-mile hike of the Appalachian Trail by PATC member George Frederick Miller, age 72. This article captured my imagination. Quite possibly, that was when I first entertained vague thoughts of someday hiking the entire Trail myself. Some 16 years later, when my plans for my own hike became rather definite, I went to my stock of *PATC Bulletins*, and from near the bottom of the pile, pulled the one on Miller's hike. One feature of his hike was a preprinted daily log form on which he recorded pertinent information each day of the hike. This idea I borrowed lock, stock, and barrel.

In 1953, two other events occurred that gave indication of my growing involvement with the Trail and its maintenance. I volunteered to become an overseer for a three-mile section of the Trail in Maryland . . . some 70 miles from my home. As an overseer, it was necessary for me to make from three to five trips a year to my section of the Trail to remove any fallen logs or trees, to cut out summer growth, and to see that the Trail was properly identified by white paint blazes, by the four-inch diamond-shaped metal marker, and by wooden directional signs. In addition to the overseer job, I did the planning for, and participated in, the first Trail hike of any consequence conducted by Boy Scout Troop 681. This first hike was a modest affair in which two adult leaders, each with seven or eight boys, began hiking on the Trail at either end of the Shenandoah National Park. One group hiked north, the other south. After four days of hiking, staying each night at a trailside shelter, each group arrived at the Herbert Hoover Boy Scout Camp where they stayed for another week. I participated in these annual hikes for two more years and did the planning for another two before bowing out. The same Boy Scout Troop still conducts these annual hikes along the Trail.

During the years 1952, 1953, and 1954, I became increasingly aware of the Appalachian Trail Conference (ATC) and the role it played in coordinating the activities of the many clubs that maintain the Trail. In 1956, while on a three-week business trip to South Carolina, I attended the three-day Labor Day Get-Together at Roan Mountain, Tennessee, a meeting of the five hiking clubs that maintain the Trail in Georgia, North Carolina, Tennessee, and southwestern Virginia. At this gathering I was gradually extending my knowledge of the Trail and the hiking clubs that maintain it.

My involvement in affairs of both the PATC and ATC became increasingly heavy in the next few years. I became Supervisor of the Trails for PATC in 1959 and served in that capacity for six years, directing the efforts of some 60 volunteer overseers in trail maintenance work, and, in one season, 1962, directing the renovation of the Club's 19 trailside shelters. In 1960, I spent the night at the Indian Run Shelter in Shenandoah National Park and chanced to meet Lochlen Gregory and Owen Allen on their 99-day hike from Georgia to Maine. In the next few years I met on the Trail a number of thru-hikers: Ray Baker in 1964;

Elmer Onstott and Everett and Nell Skinner in 1968; and Jeff Hancock and Eric Ryback in 1969. I met and talked to many others who had hiked the entire Trail—to such an extent, that I had become acquainted with over half of the small fraternity of some 40 people who had hiked the entire Trail through 1969.

During these years I had also extended my own hiking on the Trail. Hiking frequently with Maurice A. (Gus) Crews of Bethesda, Maryland, I had covered all of the 462 miles in Virginia, Maryland's 37 miles, and sizeable chunks of the Trail in Pennsylvania and Maine. These, plus bits and pieces of hiking in Georgia, North Carolina, Tennessee, and New Hampshire, had given me a pretty good idea of what I could expect over the entire Trail. I had become active in the affairs of the ATC, serving as Secretary from 1964 to 1967 and remaining as a member of the Board of Managers from 1967 to 1972 and from 1977 to 1981.

On March 18, 1935, I became an employee of the federal government. As each St. Patrick's Day rolled around, I completed exactly one more year of service. I worked 23 years for the Soil Conservation Service in the Department of Agriculture; and then, in October 1958, I accepted the position of Finance Officer with the National Science Foundation, which I held until I retired. For years, I planned to retire on March 17, 1975. That would have given me exactly 40 years of service; and for a person of Irish descent, March 17 seemed like an appropriate day to have a retirement party and call it quits. Unanticipated circumstances, however, can cause a change in even the best laid plans. The National Science Foundation underwent a major reorganization in 1969; this included extensive personnel changes. In October of that year I suddenly faced a situation in which retirement, then and there, seemed to be the expedient thing to do. Retire I did on October 31, 1969.

With retirement a reality, my long-held dream to hike the entire Trail moved from the realm of the possible to the feasible . . . even to the probable. True, I had a wife to consider; moreover, the two youngest of our five children were still of school age. There was the distinct possibility that my wife would take a very dim view of her husband's being on the Trail for over five months. Married men reading this book will certainly appreciate my predicament. I sent up a few tentative smoke signals. No outward reaction. I sent up more and stronger signals. Still no reaction. I interpreted this as calm acceptance of the inevitable, and I proceeded to make definite plans.

There are two ways to plan a hike of this magnitude. One way is to tell no one of your plans. Then, if you decide you have had enough after a few days or a few weeks, no one is the wiser, and no embarrassing explanations are in order. The other way is to tell everyone of your plans. Then, you have no choice. Unless death or injury intervenes, you must complete the entire hike. I chose the latter method. Notice of my hike appeared in the January 1970 issue of Trailway News. Shortly before my hike began, I gave a midday talk to members of PATC on my plans and preparations. I was totally committed.

In late March, my wife, my 11-year-old son Kevin, and I took a short Easter-week vacation trip to the Florida Everglades. On our return, we arrived at Amicalola Falls State Park in northern Georgia on the afternoon of April 3. Bob Harrell, outdoor editor for the *Atlanta Constitution* was there, and we talked at some length about my hike, my equipment, and my plans for inspecting trailside shelters and Trail conditions. The Henry Morrises, the Ed Seiferles, and the Al Thompsons of the Georgia Appalachian Trail Club also arrived at the Park about the same time we did. We stayed overnight at a cabin with the Morrises and the Seiferles. After an early Saturday morning breakfast, we set out in a six-car caravan to Nimblewill Gap. There I met for the first time my hiking companion from Kansas City, Elmer Schwengel. Picture-taking, a few words of prayer by Jim Engle of the Georgia club, a farewell to my wife and son, and I was hiking with Schwengel toward Springer Mountain, the southern terminus of the Trail. I reached the summit of Springer at noon on a beautiful spring day; the temperature was 68 degrees. I signed the register and noted that one Branley C. Owen of Brevard, North Carolina, had signed the register on April 3, one day ahead of me. He had indicated on the register sheet that he was hiking all the way to Maine. I thought it quite possible that I might catch up with Owen somewhere along the Trail, but this was not meant to be. Owen broke all existing records for speed, arriving at Katahdin in Maine on June 12, 1970, a mere 117 days ahead of me.

After signing the register at Springer, I walked a few yards south to the viewpoint directly beside the bronze plaque marking the southern terminus of the Trail. There I met Major Garnett W. Martin of Denver, Colorado, who had hiked the entire Trail in 1964. Martin had come back to revisit some of the more interesting points along the Trail. I finished the trail 187 days later, on October 7, 1970. Twenty years later, I returned to hike the Trail again.

The 20-year interval marked a very exciting period of my life. I continued to be active in both the ATC and the PATC. I worked on a part-time basis for 10 years at Appalachian Outfitters, an outdoor store in Oakton, Virginia, some eight miles from my home. I was employed by the U.S. Information Agency on a short-term contract to participate in five outdoor recreation exhibits in such places as Yugoslavia, the USSR, and Hungary. The two Soviet exhibits lasted six weeks each, with one of them in Moscow, the other in Irkutsk in eastern Siberia. I traveled via the TranSiberian railway for four days and nights in order to reach Irkutsk near the shore of Lake Baikal. The country of Yugoslavia fascinated me and I took five trips there on my own, leading groups of hikers over the mountains of Slovenia and Croatia. My final trip in 1989 found me hiking in the mountains of Serbia. And, I continued my hiking on the Trail with three friends of mine—Ed Hanlon, Bill Husic, and Cletus Quick. I hiked all of the Trail from Wesser, North Carolina, to Springer Mountain, Georgia, in 1976; all of it from Katahdin to Monson, Maine, in 1977, as well as sizeable distances in the other 11 Trail states.

Before I talk about those five million steps required to propel me to Katahdin in Maine, let me explain just what this Appalachian Trail is, who conceived it, who constructed it, who maintains it, and why so many people have the desire to hike it. The Appalachian Trail is a 2,000-mile-long footpath extending from Maine to Georgia generally along the crest of the Appalachian Mountain chain. It is one of the longest continuous marked footpaths in the world.

The idea for the Trail was first conceived by a young man, Benton MacKaye, in the early 1900s. It was not until 1921, however, that MacKaye put his thoughts down on paper; his article, "An Appalachian Trail, A Project in Regional Planning," appeared in the October 1921 issue of the *Journal of the American Institute of Architects*. MacKaye's proposal for a long-distance hiking trail caught the public fancy. Meetings were held, and work was begun. The first sections of the Trail were constructed and marked in 1922 and 1923 in the Palisades Interstate Park in New York. The first meeting of the Appalachian Trail Conference was held in Washington, D.C., in 1925.

Unfortunately, this early enthusiasm soon waned, until Arthur Perkins, a retired lawyer of Hartford, Connecticut, rescued the project in 1926. Perkins promptly enlisted the aid of Myron H. Avery. For the next four years, Perkins, as Chairman of the Conference, and Avery, as a loyal hardworking assistant, ensured the eventual success of the Appalachian Trail project. Not only did they work assiduously on the project themselves, but they also enlisted the support of scores of other capable people from Maine to Georgia. In 1930, Perkins died, and Avery was elected Chairman of the Conference in 1931. He occupied that post for 21 years, and during most of those same years he served as President of the Washington, D.C.–based PATC. It was under Avery's stewardship that the Appalachian Trail was finally completed and the "Golden Spike" (to borrow the railroad term for completion of the first transcontinental railway) was driven on the final few miles of the Trail in Maine on August 15, 1937.

A complete history of the Trail appears in the member handbook of the ATC. It was compiled largely by Dr. Jean Stephenson, herself a veteran of almost half a century in the Appalachian Trail Project. Although I have been involved in this project for almost 40 years, I still read this history with awe, marveling that people like Perkins, Avery, and others could have accomplished so much in so short a time. It strikes me that this was an amateur volunteer recreation effort with few, if any, parallels. It was, first of all, a tremendous promotional effort to inform and to stir up enthusiasm for the project, to stimulate the formation of hiking clubs, and to obtain commitments from people and organizations—first to create the Trail and then to maintain it. During the 15-year trail-building period, various groups were involved in studying feasible routes, in actually laying out the Trail, in clearing it, in marking it with paint blazes and directional signs, and in measuring it with a bicycle wheel calibrated to hundredths of a mile. Finally, there was the job of developing narrative descriptions of the Trail, north to south, and south to north, so that guidebooks could be printed to assist hikers in their traverse of the Trail. That these things could have been accomplished by volunteers seems truly amazing. The ATC had no paid employees for the first 40 years of its existence. Those who worked on behalf of the project did so on their own time, and rarely were they reimbursed for expenses incurred.

In these few words, I have described how the Trail came to be. But what is it? Primarily a wilderness foot trail, the Trail exists for those who wish to hike a few hours, a few days, a few weeks, or for several months. The Trail is marked with an extensive side-trail system that permits hikers to plan a variety of side hikes and circuit hikes while using the Trail as a base of operations. The Trail is studded with simple, rustic, overnight trailside shelters available to hikers on a first-come, first-serve basis. Although the Trail generally follows the crests of the mountain ranges, it frequently cuts across valleys, through rural areas, and either skirts or passes directly through small villages and towns. It can be beastly hot in summer and alarmingly cold in midwinter. There are days in midsummer when you drip with perspiration, and gnats, mosquitos, deerflies, and no-see-ums make life miserable. There are days when you walk through stinging nettles and poison ivy; times when your feet are wet for days on end due to rain, heavy dew, or wet spots on the Trail; days when firewood is wet and campfire smoke seeks you out with an unerring sensor system and makes your eyes water and your nose run.

But more than compensating for these things are spring days, clear and sunny, cool at night, warm at midday, when you walk through thousands of acres of wildflowers—bluets, spring beauties, and trilliums. There are summer days, when you can hike lightly clad, with a cool breeze on your face, a song in your heart, and not a care in the world. There are autumn days in Maine when you can look across a mirror-calm lake framed by white birch and flaming red maples while spruce and fir trees provide a dark green background. There are times when, hot and thirsty, you come across delightful ice cold springs, and the simple act of drinking deeply of cold, clear water fills you with a feeling of gratitude and appreciation that you would never have thought possible. There are cool nights when you put on additional clothes and sit quietly beside a campfire, watch it slowly die, and crawl into your sleeping bag and revel in the delightful warmth that only a 98.6 degree body and a good sleeping bag can produce. There are nights when you are overcome with the incredible sense of well-being that results from strenuous exertion, a good meal, and a mind free from worry; nights when sleep comes so quickly you barely have time to recall and fix in your mind some of the more outstanding sights and events of the day; nights when you will thank God for having the good health and great fortune to be where you are, enjoying some of Nature's best. This is the Appalachian Trail. Neither words nor pictures can adequately describe it. Only those who have partaken of its pleasures and endured its hardships can fully appreciate it.

2

An Appalachian Hiker— At Age 75

THE CALIFORNIA PRELUDE

My Appalachian Trail hike was scheduled to begin in Georgia on April 14, 1990, but first I had to get there, and strange as it may seem, I began my journey south by heading west. I left my home in Falls Church, Virginia, on March 30 and flew to California, where it so happened I had some unfinished hiking activities. These activities would also serve to complete my conditioning for the Trail hike. My reason for going to California at this particular time was an economic one. I had two Delta Airlines senior citizen tickets good anywhere in Delta territory, and those tickets were set to expire as of April 13.

In 1985, on a visit to California, I had become intensely interested in the history of the 21 Spanish Missions built between 1760 and 1824 in a line stretching from San Diego in the south to Sonoma in the north. Inspired by the book *Christwalk*, by Richard Roos, S.J., I decided to make a pilgrimage of sorts, during which I would visit all 21 missions on foot. The spring of 1986 found me at the Franciscan mission in San Diego, from which I hiked northward for 392 miles to Mission San Luis Obispo. In 1989, I hiked another 362 miles from San Luis Obispo to Mission Dolores in San Francisco. I had planned to hike all the way to Sonoma, but my companion, Karl Ellingston, a man who in his earlier years had hiked the entire Appalachian Trail and later the entire Pacific Crest Trail, decided that he had had enough by the time we reached San Francisco; so I likewise terminated my 1989 hike at that point.

But now it was 1990 and I was in San Francisco to complete the remaining miles of my pilgrimage. On the morning of March 31, eight of us gathered at Mission Dolores. Among the group were Stan and Jane Bergler Turnbull of PATC, plus one or two others who had hiked with me for one day in 1989 on the route from Mission Santa Clara to Mission San Jose. Also in the group were Arthur and Myrtis Benoit of Pebble Beach, California, who had hiked with me for several weeks in Yugoslavia in 1986.

It was a pleasant three-day walk with friends through the steep streets of San Francisco, across the Golden Gate Bridge, and along the shore of the Bay of San Francisco with Alcatraz clearly visible. We stopped on the first night at San Rafael, where I attended church services at the mission on Sunday morning. Our group arrived at Sonoma mid-afternoon on April 2. Sonoma is one of the two missions that is no longer church affiliated. It is operated as a state park, and one of the park officials, Christian Boyer, greeted us. When the Benoits explained to him that I had hiked all the way from San Diego, visiting each mission en route, Mr. Boyer became very attentive. He provided us with a personal tour of the mission, gave us a few mementos, and had me sign the VIP guest book, pointing out that Lady Bird Johnson had signed just three lines above me. I was flattered by this extra attention, but after hiking more than 800 miles to reach Sonoma I felt I had earned my spurs. Mr. Boyer told us his name is of French origin and is pronounced Christy-ANNE Boy-AIRE. He is the great, great grandson of General Vallejo, who owned vast acreages in California and who was successively a citizen of Spain, Mexico, and the United States, reflecting the changing ownership of California in the 19th century.

Still, my mission hike was not quite officially over because there was one small stretch I had missed. On my 1989 hike, I had heeded the wishes of Father Clifford, the Franciscan in charge of the San Miguel mission near Paso Robles, and skipped a 23-mile section of the mission route just north of San Miguel. The good father stoutly maintained that there were no overnight accommodations for the next 40 miles north, and that he wished to give me a ride for 23 miles, after which I could hike the remaining 17 miles or so to Mission San Antonio de Padua. My son Kevin, who was hiking with me at the time, concurred with the priest; so it was that I skipped the 23 miles.

Now in 1990, I took the bus to San Miguel Mission, and the next morning Father Clifford drove me 23 miles to the same point where he had dropped me off the previous year. I began hiking south through the rolling hill country of the Valley of the Oaks. It was a great day for hiking and I arrived back at the mission in late afternoon.

The next day I went down to the Los Angeles area by bus to visit my two sons and their families, and to get in another day of hiking and conditioning in the Angeles National Forest. I had done much strenuous conditioning all during the spring of 1990 to prepare for my thru-hike of the Trail, and during those two weeks in California I carried my heavy Kelty backpack almost every day, including the arduous day of hiking in Angeles National Forest.

THE HIKE

Thursday, April 12
Los Angeles, California, to Atlanta, Georgia

"This, the last day my air ticket was valid, I flew to Atlanta, Georgia, and was met late in the afternoon by Chuck Logan, a fellow member of the 'Old Pros,' a group of friends with whom I had hiked for the last five years, and whose motto is proudly displayed on our t-shirts: 'Often Wrong, Never in Doubt.' Chuck took me directly to a church supper being conducted at the Tenth Street United Methodist Church.

"After the meal, I attended the impressive Holy Thursday services at the same church. The services were conducted by the Reverend George Owen, another member of the Old Pros.

"George is a hard-working member of the Benton MacKaye Trail Association, which is presently building a new 250-mile trail in Georgia, Tennessee, and North Carolina along the route recommended by Benton MacKaye at the time he wrote about the need for the long-distance Appalachian Trail. George had also done much work to see that my 1990 Trail hike would begin in an auspicious manner. He had written articles, arranged for a send-off breakfast, and a host of other things. After the church services that evening, George and his wife, Sandra, took me on a nighttime tour of the unbelievably fast-growing city of Atlanta. I was amazed at the number of 40-, 50-, and 60-story skyscrapers that had been built recently or were under construction. I got to bed at midnight at the Owens' home."

Friday, April 13
Take-Off Day Minus One!

"After breakfast at the Owens' house, George drove me to the regional office of the U.S. Forest Service. The Atlanta regional office is responsible for Forest Service work in eight southeastern states, including six of the eight national forests through which the Appalachian Trail passes.

"The first person I met was Charlie Huppuch, whose responsibilities include the Appalachian Trail. I had first met Charlie during my 1970 hike, when he was stationed with the George Washington National Forest in Harrisonburg, Virginia. At that time, he and a companion intercepted me on the Trail, took my two companions and me to the Lake Sherando Recreation Area, cooked us a steak dinner, and then put us up at a Forest Service bunkhouse. Such courtesies are never forgotten. Charlie was also active in the design and building of some innovative Appalachian Trail shelters. (See entry for July 9)

"Later that day, I met Jim Milner, who had hiked with me for a day in 1970 when he was still working out of the supervisor's office in Gainesville, Georgia. Our conversations on that day centered on trails and shelters. After that hike in

1970, during which not only Jim Milner, but also Paul Sweetland, the assistant regional engineer, and Neil Hunt, then of the *Gainesville Daily Times*, participated, the Forest Service produced a very attractive and functional trail-shelter design, which has been embodied in shelters at Low Gap and Tray Mountain, to name just two.

"From the time I first became active in the Appalachian Trail movement, about 1953, and for about 15 years thereafter, my principal interest was in the maintenance of the Trail and the Trail shelters. Beginning in about 1968, when the National Scenic Trails System Act was passed, I began to focus increasingly on the land-acquisition program. I reasoned that, even if the Trail became badly neglected and the shelters fell into disrepair (neither of these things has happened), the important thing was to acquire the land. If we were able to acquire a corridor of sufficient width, stretching from Springer to Katahdin, we could, in time, remedy other shortcomings.

"In personal conversations, in letters, in articles written for publication, and, occasionally, in testimony before Congressional committees, I expressed my strong feelings on this subject. In the southeastern states, most of the land needed for the Trail corridor lay within the boundaries of the six national forests under the jurisdiction of the Atlanta regional office. Therefore, I made it a point to visit with the land-acquisition people in that office. My notes are not as complete as they might be, but they show that I visited with Bill Kane and Chuck Steele, who headed the land-acquisition effort for the entire region. I was cour-

Breakfast with Rev. George Owen of the Benton MacKaye Trail Association.

teously received, and we had some interesting and productive conversations about land acquisition.

"After leaving the Forest Service office, I visited Peter Kirby, regional director of The Wilderness Society. Then it was a quick lunch with Peter, and George and Sandra Owen, and a visit to the Catholic church in downtown Atlanta to participate in Good Friday services. I knew from my 1970 experience that I would not have many opportunities to attend church during the next five months.

"Dinner that night was at the Owens' home. Then at 7:30 P.M., there was a special reception with several trail enthusiasts, including Margaret Drummond, the ATC Chairman. Other Trail enthusiasts attending included Nancy Shofner, Ted and Kay Reissing, Marty Dominy, Chuck Logan and his friend, Joyce Guillory. Kay gave me three sacks of goodies and Joyce presented Chuck and me each with a loaf of nut bread. Chuck would accompany me for the first 14 days of the hike, all the way to Fontana. It was a very pleasant evening."

Saturday, April 14
Springer Mountain to Hawk Mountain Shelter, Georgia
2.6 miles

"Day One! D-Day! Take-Off Day! Up at 5 A.M., starting off the day with coffee and one half of a huge muffin. George and I drove to the Wagon Wheel restaurant in Dahlonega. Some 25 Trail enthusiasts were already there, the result of planning by George Owen. People were in high spirits, and conversation buzzed with the spirit of excitement and anticipation in the air. I met many old friends, some new ones, and people with whom I had corresponded but had never seen.

"Among this latter group was David Hughes, a young man who had written me that he would provide any shuttle service I might need, and who shot a whole roll of film at breakfast and the send-off. He later sent me a complete set of slides of the occasion. There was Van Hill, who made arrangements with the Claxton Bakery to provide me with fruitcake throughout my hike; he mailed the one-pound cakes to me at various points along the Trail. Also sending me off was Tillie Wood, owner of a restored house and bunkhouse for Appalachian Trail hikers, just south of Pearisburg, Virginia; she extended me a warm invitation to stay there when I reached that area (I did!). Another man I had met before, but had not seen for years, was Jim Davis. Jim was stationed with the armed services in Germany when he obtained and read my first *Appalachian Hiker* book. He promptly became a member of the ATC. Later he became a life member; still later, he enrolled his two sons as life members.

"The group departed after breakfast in 12 cars bound for the parking area near Springer Mountain. We hiked the one-and-a-half miles from the parking area to the official starting point of the Trail. Almost everyone signed the register that is housed in a large rural-type mailbox atop Springer. There was much picture-taking before we gathered in a semi-circle, and I addressed the group, thanking them for the enthusiastic send-off and expressing my thanks to the volunteers who maintain the Trail. The Reverend George Owen then offered a fine blessing and the group of 30 or more was ready to begin hiking.

"Our group, augmented by seven or eight others who also happened to be starting the long hike on this particular day, began hiking north from Springer Mountain at 10 A.M. Those who wished to hike just a few miles had rides waiting for them at various stop-off points. Good planning by George Owen. The most prominent of these stop-off points was a place called Three Forks, where a small delegation was waiting for us. Among the group was Marty Dominy, then president of the BMTA, who provided a bottle of champagne to properly celebrate 'Take-Off Day.' Another greeter was Edwin Dale, also an active member and former president of the BMTA, who provided an ample supply of cold beer for us thirsty hikers. Finally, there was Carol Moore of Laguna Beach, California, a 1989 Appalachian Trail thru-hiker who was now back to make a video of 1990 hikers. (A year later, I would see the results of her work at the premier showing of her videotape at Appalachian Trail Days in Damascus, Virginia.) Good-byes were said to those who were discontinuing their hike at that point. The rest of us proceeded to Hawk Mountain shelter, arriving there at 4:20 P.M. There were 14 people staying at the shelter, six of us inside, eight in tents outside.

"I found myself sleeping next to a man to whom I had spoken at length on the telephone, but whom I had never met. His name was Dick Cates, a prosecuting attorney from Madison, Wisconsin. His prominence can be gauged by the fact that, in 1974, when impeachment proceedings were being contemplated for President Nixon, Cates was brought to Washington, D.C., to assist in the prosecution work. Cates remained in Washington for nine long months, but his services were no longer required once President Nixon resigned from office. When Cates contemplated hiking the Trail, he mentioned it to his old friend, former Senator Gaylord Nelson. Nelson gave him my name, and I received a phone call from Cates.

"The Hawk Mountain shelter is old and rather small. Its capacity is about six people (more if it's raining!). In such cases, it is difficult NOT to become acquainted with shelter occupants who are sleeping only inches away from you on either side.

"At the shelter, many members of both the GATC and the BMTA bid me farewell and headed for home. But, before leaving, they picked up all the litter, about 25 pieces, around the shelter and carried it out. The Trail from Springer Mountain to Hawk Mountain had been very clean; there was perhaps a total of 10 pieces of litter.

"My pack weight was 37 pounds, plus two pounds for the camera. I was carrying very little food because I had a hefty food box waiting for me at Neels Gap, about 30 miles from the starting point.

Hikers and Trail enthusiasts gathered at Springer Mountain on Take-Off Day. Chuck Logan stands at far left.

Edwin Dale and author at Three Forks, Georgia, first day of hike. (Note invitation to "Champagne Brunch" on sign.)

"So ended Day One, a day I shall never forget. And, I shall always be grateful to those who contributed so generously to make it such a joyous event."

On this day, and for the next 136 days, I was to find very little litter. This was a VERY pleasant improvement over my first hike in 1970, when picking up litter became a real chore.

■ ■ ■

Let me explain the type of record keeping that I attempted for each day of the hike. First, I used a 5- x 8-inch bound and unlined journal in which I filled about a page a day with notes indicating the beginning and ending points of each day's hike, as well as any events of particular interest. In the back of the book, I recorded names and addresses of people I met, and with whom I planned to correspond at a later date. The second type of record was a printed daily log. I accumulated these logs until I had perhaps 10 to 12 of them, and then mailed them to the ATC headquarters in Harpers Ferry. The ATC office made copies and mailed them to the pertinent maintaining Trail club. Copies were also distributed to offices of the National Park Service and the U.S. Forest Service where those offices shared trail-maintenance responsibilities.

A third record I maintained were the guidebooks. There are 10 guidebooks covering every mile of the Trail, and each includes north-to-south and south-to-north descriptions. In 1970, the ATC provided me with the south-to-north portions of the guidebooks, and I religiously signed and dated each sheet as I hiked, correcting the information as needed. I planned to perform the same chore in 1990, and the ATC once again mailed the books to me along the Trail, as I needed them. Unfortunately, I had neither the time nor the energy to complete each sheet in the same meticulous manner as I had done in 1970. I am apologetic about this aspect of my hike, but I did refer to the guidebooks frequently enough to observe that there is a lack of uniformity among the 10 books. So much for the record keeping, a very necessary part of the hike if one is to do any writing on the subject.

Sunday, April 15
Hawk Mountain Shelter to Woody Gap (GA 60)
12.4 miles

"With the excitement of Take-Off Day behind me, I began the routine of rising early, eating a light breakfast (frequently cold), and heading on my way as soon as I could make it. This was Easter Sunday, and I began hiking at 8:10 A.M. I fell into step very shortly with Eddie Bannon, 57, from New Jersey.

"Eddie, a second-generation Irish-American, recounted another Easter Sunday some 70 years earlier, when his father, who was then living near Dublin, Ireland, had set out on foot with a machine gun to participate in the Easter Rebellion against the British. The British had all bridges secured, so the elder Bannon forded a river and reached Dublin only to find that the rebellion had been quelled. Had it been otherwise, Eddie might not have been hiking the Trail and telling me the story!

"The hiking today was tough and exhausting. I had hiked through these mountains on my 1970 trip, and again in 1977, when Ed Hanlon, Bill Husic, and I hiked south from Wesser, North Carolina, to Springer Mountain. But, I was 55 years of age in 1970 and 62 in 1977. Now, I was 75 and I began to find the climbs from gaps to summits really grueling. I found these four ominous words in my notes: 'beginning to have doubts!'

"At one of the gaps, we encountered a young man, Lee Selman. He told me that he and his two children had risen at 3:30 A.M. to drive to the Trail and intercept me. He was not a member of the ATC or the Georgia club. I do not know how he knew I was coming through at that particular time. He said he had read my book through and through, and he asked me about certain people whose names had appeared in the book. He said he just wished to meet me and take my picture. Chuck Logan agreed to take the photo with Selman's camera. I posed with Selman and his children. That done, Selman thanked us, shook our hands, and departed. His mission was accomplished. I'm still puzzled on that one; perhaps some day I'll learn the answer.

"I had planned to spend the night at Gooch Gap shelter, but Jim Davis, who was hiking with us, suggested we push on for another 3.6 miles to Woody's Gap and be his guests overnight at the 1,000-acre R Ranch for which he was the executive director. We readily agreed. When we did reach Gooch Gap, we found Edwin Dale there with a cooler of cold Strohs beer! We also learned that Carol Moore had been there earlier and had left food for me at the shelter. I left it to be enjoyed by those staying there.

"Chuck Logan, Davis, another hiker, Pierce Cline, I believe, and I reached Woody Gap at 6:40 P.M., and were whisked over to the R Ranch by Mrs. Davis, where we were treated to a big pizza. I settled into bed at 10 P.M. It was a great day, even though those steep grades were killing me."

Monday, April 16
Woody Gap to Neels Gap
10.7 miles

"Up at 5:30 A.M., showered and shaved. Cereal breakfast . . . heated water on the hot plate . . . how convenient. Got an early start. Driven to Woody Gap by Jim Davis. Began hiking at 8:10 A.M., carrying light day-packs only. Beautiful day. Excellent views through the leafless trees. Especially sensational views from summit of Blood Mountain.

"Reached Neels Gap at 4:30 P.M. Coming down from Blood Mountain, found Marty Dominy waiting for us with a cooler of beer! What a treat! How thoughtful. The big food box I had prepared at home was waiting for me. Ate the house dinner—spaghetti and meat sauce with salad. The salad was the best part, that and the homemade bread.

"Drove with George Owen the 11 miles to Hiawassee to hear an evening performance of the Dekalb County Symphony. Back at Neels Gap at 10:45 P.M. To bed in dorm, to sleep immediately."

Tuesday, April 17
Neels Gap to Low Gap Shelter
10.6 miles

"Good sleep, did not have to make nightly visit(s) to toilet! Up at 6:55 A.M. Bought the house breakfast, excellent at $3.13—scrambled eggs, muffin cake, juice, orange slices. Left Neels Gap at 9:10 A.M. Slow, slow going the 5.5 miles to Tesnatee Gap. Trail steep and eroded to rock. Reached Tesnatee Gap at 2 P.M. Enjoyed lunch on top of Cow Rock with Andy and Lorraine Arroms of Ohio. Continued with the grind after lunch—trails not so steep. Encountered two smart-ass teenagers who defiantly discarded litter and cut switchbacks. Unpleasant. Picked up their litter, finally caught up with them, and discussed their behavior. Reached Low Gap shelter at 6:30 P.M. Room for me in shelter. Chuck put up his tent. Rain and wind threatened, so Chuck put my tarp over his tent. Others tied their tarps over the front of the shelter. Shelter floor 3- to 4½-feet off the ground. Using table to get into shelter. Shelter also had ample service table outside under the eave.

"Rain still threatening, sprinkled a bit. Everyone in the sack. For evening meal, can of chili plus Joyce Guillory's homemade cake and cookies. Wrote a few notes until light rain put a stop to it. Rained hard during the night."

Wednesday, April 18
Low Gap Shelter to Tray Mountain Shelter
15 miles

"Up once during night. I slept poorly—the coffee, perhaps, but I did NOT hear the howling of hunting dogs reported by others. Up at 6:50 A.M., cold (42 degrees) and windy. Put my shirt and pants on over my pajamas. Ate cold cereal, then HOT coffee with banana bread. On our way at 8:10 A.M. Extremely pleasant hiking in the warm sun. Wore our long-sleeved shirts and warm caps until lunch. Reached the new, and rather small, Blue Mountain shelter at 12:40 A.M. Excellent view. Ate another of Sandra Owen's chicken sandwiches. Writing these notes at 1:15 P.M. at shelter. Have hiked eight miles, seven more to go!

"Staggered into Tray Mountain shelter at 7:40 P.M., dead tired. Ate a light supper—a three-ounce can of tuna plus bread, an egg, much coffee. All in bed by 8:20 P.M., with seven or eight of us in the big shelter. Wind howled all night. Slept well in the sack for 11 hours. Had no time for any paperwork. Hiked some 15 miles. Too much for me. Others arrived in shelter from 4:30 P.M. on. I just don't have it anymore."

In 1970, following roughly the same route, I arrived at Tray Mountain shelter at 4:45 P.M. I was then age 55. Now, at 75, it took me three hours longer. Those 20 years did take their toll!

Thursday, April 19
Tray Mountain Shelter to Plum Orchard Gap Shelter
15 miles

"All of us overslept (6 in the shelter, 25 camping nearby). Up at 7:20 A.M., sun shining, but wind blowing at 20 to 25 miles-per-hour from the east. All of the hikers hastily put on warm clothes. I began hiking without breakfast. Ate breakfast on the Trail around 9 A.M. Another grueling day. Reached Addis Gap about noon, but did not walk the 0.3 miles down to the shelter. Ate lunch on the Trail around 1 P.M. Reached Dicks Creek Gap after crossing Kelly Knob at around 3,800- to 4,000-foot elevations. Kept on trudging. Good grades coming north from Dicks Creek Gap, but even moderate grades are murder for me. Am having some back problems.

"Arrived at Plum Orchard Gap shelter around 6:20 P.M. Karyn Hartel (and others) had a fire going. Great! Heated water for coffee. The two Weithman brothers from Ohio gave us extra food, including a noodle and cheese dinner, which Chuck Logan promptly prepared for our supper. All of us watched the fire until 9:20 P.M., when I was the last of the six in the shelter to call it a day. A most enjoyable evening, great camaraderie.

"On my daily logs, which I have mailed to the Appalachian Trail Conference, I appended the following note for the April 18 and 19 logs: 'Apologies for the lack of data. Two dawn-to-dusk hikes have left no time for writing up notes!'"

Friday, April 20
Plum Orchard Gap Shelter, Georgia, to Deep Gap, North Carolina
12 miles

"Up at 5 A.M.; put more wood on fire, but it failed to catch. Up for good at 6:30 A.M.; put leaves on the coals in the fireplace, and got a good fire going. Heated water for many; served John Keane coffee in his tent. He was startled,

The Walasi-Yi Center at Neels Gap, GA.

but pleased. Left shelter at 8:20 A.M. Our destination, Standing Indian shelter across the border into North Carolina. Temperature was 42 degrees at 7 A.M. Foggy all day, poor visibility, much warmer, some wind. Wore a long-sleeved shirt most of the day. Walking not too strenuous except northbound at Bly Gap, entering North Carolina where it is extremely steep. A group of five of us walked together most of the day. Ate lunch at the big A-frame Muskrat Creek shelter, capacity 20 people or more. Began hiking again at 2 P.M., four miles to go to Standing Indian shelter.

"As we hiked north from Muskrat Creek shelter I observed the biggest stands of ramps (rampions) I had ever seen. One field of a half acre, another of two acres. The others in the group had not recognized them, but now, having done so, they stopped hiking and picked a goodly supply for future consumption.

"Around 3:30 P.M., we were surprised to be greeted by George Owen, who had driven 156 miles to meet us. He suggested that Chuck Logan and I drive with him to Franklin, North Carolina, and stay overnight there. We agreed immediately. Walked to within a half mile of Standing Indian shelter and left the Trail at Deep Gap and drove into Franklin. Ate dinner at the very good B & D restaurant. Then, over to Henry Motel, $18 for a double for Chuck and George; a single for me at $16.20. Very reasonable.

"I phoned Jack Coriell, a long-time trail worker for the Nantahala Hiking Club, over whose trails we would be hiking for the next several days. We agreed to meet for breakfast and to hike together the next day. George and Chuck took all our dirty clothes and washed them at a laundromat. After that, George and I reviewed my itinerary and changed my expected time of arrival at the Outdoor Center in Wesser, North Carolina, from April 23 to April 25. I promptly phoned Dr. William B. (Chan) Chandler in Hendersonville, North Carolina, one of the Old Pros, to alert him to the schedule change. I expected to meet him about April 24 or 25 on the Trail.

"I'm afraid I'm the victim of drinking some bad water; my bowels are getting very loose. Chuck is having the same trouble.

"Finishing these notes at 11:30 P.M. in the motel, and have not even begun my daily logs for the past three days. Have a seven-mile day tomorrow. Will try to do some catch-up work at Carter Gap shelter. George delivered to me a cablegram from Belgrade, Yugoslavia, from my two young hiking friends, Misko and Maja, extending best wishes for a successful hike of the Appalachian Trail! How very thoughtful."

Saturday, April 21
Deep Gap to Carter Gap Shelter
9 miles

"Up at 5:30 A.M., overcast day. Finished my packing. Over to B & D restaurant for pancakes and sausage breakfast with old friend Jack Coriell, Don and

Beth Bradley, Bob and Judy Hughes—all veteran hikers. Jack had been supervisor of trails for the Nantahala Hiking Club for many years. Don had recently succeeded him in that position.

"After breakfast, we returned to the motel and weighed our packs. I weighed 162 without pack, 207 with pack. A 45-pound pack! Must get rid of some of that stuff!

"Drove back to Deep Gap in two cars. Started hiking around 9:30 A.M. Foggy and drippy. Began raining shortly, and continued for a good part of the day. Five were in our group, including George Owen, who carried my pack until noon, at which time he returned to Deep Gap and drove home to Atlanta. From that point on, Don Bradley carried my 45-pound pack, and I carried his day pack. Everybody was quite anxious to help an old man.

"I was very impressed with the eight miles of trail work I observed from Deep Gap to Carter Gap shelter, including a unique method of installing waterbars. Ate lunch at 2 P.M. at Beech Gap, then hiked on to Carter Gap shelter. Two hikers were already there, including Eddie Bannon.

"After an hour of trying, Chuck and I got a fire going in the makeshift fireplace in front of the shelter. By 6 P.M., we had a real fire, and did our cooking on it rather than the propane stove. Made a cream sauce and one six-ounce can of tuna for Chuck and myself.

"After supper, Marty Dominy arrived with a cooler of Budweiser beer. Greatly enjoyed by all. Later, we walked with Marty to Timber Ridge, where he returned to his car, drove into Franklin, and stayed at the same motel we had the previous night.

"Five of us in the shelter, none outside. All of us in the sack around 8:30 P.M. Watched our big fire blaze. Went to sleep around 9:30 P.M. Up at 11 P.M. to heed the call of nature and to put more wood on the fire.

"(Had expected a mere seven miles today; turned out to be nine!)"

Although I make no mention of it in my notes, I distinctly recall how impressed we were when it neared the time for Jack and Don to leave us. Jack simply opened his day pack, took out a tiny two-way radio, raised the antenna, and contacted his wife. The conversation went something like this: "Kay, this is Jack. We're here at Beech Gap having lunch. Expect to reach Carter Gap shelter at 4. Could you pick us up at the trailhead near Timber Ridge at 5? Good. See you at 5." Wow! It's hard for me to comprehend the changes that have occurred during my lifetime: from horse and buggy and horse-drawn sleds in winter, oil lamps, and outside plumbing, to airplanes, spaceships, television, computers, and even two-way radios on the Appalachian Trail!

Sunday, April 22
Carter Gap Shelter to Rock Gap Shelter
12 miles

"Up at 6:40 A.M. On our way at 8:15 A.M. Very pleasant day, beautiful trail, excellent views; walking through tunnels of rhododendron; nicest day of the trip so far. Moderate grades on the Trail, not nearly so tiring. Exception: the last 0.3 mile up a 30-percent grade on a rocky trail to the Big Albert firetower. Brutal! Ate lunch at the base of the firetower, then continued on the Trail to Big Spring shelter.

"Walked about a mile farther on the Trail when 'good ole' Marty Dominy caught up with us. With an ice cooler and beer in hand, he had both run and walked down the Trail to catch us. Chuck and I each enjoyed a beer, then took one can each with us to the Rock Gap shelter. We reached the shelter at 4:45 P.M. Enjoyed our beer, which we shared with Tim Gfroerer, a Georgia Tech graduate student.

"Chuck and I then proceeded to gather a supply of firewood. I worked on my notes until a light rain intervened. We used Chuck's stove to cook the evening meal, freeze-dried beef stew. It was adequate and filling, but I would not wish to eat it too often. It does not improve with age.

"Shaved after supper. Chuck got a large fire going. In bed around 8:30 P.M. Enjoyed the fire until 9:30 P.M. or later. Just three of us in the shelter, nobody camping outside. One of our more enjoyable nights, as were Plum Orchard and Carter Gap shelters."

Monday, April 23
Rock Gap Shelter to Siler Bald Shelter
8 miles

"Up at 6:30 A.M., put more wood on the fire but it did not catch. Chuck got it going at breakfast time. On our way at 7:40 A.M. Like yesterday, pleasant walking over well-maintained trail. Reached Winding Stair Gap at 10 A.M. Earlier, around 8 A.M., Ken Cruise intercepted me. He said he was a friend of Dan Bruce's. Chatted with him for about 10 minutes. Ate a light trail lunch around 10 A.M. Walked along good grades mostly over 4,000 feet. Excellent trail maintenance. Very frequent evidence of chain saw work from winter and spring blowdowns. Reached Siler Bald shelter at 1:10 P.M. and had lunch—hot soup, one egg, hot coffee, peanuts, and raisins. Robert Mackey of Williamsburg, Virginia, was already at the shelter.

"After lunch, I got busy on these notes, became drowsy, took a short nap. Robert built a big fire directly in front of the shelter, which is in a grassy area, and has a concrete table and wooden bench. Finishing these notes at 4:15 P.M. Will now get busy on daily logs.

"Worked 'til darkness, then to bed. Startled around 7:30 P.M. when Chuck, working some 20 feet in front of the shelter, let out a yell! He had almost

24

stepped on the resident skunk. The skunk scurried away, no more to be seen. I lay on top of my sleeping bag until 10 P.M., then crawled into it. A mouse ran over me once. Also, a busy rat made much noise."

Tuesday, April 24
Siler Bald Shelter to Cold Spring Shelter
12.4 miles

"Up twice during the night, second time around 3 A.M. when I put leaves and wood on the remains of our evening fire. Some time later, I was startled when leaves and wood suddenly burst into flame.

"Up for good at 6:30 A.M. Still some fire, but Chuck and I used his stove for hot cereal and coffee. I was the first to leave at 7:20 A.M., my earliest start so far. Hiked on blue-blazed trail 0.6 miles to the Appalachian Trail, and 20 minutes later, I climbed the steep 0.2-mile trail to the summit of Siler Bald, which has excellent views of the mountains north to the Smoky Mountains National Park and south to Georgia.

"Chuck caught up with me at 9 A.M. Pleasant hiking all day. Ate two light trailside lunches. Climbed to Wayah Tower at around 2:30 P.M. Reached Cold Spring shelter in the rain. Three days in a row for the afternoon rain. One of the locals informed us that the pattern was pretty routine.

"Chuck and I located two fields of ramps. We picked some and sauteed them for supper, mixing them with the freeze-dried beef stew. This made the stew much better. Ate the green tops as a salad, a part of my diet that suffers on these trips. Tomorrow, it's 12 miles into Wesser, and we hope to get there for dinner. Also hope to meet Chan Chandler there. Finishing these notes at 8:15 P.M., writing while standing at the serving table that rests on the 10-inch chestnut beams used by the Civilian Conservation Corps while building this shelter some 50 years ago. Chuck has a nice fire going. All enjoy it, but none of the young men offer to help gather wood. To bed around 9 P.M."

Wednesday, April 25
Cold Spring Shelter to Wesser, North Carolina
12 miles

"Up as soon as it was light enough to see. Temperature 52 degrees at 7 A.M. On our way at 7:30 A.M. Absolutely fantastic hiking, nice vistas, temperature just right. Stopped many times just to look and enjoy. Reached Tellico Gap at 9:50 A.M. Pushed on to Wesser Bald with its sweeping views. Ate lunch there. Proceeded north and was surprised to meet Chan Chandler and Dave Denison around 2:30 P.M. Enjoyed a snack from Chan's larder, including fresh fruit. Reached Rufus Morgan shelter around 3:15 P.M., and was disappointed—unimpressive, very small, low ceiling, made from 8- and 10-inch logs."

"Reached Nantahala Outdoor Center at 4 P.M. Enjoyed a huge dinner in the restaurant for $10, including soup and ice cream. Main dish was Sherpa Rice, with the same ingredients as Appalachian Trail Mix, with excellent seasonings, plus cheddar cheese and small sausages.

"Chan had reserved a four-bunk room in a house bearing the name 'Bartram 3.' We bought food supplies at a camp store, then headed to our room. Took a shower, washed clothes. What a treat! I returned to the campers' dining room, a mere 20 yards from our bunkhouse. Chan attempted to pop corn, a dismal failure. Worked on my notes while I toyed with burnt popcorn."

Thursday, April 26
Wesser, North Carolina, to Sweetwater Gap
15 miles

"We were up early and ate breakfast at the N.O.C. restaurant. I said goodbye to Dave Denison, who drove back to Hendersonville, North Carolina. I phoned my wife, because our 52nd wedding anniversary is April 27, but there would be no phones available to me that day! The three of us—Chuck Logan, Chan Chandler, and I—would now be hiking together for three days.

"The Trail over Swim and Cheoah balds, (very formidable in 1970) has been relocated to a large extent. Much easier grades, but still a strenuous climb from some 1,700-foot elevations at Wesser to 4,700 feet at Swim Bald, then a long descent, followed by the 5,062 foot climb up to Cheoah Bald. We spent a pleasant 45 minutes at Sassafras Shelter, ate lunch there, and pushed on to Cheoah.

"At that point, Chuck went ahead rapidly, stating we would camp at Stekoah Gap instead of Sassafras as originally planned. That would make it a 13-mile day, instead of 7. Chan and I stopped for 10 minutes atop Cheoah, which offers a spectacular view of the southern Appalachians and an attractive grassy vista, which is kept cleared. There is no water, but what a place to camp! Regretfully, Chan and I pushed on, arriving at Stekoah Gap at 7:30 P.M. to find Chuck just coming from Sweetwater Gap to the north, where he had left his pack. No camping is permitted at Stekoah Gap so we were forced to walk farther. Chuck carried my pack and we climbed two steep peaks before reaching Sweetwater Gap at 9 P.M.

"Connie Conover and Milton Herndon had a nice fire going. I put my sleeping gear under Connie's big tarp. Chan and Chuck wrapped themselves in tarps and fared passably. We all ate a quick cold cereal supper, plus bread. I slept well."

Friday, April 27
Sweetwater Gap to Cable Gap Shelter
7 miles

"52nd wedding anniversary. Up at 6:30 A.M., clear, beautiful red sunrise. Hot coffee, granola with dry milk, bread, and peanut butter hit the spot. Broke camp at 7:52 A.M. Leisurely, but strenuous, hiking over tops of several peaks. Would have been better if it had been slabbed. Saw a cluster of five pink lady's slippers.

"The three of us ate lunch at Cody Gap at 11:45 A.M. Excellent ice-cold spring. Surrounded by two acres of May apples and trillium in bloom. Tarried there a full hour. Drank a full quart of that excellent water.

"Reached Cable Gap shelter at 3 P.M. The shelter was renovated in 1988, was very clean. It had no table, but a good toilet. Loafed, snacked, worked on notes. Washed our t-shirts, partially dried them in the hot sun, put them on again.

"Coffee and bread with peanut butter at 4 P.M. Feels so-o-o good to have a few hours to relax. Difficult for me to write without a table. My back gives me fits. Writing these notes in stocking feet with my back propped against a wall. Now to complete my daily logs for yesterday and today."

"Had early supper. Finished the last of my freeze-dried beef stew, topped off with instant chocolate pudding, which I had prepared minutes after reaching the shelter. Chuck's fire lasted only 30 minutes before all the wood was gone. Three of us sleeping in the shelter. Chuck and one other fellow are in tents outside. Enjoyed a good night's sleep."

Cable Gap Shelter.

During some 35 years of backpacking, I have rarely had any back problems, but on this trip, my back gave me much trouble for nearly three weeks. The pain from carrying the heavy pack was matched by the pain from trying to write without a table or some other support. I tried writing while stretched out full length on a shelter floor, and found relief by propping my pack up against a tree or the shelter wall and leaning back against the pack. But, these were awkward ways to write. At the end of nearly three weeks, the pain began to diminish and gradually ceased altogether.

Saturday, April 28
Cable Gap Shelter to Fontana Dam
7.9 miles

"Up at 6:20 A.M.; dark. Finished the granola purchased at Wesser. Much hot coffee, bread and peanut butter. Almost all of our food gone. Rain began around 8 A.M. Pleasant walking, in spite of rain, and no really strenuous climbs. We had a 2 P.M. rendezvous with Dave Denison at NC 28, so we were in no real hurry. A most pleasant way to hike!

"Among the three of us, Chuck, Chan, and myself, we had fairly good knowledge of many plants and we taught each other. Saw perhaps seven to eight of the rare yellow lady's slippers. Saw jack-in-the-pulpit, acres of trillium, more acres of May apple—photographed one that was 16 inches in diameter.

"Rain stopped around 10 A.M. We continued our slow, enjoyable walking. Reached NC 28 an hour ahead of schedule. Chan remained on the road, waiting for Dave. Chuck and I proceeded on the Appalachian Trail to Fontana Dam, the biggest dam in the eastern United States. Chuck got a ride to the village to check on mail and messages. I waited for Dave and Chan. They arrived about 2:30 P.M.

"We drove to the registration center for rooms at the village. Cost of a room was listed in *The Philosopher's Guide* as $40 in 1989, but, reportedly, was much higher now. While I was cogitating over that information, a Dr. Fletcher Raiford, who had driven over from Hendersonville with Dave, offered to let us stay at his home in Hendersonville. I accepted!

"Chuck had learned that his lady friend, Joyce, was on the way from Atlanta in Chuck's car. We said goodbye to Chuck and the four of us drove to Hendersonville, a two-hour trip in heavy rain. Drove to Dave's home first for cake and coffee, then to the Raiford residence, a large house with space galore. More snacks, then a light supper.

"I learned that Fletcher, in his grammar school days, had visited the Natural History Museum in Washington, D.C. While at the museum, he had viewed with great interest a display showing the concept of the Appalachian Trail! He is a long-time ATC member and has done much Appalachian Trail hiking, including the section from Wesser to Fontana, which Chuck, Chan, and I had just completed.

"Weighed myself on the ancient bathroom scale—145 pounds, stripped, a loss of about 12 to 13 pounds since the beginning of my hike, and about the same as I had experienced on my 1970 hike. Still have a bit of blubber around the tummy, but my clothes are much looser.

"Phoned my wife, Mary, at 9:30 P.M. Learned that she and her friend, Lorraine Hanlon, were planning a trip to Hawaii, and then on to Singapore and Hong Kong, beginning May 15. Could not help but think this was a slight variation of the proverb, 'What's sauce for the goose is sauce for the gander!'"

A comment on Chuck Logan, a man in his upper 40s with a grown daughter. He was an inveterate weekend hiker and trail maintainer, but had never done any consistent day-to-day backpacking such as we had just accomplished. At the conclusion of our 15-day, 164-mile hike, I judged that he was definitely afflicted with "the bug," the desire to hike the entire Appalachian Trail! In the spring of 1991, he hiked from Fontana Dam to the north end of the Great Smoky Mountains National Park, about 70 miles. I'm confident he will accomplish his goal, with retirement not too many years away.

Sunday, April 29
Hendersonville, North Carolina

"Up at 5 A.M., made coffee, and snacked on peanuts and chocolate. Not your usual breakfast menu. Brought diary up to date for last two days. Went to 9 A.M. Mass with Chan at a pretty stone church. Nice service. Back at Raifords, worked rest of morning and most of afternoon on my trail notes and logs. Took a 20-minute walk after lunch and visited the pediatric clinic that Fletcher helped develop. Wrote many, many postcards. In late afternoon, walked to the nearby Chandler residence for dinner . . . a vegetarian stew plus some wonderful corn-bread. Met Chan's very likeable wife, Judy, and his 15-year-old daughter, Kate. Back at Raiford's at 9 P.M., and we compared notes on our trail food. Both Chan and Fletcher purchased mountains of food. And I've got a food drop waiting for me at Fontana! To bed at 10 A.M. Very pleasant day . . . got much done."

This was a day of rest. No hiking. Hikers love these occasional days, whether they fall on a Sunday or some other day. Two 2,000-milers who adhered to the "walk six then a day of rest" routine were Murray Chism and Ed Little, who hiked the entire Trail from March to November (yes, with snow on Katahdin!) in 1958. From Monday through Saturday, they hiked. On Saturday afternoon or evening, the wife of one of the two hikers would pick them up and drive them to a motel. Then, they treated themselves to a day of cleaning up and resting. On Monday, they would be deposited back on the Trail for another six days. Not a bad routine! But it's hard to come by wives who are willing to twiddle their thumbs in a lonely mountain area for five-and-a-half days a week while their ever-loving husbands are out hiking the Trail. Quite probably, a story written by Mrs. Little or Mrs. Chism as to how they spent *their* time from March to November of 1958 would have made good reading.

Monday, April 30
Fontana Dam to Birch Spring Shelter
5.2 miles

"Up at 5:30 A.M., drank coffee and had a few crackers. Finished my packing. At 7 A.M., Fletcher and I took off after bidding good-bye to his wife, Joyce. Drove to Chan's place, then to the home of Mead Parce, former reporter, editor, and much-traveled, very knowledgeable guy. The four of us then drove toward Fontana, stopping at McDonald's in Waynesville for breakfast. Reached Fontana at 10 A.M. Picked up my food box mailed from home, as well as eight pieces of mail. Sorted hurriedly through the mail, then repacked all the food into my pack. At 11:30 A.M., we drove over to the dam and examined the "Hilton" trail shelter built by the Tennessee Valley Authority, which sleeps 28 and has bathrooms, showers, and picnic tables. Said good-bye to Mead Parce, who drove Fletcher's car back to Hendersonville. Chan, Fletcher, and I began hiking over the dam at 12:10 P.M. A three-and-a-half hour hike . . . up, up, up, but generally on acceptable grades. Gained 2,000 feet in elevation by 3 P.M. Snacked at Shuckstack firetower and then walked the remaining mile to the Birch Spring shelter. This shelter is a rather dismal affair, even since the Park Service removed the wire bunks and installed wood sleeping platforms. No broom, toilet, or table, and sleeping platform rather dirty. This shelter area is used by horses. That plus the several small springs that seep through the shelter area give it an almost constant muddy aspect. We boiled our water. All of us in the sack by 8:30 P.M.

The trailside shelters in the Smokies are different from those elsewhere on the Trail. The typical Smoky Mountains shelter is 24 x 18 feet, is built of stone with a metal roof and a bear-proof cage across the open side, and has one 36-inch, indoor fireplace.

The shelter has six double-deck bunks (capacity 12), with floor space providing additional sleeping area. For perhaps 30 or more years, the bunks were covered with taughtly stretched wire. In 1989-1990, the Park Service began replacing the unpopular wire sleeping area with wooden sleeping platforms, a big improvement. There are no tables and no shelf spaces. All walls are stone, and straight up-and-down, with not even a fireplace shelf on which to put articles.

In 1970, each shelter had a latrine, but in 1990, there were none. Instead, open areas were designated by a sign, "Toilet Area," in which people of both sexes were expected to do their thing. It was the lack of toilet facilities that most bothered the 1990 hikers. This was the Great Smoky Mountains National Park, one of the crown jewels in the park system, and no privies? Some 400 miles to the north, in the Shenandoah National Park, each shelter along the 94 miles of the Trail has a table and a latrine. And, still farther north, way up in Maine, there are 28 shelters along the northernmost 264 miles of the Trail. All of them have latrines.

Perhaps the lack of latrines in the Smokies is due to the indifference of those maintaining the Trail and the shelters. In Maine, the work is done by volunteer members of the Maine Appalachian Trail Club; in the Shenandoah National Park, by volunteer members of the Potomac Appalachian Trail Club; in the Smokies, by paid employees of the National Park Service.

Tuesday, May 1
Birch Spring Shelter to Spence Field Shelter
9 miles

"Up four times during the night at Birch Spring shelter, but I slept well otherwise. Up at 6:30 A.M. and brewed a pot of real coffee. Left shelter at 8:30 A.M., reached Eklaneetlee Gap at 10:45 A.M., and Mollies Ridge shelter at 11:30 A.M. Ate lunch there. Evidence of horses using the Trail, horse droppings and trail damage. Pleasant two-hour stay at Mollies Ridge shelter. Fletcher arrived 45 minutes after Chan and I. Not sure Fletcher should have attempted this.

"Left shelter at 1:30 P.M., hiked steadily by myself. Chan was more or less looking out for Fletcher. Skies darkened around 3:30 P.M., and I put on rain gear. Reached Spence Field shelter about 4:45 P.M. A lady, Aurelia Kennedy, in upper bunk, informed me that eight more women would be arriving shortly. Mrs. Kennedy is the wife of Payson Kennedy, who owns and operates the Nantahala Outdoor Center at Wesser, North Carolina. I hustled down to the spring on the 150-yard gullied trail and filled a three-pound coffee tin and a two-gallon water bag. Back to the shelter, then it began to rain in sheets.

"Chan arrived shortly, then Charles (Santa Claus) Ellis. Finally, around 6 P.M., Fletcher arrived. I used my wood-burning stove. I had broken up a good supply of small twigs along the Trail, and found more around the shelter. I cooked up a full box of Tuna Helper, using chicken in place of tuna. Chan and I ate, then got some of the hot food into Santa and Fletcher, who had arrived wet and cold. Fletcher had even hiked through hail.

"Minutes later, the eight women straggled in, one by one. All soaking wet. We kept hot water boiling for 45 minutes, giving each wet and cold person a cup of hot tea, coffee, or whatever."

"Eventually, we cleared away from the fireplace area and the ladies took over with two other conventional stoves. My little Sierra wood-burner does wonders, but it must be tended constantly. Much banter and clothes changing until around 9 P.M."

Santa Claus Ellis, a man probably in his late 60s from Baltimore, Maryland, has a full, flowing, snow-white beard. He actually does portray Santa Claus during the Christmas season, so his trail name was a natural. He and Fletcher told us the following story, which occurred after Chan and I left Spence Field. Fletcher and Santa Claus did not leave until much later. It seems that one of the ladies, whom I call the 'Constipated Lady,' was in dire straits. She had not had a bowel movement for some five or six days. She was mightily concerned, as were her fellow hikers. That morning at Spence Field, the Constipated Lady walked away from the shelter, past the aforementioned 'Toilet Area' sign, and became lost to view. The others, including Santa Claus and Fletcher, who had been apprised of the situation, waited expectantly at the shelter. Some minutes later, the lady could be seen approaching the shelter, but with no obvious sign of victory or defeat. When she was very close to the waiting group, her face broke into a broad smile and she held her hand high, giving the victory sign. A loud cheer went up from the other women and they immediately burst into song, each verse recounting the Constipated Lady's triumph over adversity (I will not recite the exact words), and ending with a couple of enthusiastic Alleluias!

Life has its lighter moments, even on a long-distance hike.

Spence Field Shelter. The men (from l to r.): Chan Chandler, Santa Clause Ellis, and Fletcher Raiford.

Wednesday, May 2
Spence Field Shelter to Derrick Knob Shelter
6 miles

"Up at 6:30 A.M. I began hiking at 8:20 A.M., up the 5,500-foot Thunderhead. The trail was horribly gullied for most of the route until within one-quarter mile of the first peak, then it had more moderate grades. Beautiful views from West Peak of Thunderhead, but no views from the summit. After leaving Thunderhead, the gullies reappeared; some waterbar work, but inadequate. Reached Derrick Knob shelter at 1:15 P.M., no one there. Shelter is situated on a nice grassy area. Chan arrived at 2 P.M. He would have arrived much earlier, but he had waited for Fletcher. That killed our chances of reaching Siler Bald shelter as planned. So, instead of an 11.4-mile day, we have only a 6-mile day.

"During the day I had observed tens of thousands of the very pretty spring beauty flowers, one of my favorites. Entire hillsides were covered with them. Santa Claus arrived about 5:30 P.M., and Fletcher somewhat later. For dinner, we used both my wood stove and Chan's Peak One to cook freeze-dried Mandarin chicken. Fletcher made bannock bread and cooked dry, mixed fruit.

Spring Beauty.

Super dinner and plenty of coffee. All of us in the sack around 8:30 P.M. Conversation ceased around 9 P.M."

Thursday, May 3
Derrick Knob Shelter to Double Spring Gap Shelter
7 miles

"Up at 6:10 A.M., barely light enough to see. Used Chan's gasoline stove to make coffee and instant oatmeal. Coffee tasted so good. On our way at 7:40 A.M. on well-graded trail. Counted 11 blowdowns, but saw no evidence of blowdown work this year. Observed some excellent waterbar work. Bars are made with 10-inch diameter hardwoods, 20 to 25 feet in length. Almost all of them are still functioning, spaced at 60- to 70-yard intervals. Some of the best waterbar work I've seen. In 1970, there were none in the entire park.

"Saw no check dams, but did see some excellent paint blazing—too infrequent, but excellent quality and freshly painted. Reached Siler Bald shelter at 11:55 A.M. Made another batch of that good ground coffee.

"Left Siler Bald shelter at 12:35 P.M., arrived Double Spring at 1:40 P.M. Decided to call it a day and to head for Mt. Collins shelter Friday night, then on to Newfound Gap Saturday. Chan and Fletcher will leave for home from there. Brought my notes up to date. Wrote a letter to my wife and many post-cards. Chan and Fletcher collaborated on the dinner; Fletcher cut up all the ramps we had picked earlier.

"People kept coming into the shelter until darkness. Eleven people in all, including Dick Cates, who had shared a shelter with me in Georgia on the first day of my hike. This time his son, a medical student, was with him. Great group of hikers. I gave a number of postcards to hiker Gregg Long to mail, because he was leaving the trail the next day. Chan also gave Gregg some telephone instructions so Chan and Fletcher could be picked up Saturday at Newfound Gap.

"I met only one unpleasant person on my entire 1990 hike, and that meeting occurred in Georgia during the first few days of my hike. At that time, he was headed south. Now heading north, he appeared while our group was sitting outside the shelter. He asked if there was space in the shelter, and we told him there was one more space. He decided to go on! At 9 P.M.?

"I had a fairly good sleep, although it rained in torrents and I needed to relieve myself. Fortunately, Fletcher had brought with him two large plastic bottles, which were put to use, as I would have been soaked in seconds if I had gone outside."

Friday, May 4
Double Spring Shelter to Mt. Collins Shelter
6 miles

"Up at 6:30 A.M. Hot brewed coffee, instant oatmeal. I should get some variety in these breakfasts! Left shelter at 8:30 A.M.

"At the shelter, before leaving, I became acquainted with a very pleasant young man from the Cincinnati area, Ed Seibert. Much picture-taking at the shelter before we began the day's hike. Climbed steadily all morning on gullied trail; not really steep, perhaps a 10 percent grade, but steep enough for gullies to appear. We had rain covers on our packs all day, but it did not rain until mid-afternoon. Heavy fog, plus 20-miles-per-hour winds kept us somewhat damp. Reached Clingmans Dome (highest point on the entire Trail at 6,643 feet) after 5.5 miles. Place deserted and no views.

"Writing these notes at Mt. Collins Shelter at 4 P.M. Chan is looking for Fletcher. It rained very hard after I reached the shelter. Minutes before, I had met Bill Kerr, age 60 to 65, from Smoky Mountains Hiking Club (SMHC), who was cleaning out waterbars on the side trail going from the Trail to Mt. Collins shelter. He informed me that SMHC had recently done much chainsaw work on the Trail from Clingmans Dome to Newfound Gap, the only area in the entire Park over which the trail club has jurisdiction.

"In view of dense fog, Chan, Fletcher, and I tried to stay together during the day, but, at 2 P.M., Fletcher remained on the Trail talking to Bill Kerr, and we haven't heard from or seen Fletcher since.

"Moments after writing the entry above, Chan appeared with Fletcher in tow! Fletcher had realized he was lost, and, when Chan found him, Fletcher had already set up his tarp in lean-to style. All's well that ends well! But . . . ! The trail to the shelter is not blue blazed.

"Chan cooked supper: Ramen noodles and a freeze-dried dish with chicken made a great combination, plus it was hot. Six more young men arrived, two by two, before 6 P.M.—a very pleasant group. Visited until about 9 P.M., then to sleep. Awakened just before midnight by torrential rains. The rain roared on the metal roof off and on all night."

Oddly enough, at this same shelter 20 years before, it had rained just as heavily and for a longer period of time, so much so that the next day, I dubbed the Appalachian Trail, the 'Appalachian Creek' as I sloshed along the route to Newfound Gap.

Saturday, May 5
Mount Collins Shelter to Icewater Springs Shelter
7 miles

"Up at 6:30 A.M. Got stove going promptly. Hot coffee, so good, plus instant oatmeal and diced dates. On our way by 8:30 A.M. The Trail was a horrible mess, with many muddy ponds caused by the rain and by waterbars that had filled in and acted as dams. All the waterbars Bill Kerr worked on yesterday were functioning perfectly. Two solid days of muddy, soupy walking. Evidence of much recent blowdown removal. About two miles south of Newfound Gap, I observed about a half mile of highly professional water control work—waterbars, check dams, water-channeling, and stair steps—almost as though it were a model demonstration.

"We reached Indian Gap about 10:20 A.M. Chan pushed on to Newfound Gap. I waited for Fletcher to be sure I got him on the correct trail. Then I pushed on to Newfound Gap, arriving at 11:50 A.M. Visited with Chan. Then, about 12:15 P.M., Fletcher emerged from the woods, and simultaneously, his son-in-law, Joe Bell, arrived by car from Hendersonville. U.S. 441 goes through Newfound Gap, and there are restrooms, water, and a pleasant grassy area there. We took advantage of the grassy area to eat sandwiches and a host of other goodies Joe Bell had brought with him. Chan and Fletcher had planned to go all the way through the Smokies with me, but, in view of our slow pace, they would now stop hiking. They returned to Hendersonville with Joe, but not before giving me a substantial amount of their unneeded food. Said our good-byes, and, at 12:40 P.M., I began hiking with my much heavier pack.

Wooden Appalachian Trail sign with specific trail information.

"Stiff climb out of the Gap. Arrived at Icewater Spring shelter at 3 P.M. to find it occupied by Tim Gfroerer, Bill Waller, and the Milton Brown family of five. Later, at 6 P.M., two hikers arrived who had come all the way from Derrick Knob, some 20 miles south. Cooked a light supper using my wood-burning stove. Wood very scarce in the area. Getting very cold, temperature 43 degrees, at 6 P.M. Have my heavy pajamas on underneath my outer clothes. Difficult to write. All of us in the sack by 7 P.M. I conversed at length with another late arrival, Bill Stokes, a member of the Charlottesville, Virginia, chapter of the PATC. He works as a volunteer the first two weekends in October at the annual apple festival at Syria, Virginia. I made a note to attend one such festival, which is only 75 miles from my home."

Sunday, May 6
Icewater Spring Shelter to Tri Corner Knob Shelter
12 miles

"Up at 6:15 A.M. Used Bill Waller's Coleman stove to heat water for breakfast and for shaving. Temperature 28 degrees, frost on trees, 10-miles-per-hour wind! Chilly! On my way at 7:30 A.M., first one out of camp. Pleasant walk all morning, much better trail, nice grades, occasional waterbars, half of which are all or partly filled in. Walked through many muddy areas. Encountered 11 blowdowns during my first seven miles of hiking, three of them real trail blockers. Ate lunch at Pecks Corner at noon. My back is killing me as I try to write notes while sitting on a log. Walked through some 60 to 70 muddy ponded areas; have hiked with wet feet for another day.

"Arrived at Tri Corner Knob shelter at 4 P.M. Got my little wood-burning stove going speedily, boiled water, then put a package of freeze-dried Mandarin chicken for two into the pot. Delicious, with coffee. Ate three-fourths of it and put the balance in my plastic shaker for breakfast. At 5 P.M., it began to hail, then rain. And at 6 P.M., it began to snow, heavily, one inch in a few minutes. Crazy weather. Too dark to work on notes. There was no sign and no blue blaze trail to the shelter. Almost missed it.

"Got into my sleeping bag by 7 P.M., temperature around 43 degrees and damp. It was a long night, but I was pleasantly warm. Wore my long-sleeved shirt and light nylon jacket over my pajamas."

Monday, May 7
Tri Corner Knob Shelter to Davenport Gap Shelter
15 miles

"Up at 6 A.M. Ate my cold chicken from previous evening, plus hot coffee and oatmeal. Left camp at 7 A.M., temperature around 28 degrees. Snow still on ground, ice in ponds on the Trail. Beautiful effect, with snow-covered trees and

Snowy Trail between Tri Corner Knob shelter and Cosby Knob shelter.

the sun shining. As the sun rose, it penetrated the trees and snow began dropping. Trail had good grades, but much rocky terrain and mud. Reached Cosby Knob shelter at 11:45 A.M. Spent two hours at the shelter. Tim Gfroerer was already there. Washed underwear and hung it to dry. Took a spit bath (that is, I washed with a soapy cloth). Had a good lunch. Very nice shelter; would have enjoyed staying overnight with Tim, but I had set a goal of being in Hot Springs by Thursday night. Laid on my stomach in the shelter, writing my notes. No table. Left Cosby shelter at 1:45 P.M., having thoroughly enjoyed my two-hour midday break there. Made steady progress, some nice views. Finally climbed the last summit, a 700-foot ascent on excellently graded trail. Began the long 4- to 5-mile moderate descent to Davenport Gap shelter, a route bordered at frequent places with dwarf irises, spring beauties, and trout lilies. Met two National Park Service employees doing trail clearing work.

"Reached the shelter at 5:45 P.M. Eric Jacobsen had arrived earlier and had gone into Waterville for groceries and goodies. Shortly after, Mike Church and two young ladies returned from a trip to Knoxville, Tennessee. I learned that my friend, Marty Dominy, had been there the day before with a cooler of beer! I looked in the spring box in front of the shelter, hoping that one beer might have been left for me, but no such luck. I cooked a package of beef stroganoff for supper and put aside a generous portion for breakfast. In my sleeping bag at 8:15 P.M., much warmer at the lower elevation than during the previous two nights. I went to sleep promptly. Woke up suddenly 25 minutes later. Still half asleep, but thinking it was morning, I started to get dressed when Mike Church informed me that it was still Monday evening and only 8:40 P.M.! As members of my family will attest, any time I am awakened during the first three hours of a sound sleep, I am like a drugged person, and I do strange things. The above incident was just one of several on my 1990 hike."

The Davenport Gap shelter is a scant mile from Davenport Gap and the highway (TN 32/NC 17), and marks the northernmost section of 97 miles maintained by the Smoky Mountains Hiking Club and the beginning of some 90 miles maintained by the Carolina Mountain Club. In 1970, I hiked through the park in four-and-a-half days and lamented the fact that I had done it too rapidly. In 1990, it took me seven-and-a-half days to traverse the same trail, one more day than I had planned.

There are really two vastly different Appalachian Trails in the Smokies— the western 38 miles and the eastern 30 miles. In the western part, the Trail seems to have been designed with no effort to maintain a moderate grade by using switchbacks. Consequently, hiking in the western part is a rather exhausting experience, and much of the trail is seriously eroded. In the eastern 30 part, it is obvious that the trail was designed by someone with engineering experience. Good grades have been achieved. In some places, low areas have been built up with rocks as high as 9 or 10 feet to the desired grade. The one problem on the eastern part is drainage. My notes show I walked through muddy ponds some 60 to 70 times in the 15 miles from Tri Corner Knob shelter to Davenport Gap. Nevertheless, the Smokies are beautiful and majestic.

One reason for beginning my hike 10 days later in 1990 than I did in 1970 was so I could enjoy the flowers and foliage to a greater extent in the Smokies. It was a good decision. And the Trail was exceptionally free of litter.

Tuesday, May 8
Davenport Gap Shelter to Groundhog Creek Shelter
11 miles

"Up at 6:20 A.M. Got my wood stove going first thing. Had hot coffee and stroganoff in minutes. Heated more water for shaving. I am liking the stove more all the time. It uses very little wood and the tiny electric fan produces a hot flame. Left camp at 7:25 A.M. Nice sunny day, light breeze. Reached Interstate 40 at 9 A.M. Began the long, slow 2,300-foot climb to Groundhog Creek shelter. Ate my lunch and worked on my notes at a campsite beside a fast-flowing stream named Painter Branch. (Included in my lunch was the last of my hard-boiled eggs cooked on April 29, ten days ago!)

"Pleasant hiking the rest of the day. Stopped briefly at the brilliant white tower maintained by the Federal Aviation Agency. Looks like a freshly landed spaceship! Reached Groundhog shelter at 4 P.M. Broke up more wood, got my stove going, cooked a package of Ramen noodles, adding a can of chicken Chan had given me. Ate three-fourths of it, saved the rest for breakfast. Worked on my notes for the past three days. This shelter has a table, first one since Georgia. Having a table is a great help, both for cooking and writing. The shelter also has a privy, another plus.

"Climbed 2,300 feet today, good grades but still very tiring. My back and my left leg still giving me much trouble. Walked with dry feet today, a real treat after four days of wet feet. Six at the shelter, three sleeping inside, three in tents. One of the young men collected wood and we had a very pleasant fire in the fire ring."

> Although seldom used by hikers, hard-boiled eggs are an excellent trail food. They keep for long periods of time and are relatively inexpensive. They were one of the principal items in my lunch menu for the entire hike.

Wednesday, May 9
Groundhog Creek Shelter to Roaring Fork Shelter
11 miles

"Up at 6:10 A.M., ate breakfast eaten and on my way at 7:05 A.M.. Weather looked ominous so I stopped and broke up wood chips for my evening meal, a very wise precaution. Began raining at 9 A.M., rained steadily all day, and my pack rain cover leaked! Kept walking straight through, no stop for food or water until I reached the Roaring Fork shelter at 2:15 P.M., cold and wet. Got my stove going promptly. All wood outside the shelter was soaking wet so I used the wood I had picked up earlier, plus wood chips I found on the dirt floor of the shelter. Got a hot noodle and bean dish under my belt, plus hot coffee, even a candy bar. Then I washed dishes and hit the sack. My foam pad was wet, so I put the ground cloth on the floor and took a nap. My back and leg much less painful than yesterday.

"On my hike in 1970, I walked for more than three miles on the Max Patch Road. Since that time, the U.S. Forest Service has acquired the fantastic Max Patch Mountain, a huge bald that required years of negotiation to bring into the Forest Service system. The Trail was promptly rerouted over Max Patch, and I had quite an experience hiking it in a cold rain, driven by a 15-miles-per-hour wind. I was surprised to come upon it so soon. It just sort of loomed up ahead of me, this immense grassy bald. There were no identification signs, but after hearing about the famous Max Patch Bald for years, I assumed correctly that this huge bald over which I was hiking just had to be it.

"After leaving Max Patch, the Trail became very muddy and slippery, and I was relieved and again surprised to come upon the very new Roaring Fork shelter. The shelter was of a new and very clever design, and a sign indicated that it had been donated by the 'Mountain Marching Mamas.' Passed through acres of trillium today and saw thousands of them, including perhaps 100 wake robins, the rather rare purple variety, 15 of them in one bunch."

Thusday, May 10
Roaring Fork Shelter to Hot Springs Hikers Hostel
15 miles

"A wild, wild day! Up at 5:55:55 A.M.! (Ah, these modern watches). Hot breakfast, shaved, and on my way at 7:20 A.M., everything wet. It had rained during the night and early morning. Wore rain gear on my pack and myself. Cool. Ten-miles-per-hour wind finally stopped by late morning. Very pleasant hiking through fantastically beautiful country. Had only one stiff climb all day, over 4,600-foot Bluff Mountain where, on the summit, I was surprised to find a dense 20-yard circle of orange-yellow flowers. Later, a Mr. Cameron at Hot Springs identified them as 'Senecio'? Also saw many May apples in bloom, plus acres of trillium, including the wake robins.

"Beautifully graded trail and very little erosion. Infrequent waterbars but, with the good grade, not many are needed. Half of the waterbars were filled in with debris. Met Mike Church several times and we ate lunch together around noon. He is very thin, and has obviously lost weight. In the forenoon, we reached the very old Walnut Mountain shelter. The shelter, built in 1938, was in bad shape and scheduled to be demolished. When Gus Crews and I visited the shelter in 1970, we had found two young ladies, Anne and Pat, comfortably ensconced. They had finished their academic requirements at Wittenburg University in Ohio, and had a three month interval before receiving their diplomas. What better way to spend the three months than to take a leisurely hike on the Appalachian Trail.

"Around 2:30 P.M., I reached Deer Park Mountain shelter. Several of those who stayed at the Roaring Fork shelter the previous evening were staying at Deer Park tonight. The shelter was a big improvement over what it was some 10 years ago when I last saw it on a dark rainy day in the late afternoon. At that time, my examination of the shelter as a place to spend the night revealed a dismal looking interior with four of the five wire bunks totally unuseable. Even though my companion, Ed Hanlon, and I were exhausted after 20 miles of hiking, we nevertheless pushed on the additional three miles to the hikers hostel at Hot Springs. This time at Deer Park, Mike Church and I found the wire bunks had been replaced with wood flooring; there was also a new roof and two large benches.

"Around noon we had seen our first information sign of any consequence, a U.S. Forest Service sign stating that Hot Springs was 6.52 miles away. It was the first such sign in 25 miles! Deplorable. Reached Hot Springs at 4 P.M., 15 miles from Roaring Fork shelter. A good day's hike through country as pretty as one could ask for. Saw only about five blowdowns for the day, five small pieces of litter!

"First thing after arriving at Hot Springs Hikers Hostel, we took much needed showers! Then we weighed ourselves. Mike Church, normally 140 pounds, now weighed 110. Lost a pound a day for 30 days. I was down from 157 to 142. Mike is thinking of ways and means of increasing his calorie intake. A walk downtown ended with a so-so T-bone steak dinner, my first such luxury since leaving Fontana on April 30. Back at the hostel, I used the rectory phone to make a number of long distance calls, trying, among other things, to work out a rendezvous for the annual spring get-together of several people from Georgia and others from the Washington, D.C., area. These arrangements are difficult at best, but doubly so when hiking each day and spending the night where there is no phone service. I learned that we would meet at the Roan Mountain Inn on May 15 in Roan Mountain State Park, which, on my part, would involve both hiking and hitchhiking. After the phone calls, I returned to the hostel, worked on my notes until 10 P.M., then went to bed. I learned that, for some reason, there is a big influx of hikers in Hot Springs, almost 20 staying either at the hostel or at the inn run by Elmer Hall."

Hot Springs is one of my favorite stop-over points on the entire Trail. I have made it a point to stop there many times over the years. The hostel is situated on about 1.5 acres of land on the edge of and above the town. In addition to a sizeable rectory and church, it has two buildings for the use of hikers—a dormitory with bunks and mattresses, and another containing a kitchen, dining room, and living room. The two buildings are connected by a covered breezeway. All the comforts of home!

Friday, May 11
Relaxing at Hot Springs, North Carolina
No hiking

"Up at 4 A.M., worked on diary and daily logs, studied maps, had big breakfast at downtown restaurant. Got my dirty clothes washed. No luck on haircut. The one lady barber had a full schedule. Attended morning Mass in the Jesuit chapel. The congregation consisted of one person—me! Later, picked up 12 pieces of mail at post office and proceeded to write answers. Mike Church and I collaborated on cooking cheese sandwiches and fried onions for lunch. In midafternoon, bought popcorn and enjoyed it down by the river. All in all, a pleasant day of relaxation. Ate a vegetarian dinner at the inn with 23 other hikers. Also met with Thurman Harp, the U.S. Forest Service district ranger. We discussed the almost total lack of signs on the Trail in his district.

"During the 10 days of hiking from Fontana to Hot Springs, I had spent no money. There was no place to spend it! Now, in two days in Hot Springs, I spent $72 on lodging, meals, and groceries. My cumulative expenses for 268 miles of hiking came to $278, and that included my airfare of $95 to Atlanta, Georgia."

Saturday, May 12
Hot Springs to Spring Mountain Shelter
11 miles

"Up at 4:40 A.M., Cooked a big breakfast on the hostel stove. Eggs, toast, sweet roll and coffee. Still having intestinal troubles so I took one of the two-a-day pills. Wrote a number of cards and letters including one to the aged Father Andrew Graves, the first Jesuit priest to serve the Hot Springs area some 40 years ago. Got all my gear together and left the hostel at 8:30 A.M. I took the new route along the river that joins the existing Trail north of Lovers Leap. Pleasant, but slow walking. North of Hurricane Gap, I stopped to view the monument which reads:

In Memory
Rex R. Pulford
September 22, 1920
April 21, 1983

"Mr. Pulford was the father of Dorothy Hansen of the Walasi-Yi Center on the Trail in Neels Gap, Georgia. Surrounding the monument is a very impressive flower arrangement of gladiolus, bluets, and daisies maintained regularly by Sam Waddle.

"I walked with Joe Wolff for part of the day. Joe is renowned among 1990 hikers for having won the ramp-eating contest at Waynesville, North Carolina. He managed to eat 43 ramps in three minutes!

"I did not each lunch until 2 P.M. Very pleasant hiking today over a well-maintained Trail with a moderate grade, which had almost no litter and only two to three blowdowns. Paint blazing is very old for four to five miles south of the Spring Mountain shelter, which I reached at 4:40 P.M. I collected wood for my little stove, but it was very windy and two short-term hikers, Dr. Sam Corbin and Dave Goldman, who had a Peak I stove with lots of fuel, performed the heating chores. Much appreciated. Cold windy day, have all my warm clothes on as I write these notes at 7:20 P.M. Some six to eight people sleeping in the shelter tonight."

Sunday, May 13
Spring Mountain Shelter to Jerry Cabin Shelter
15 miles

"Up at 5:55 A.M. The two men gave me hot water for instant breakfast and coffee. On my way at 7:15 A.M.—good start. Got to the highway in Allen Gap at 9:10 A.M. Proceeded up the long climb out of the gap. Made reasonably good time, reached Little Laurel shelter at noon and ate lunch there with six to seven other hikers. Pushed on at 12:40 P.M.—another long steep climb of over half a mile. Reached the trail leading to the Camp Creek Bald firetower, but did not climb it. Very pleasant trail all day. I reached the Jerry Cabin shelter at 4:45 P.M., 15 miles for the day, and I felt pretty good. Hikers had passed me all day, but I did beat three of them—Pete Hudson and the two girls whom we knew simply as Ginney and Gigi. Two elderly hikers, Irv Winkler and Johnson Page, were already at the shelter when I arrived, and they had collected wood for an evening fire.

"I had encountered only about six blowdowns all day, and had picked up five small pieces of litter, which was all there was to be found. Paint blazing was generally very good. Did go through a goodly number of low muddy areas.

"Used my wood stove to cook the second half of the Mandarin chicken from the previous day. After all of us had eaten, we enjoyed our fire. All of us in the sack by 9 P.M., five inside the shelter, the two girls in their tents outside.

"Love the camaraderie of the evenings at the shelters, especially with a nice fire going. This shelter is immeasurably different from the filthy place I found in 1970. Sam Waddle has done a wonderful job these past 13 years or so in keeping the shelter in first-class shape."

Monday, May 14
Jerry Cabin Shelter to Devils Fork Gap, Tennessee
8 miles

"Good night's sleep; I was up twice and could see the moonlight shining on the grassy clearing in front of the shelter. Pleasantly cool. Up at 6:30 A.M., later than usual, but in no hurry as I will not leave the shelter until after Sam Waddle arrives. Ate two packages of instant oatmeal and drank coffee for breakfast. Had the privilege of using the open air privy with the fancy stained-oak toilet seat, a gift from a Georgia hiker. Real class! Sam Waddle and a friend, Richard Burgess, arrived at 7:30 A.M.

"I finished packing, and six of us left the shelter at the same time. We stopped for a few minutes at the Howard Bassett monument. Howie, a soft-spoken, lovable man, had hiked the entire Trail in 1968, and came back frequently to revisit parts of it. Sam took advantage of our stop there to dig into his pack and distribute a soft drink to each of us, plus a candy bar. A courtesy he has performed hundreds of times. Sam's devotion to the shelter, to the hikers who use it, and to the Trail he maintains is unbelievable. He operates a farm near Chuckey, Tennessee, and it's a long way by vehicle and then by foot to reach the shelter. But, he makes the trip regularly, helps the hikers in any way he can, and, in the colder months, he provides a plastic protection on the open side of the shelter. He also brings in firewood.

"The name 'Jerry Cabin shelter' does not really have any great significance, and I would like to see the shelter renamed the Sam Waddle shelter."

After the completion of my 1990 hike, I wrote a joint letter to the U.S. Forest Service and the Carolina Mountain Club asking that they give consideration to changing the name of the shelter from Jerry Cabin to Sam Waddle shelter. To date, I have not received a response.

"We walked with Sam and Richard to the point where Sam's responsibility ends, said our good-byes, and proceeded toward the new (1988) Flint Mountain shelter, reaching it at 11:45 A.M. Ate lunch there with Irv, Johnson, and Pete Hudson. I then proceeded by myself and reached NC 212 at Devils Fork Gap, North Carolina, at 2 P.M.

"I waited 20 minutes, in vain, for even one eastbound vehicle to appear. No luck, so I began walking. I walked three miles before catching three quick rides that took me all the way to Erwin, Tennessee. Headed directly for the Elms Restaurant, where I had eaten a number of times on previous occasions. I located a table with a good light for writing, ordered a big fish platter, much coffee, and a couple of desserts while I worked on my notes.

"Called the U.S. Forest Service to obtain directions to their Rock Creek Park. Hitched a ride almost immediately with a fellow who took me all the way to the park, a good six miles. I quickly found a campsite with a table and fireplace, built my bed on top of the table, put my nylon tarp over the sleeping gear, and anchored it down so that in the event of wind or rain I could raise the tarp over my head and grit it out. I had a good night's sleep; I woke up several times, and was reassured to see stars shining directly overhead. It had been a great day weather-wise, and I had enjoyed the variety, ending up with my sashay into the attractive and well-maintained Rock Creek Park."

During the next two weeks, I would hike various sections of the trail with friends from Georgia and Washington, D.C., on a planned semi-annual get-together. It would be almost two weeks of varied activity before I would get back into the daily routine of shelter-to-shelter hiking.

Tuesday, May 15
Rock Creek Camp Ground, Erwin, Tennessee, to Cabin 12 at Roan Mountain State Park, Tennessee
No hiking

"A wild day. Up at 6:20 A.M. and got my stove going immediately with wood I had gathered the night before. Ate breakfast and got out to the highway by 8:10 A.M. Obtained a ride from the first motorist I hailed, a lady in a Volkswagen bug who passed me up, then turned around and came back! Her fears of hitchhikers were probably allayed by my age and white hair. She dropped me off in north Erwin, at the U.S. Forest Service office.

"Had a very good 20 minute discussion with the district ranger, Olin Mason. He is very professional, very knowledgeable, very tall (6 feet, 6 inches!) and very interested in the Appalachian Trail. He is systematically hiking every mile of the

Trail in his district. He expressed an interest in hiking with me for at least a part of a day when I was to return the following week. Mason also described the problems the Forest Service is having with some local landowners who dispute the Trail. The Don Nelan shelter, just north of U.S. 19 East, had been burned by arsonists some two months earlier. One of the meetings held with landowners had ended in open hostility approaching violence. The U.S. Congressman from eastern Tennessee, Jamie Quillen, had requested meetings with the chief of the Forest Service on two occasions.

"On another subject, I found that Mason shared my feelings on the need to identify by signs on the ground those gaps and mountain summits mentioned in the *Appalachian Trail Data Book*. He said he had already expressed his thoughts on the issue to the Carolina Mountain Club.

"From the Forest Service office, I walked across the street to McDonald's and had a second and more substantial breakfast. I visited with a group of elderly men who were enjoying coffee and discusssing the affairs of the world. I had much in common with them, because I do the same thing every morning at the McDonald's near my home.

"One of the men gave me a ride to the post office where I picked up three pieces of mail. From there, it was a one-mile walk to a barber shop for a haircut. One of the customers at the shop gave me a ride all the way to Unicoi, Tennessee, where I obtained another ride with Byrl McKinney of Limestone Cove. My destination was the inn at Roan Mountain State Park, but first, McKinney took me to his rural home near Limestone Cove and proceeded to fix me a bologna and tomato sandwich. After that, a trip to Roan Mountain State Park and a fruitless search for the inn. It finally developed that there was no inn, but the park people did have a reservation in the name of David Sherman for Cabins 11 and 12. No problem finding the cabins and I promptly ensconced myself in Cabin 11. I promised to send Byrl McKinney a copy of the *Appalachian Hiker II*. A most helpful fellow.

"After Byrl left, I washed clothes and took a much-needed shower. The cabins are very complete, with beds upstairs and down, a complete kitchen, dining room table, and a wood-burning stove with wood freshly cut and split on the porch. Somewhat different accomodations from sleeping on a picnic table, as I had the previous night, although I had no problem with that either. Having the cabin all to myself, I proceeded to work on my notes and write some cards. Then I sauntered down to the camp restaurant, ate an early and excellent chicken dinner, and returned later for coffee and cherry cobbler.

"Ron Tipton arrived from Washington, D.C., at 9 P.M. We visited until 11 P.M. before going to bed. At 1 A.M. George Owen and Marty Dominy arrived from Atlanta, Georgia. I was completely unaware of their arrival until I woke up Wednesday morning."

Wednesday, May 16
Indian Grave Gap to Iron Mountain Gap
11 miles

"Up at 6 A.M. The others woke up later. Breakfast at the park restaurant. We then took off in two cars. Placed one at Iron Mountain Gap and then drove south through Erwin to the Nolichuckey River Expeditions where Ron, Marty, and George began hiking north on the Trail. I drove back to Erwin, cashed an American Express check, made some purchases and later bought a take-out lunch and ate at Rock Creek Park, where I had camped two nights previously. Then I drove to Indian Grave Gap, where I found Joe and Tom Wolff.

"Gave each a cold beer and enjoyed one myself. The three hikers arrived at 1:30 P.M. and they ate lunch at the gap. We all began hiking at 2 P.M., late in the day with 11 tough miles ahead of us! I predicted it would be 8 P.M. before we reached Iron Mountain Gap. It was 7:58 P.M. when we reached it and retrieved the first car; it was after 9 P.M. when we retrieved the second car at Indian Grave Gap; and it was 9:45 P.M. when we entered the Elms Restaurant just minutes before they were scheduled to close. Some of the kitchen help had already left, and we hurriedly ate the overcooked chicken most of us ordered. We arrived back at our cabin after 11 P.M. to find Chuck Logan, who had driven up from Atlanta and waited three hours for us.

"I was outspoken about the overambitious hike schedule, especially since we had to spot cars in two places and do much driving even before we began the day's hike, and again after we finished. We popped corn and hit the sack about midnight. On the 12 miles hiked that day, we observed 19 blowdowns and generally poor blazing. Many of the blazes were misshapen with unsightly paint drips. There were very few signs to aid a hiker, except for the very helpful diamond-shaped metal markers showing 'water' with a directional arrow, a technique that could be used advantageously throughout the entire Trail. There was a dangerous lack of blazing in the open area near the place called Beauty Spot."

Thursday, May 17
Roan Mountain—Carvers Gap to Iron Mountain Gap
13 miles

"Overslept! All of us up at 7 A.M. or later. The others walked to restaurant in the rain. I stayed in the cabin, made my own breakfast, and worked on my notes. The others returned at 9 A.M., and, shortly, we took off in three cars, two bound for Carvers Gap, the other for Iron Mountain Gap. George, Marty, and I began hiking south from the gap at 10:40 A.M., in light rain. The Trail is too steep, badly eroded. Climbed the 800 feet to the summit. Continued south on a very steep, badly eroded Trail. A 3-R situation (rocks, roots, erosion). Marty eventually went on ahead. Case of youth versus old age. Marty is about 32, the same age as my youngest son!

"Rain stopped around 10 A.M., but fog continued. We walked steadily but slowly because of hazardous footing. Reached Hughes Gap around 11:30 A.M. Began ascending, and at one-tenth of a mile south of the Gap, on our left, some 80 yards from the Trail, we observed a very new and substantial home. What happened? Was neither the Tennessee Eastman Hiking Club nor the U.S. Forest Service aware of the construction of this building? It seems incredible, but there it was. The National Trails System Act provides that the purchasing agencies strive for a right of way of 500 to 1,000 feet from the center of the Trail.

"George and I ate lunch at a nice viewpoint on the Trail. Met four or five northbound hikers, including the Wolff brothers, whom I seem to bump into at various points during my hike. Skies cleared around noon; excellent hiking temperatures the rest of the day, with a brisk wind blowing.

"It was 6:10 P.M. when we reached our car at Iron Mountain Gap. Drove directly to the Celo Inn, a remarkable place in the village of Celo, North Carolina, in a very secluded area. Checked in immediately for a trout dinner, supplied by the large trout grown on the premises. It was a super meal, with Chuck Logan providing a bottle of my favorite Yugoslavian Avia Riesling wine. Homemade hot apple pie and coffee for dessert. After weeks of simple hiking fare for my evening meal, this meal at Celo was a bonanza.

"I finally, after several efforts, got through a phone call to my friend, Ed Hanlon, in northern Virginia. He will meet me in Damascus, Virginia, on Saturday, May 19, and bring me back to Erwin, Tennessee, so that I can fill in the gaps of my hiking activities since leaving the Trail at Devils Fork Gap on Monday, May 14. Great! Worked on my notes until 10:30 P.M., then to bed. Three of us are sleeping in 'the cottage' that was built by the original owners when they built the inn. Most interesting. I love this cottage and would like to bring my wife down here. Made a disturbing discovery—I lost my reading glasses!"

Friday, May 18
Carvers Gap to Elk Park
13 miles

"Up several times during the night. Discovered that my loose bowel problem is back. Will resume the pills. Arose a few minutes past 5 A.M., resumed working on my notes at the kitchen table while enjoying peanut butter and hot coffee. Later ate breakfast in the dining room with the group. Extremely nice breakfast of hot muffins, toast, eggs, grits, and grapefruit.

"Drove to Carvers Gap, left our car there, and began hiking north. Sunny but quite windy. I put away my felt hat and switched to my pullover warm cap.

Wore a long-sleeved shirt. After a half hour of hiking, I put on my rain parka to ward off the wind. Once we got out of the gap, the wind decreased, and things were more bearable.

"George and Chuck walked to the summit. I followed the Trail and reached Roan Highlands shelter at 11:20 A.M., meeting the Wolff brothers and Ed Seibert there. Beautiful day, excellent visibility for miles. Chuck and George caught up with me at 12:30 P.M., as I was eating lunch with Ed Seibert, just north of the Overmountain Trail intersection. From our vantage point, we could see clearly the Overmountain shelter which, in reality, is a big barn that can accommodate 20 or more hikers.

"Started hiking again, but in minutes, I met Ron, Marty, and Ron's friend, who were hiking south from Route 19E. We visited a bit and exchanged car keys so each group would have a car available at the end of the day's hike. Our group then began hiking toward the summit of Little Hump Mountain (elevation 5,459 feet), and from there it was a 40-minute climb to the summit of The Hump (elevation 5,587 feet), which we reached at 3:15 P.M. Enjoyed views at some length, then made the long, slow, five-mile descent to Route 19E, reaching it at 6 P.M. Drove to Roan Mountain State Park where Park Ranger Everette Cox had found my missing spectacles.

"From the park, it was an hour's drive to Celo Inn and another wonderful dinner at Truxelle's Trout Farm. At that place, 'fresh trout' really means fresh! Probably the best trout I've ever eaten, almost no bones. After dinner, we repaired to the cottage and reviewed the color pictures Chuck Logan had taken during the first two weeks of our hike.

"Along the Trail today, there were an excessive number of blowdowns, mostly north of the Hump, and many unsightly paint blazes with long paint drips down the trees. I began to wonder, was it the fault of the painter or the consistency of the paint?

"But the day had been exciting with beautiful views—breathtaking—almost the entire day. I probably will not see the equal until I reach the White Mountains of New Hampshire. Worked on my notes until 11 P.M."

Saturday, May 19
Celo Inn to Damascus, Virginia, to Erwin, Tennessee
No hiking

"Up at 5:30 A.M. Yesterday's trout and baked potato for breakfast! Showered, shaved, paid for two nights of lodging and breakfast, and said good-bye to the Georgians, after which Ron Tipton and I drove in his car straight through to Damascus, Virginia. Found Ed Hanlon at the hikers' hostel known simply as The Place. I transferred all my gear to Ed's car, but, unfortunately, left my wool rain hat in Ron's car.

Ed Hanlon at "The Place" in Damascus, VA, during the Trail Days festival.

"The Appalachian Trail Days celebration was in full swing, and I hustled over to the gazebo and onto the speaker's platform to give a short talk on my hike. Ceremonies were over by 1 P.M. Ed and I then had lunch at a small restaurant. I was meeting many hikers, from this and past years. Had time merely to extend greetings. Watched the parade. Very friendly atmosphere permeating entire community. Some 60 tents on the hostel grounds and more across the river. Tried to find a motel, but nothing available. Around 3 P.M., we left Damascus and drove to Erwin, and put up at the Brotherton Motel. Very nice place. Enjoyed chips and dip, then went over to the Elm's for chicken dinner. Napped in our room. Awoke at 10 P.M., made our plans for the next three days. To bed at 1:30 A.M."

A few words about the town of Damascus, Virginia: The town has taken the hikers into its bosom. First, it was Paschal Grindstaff, the postmaster, and a little welcome area with a trail register, established in conjunction with the U.S. Forest Service, in the outer room of the post office. Then, in 1975, the Methodist Church in Damascus had a large frame building, a former rectory, of which it wished to dispose. Paschal Grindstaff and others persuaded church authorities to make the building available to hikers. The result was "The Place," with six large rooms available for sleeping, plus a kitchen and dining room. It has become one of the most talked about hostels on the entire Trail. No fixed price was charged for an overnight stay, but, in later years, a donation of $2 a night was recommended. From the day of its beginning as a hostel until 1990, the donations took care of day-to-day expenses and accumulated to a tidy $6,000.

Charlie Trivett, although not a member of the Methodist parish, became the principal monitor of the hostel, and Paschal Grindstaff and Paul Lethcoe also contributed regularly to its success. In 1990-1991, much of the $6,000 was used to shore up the foundation, to add toilets and showers, and to paint the interior rooms.

In 1987, the town instituted a week-long celebration known as Appalachian Trail Days, which has become a very popular get-together for hikers. There's somewhat of an atmosphere of a college homecoming event, mixed in with a country fair, parades, pageants, temporary eating places, exhibits, dancing, music, etc.

During the hostel's first year, Charlie Trivett and his wife, Alice, provided a free dinner for each hiker. After one year of this generosity, the Trivetts were forced to discontinue the practice. Such is Damascus. The town designs new t-shirts proclaiming Damascus to be the friendliest town on the Trail. I haven't heard of anyone disputing the claim.

Sunday, May 20
Spivey Gap to Indian Grave Gap, Tennessee
19 miles

"Hiked in two directions today, north-to-south in the morning and south-to-north in the afternoon. Up at 5:45 A.M., breakfast in our room. Ed Hanlon then drove me out of Indian Grave Gap, and I began hiking in the rain at 7:20 A.M. Pleasant hiking, rain stopped between 9:30 and 10 A.M. Reached Nolichucky Expeditions at 10:45 A.M., earlier than Ed had anticipated. Ate my lunch while waiting for him. He arrived at 11:15 A.M., and we drove to Spivey Gap on Route 19W. Began hiking at exactly noon. Skies had cleared, very pleasant hiking. Reached the No Business Knob shelter at 2:30 P.M. Nice shelter, but toilet facilities are a shambles, as they were some 10 years earlier when I was last in this area.

"During the day, I saw wild azaleas in bloom, a few Catawba rhododendrons, one lone pink lady's slipper. Located two junco nests when the parent bird flew out from the bank beside the Trail. One nest had baby birds, the other four eggs. The nests were cleverly hidden, and, frequently, I would give up the search after a few minutes, but on this day I did find two of them.

"Reached the Nolichucky River at the Chestoa Bridge at 5:30 P.M. Ed had been waiting for an hour. Drove directly to Brotherton Motel, showered, then went to the Elm's for a dinner of excellent filet mignon steak. Back at our room, we watched Sunday night televiaion.

"I had hiked 19 miles today with a day pack and saw very few blowdowns, almost no litter, excellent paint blazing from Spivey to one-half-mile north of the shelter. The side hill trail north and south of No Business Knob shelter is sliding down the mountain. Much work will be needed to shore up the deteriorating trail. I was very tired from the day's hiking, and went to bed without finishing my notes. Met 12 people while hiking today, 5 of them just back from the festivities at Damascus.

Monday, May 21
Spivey Gap to Devils Fork Gap
20 miles

"Up very early, breakfast in room. Ed got me on the Trail at 6:45 A.M. Overcast. Began climbing almost immediately and continued climbing until 10:30 A.M. when I reached the summit of Big Bald (elevation 5,516) at mile 6.2, a 2,300-foot elevation gain from Spivey Gap. From the summit, I could see the lodge partway down the mountain, and I recalled a day in 1975 when Ned

Greist, a notable Trail enthusiast and scouting leader, completed a 45-year effort of hiking the entire Trail at this point. We had a big dinner for him at the lodge, complete with champagne to celebrate the event. Had planned to eat my lunch at the summit and to admire the 360-degree views, but it was very cold, windy, and foggy. Shortly, I descended to a more sheltered spot and had lunch. Made steady time all day, with very few stops. But, that 2,300-foot climb had taken time and sapped a certain amount of my strength. Reached Sams Gap at 1:55 P.M. and began the 7.7-mile hike to Devils Fork Gap. Pushed hard, hoping to reach the gap by 5:30 P.M. Had one last peak to climb. Thought for sure I would reach the gap by 5:40 P.M., and reached what I thought was it at 5:45 P.M. Came out on a paved road, but it was not Route 212! Hustled back down the road, found the Trail and climbed one more ridge. Reached Hanlon's car at 6:15 P.M. after 11¹/₂ hours of almost nonstop hiking. Enjoyed one cold beer from Ed's cooler, and we headed for Erwin.

"The point where I met Hanlon was Devils Fork Gap, the same place I had left the Trail one week earlier to join my friends at Roan Mountain State Park. Much had happened in that seven-day span.

"At the motel, I took a shower, cleaned up, then went over to Elm's for our final meal there. Back at my room, I collapsed on my bed, fully dressed. I slept deeply for almost two hours, then roused myself. Did no writing, too exhausted, but the 39 miles in two days meant I had completed all of the Trail from Springer Mountain, Georgia, to Route 19E in Tennessee—381 miles. And I was most grateful to my longtime friend, Ed Hanlon, for chauffering me around the mountains to fill in the gaps in my hike."

Tuesday, May 22
Route 19E to Moreland Gap Shelter
14 miles

"Up at 5 A.M. Got all gear packed—my backpack, a sack to be given to Charlie Trivett in Damascus, and my blue carry-on bag that has followed me from San Francisco to Carmel to Hollywood (California), and from Atlanta to Hendersonville to Roan Mountain State Park on the Trail. Left motel in the rain. Big breakfast at McDonald's, then to U.S. 19E and the Trail intersection. Said good-bye to Ed, got my pack on, and went into the heavy and steady rain at 8:30 A.M.

"I began slipping, sliding, falling on trails soaked from an all-night rain. For nearly 11 hours, I trudged north, heading for Moreland Gap shelter. It was one of the most dismal days I've ever spent on the Trail. The guidebook was almost useless as a means of telling me where I was.

"Pete Hudson met me near the ruins of the Don Nelan shelter, which recently was burned by arsonists, and we walked in to examine it. The roof was on the ground and there were very few burned timbers. Both Pete and I puzzled. It made me think of the former Mosby shelter, just north of Shenandoah National

Park in Virginia, where its valuable chestnut timbers were stolen and the rest of it was burned to lessen any suspicion of theft.

"As the hours passed, I kept stumbling and sliding over the narrow summits; I worried that I might not reach the shelter before dark, or that I might miss it in the gathering darkness. The guidebook made no mention of the shelter being on a side trail, so I assumed it was directly on the Trail. The guidebook further stated that at mile 13.3, 'Reach first major summit (4,121 feet)—shelter 0.2 miles beyond summit.'

"I reached what I thought MUST be that summit around 7 P.M., descended for 15 minutes, began hailing anyone within earshot, and finally got an answering hail as Pete Hudson came out to greet me! He and two others, Mark Elliott and Sandra Bernoi, were already there. Unpacked and all my sleeping gear was dry, thank God. Had a scanty meal. Pete gave me some hot water for coffee. Then, I crawled into my warm pajamas and into the sleeping bag. What a treat to be warm and dry! Visited with others, then went to sleep around 9:30 P.M.

"And so ended a day in which I found not one sign in the entire 14 miles, either giving mileages or identifying a gap or a summit! Oh, yes, the 20-year-old cinder block shelter, turned dark green over the years, exuded all the warmth and brightness of a dungeon."

> In the 1950s, as a newer member of the Potomac Appalachian Trail Club (PATC), I remember attending an annual meeting at which the outgoing president read from a list of unrealized goals. One of them related to the locked cabins (some 12 to 14 at that time) that PATC operated. He had wanted the interiors painted with a light color to alleviate the dungeon-like darkness that pervaded most of them (and still does!). In 1962, I volunteered to oversee the renovation of PATC's 18 trailside shelters, and with that painting issue in my memory, I suggested that each shelter be painted white on the interior. When our renovation program was completed in the fall of 1962, all 18 of those shelters were painted white. It does make a difference in the light effectiveness of a candle, a flashlight, or even a Coleman lantern.

Wednesday, May 23
Moreland Gap Shelter to Hampton, Tennessee
7 miles on the Appalachian Trail, 3 miles other

"Up at 6:30 A.M., and now, after sponging gasoline from Pete Hudson for some time, I paid my dues. For one dollar, he gave me more hot water, and then, using a tiny coffeemaker he had, he brewed me two cups of real coffee. What a treat! Mark Elliott gave me a massage to relieve my back problem. Left shelter at

9 A.M. after saying good-bye to the others. No one seemed to be in too much of a hurry today. Terry Simpson, who had arrived very late at the shelter, caught up with me and walked with me almost to the Laurel Fork shelter. I took the blue blaze trail along the former bed of the railroad. Was spellbound by the beauty of the trail through the Laurel Fork area—one of the more spectacular areas on the entire Trail. Ate lunch at the run-down Laurel Fork shelter. Joined briefly by two van drivers from the Warren Doyle expedition—Ken Miller (Georgia-Maine 1989) and Diane Watt. I reached Hampton around 3:30 P.M. Stopped at Brown's grocery to inquire of Sutton Brown as to availability of a room in 'Braemer Castle,' mentioned in the *Philosopher's Guide*. Sutton took me to the castle, but the rooms and apartments were under renovation. I was offered a room with absolutely nothing in it for eight dollars. I demurred, after which Sutton was good enough to call an elderly lady in town who also takes roomers. I walked another mile and obtained, for the same eight dollars, a wonderful, spotless, furnished room with a private bath. The lady also washed and dried my clothes that were still muddy after that all-day trek in the rain to Moreland Gap shelter. I enjoyed a real tub bath, first one in years, put on clean clothes, and felt like a new man. What a change in one day! Walked to the 7-11 Restaurant and had a big ham and pancake meal. Back at the rooming house, I worked on my notes at the kitchen table. At 8 P.M., the landlady brought me a dish of dessert and a cup of coffee. Such service. I thanked my lucky stars that I had not stayed at the Castle. According to the *Data Book*, I have 41 miles to go to Damascus, Virginia. Will probably reach there Saturday after the post office closes.

"Litter. In a number of my daily writings I have commented on the cleanliness of the Trail. Not so in the past two days. Yesterday, I counted some 25–30 pieces of litter on the Trail and about 50–60 more pieces deliberately dumped on the Trail near Buck Mountain Road. Nice people—burn shelter, dump litter! Today, I noticed another 35 pieces of litter. In the past two days, there has been more litter on the Trail than all I have seen in the previous months."

Tuesday, May 24
Hampton to Watagua Dam Road
12 miles

"Awake at 2 A.M. to visit the bathroom and no sleep thereafter. Using VERY hot tap water, I enjoyed a cup of coffee and a packet of cereal. The landlady opened things up at 5:45 A.M., and I noticed that, in addition to locking doors with a key, she also had installed a two-by-four-inch wooden bar across each door to further reduce the possibility of an unauthorized entrance. I resumed my paperwork and got everything up to date. Even wrote a number of postcards.

"Left the rooming house around 8:45 A.M., and caught a ride almost immediately to the trailhead. Before leaving, I noticed that the landlady appeared to be in deep thought. She asked me if I thought the other roomer in her home would be trying to sneak some of his friends into her house! I assured her that it was very unlikely. She had been so nice to me that I paid her more than her asking price and, instead of disturbing either of those immaculately made beds in my room, I slept on the floor. It was no sacrifice on my part, as the thick rug and pad were like heaven compared to the wooden floors of the shelters. And, she would have little work to do, other than to launder the one towel I used.

"It was a blessing that I was able to get all of my paperwork done in Hampton before leaving, because the next three days were so hectic that I did not get back to the onerous task until Sunday morning in Damascus. After reaching the trail-head on Route 321, I walked on the blue blaze trail for a mile to its intersection with the Trail. At that point, I met Warren Doyle, who was measuring the entire Trail from Georgia to Maine with a wheel. Doyle is the founder of the Appalachian Long Distance Hiking Association (ALDHA). The figure, compiled when he reached Katahdin in Maine, some months later, was 2,144 miles."

"The time of my meeting with Warren was 10 A.M., and I was about to begin the long climbs up and down Pond Mountain, a hike that would take six hours! Ate my lunch at a small spring near the summit. Met Warren again. He invited me to join his group at a beach party in the U. S. Forest Service's Shook Branch Recreation Area. At 4 P.M., I reached Route 321 and walked along it to the near-by store where I enjoyed a beer. Met Warren and one of his fellow hikers, Jamie. They were having a snack and, again, I was urged to join their group. At the store, I called the store where I thought I had left my camera. Yes, they had it! Lucky me. I made arrangements with Warren to have it picked up by his support driver.

"I walked another mile or so on the Trail to where the beach party was in progress. Snacked from my pack. Around 6:30 P.M., I began hiking on the Trail with the group of about 14 to an overnight campsite at Watauga Dam Road, which we reached at 7:30 P.M. I set up my nylon tarp and was in bed around 9 P.M. It was the first time I had to use the tarp for that purpose since my hike began.

"I encountered 34 blowdowns between Laurel Fork shelter and Route 321, and an additional 12 blowdowns from Route 321 to where we camped along Watauga Dam Road. There was no evidence of any blowdown removal this year."

Friday, May 25
Watauga Dam Road to Low Gap at intersection of Appalachian Trail and U.S. 421
24 miles

"Up at 3 A.M.—something's still not right in my system! Up for good at 5:40 A.M., got my gear together, ate a cold breakfast. Began hiking at 6:20 A.M., earliest start to date. Reached Vandeventer Shelter at 9 A.M., and met Mark Elliott and Sandra Bernoi again. Pushed on steadily, ate lunch at the Iron Mountain shelter (new since my 1970 hike). From the shelter, I pushed on to Double Springs shelter. Had planned to stay overnight there, but changed my mind and hiked another three-plus miles to where Doyle's group was camping at Low Gap, giving me 23.7 miles for the day.

"Made arrangements to sleep overnight in the group support van. Used driver Ken Miller's stove to cook a Richmoor beef stew dinner and gave half to Ken. All worked out well except for a most unfortunate accident. In trying to make a long awkward reach to unlock the front door of the van, something snapped in my left shoulder blade and I felt excruciating pain. Must be VERY careful in moving my left arm and expect it will be weeks before it heals. (I underestimated; it still bothered me more than a year later!) I slept well in the van on the floor between piled-up milk bottle crates.

"Interesting incident occurred mid-afternoon when I was passed by Brian Hart and Milton Herndon. They were walking rapidly, trying to make it all the way to Damascus—a 40-mile jaunt with packs from Watauga Lake shelter. Learned the next day that they arrived at Damascus at 9 P.M.!

"Saw a patch of Catawba rhododendron in bloom near several bushes of flame azalea. Also saw a big bunch of mountain laurel in full bloom, a gorgeous sight.

"Today, after some 40–50 miles of hiking, I saw the FIRST sign identifying a gap—Turkey Pen Gap (elevation 3,970). Consensus of hikers is that points considered important enough to list in the *Appalachian Trail Data Book* should be identified by a sign on the Trail."

Saturday, May 26
Route 421 to Damascus, Virginia
14 miles

"Up at 4:30 A.M. Cooked hot breakfast of cereal, hot chocolate, coffee. My left shoulder blade is hurting like hell whenever I make a false move. Heated more water on the roaring Svea stove and shaved. On my way again at 6:20 A.M. Pleasant day. Reached Abingdon Gap shelter at 8:56 A.M. Tarried but briefly at a shelter (one of many) in which plywood has been placed atop the wire screen bunks. The plywood is not so good; it begins to chip off in use. Ate lunch on the Trail. Met Henry Childs of Rockaway Beach, Long Island, New York, who said he was delighted to meet me. He had read my first book, had systematically backpacked much of the Trail, and now, in his later years, was day-hiking while his wife met him at selected points.

"I arrived on the outskirts of Damascus shortly after 1 P.M., and was downtown at 1:30 P.M. Walked directly to C & J Grocery. Met Dick Cates and ate dinner with him at a seafood restaurant. Received 12 pieces of personal mail at Damascus, plus two envelopes from ATC in Harpers Ferry, a guidebook for Central and Southwestern Virginia, and more daily log forms. Jean Cashin enclosed a note mentioning that the thru-hiker count was down this year by almost one-half! My other mail disclosed, among other things, that my daughter, Sharon, and Judy Jenner, the longtime editor of the *Appalachian Trail News*, planned to hike in southwestern Virginia in the early part of June, so I am looking forward to hiking with both. I went to bed at 10 P.M. on the first floor of The Place—no beds as such but three-inch-thick foam pads and much softer than the wooden floors of the shelters!"

It later turned out that a late surge of hikers starting in Georgia that year resulted in a record 203 finishing the Trail.

Sunday, May 27
The Place
No hiking

"Up at 6 A.M. Members of the Warren Doyle expedition were already up and getting ready to move on. They operate on a very fixed schedule; they hike rain or shine, and make tremendous mileages each day. I had hiked with them for two days, but it would not be my cup of tea as a steady diet. Had breakfast at the Cowboys Restaurant with Dick Cates and the van driver, Ken Miller. Went back to The Place and worked on my notes. At lunchtime, Mark Elliott cooked me two big pancakes with butter and syrup, as well as real coffee. At 6 P.M., the 'fighting deacon' of the Methodist Church came into The Place and gave us a lecture on alcohol and rowdyism. I think he was talking to the wrong group because the hikers this week were as peaceable and as orderly as a group of Quakers at a Sunday meeting. Somewhat later, I walked the two-minute stretch to Quincy's Pizza.

"Back at The Place, we received another visitor, Dorothy Mauldin, who dropped in on her way back from Tillie Wood's 'Woodshole' just south of Pearisburg, Virginia. Badly crippled in an accident, Dorothy gets around very well with two special crutches. She sleeps in her van and is a tremendous lover of the Trail and of all the hikers who use it. To bed at 10 P.M. after taking care of most of my paperwork and correspondence. How I love these stop-over points, with a day or so to catch up on washing, writing, and even eating!"

Monday, May 28
Damascus to Taylor Valley
7 miles

"Up at 5:45 A.M. and went to Cowboys for breakfast with Dorothy. Back to the hostel and in a few minutes she took off for her home in Georgia. Back to that dining room table to write cards and letters, and to get my guidebook and daily logs ready for mailing to ATC. After getting all my gear sorted and packed, I said my good-byes to Charlie Trivett, Dick Cates, and others. Left hostel about 1:45 P.M. Had a final lunch at Cowboys and walked past Dot's Restaurant on the outskirts of town.

60

"Two young ladies with whom I had hiked at various times during the past weeks, came out and waved good-bye. They were leaving the Trail at this point and going home, a ritual experienced by perhaps 800 others of the 1,000 who start each year with the high hopes of doing the entire Trail. And, yet, for none of them has the trip been a failure. For each, it will have been a rich experience, walking through tunnels of rhododendrons, seeing trillium, spring beauties, bluets, wild azalea, mountain laurel, acres of ferns, and many more. The cama-raderie of sitting around a campfire at the trailside shelters at night, of waking up to the sounds of birds singing. . . . 'Better to have loved and lost than never to have loved at all!'

"Some of the enthusiastic letters I receive are from people who, late in life, hike for a week or more before being forced to discontinue. But they are so happy to have done what they did, to put a pack on their back, to strike out on the Trail, to have met other people at the shelters and on the Trail. And, each of us who has helped even a little bit to make this Trail a reality can take righteous pride in our efforts.

"Now back to Dot's Restaurant! Had difficulty following the Trail beyond the restaurant, as it was very poorly blazed. Missed the abrupt left turn off the left side of the road where the Trail ascends the mountain. Finally, after two inquiries, I found the Trail and hiked about half an hour before the heavens opened up. Got my pack and myself covered with rain gear and kept slogging along. It became very dark, and somehow or other I got off the white-blazed Trail and onto the yellow-blazed Iron Mountain Trail. Finally, I realized my mistake, and spotted the parallel Virginia Creeper Trail 30 feet away. I walked over to it, and met two men who suggested I continue on the Creeper Trail for half an hour and I would pick up the Trail again. Found it with signs showing six miles to Damascus and two miles to the Trail.

"It was about 7 P.M., and I decided not to risk it. Saw two houses ahead of me on the Virginia Creeper Trail, stopped at the first, and wound up at the second, occupied by Carl McMurray and family. He put me up at the adja-cent former general store and laid out a mattress for me. Ate a light supper in the store and later I was invited over for apple pie and coffee. Met his wife, Linda, and son, Eric, who towered over me at six feet, eight inches. Then, back to the store. Reflected that I was better off than my friends in the shel-ter! Still raining and chilly outside. Crawled into bed at 10:20 P.M. and had a good night's sleep."

Tuesday, May 29
Taylor Valley to Route 601 near Konnarock, Virginia
11 miles

"Up at 6 A.M., and over to the McMurray's, where I shaved and enjoyed a bacon and egg breakfast with toast and grits. A most hospitable couple. Back to the store, finished packing and took off at 7:50 A.M. In 5 to 10 minutes, I reached the Appalachian Trail sign, and by 8:15 A.M., I was hiking on the Trail. Reached the Saunders shelter at 9:15 A.M. I could have easily made the shelter the previous evening if I had not been misled by that two mile sign.

"The shelter is only three years old. It has a nice design, made from carefully joined, preformed timbers. It sports a wood table made from three-inch-thick wood boards.

"Off and on rain most of the day, temperature around 50 degrees; miserable weather but fantastic wooded and flowered areas, rushing and roaring streams. Got back on the Virginia Creeper Trail four miles north of Taylor Valley. Reached U.S. 58 at 2:15 P.M. Decided it was unlikely that I could reach Deep Gap shelter before dark. Tried to hitch a ride with no luck; it is difficult to obtain rides when you and your pack are soaking wet. Learned to my dismay that the rain cover on my pack had slipped, and that rain had fallen on my unprotected pack. Luckily, I had much of my clothing in plastic bags, but the guidebook and other paper material got somewhat wet.

"Began hiking again; still cold and raining. Reached Route 601 near Konnarock at 3 P.M. Stopped at the only house visible, where Barbara Tolbert immediately provided me with hot coffee, a hot shower, and a tuna sandwich with hot chocolate. What a break! Barbara occupies a U.S. Forest Service–owned house, acquired as part of an Appalachian Trail land purchase. She has put up a number of hikers. The house has almost no furniture, but it does have heat and electric lights. Will get my notes up to date for two days.

"Drove with her to nearby store in Konnarock. My purchase—three candy bars. Back to Tolbert place for a sweet roll and glass of milk. The house is *very* exposed. Winds shake the windows and blow hard down the fireplace. So, I lost another day, but I dreaded trying to climb another 1,000 feet or more over an eight-mile trek to reach Deep Gap Shelter. Weighed myself after the shower—142—same as at Hot Springs, North Carolina. Around 8:30 P.M., we heated up the remaining half of a four-man beef stew package from my pack. Eaten with two pieces of bread, it was sufficient.

"My left shoulder blade is still very touchy. A slightly incorrect move and I get a most painful twinge. To bed at 10 P.M. on floor in empty room."

Wednesday, May 30
Route 601 to Deep Gap Shelter
8 miles

"Up several times during night, and up for good at 6:10 A.M. Barbara up at same time to make an excellent pancake breakfast. Reread some of my diary notes; I *have* had a most *interesting* trip so far, no question about that! At 8:10 A.M., the weather looked somewhat more promising, but not much. Wrote a few cards while the weather cleared.

"It turned out to be a fine day. Ate lunch before I left Barbara's place. Took her picture. She drove me to White Top Post Office where I mailed stuff to home and to Pearisburg, Virginia, which I expected to reach in about 10 days. Weighed my pack—40 pounds with camera and one pint of water. Began hiking at 12:30 P.M. Within a minute or two, I found the big, but unmarked spring, a scant 100 feet from Barbara's home. No sign, easily missed. Hiked steadily up, up, up. Beautiful views from Buzzard Rock. Ed Seibert caught up with me as I neared White Top Mountain Road and we walked together to Deep Gap shelter, arriving at 5:30 P.M.

"Three others were there, including Mark Dusanberry from Alexandria, Virginia, which is about 12 miles from my home in Falls Church, Virginia. My wood stove worked to perfection. I made a batch of Stove Top dressing and heated up remains of the beef stew I had cooked the previous night. With Claxton fruit cake and a big pot of coffee, it made for a good supper. A cool night, not too far below the summit of Mt. Rogers (5,700 feet), the highest point in Virginia. Did not sleep well, perhaps I had too much coffee. But I kept warm in my lightweight sleeping bag with a long-sleeved shirt over my pajamas. A very good day. Would not wish to have missed the White Top Mountain hike and those views. White Top is the second highest peak in Virginia. To bed at 9 P.M. Several deer around the shelter, very tame."

Thursday, May 31
Deep Gap Shelter to Old Orchard Shelter
13 miles

"Up at 6 A.M., temperature 44 degrees. Got stove going within minutes and had two packages of instant oatmeal, peanut butter, and coffee. Seibert was one of perhaps three or four others I met who were also using a wood stove, so we had a little competition for wood. The tiny stove uses so little fuel, there is generally plenty for all. Brought my notes up to date, a bit difficult in the chilly weather. Left shelter at 8 A.M., pleasant walking. During this day, Seibert and I would be hiking in the Mt. Rogers National Recreation Area and in the adjoining Grayson Highlands State Park. The two areas combine to provide one of the more unusual types of hiking on the entire Trail. These are high-elevation highland areas, around 4,500 to 5,000 feet, reminiscent of mountain-grazing areas in our western states. Western cattle and horses graze all year round in a natural setting that one does not often see in the east. Passed the intersection leading to the summit of Mt. Rogers, but did not climb on the side trail to the summit, as it is wooded and offers no view.

"Ate lunch at 5,400 feet at Rhododendron Gap. Beautiful spot, aptly named, as it has a dense growth of rhododendron. The morning was mostly sunny. Thoroughly enjoyed the vast open areas, huge rock outcroppings, the ponies, and cows. Took a picture of a horse with a new colt. Had another snack around 2 P.M.

at an intersection of the Trail and the Little Wilson River, a very wild and pretty spot. Reached the livestock corral called 'Scales' around 3 P.M., and pushed on steadily. The sky was becoming overcast, so we gathered wood for our small stoves.

"We reached Old Orchard shelter at exactly 5 P.M. Like the rest of working America, we too had experienced an 8-to-5 day. But, although strenuous, our day could not be called 'work.' Instead, it had been a grand day of excellent hiking over a wide variety of terrain in the highland areas. Promptly after reaching the shelter, I swept it out with a 'Russell Norton' wallpaper brush. More on that later. Then I spread my sleeping gear out.

"Seibert and I were joined at the shelter by Bill Miller of New Jersey, with whom we would hike for the next nine days. Ate a light supper of soup, one serving of instant potatoes, and hot chocolate. No coffee this time. To bed around 8:30 P.M. and had an excellent night's sleep. All in all, a very good day. And, two observations on Trail conditions . . . some excellent paint blazing across the open areas of the highlands—four- and five-foot fence posts with clear white paint blazes. On the litter front, only one piece in 13 miles. Fantastic. My gratitude to a new generation of hikers who refrain from littering and to a growing group of others who are willing to stoop down and pick up litter left by a few less thoughtful hikers."

Friday, June 1
Old Orchard Shelter to Trimpi Shelter
14 miles

"Up at 5:50 A.M. Light breakfast, two instant cereals. But I consumed two hours breaking camp. Not good. Left camp at 7:50 a.m., clear and sunny. Made good time, hiking by myself until 2 P.M. when Ed Seibert caught up with me. Tremendous storm damage by Hurricane Hugo. The freshly sawed end of one giant tree that had fallen across the Trail bore this painted message: HUGO WAS HERE. Bob. 9-22-89!

"Ate lunch on the Trail. At around 3 P.M., we heard what sounded like a turkey call, but did not hear it enough to be certain. Moments later, Ed Seibert called my name sharply. The alarm in his voice caused me to stop in mid-stride. Had I not heeded his alarm, I probably would have stepped directly on a turkey poult. It made no move, and as we studied it we observed another poult only two feet away, then a third. Quite likely there were a number of poults likewise glued to the ground after Mama had sounded her alarm, but we saw only the three. One of them abandoned its motionless ploy and ran for cover. The other two made no move during the time we studied them. We were surprised that Mama did not reappear.

"I did not see it, but earlier at a point one mile north of the Old Orchard shelter, both Ed and Bill had seen the clear, big tracks of a bear.

"We reached Trimpi Shelter at 4 P.M. Enjoyed a supper of macaroni and cheese with a can of tuna contributed by Seibert. Coffee and Claxton fruit cake topped it off. Seibert built an outdoor fire after supper, and we stoked it until bedtime around 9 P.M."

Saturday, June 2
Trimpi Shelter to Chatfield Shelter
17 miles

"Up at 5:50 A.M. Cold breakfast. On my way at 6:27 A.M.—37 minutes from wake-up to take-off. Much better than yesterday. Bill and Ed left later. I made good time in very interesting country. Thought I would never reach the summit of Brushy Mountain. Scared up a hen turkey with poults. I stayed in one spot for five minutes watching and listening to the hen turkey, while she crossed and recrossed the Trail repeatedly uttering warning calls to the poults.

"Reached the visitor center and the headquarters of the Mt. Rogers National Recreation Area at 11:45 A.M., and remained there until 2 P.M. Received messages from my daughter, Sharon, and Judy Jenner. Called my daughter and agreed to meet her at Levi Long's hostel at Bastian, Virginia, on June 7. My problem is catching up with Judy Jenner. Her husband, Dave Startzell, had left her off at the Mt. Roger's visitor center a day or so before I arrived. I had lost a day or more after leaving Damascus, Virginia. I just can't make the miles anymore with a 40-pound pack, and my back still gives me fits when I go much more than 12 miles per day. Also, I realize my age when I climb those steep, wooden stiles across fence lines.

"Seibert and I arrived at the Chatfield shelter in late afternoon. We heated up half of a four-man Richmoor freeze-dried beef stew. Along with bread, coffee, and a candy bar, I made out okay. But I don't think I will buy any more freeze-dried beef stew after this package is finished. Crawled in sleeping bag and visited until 10 P.M. with fellow hiker Scott, one of the two Florida Flyers whose paths I have crossed several times. Moon shining brightly in clearing in front of shelter. The noise of the stream some 50 feet in front of the cabin is clearly audible. A good day, but 17 miles is a bit too much for me."

Sunday, June 3
Chatfield Shelter to U.S. 11, Atkins, Virginia
5 miles

"Up at 6:20 A.M. Hot cereal for breakfast and coffee. Had to hustle to get things packed—rain imminent. Still taking the Lomotil pills, but they are not too effective. While at Chatfield shelter, we boiled all our water from the stream. Began raining at 8 A.M.; we began hiking at 8:20 A.M. It rained all the way to U.S. 11. Trail route very muddy. Feet thoroughly wet in short order. Bill left before Seibert and I did, with the intention of getting a room at the Village Motel. His trail name is Motel Al—a motel every three or four days, but he wasn't quite able to achieve that goal on this trip.

"Seibert and I had trouble finding our way across the open areas and across the railroad. Puzzled by all the white paint blazes on the railroad ties and on the rails themselves?! Terribly wet route. Met Mike Dawson, the regional representative of the ATC with headquarters in Blacksburg, Virginia. He was accompanied by two people whom I presumed to be members of the Konnarock Crew. Since we met in a driving rain our visit was very short!

"We arrived at the Village Motel on U.S. 11 at 11 A.M. Bill was already ensconced in Room 13. I promptly moved in with him, took off my muddy, filthy clothes, and tossed them in the bathtub; then washed them and myself and put on clean, dry clothes and shoes. Walked over to the restaurant to eat with Bill and Ed. Ate a mammoth brunch—sausage, eggs, hashbrowns, toast, and to top it off, ice cream!

"At 2 P.M., I returned to the restaurant to work on my diary and trail logs. At 3:30 P.M., Rob Fries, Mike Dawson's assistant, came into the restaurant to meet me and to invite me to a 5 P.M. supper with the Konnarock Crew at their headquarters in Sugar Grove. I accepted the invitation. I then walked to the nearby grocery store to purchase supplies for the next three days. At 4:40 P.M., Mike Dawson arrived, and we drove to Sugar Grove to the former Youth Conservation Corps buildings, which now house the Konnarock Crew. I enjoyed the Mexican dinner with about 20 of the crew. Asked to make a few comments, I described some of the excessively steep trails over which I had hiked, and urged the crew to observe moderate grades in their trail relocation work.

"After the dinner, I participated in a videotaped discussion of my hike, and visited with a number of people in the very dedicated Konnarock Crew, a great group of trail workers having done much to improve the caliber of trail maintenance and trail construction. Rob Fries brought me back to the motel, and we enjoyed ice cream and coffee. Then I wrote cards to five of my friends and went to bed at 10:30 P.M."

Monday, June 4
U.S. 11 to Knot Maul Branch Shelter
14 miles

"Good night's sleep. Up at 5:10 A.M., shaved and over to the dining room at 5:40 A.M. Lowering skies. Another day of wearing rain gear!

"Crazy day, weather-wise. Rain threatened several times, then sunshine. It ended up on the sunny but cool side as we supped at the very pleasant Knot Maul shelter, which has a table, privy, and spring.

"Met Ken Rose and Gordon Burges of the Konnarock Crew twice as they were putting on finishing touches and wheel-measuring the new trail relocation installed over the meadow the previous day. The fresh cuts in the turf were muddy as hell, but it was excellent work, especially on the stiles constructed by some of the ladies I had met Sunday night. I made good time. Had to wrap my towel across the crossbar on my pack frame to ease pain in my left shoulder blade.

"Bill and Ed caught up with me near the O'Lystery Community Park, where our group stayed overnight in 1981. Tried to contact Wayne Bruce, the fire warden, but no one was home. Clothes on the line, doors unlocked? All of us snacked on the picnic table at the pavillion, then proceeded to the Knot Maul Branch shelter, reaching it in an hour. Fired up my Zip Ztove, made a one-man portion of my freeze-dried beef stew with Stove Top dressing, and had a candy bar and coffee. All I wanted. Stove continues to work like a charm. Found note from Judy Jenner. She is still one shelter ahead of us—nine miles. All in all a very pleasant day. Temperature a cool 60 degrees at 8 P.M. Went past many poke salad (poke weed) plants during the day. Had they been near the shelter I would have gathered and cooked them for the evening meal. Had fire going after supper; made a late pot of tea. Loath to go to bed. Almost a full moon shining through the trees."

Tuesday, June 5
Knot Maul Branch Shelter to Jenkins Shelter
20 miles

"Up at 5:40 A.M. and on my way at 7:00 A.M.; others later. Our goal for the day—the Davis Farm Campsite, an 18-mile day. Made good time all day through more beautiful country. Ate lunch at Chestnut Knob shelter at elevation 4,309 feet. Excellent views, but horribly blazed trail through almost a mile of open-field walking. There was one post and a directional arrow at the beginning, no posts after that, and only an occasional blaze on a rock half hidden by waist-high grass! Found note from Judy Jenner written earlier in the day.

"Ed and Bill arrived as I was leaving the shelter, and they remained for lunch. I continued on alone. Ed caught up with me late in the afternoon. We stopped at two viewpoints off the Trail to view Burkes Garden from above, quite a sight, the Garden seemingly formed in a crater.

"At 5:30 P.M., we reached a gravel road, VA 623, where our group of six had camped in 1981 after the biannual ATC meeting in Cullowee, North Carolina. From there, we walked steadily north looking for a sign to Davis Farm Campsite. Realized we had missed it. Left a note on the Trail for Bill and hurried on. In a surprisingly short time, we came to a sign reading 'Shelter Trail,' and in moments we were at Jenkins shelter being greeted by Judy. We were most happy to have shelter, and Judy was equally happy to have companionship. I ate a cold supper—slices of Spam with bread and margarine, plus coffee. Judy built a fire, which was most welcome. Surprised to have Bill walk in at 9:30 P.M.! He had seen a blue blaze trail and followed it down the mountain to the Davis Farm Campsite, which he reported to be very poor and seemingly unused. In any event, we were all together but dead tired after a 20-mile hike! In bed at 9:45 P.M., the other three visiting at the table. Very nice, roomy shelter."

Wednesday, June 6
Jenkins Shelter to Bastian, Virginia
12 miles

"Up at a late 6:30 A.M. Leisurely breakfast, clear day. Left shelter at 8:40 A.M. Hard to get legs moving after yesterday's marathon! Some 20 to 25 stream crossings in a space of three to four miles. Really beautiful country. Judy was the first to leave camp. Ed and Bill passed me, but the three of us joined Judy at the end of the section at the junction of U.S. 21 and U.S. 52 at 3 P.M. Judy had already called Levi Long, and within two to three minutes Jan Long appeared in her van. She drove us first to a grocery store for beer and snacks then to the Levi Long Hostel.

"Ed's trail name is 'Budman.' Bud as in Budweiser. There is a refrigerator in the Long Hostel, so we laid in a good supply of beer and left quite a bit for later arrivals. Judy and Bill had taken one brief look at the condition of the old mattresses in the Long Hostel and decided they wished to stay in a motel. Levi obligingly took them over to Bland for the motel. All of us, however, ate dinner at Long's Corner Cafe—hamburger steak, three vegetables, fresh corn bread, coffee, and a sundae for dessert. Found to my surprise that my bill had already been paid by Dorothy Mauldin, who had made the arrangements a week before. Bless her!

"After supper, Ed and I made long distance phone calls. I called my daughter, Sharon, in Harpers Ferry, and asked her to bring certain items down to Bastian. Her out-of-town friend had arrived the previous day, and they, plus another friend, are to arrive Thursday. At 10:30 P.M., as we prepared for bed, I took a close look at the mattress on the floor of my bedroom. It bore the dirt and grime of ages and I could see why Judy and Motel Al were repulsed. I simply put my five-by-seven-foot ground cloth over the entire mattress. No problem.

"Before going to sleep, I reflected a bit on this pleasant stopover at the village of Bastian and the warm hospitality displayed by Jan and Levi Long, and by Jan's mother, who helps in the kitchen. Their van has the eight-inch green and white National Scenic Trail sign on the front. Their state license tags read 'Hiker AT.' The meals bear the Long trademark, each plate having a slice of red tomato and a big slice of white onion. Great stuff for fresh-vegetable-starved hikers. A hiker there on a Sunday receives a special treat—mountain music performed by neighborhood people who gather at the Long's Corner Cafe, and with Levi playing the fiddle, they entertain anyone within earshot. After my hiking days are over (not too far distant!), I would like to take a trip by car and visit many of these places. I would arrange such a trip so that I would certainly be at Bastian on a Sunday!"

Jan and Levi Long at Bastian, Virginia.

Thursday, June 7
Bastian, Virginia, to Jenny Knob Shelter
12 miles

"Up at 5:30 A.M. Worked on my notes, then washed my dirty clothes in cold water in the kitchen sink and hung them on the clothesline to dry. At 8 A.M., Levi drove over (only 100 yards!) to tell me that Sharon would call me in 15 minutes. I went right over to the diner and ordered the house breakfast—eggs (seemed like 3), a big slice of ham, hashbrowns, toast, and coffee. Sharon did call; she and her friends are not coming! Complication with work schedule of one of the friends. So be it. Sharon will hike with me as I near Shenandoah National Park.

"At breakfast, I met Henry Ford and his wife, Doris, formerly of Greensboro, North Carolina, now in this area (Max Meadows), indefatigable workers on the Trail. We discussed the lack of paint blazing in the open area around Chestnut Knob shelter. Back at the hostel, I continued working on my notes and got all my gear packed, after which Ed and I had an early noonday meal at the diner— chicken and dumplings with all the other 'fixins.'

"At 12:30 P.M., Levi drove the two of us back to the trailhead on U.S. 21-52, and we began hiking up, up to regain the elevation we lost on Wednesday. Hot day. Went through much more Hurricane Hugo damage, most of which the trail club has removed. Got into Jenny Knob shelter at 7 P.M. Ate a light supper, all I needed after those two big meals at Levi's diner.

"At the shelter, I enjoyed meeting and visiting with the British couple, Tim Osman and Melanie Dean. The story of how they happened to be on the Trail is interesting. Melanie had worked in the United States for a short time and had seen a poster about the Trail, on which was listed the address and phone number of the ATC. Back in London, she and Tim discussed the possibility of hiking the Trail. One Friday night (afternoon our time), on impulse, they phoned the ATC, made a few inquiries, and asked if there was a book available that would be helpful to them. My book, *Appalachian Hiker*, was mentioned. Credit card number furnished, the book was mailed. After reading the book and discussing it, one of them said, 'Let's do it.' The other promptly agreed. They sold their two cars, rented their apartment for a year, came to the U.S., and shortly found themselves on the Trail in Georgia. So here they were, having finished more than one-fourth of the Trail, and obviously thoroughly enjoying it. They dutifully made entries in the shelter log books and signed their entries simply as 'Thatcher's Children.'"

Tim and Melanie did finish the entire Trail in September, after which they rented a car and visited many points in the United States, including a number of Trail towns before returning to England.

Friday, June 8
Jenny Knob Shelter to Wapiti Shelter
13 miles

"Up at 5:25 A.M. Left shelter at 6:40 A.M. Ed caught up with me about 9 A.M. Very steep (20 to 25 percent) grades over Brushy Mountain. Wild country. Descent very rocky and steep. Approaches to VA 42 go through open field area that needs more posts to identify the Trail. Only two posts in some 300 yards of shoulder-high grass!

"Visited the Trent grocery store at 10 A.M., a scant 0.2 miles off the Trail on VA 606. Had a cheese sandwich from my pack, plus one pint of ice cream—my undoing! Had a hard time finding enthusiasm to continue the hike. Had said good-bye to Ed, who is going on to Doc's Knob shelter then early into Pearisburg. Had hiked with him the past 10 days; he is a very nice hiking companion. Walked with Judy Jenner in the afternoon, crossing Dismal Creek many times. Seemed as though we would never get to Wapiti shelter. Rested a number of times; finally reached it around 5 P.M. The two Brits, Tim and Melanie, were already there, as was David Poole, a southbounder. Worked on my notes until supper time. Bill arrived at about 6 P.M.

"Enjoyed a wonderful evening visiting with the two Brits. Had a big fire going, which we stoked until bedtime. It burned brightly for hours after we went to bed. A full moon shone through the trees at about 10:30 P.M., and continued to shine all night long. The shelter is about 150 yards from Dismal Creek at a Trail bridge crossing where the water is three feet deep. A most pleasant location. We drank water from the creek, but we boiled it."

Saturday, June 9
Wapiti Shelter to Woodshole
6 miles

"Up at 5:25 A.M., same as yesterday. Not using an alarm, but I seem to be geared to getting up about 5:30 to 6:00 A.M. The moon was just going down and the sun's light (before dawn) made the change in light sources almost imperceptible. I had prepared plenty of wood for my wood stove, but used it neither for the evening meal, nor for breakfast. In both cases, Bill's propane stove provided enough hot water for my two simple meals. Bill, the first to leave camp, was heading directly for Pearisburg in one day (about 16 miles).

"Judy and I left at 6:40 A.M. Very pleasant Trail with moderate grades. We dawdled a bit, enjoying the views at the rock outcroppings. We also left the Trail for about 200 yards to enjoy the views from the summit of Flat Top where three or four communication towers are located. Arrived at Woodshole at noon, greeted by Tillie Wood, whom I had last seen at my send-off breakfast at Dahlonega, Georgia, on April 14. Tillie invited Judy and me to her porch for a glass of wine. She also handed me some 10 pieces of mail which she had picked up at the general delivery window at the post office in Pearisburg. After a bit of visiting, I retired to the hostel to read and answer my mail.

"Among the usual cards and letters from my friends was a package from Sharon with some medicine and clothes I had requested. Also, a small package from Appalachian Outfitters in Oakton, Virginia, contained a new rain cover for my 20-year-old Kelty backpack. In 1970, I had sent an S.O.S. to them asking them for a new and larger Kelty pack, which I received three days later at Delaware Water Gap, Pennsylvania. Now it was a rain cover to protect that same pack.

"Judy and I enjoyed lunch in the covered dining room in the hostel—real class. Shortly afterward, her husband, Dave Startzell, arrived from Harpers Ferry to spirit his wife away from the Trail for the rest of the weekend. Hikers began strolling in from 4 P.M. on. Then Bill arrived from Pearisburg in his car. I arranged to meet him the next night for pizza. Still later, a retired U.S. Forest Service employee, Bane Burton, arrived. Bane was the fellow who gave me a quart of good drinking water in 1970 as I approached the pollen-covered pond at my destination for the night, Big Pond shelter. Enjoyed a visit with him. I also gave a demonstration on the use of my tiny woodburning stove to the other hikers and to Tillie and her houseguests.

"At around 9 P.M., I phoned my wife, Mary. She and her friend, Lorraine Hanlon, had returned earlier in the day from the Far East—Singapore and Hong Kong. She learned on her return that our hot water heater had sprung a leak, and had to be replaced at a cost of $800. Such is life in the big city!"

Sunday, June 10
Woodshole to Holy Family Hospice, Pearisburg, Virginia
10 miles

"Up very early and downstairs to the dining room in the hostel. Wrote more cards and letters. Very cool breeze in that open air breezeway, and I eventually moved into the warmer confines of the main house. At 7:30 A.M., Tillie served all the hikers a super breakfast—orange juice, link sausage, eggs, grits, home-made biscuits, and coffee! A wonderful experience that was discussed later by hikers who had enjoyed it. Some of the younger hikers do become a bit home-sick after weeks on the Trail, and a Sunday morning breakfast with the family touch Tillie provides is deeply appreciated.

"At 8:40 A.M., I put my heavy Kelty pack in Tillie's car and set forth for Pearisburg carrying a light day pack only. An absolutely delightful walk, very mod-erate grades, rhododendron, azalea, and other flowers in bloom. Just plain beau-tiful country. A sunny morning, light breeze, temperature around 65 degrees, excellent hiking weather. Some breathtaking views of the valley, of Pearisburg, and of nearby mountain ranges. On reaching Angels Rest, which overlooks the city of Pearisburg, I found an ice cooler on the Trail. I hefted it, heavy! I hailed anyone

Tillie Wood's rustic bunkhouse at Woodshole.

within earshot. An answering call came, and who should emerge from the cover of the trees but, you guessed it, Marty Dominy! This time he had managed to buy some of my favorite beer, Stroh's, and we each drank a can with great relish.

"He then departed, carrying the heavy cooler, planning to meet me again within a half hour at the Trail intersection on VA 100. At that point, I also met hikers Mark Elliott and Sandra Bernoi. Marty joined us and gave us all a ride to the Holy Family Hospice where we would spend the night.

"Marty took off shortly, bound for his place of work at Macon in middle Georgia. After he left, Mark, Sandra, and I sat in the shade of one of the big trees on the hospice lawn and discussed Marty's exploits. He had met me on April 14, the first day of my hike. At Three Forks, some three miles from Springer, he was present with a bottle of champagne as an auspicious send-off gesture. He had met me at many odd and unexpected places ever since. And here at Pearisburg, almost two months later and 615 miles into my hike, he had done it again.

"Back at the unusual building that serves as a place of rest and recreation for hikers, I took a much-needed shower. Gave special attention to the crotch area, where I was beginning to suffer from the chafing caused by infrequent bathing, a not uncommon problem on these long hikes. I used the term 'unusual building,' because it was formerly a barn out in the country. It was cut into four pieces and brought to the church property where the pieces were reunited, and a shower, kitchen, and library added. The former loft of the barn now serves as the sleeping area.

"Many of the hikers in 1977 interrupted their hikes for long periods of time to assist in the construction of the new hospice. And why the term hospice instead of hostel? Father Charles, a much-loved former priest of the Holy Family Church, favored the word hospice as being more in keeping with the old-world meaning of the type of service he was providing at Pearisburg. I checked *The American Heritage Dictionary*: 'hospice—a shelter or lodging for travelers, children, or the destitute often maintained by a monastic order.' And the same dictionary, under hostel: a supervised, inexpensive lodging for youthful travelers.' Also called 'youth hostel.' I will let the reader or the thru-hiker make his own decision as to whether the facilities along the Trail are hospices or hostels. I have made my own decision. But I think Father Charles was correct in his choice of the word 'hospice' for his operation.

"At 7 P.M., Bill arrived and took Sandra, Mark, and me to the Pizza Hut, where we joined other Trail hikers. First, two trips to the salad bar, then Bill and I shared a pizza. A great day. Back to the hospice, where Mark and Sandra took my dirty clothes to the laundromat and washed them with theirs. Very thoughtful. But then I had been the recipient of a tremendous amount of such thoughtfulness all during the hike, and especially during the past four days, from the Longs at Bastian, to Tillie Wood at Woodshole, to Marty Dominy, Dorothy

Mauldin, and various people here at Pearisburg. The Appalachian Trail family takes care of its own. To bed at 10:30 P.M., a long and interesting day."

Marty had driven all the way up from Georgia to make this one final contact with me on my 1990 hike. Marty's ability to find me at odd places bordered on the phenomenal. I was not operating on a fixed schedule, as readers will have already deduced. Therefore, Marty had to stop many times, charge into one of the trailside shelters, examine the log book, check with other hikers, and then carry that heavy cooler up the mountain and take a stand. Unbelievable. We had time only for a short visit on the grounds of the hospice, as Marty had miles left to travel.

I would not see him again until late April of 1991, when we were privileged to have him as our houseguest for two days of festivities conducted by the U.S. Forest Service in Washington, D.C. The culmination of those activities was the Forest Service's presentation of an award to Marty, as president of the BMTA, for extraordinary contributions in the construction and maintenance of that organization's trail in Georgia. I attended the very impressive award ceremonies.

Monday, June 11
Pearisburg to Symms Gap Meadow
10 miles

"Up at 5:30 A.M. Using the electric stove in the hospice, I had breakfast number one, coffee and granola. Later, Dave Startzell and Judy arrived at the hospice, and Judy announced she was discontinuing her hike and going back to Harpers Ferry with Dave. I was being discarded in favor of a younger man, her husband! Such is life. I felt that perhaps Judy was discouraged at the thought of that 18-mile hike over Peters Mountain with no shelter in that stretch. In any event, Judy and Dave drove me over to the Virginia Restaurant where I met the Brits and I had breakfast number two, a whopping combination of pancakes, sausages, and home-fried potatoes.

"Bill was also there and after breakfast he took us to the Food Lion, an excellent grocery, and I purchased almost $10 worth of groceries. Then over to the hospice to boil my six eggs and to pack all the newly purchased groceries into my pack, the routine which all thru-hikers dread! Bill drove the Brits and me to the Shumate Bridge, where we would begin the day's hike. Said good-bye to Bill, who had hiked with me for more than 10 days. He was driving back to his home in New Jersey. He was another one of those pleasant friendships one makes on a long-distance hike of the Trail.

"The hike over the summit of Peters Mountain was not too difficult. We reached the summit at 11:30 A.M., but found the guidebook very confusing as to this stretch of the Trail. The three of us ate lunch on the Trail at 1 P.M., then continued hiking through very interesting country on this, our first day in West Virginia. The Trail straddles the border of Virginia and West Virginia along Peters Mountain. We enjoyed tremendous views from some of the open areas we traversed. In mid-afternoon, we met a group of about 16 young people from several Catholic churches in Toledo, Ohio. They were hiking for two days and then spending perhaps a week or so doing manual work for the less fortunate members of the Holy Family parish in Pearisburg, Virginia. A very worthy program.

"The Brits and I, plus the young people, all camped at Symms Gap Meadow. I set up my tarp for shelter, one of the very few times it was necessary during my entire hike. I used my stove to cook a Lipton chicken-flavored dinner plus a half-can of chunky soup given to me by a member of the church group. We had a large fire going and roasted marshmallows later in the evening. It was a cool, windy night and I soaked up much wood smoke standing around the fire with the wind shifting frequently. The campsite, located on a high open area, provided excellent views of the villages and homes in the valley below. To bed under my tarp at 9:45 P.M."

Tuesday, June 12
Symms Gap Meadow Campsite to Baileys Gap Shelter
13 miles

"Up at 12:30 A.M. and again at 3:30 A.M., to put more wood on the fire. Up for good at 5:30 A.M. Got the fire going from the coals. Made coffee for myself and for the Brits. Had the usual instant oatmeal and this time some granola for breakfast. Woke up the Brits. Got my tarp packed away.

"Left camp at 6:40 A.M. Uneventful but pleasant hiking. The U.S. Forest Service has the Trail well-marked, but the hikers' consensus for the day was that the sign reading 'Pine Swamp Shelter 1.3 miles' was off by one mile; it was more like 2.3. The Brits, plus Larry Young and Rob Bossert, were at the shelter when I arrived. Most of them going on to War Spur shelter before nightfall, whereas I will go only the four miles to Bailey Gap shelter.

"I ate a substantial lunch at the shelter, my usual noonday lunch—one hard-boiled egg, one muffin, some peanut butter, and this time a candy bar. The group of young people with whom we camped last night arrived at the shelter as I was leaving at 12:15 P.M. Worked on my notes at the shelter, the kind of routine I prefer. Notes made currently are infinitely more accurate than those made a day or two later.

"My four-mile hike to Bailey Gap shelter was uneventful, except that I did note much new trail relocation work done by the Konnarock Crew. I found

Larry Young at the shelter when I arrived. We found two springs, neither very statisfactory. Later, we found a good spring marked with a sign. Had a better-than-usual evening meal—a one-pound, three-ounce can of Campbell's Chunky Sirloin Burger soup, plus a pot of coffee and some peanut butter and granola. Nothing you would find at your favorite restaurant, but one learns to adapt when hiking the Trail.

"Bailey Gap shelter was rather buggy so we built a fire, which more or less discouraged the mosquitos and other insects. A most pleasant evening, with the sun sinking low and birds singing their going-to-bed songs, while we enjoyed the fire. Washed and shaved.

"Love these days when I can get into the shelter early enough to perform the needed ablutions and get my diary and daily log up to date. At 6:30 P.M., two young hikers arrived, hikers who were at Woodshole Sunday and with whom I had enjoyed that wonderful breakfast. And that concludes my account of a pleasant day's hike into Bailey Gap shelter on June 12, 1990."

In contrast to this day, let me recite the account of my hike to that same shelter on May 14, 1970, just as it appeared in my diary and in the original *Appalachian Hiker* book in 1971, a description of the most miserable night I have ever spent on the Appalachian Trail:

■ ■ ■

A wild, wild day! Up at 5:00, wrote more postcards. Breakfast with Mary Finley at 6:30. On my way at 7:30. Hiked a good mile . . . had forgotten the guide book. Dashed back to Finley place . . . 40 minutes lost. Blazing in Pearisburg streets very dim. Motorist stopped and gave me directions. Crossed two bridges, saw Highway Appalachian Trail crossing sign. Turned off U.S. 460 and blundered ahead on the old Trail where paint blazes were not obliterated. Back to U.S. 460. A State Trooper helped me out. This time found the new Trail. Rough going especially climbing the second mountain at a very steep grade on the road in the hot sun. First day I have been bothered by insects to any degree. Had to wear kerchief around my head and ears. Chugged into Interior at 6:30; reached Bailey Gap shelter at 7:45. Quickly made bed . . . put water on dehydrated food, dashed to spring with upper part of my body clad in paper-thin t-shirt. Trail to spring horrible. No sign. No blue blazes. No trail . . . period. Finally found the water and promptly got lost.

Took an East-West compass bearing trying to pick up the Trail. No luck. What a predicament. My open pack beside the table at the shelter . . . all my gear including matches and flashlight. Nothing I could do except bed down . . . bare arms and all, pull leaves over me for warmth, and grit through eight hours of misery. Slept but little . . . watched moon slowly sink. Luckily it stayed clear, no rain.

Friday, May 15. Up at 6:00, collected my water bottles, shook leaves and dirt out of clothes. Took a south reading on compass and climbed to top of mountain and found dirt road. Followed it north for 10 minutes and hit the AT. Turned left, hit shelter from the north side in 5 to 10 minutes. All my stuff OK."

Wednesday, June 13
Bailey Gap Shelter to Laurel Creek Shelter
14 miles

"Overslept. Up at 6:30 A.M. and ate a quick breakfast. Left shelter at 7:20 A.M. Made good time through very pleasant area. Enjoyed the viewpoint on the rock outcrop at Wind Rock, elevation 4,100. Good signs erected by Jefferson National Forest. Beginning at milepoint 7.8, I noticed some 40 new waterbars. Last 1.3 miles going into War Spur shelter is very steep, perhaps 20 percent grade, and badly gullied. Reached the shelter at noon. Larry Young there, later Red Climme and Bret Coffee arrived. All of us considering our options in getting to Cloverdale (near Roanoke) on a Sunday. It is a mail stop and the post office closes at 11:30 A.M. on Saturday!

"Left War Spur at 1:30 P.M. and made the big climb, 1,700 feet, up Johns Creek Mountain. Arrived at the new Laurel Creek shelter (a real jewel) at 5:50 P.M. Made dinner after first sweeping out the shelter floor and the privy. Had a bowl of soup then a big portion of Lipton's noodles and chicken sauce. Very filling. Used my wood stove for cooking, then the fireplace and cast iron grill for dishwashing and shaving.

"This was the first time since I began my hike on April 14 that I would be alone in a shelter. In 1970, it was customary. Under the circumstances, I especially enjoyed the fire. Finished my notes at 8:45 P.M.; getting too dark to write. Watched the fire from my sleeping bag. When the last flame flickered out at exactly 9:30 P.M., I lay down to sleep. And from my daily log, I note my comment that it has been 10 days in a row without rain."

Thursday, June 14, Flag Day
Laurel Creek Shelter to Niday Shelter
13 miles

"Up at 5:15 A.M. Barely light enough to see. Started fire promptly in outdoor grill. Made pot of coffee, heated water for cereal. Then worked on daily log for yesterday. Left shelter at 7:15 A.M., very rough going. Blazing not so good, especially in open pasture and rock areas; somewhat stingy with the white paint on the rocks. I missed the blue blaze trail to Sarver Cabin as did many others. Apparently there is no sign. Some good views from the rock overlooks from mile 6.8 to 8.0, but very slow going over the steep rocky area. Not a particularly interesting 13 miles.

"Arrived at Niday shelter at 4:15 P.M. Met the Wynns (Ma and Pa) at the shelter as they were heading back to their car on VA 42. They spoke highly of the campsite at VA 624, which I planned to reach the following day. At the shelter, I obtained water from the creek some 0.1 mile away. Someone had been thoughtful enough to leave an empty two-quart Gatorade bottle at the shelter and I filled that also. Used my wood stove for Virginia Pea soup (very tasty, used it often) and to make Stove Top dressing. A bit of the ever-ready peanut butter and three cups of coffee made an adequate meal. Took a spit bath, washed my underwear, and hung them on the line to dry. Resolved to get a motel in Cloverdale and to wash things properly. To bed at 9:30 P.M., again the only occupant."

Friday, June 15
Niday Shelter to VA 624
14 miles

"Up at 5:30 A.M., cold breakfast and on my way at 6:30 A.M. Began raining even before I began hiking and I encountered intermittent rain all day. Crossed VA 621 at 7:20 A.M. Shortly thereafter, I began hiking toward the summit of Brush Mountain on a new Konnarock-ALDHA relocation installed from November 8 to 11, 1988, according to a plaque on a Chuck Wood birdhouse located directly beside the Trail.

Chuck Wood, a resident of Norristown, Pennsylvania, has been making bluebird houses for years. Each one is numbered and a plaque gives the name of the recipient. Mine is number 729, which Chuck had delivered to me in March of 1990, shortly before I began my hike. His son, also named Chuck, is a member of ALDHA who participated in the relocation.

"This is an excellent trail construction job, a sidehill trail with the downhill side buttressed throughout with eight-inch diameter logs. One of the best jobs I have ever witnessed. Walked all the way to the summit without taking off my pack. Very proud of my accomplishment but more proud of the expertise of the trail crews in constructing a trail that permitted me to do it.

"Reached VA 620 around noon. Raining. There were several trash containers at the intersection and I got rid of my tiny, three-day accumulation of trash.

"I ate lunch near the well-signed side trail leading to Pickle Branch shelter. Very rough going thereafter until I reached the summit of Cove Mountain around 3:30 P.M. Around 4 P.M., I became concerned as my compass showed I was hiking due south. By itself, this is not too alarming because sometimes one has to hike south to reach Katahdin up north. But I had been hiking south for some time; hence the concern. I examined the guidebook and map, but neither was of help. Shortly thereafter, I arrived at a heavily signed and blazed trail intersection which showed the route to the parking area on VA 311.

"From there it was a slow, dangerous descent over huge rocks, wet and slippery, and at a very steep grade. To make matters worse, the Trail was poorly blazed in some areas. Eventually, around 5 P.M., I reached another junction with more signs, one to the VA 311 parking area, the other to VA 624—my two-day destination with a grocery store and lodging.

"More dangerous descents over rocky terrain. Reached VA 624 at 6 P.M. and found the Catawba Grocery. The rain had stopped but everything was wet. I bought two hotdogs and headed for the far end of the adjoining small pond. Sat down on the spanking new picnic table built just six days earlier by two thru-hikers, Rambling Dan, of Kentucky, and Flamingo Legs, of Florida. Nice job, room for four people.

"After putting away the two hotdogs, I walked back to the store and examined the little building next to it. It is described in the *Thru-Hikers Handbook* as 'a shelter of last resort.' The Last *Philosopher's Guide* used even more deprecatory language. I have slept in some rather marginal places and my standards are pretty low, but this place looked grim even by my standards.

"I bought some more groceries in the store, including two pints of ice cream, and after polishing off the ice cream, I phoned some motels in Salem and obtained rates. Gene Martin, owner of the grocery store, offered to take me to the motel for a fee of five dollars. Fair enough.

"I put my pack in his pickup and off we went on a rainy night. Got into lively conversation with Martin, and discovered he was a member of a huge fraternity which comprises about 99.9 percent of the world's popuation. The name of the fraternity is Nice People! He took me to a motel that was much closer than the one of which I had inquired, and the cost was $10 less. And he, perhaps dimly suspecting that I might be a member of his fraternity, waived the taxi fee I had agreed to pay.

"So there I was, in an attractive motel room, and even though I was dead tired, I concluded that things could be a helluva lot worse! I could have been sleeping in the unlit 'shelter of last resort' or huddled in my sleeping bag up in the mountains under the dubious protection of my tarp. I took a much-needed shower and afterwards performed a delicate operation. During my 1989 mission hike in California, my feet had taken a severe beating on the five-mile, all upgrade, hard-surface highway going north out of San Luis Obispo. By the end of the second day of that hike, I was certain I would lose the nail from my left big toe. It took almost a year to happen but this was the time. Also, in some 700 miles of hiking from Springer Mountain this year, I must have damaged the right big toenail, as well as one of the second toenails, as all three were badly discolored. And now, after a long hot shower, it seemed the time had come for the removal job. All three came off easily.

"After the shower, I looked at myself in the big mirror and cringed a bit. I looked so skinny! To bed about 11 P.M., to sleep in minutes."

Saturday, June 16
VA 624 to Campbell Shelter
10 miles

"Up early and over to the nearby Hardee's restaurant at 7 A.M. for a pancake and sausage breakfast. I'm a loyal McDonald's fan, but their restaurant was much too far away. Back at the motel, I was surprised to hear a knock at the door. Gene Martin was there, ready to take me back to Catawba to continue my hike. Hurriedly finished packing my gear, and we drove back to the store. Bought another pint of ice cream and at 10:30 A.M., I shouldered my pack and got back on the Trail.

"Very pleasant hiking all day, quite a contrast from yesterday. The first one-and-a-half hours, I walked through pastures with big four-foot diameter rolls of hay. After noon, I was at a higher elevation. Met 8 to 10 people on the Trail during the day, including Charles Parry, the supervisor of trails for the Roanoke Appalachian Trail Club. He had a Stihl chainsaw (I was later told by members of the Roanoke Club that the chainsaw is Charlie's constant companion whenever he does any trail work). We sat down and visited for 20 minutes. I had spent many years in trail maintenance work and I have a warm spot in my heart for anyone engaged in that activity.

"Shortly after leaving Parry, I was surprised to see a five-foot black snake lolling directly across the Trail. Seeing me, he slowly moved away and when last seen he was climbing straight up a 16-inch diameter oak tree.

"Still further on, I came to VA 311 and the big parking area, which featured a big sign indicating that it was for those hiking the Appalachian Trail. We have indeed become a recognizable entity.

"Also while hiking today, I reflected on my hike the previous day, especially the long, dangerous descent over Cove Mountain, and I realized how dramatically the Trail has changed in the 20 years since I last hiked it in its entirety. It is more of a wilderness trail now, no doubt about that. One seldom sees a house. Road walking has become very infrequent, and one seldom walks on a road for more than a short distance before the Trail leads back into the woods.

"Continuing my hike, I came across the metal Boy Scouts of America 30-foot-long shelter where I had stayed in 1970. Then in another 20 to 25 minutes, I reached the Catawba shelter. Visited with Irv Warfield, an inveterate hiker and trail worker from Richmond, Virginia. Visited with another fellow who was wearing the dirtiest, once white, t-shirt I had ever seen.

"None of us hikers would win any medals for cleanliness, but this fellow seemed to be overdoing it. It made me think of the hiker we met at Long Pond shelter in Maine in 1977. He showed us his t-shirt and boasted that 'this t-shirt hasn't been washed since I left Georgia!'

"Leaving the Catawba shelter, I shortly reached the spectacular McAfees Knob. What a view! The Knob seemed to jut out into space. And how lucky we (the people) were to be able to buy it. That's a story in itself. I stood on the Knob for about 10 minutes drinking in that wonderful view and experiencing the sensation of being out in space. Visited with Henry Johnson, who was staying at the Catawba shelter.

"Walking on still further, I came upon the Pig Farm Campsite with picnic table. Noticed a father and two children camping overnight with their tent already up. Papa was poking through the fireplace to remove all the unburnable litter! What a nice example for those two young children.

"Within five minutes after leaving the campsite, I came upon the new shelter dedicated to Tom and Charlene Campbell, two wonderful people, longtime members of the Roanoke Appalachian Trail Club. I had stayed at their home in Roanoke during my 1970 hike. The shelter register described the October 1989 dedication with 30 people attending. Tom was for many years a vice-chairman of the ATC, and was made an Honorary Life Member. There are four trailside shelters within a space of nine miles in this area. Someone had affixed a placard at the Boy Scout shelter, which contained a tongue-in-cheek notice reading somewhat as follows, 'These crazy Virginians, trying to have the rockiest trails plus the most shelters per mile of any club in the 2,140 mile Appalachian Trail!'

"I can't leave this shelter or this day's hiking experience without commenting on two items: (1) the clever and very helpful entrance platform in front of the shelter, and (2) the paint blazing I observed in my 10 miles of hiking this day.

"Because of the terrain's unevenness, or for other reasons, many shelters are erected so the sleeping platform is anywhere from three to four-and-a-half feet off the ground. Frequently, no provision is made for the hiker to get into the shelter in an easy manner. At two of the shelters I had stayed in overnight, hikers had moved the picnic table over to the shelter and used the table to climb into it. Not a good arrangement. At the Campbell shelter, a landing platform has been built with stair steps on two sides, a very, very convenient arrangement. At other shelters, even a large log rolled into place would be a big help, but the platform arrangement is excellent.

"The second item is the paint blazing. My penchant for clear, precise paint blazes is well known. To achieve such blazes requires, in most cases, the bark of the tree to be scraped to provide a good base for the paint. My daily log that I mailed to the ATC contains the following passage for June 16: 'Paint Blazing: Since beginning my hike on April 14, this is the first day where I could definitely state that almost all paint blazes had been applied to areas which had first been scraped! It does make a difference.'"

Sunday, June 17
Campbell Shelter to U.S. 220, Cloverdale, Virginia
15 miles

"Awake at 5:20 A.M. and on my way at 6:15 A.M., my earliest take off to date. Pleasant hike and climb to Tinker Cliffs with its spectacular views.

"After leaving the cliffs, I got mixed up somehow and started going back south! Corrected my error but it cost me time (30 minutes), and more important, energy! Ate my lunch at Lambert Meadow shelter and then pushed on and on, a long day with plenty of climbing. Interesting route but very tiring. Finally reached U.S. 220 in Cloverdale at 5:45 P.M. There is a convenience store near the Trail intersection, and I bought a can of beer. After that it was a one-dollar ice cream cone, which I consumed with the same pleasure as the beer.

"At that point, I made an important phone call. At the Lambert Meadow shelter, and at a previous shelter, I had examined the shelter register. In each of them on the first page was an invitation from Homer and Therese Witcher to any thru-hiker to give them a call if overnight lodging was desired after reaching Cloverdale. Homer is the supervisor of the 13 trailside shelters maintained by the Roanoke club; his wife is the vice president of the club. They had listed their phone number on the registers. So now I called them and they promised to pick me up in minutes.

"While waiting, I invested another dollar in an ice cream cone and finished that off just as they arrived. They took me to their home about two miles north of the Trail intersection. They both had an evening engagement and left me at their home with other members of their family.

"I was so tired I could hardly see straight! No exaggeration, I was dead. I made one-and-a-half grilled cheese sandwiches, then went to bed on the floor of the Trail bedroom. This room has a double-decker bunk with beds all made, but I was eternally grateful for the comfort of the carpeted floor. I weighed myself, 136! Confirmed it the next morning, 136. Lightest since I finished high school in 1931. Oddly enough, on my 1970 hike my weight reached its lowest at Roanoke.

"I telephoned my daughter at Harpers Ferry, and we agreed to meet Thursday, June 21, at Peaks of Otter Restaurant on the Blue Ridge Parkway.

"During the hike this day, I had seen a young deer and had scared up a number of grouse. Had also seen prolific stands of two plants, poison ivy and pokeweed."

Monday, June 18
U.S. 220 to VA 779
2 miles

"At the home of Homer and Therese Witcher in Cloverdale. Awoke around 3 A.M. Not much sleep thereafter. Saw Homer and Therese off to their jobs at different hospitals. Coffee and toast for breakfast number one. Around 9 A.M., Homer's daughter, Kimberly, and a friend, drove me to the post office in Cloverdale. It was a real adventure to an out-of-the-way place, not recommended for a hiker mail stop. Picked up eight pieces of mail. Then stopped at Shoney's for an all-you-can-eat (AYCE) breakfast.

"Back at the Witcher house, I thoroughly greased my boots, washed and dried my clothes, and wrote a number of postcards. For lunch, I microwaved one huge potato, which I had purchased for 55¢! Made up a grocery shopping list and brought my trail notes up to date. Drove with the girls, Kimberly and Tonja, to a giant mall and bought a pair of hiking pants. Then to Winn-Dixie for $15.85 of groceries. At the grocery store, in a crowded aisle, I met none other than Mark Elliott and Sandra Bernoi for the umpteenth time, and there would be more meetings to follow.

"Went to dinner with the Witcher family at a K&W Cafeteria, seven of us in the group. On the way home, Therese dropped Homer and me off on the Trail at its intersection with VA 779, and we walked back to their home on their 'country lane' route, which Homer and Therese keep mowed to a width of eight feet—a Herculean task, as the lawnmower must be hoisted over the tops of about six stiles in the two-mile route.

"They do a tremendous amount of trail and shelter work, just two of the many trail stalwarts in the 31 trail clubs that keep the trail and the shelters in generally excellent condition. They were married on McAfees Knob, and Homer and Therese had to cut through a new trail so that the friendly sherpas could carry up the wedding cake and five gallons of punch.

"While daylight still prevailed, I played catch with a softball with them, Therese being a member of the ladies softball team. Her future softball playing may be hampered a bit. Today she had a prenatal medical exam; everything okay. Her baby is due January 30, 1991. She is very excited, as it is her first.

"To bed at 10:20 P.M., somewhat exhausted from my day of rest off the Trail!"

Tuesday, June 19
VA 779 to Fullhardt Knob Shelter
4 miles

"Slept rather poorly, up at 5:20 A.M. Weighed myself, 144! Gained eight pounds in one day. Must have been really dehydrated. Spent the day cleaning my pack, scouring cooking pots and repacking. Read the May-June issue of

Appalachian Trailway News and will leave it at Fullhardt Knob shelter. Kim and Tonja took me to Cloverdale Post Office at 2 P.M. and I mailed some articles home. They put me on VA 779 where it crosses the Appalachian Trail near U.S. 11. From there it was 3.9 miles to the shelter. Reached it at 4:45 P.M. Shortly after, Jeff Kingsbury arrived, then Mark and Sandra. I had a beer for each of them; they had one for me!

"Late supper, heated up can of corned beef hash with bread. Filling, but I don't see how Karl Ellingston could stand it as a steady diet as he did during his hike on the Pacific Crest Trail. Finishing my notes at 8 P.M. Really enjoyed my one-and-a-half days R&R at the Witcher home. Very nice people.

"Obtained our water at the shelter from the cistern arrangement, the only remaining one of the four or five cistern shelters that once existed on the Trail in the Jefferson National Forest. The water came out clear and cold."

Wednesday, June 20
Fullhardt Knob Shelter to Bobblets Gap Shelter
14 miles

"Up at 5:25 A.M., on my way at 6:25 A.M. Uneventful but pleasant, and not too strenuous hike of six miles to Wilson Gap shelter. Arrived there at 10 A.M., just as Jeff Kingsbury was leaving. Spent almost an hour there eating lunch, checking the guidebook, looking through the shelter registry.

"The hike to Bobblets Gap was likewise uneventful and not too strenuous. I had entered the domain of the 86-mile stretch of the Trail that is maintained by the Natural Bridge Appalachian Trail Club (NBATC). The quality of the blazing (old, infrequent) not nearly as good as on the Roanoke section; also the trail itself was overgrown. Crossed the Blue Ridge Parkway twice and walked beside it for more than a mile. Arrived at Bobblets Gap shelter at 3:15 P.M. Fourteen miles for the day.

"Jeff already here since 2 P.M. relaxing. He even had steaming-hot water on the fireplace for coffee.

"Skies became very dark; thinking rain was imminent, we decided to eat early. I had a small can of Campbell's Chunky Beef soup with bread, candy bar, and coffee. Later, some honey-roasted peanuts.

"Around 7 P.M., a British couple, John and Pam Carr, who are friends of Jeff's, arrived with fruit and doughnuts. They have their luggage at Chuck Young's place in Warrenton, Virginia. Good old Chuck, a regular volunteer at the ATC in Harpers Ferry, and a special friend of any hikers from outside the country. He had met many of them, some at the airport, taken them to his home, chauffered them around. Our goodwill ambassador! Agreed to meet the Carrs the next morning at the parkway at 9 A.M., and to join them for breakfast at the Peaks of Otter Restaurant.

"John is resting up from his hiking activities to let a bone spur problem in his foot heal up a bit. John and Pam left around 8 P.M., and I sat down to work on my notes, and promptly Dick Kelly, the shelter overseer, arrived and visited until 9 P.M. So much for my writing plans. The story of my life on this trip. My best bet is a restaurant where no one knows me, which is where I am writing these notes at 10:30 A.M., Thursday, at Peaks of Otter Restaurant. To bed at Bobblets Gap shelter at 9:30 P.M.

"A word about Dick Kelly. He provides the same type of loving care to this shelter as does Sam Waddle to the Jerry Cabin shelter in Tennessee. He has even provided a desk-type chair for the interior of the shelter, and he services the shelter regularly. It makes one wonder, what IS it about the Appalachian Trail that seems to bring out the best in people?"

Thursday, June 21
Bobblets Gap Shelter to VA 614
8 miles

"Poor night for sleeping, awoke many times. Rained hard around midnight, and for several hours thereafter. I got up at 6:30 A.M., Jeff likewise. He took off early for Cove Mountain shelter, the Jelly Stone Campground, and then for Cornelius Creek shelter.

"Having plenty of time, I made coffee using the dry wood I had picked up and broken the previous day for use in my wood stove. Got all my gear packed and then sat in the shelter at the writing desk so conveniently provided by Dick Kelly. Worked on my daily log sheet.

"At 8:40 A.M., I headed for the Blue Ridge Parkway. The Carrs were already waiting for me and we drove directly to the Peaks of Otter Restaurant for the AYCE breakfast, best of my trip so far. Made two trips for fresh fruit, then three trips for everything else: eggs, gravy, biscuits, hash browns, applesauce, and pancakes with blackberry syrup.

"The Carrs left at 10:30 A.M., and I removed myself to a quiet alcove just off the dining room. Brought notes up to date and wrote many cards, including one to Chuck Young to inform him that I had met his British friends, the Carrs.

"Sharon arrived at 12:30 P.M. We visited a bit, then drove in the Garvey van back to Bobblets Gap shelter. Both of us hiked on the Trail up to VA 43, then Sharon returned to the van and I continued on the Trail. I reached the Cove Mountain shelter at 4 P.M., stopped there briefly, then pushed on, reaching VA 614 and Sharon around 6:30 P.M.

"We then drove the two to three miles to the U.S. Forest Service North Creek Campground, rented a site, and cooked our evening meal on my two-burner Coleman stove. To bed around 10:15 P.M., Sharon on the floor of the van, I just outside. I slept rather poorly, up a number of times."

Friday, June 22
VA 614 to Thunder Hill Shelter
13 miles

"Up at 5:30 A.M., heated water for coffee and shaving. Woke Sharon at 6:15 A.M. Left camp around 7 A.M. for our appointment with John and Pam Carr at the Peaks of Otter Campground. On meeting the Carrs, we put our day packs in their car and then drove in two cars to Thunder Hill shelter. Left our van there and the Carrs took us down to where I had finished hiking Thursday night. Sharon and I, carrying day packs, began hiking at 9 A.M. Morning hiking was uneventful, and we made good time in spite of much climbing. Ate lunch around 10 A.M. and again at around 2:30 P.M. at a blue blaze trail intersection. Pushed on; skies darkened around 3 P.M., and it rained hard. Because of the rain, we did not go into Cornelius Creek shelter, one of my favorites for many years. Kept slogging on toward Thunder Hill. Rain stopped and skies cleared around 4 P.M.; then in 30 minutes, skies became very dark and it rained harder than ever. Sharon got soaked to the skin (no rain parka). My Kelty rain parka kept my day pack and the upper part of my body dry, but I was wet from the hips down. Skies cleared again, and we climbed to the almost 4,000-foot summit of Thunder Hill and reached our van at 5 P.M., wet. Sharon changed into dry clothes immediately. We turned the heater on in the van and drove to the campground where we obtained a camping spot. I, too, then changed clothes as we drove to the restaurant where they were having the Friday night seafood special at $33 for the two of us. A big line was waiting to be served, so I used the time to work on my notes for the past two days. Ate a delicious meal from 7:30 to 9 P.M., the works, including two desserts.

"Writing these notes in the antique room in the restaurant basement. Later we drove to Peaks of Otter Campground. Sharon took all the wet clothes outside the van and hung them to dry in the strong wind. It was after 10 P.M. before we both got settled down to sleep, she on the platform in the rear of the van, I on the floor. To sleep within minutes."

Saturday, June 23
Thunder Hill Shelter to U.S. 501
(via Matts Creek Shelter and return to Thunder Hill Shelter)
15 miles

"A wild day. Up at 6:00 A.M. Hot coffee and cereal using the Coleman stove. Drove to Thunder Hill shelter parking area. Parked the van, put food and clothes in our day packs and started out. Reached the Thunder Hill shelter in minutes to find Mark Elliott and Sandra Bernoi there. They had arrived Friday afternoon just as the heavy rain began, and wisely decided to stay over.

Near Thunder Hill shelter, Virginia.

"After visiting a bit, we proceeded on our day's hike; a very pleasant route. Especially pleased with the constructed rock viewpoint near Thunder Head. Reached Petites Gap at 10:20 A.M. and reached Marble Creek, site of a former shelter, at 11:30 A.M., and had our lunch there. Left around noon for one of the more beautiful eight-mile hikes along the Trail, which leads to the junction with U.S. 501; comparable to the earlier hike north from Woodshole to Pearisburg.

"Saw deer on three occasions, excellent views, walking on pine needles much of the way. We arrived at Matts Creek shelter at 2:30 P.M. Had half a candy bar and a sandwich, then proceeded mostly downgrade. Reached U.S. 501 around 4 P.M. Had no luck hitching a ride, so began walking the four miles to the Blue Ridge Parkway.

"After one mile of that business, we walked into the yard of Peyton Jackson, who was working on his car, and arranged a ride to our van at Thunder Hill shelter via the grocery store at Big Island.

"We bought a few groceries, but in our hurry we forgot to buy ice cream and popcorn, luxuries that are only infrequently enjoyed while backpacking. But, with my van and all the equipment I had in it (four different kinds of stoves, two Coleman lanterns, pots and pans), I was at this time car camping and I had looked forward to popping a big batch of corn.

"Peyton drove us back to our van, and Sharon and I promptly took our sleeping gear to the shelter. Found two hikers already there, and J.P. McMullen arrived shortly. We learned that there would probably be six in the shelter that night, so we left six cans of beer, which they were to put in the spring.

"Back to our van, and we enjoyed a hot lasagna supper with noodles, plus hot tea and Claxton fruitcake for dessert. Worked on my notes in the van until darkness intervened, sipping on some three-year-old plum brandy direct from the remote mountain areas of Serbia. My friend Mihailo Hadzi-Cenic had brought over several such bottles in 1987 on a visit to the U.S. No label on the bottle as it was obtained from a mountain family. It is the Yugoslavian national drink and its name is slivovica.

"At 9:30 P.M., Sharon and I, walking with the light of a Coleman lantern, returned to the shelter to sleep. Most of the hikers had already bedded down; I went to bed promptly while Sharon first visited with J.P. McMullen, another hiker I saw many times in 1990 from the first day on."

Sunday, June 24
Punch Bowl Shelter to U.S. 501
11 miles

"Up at 6 A.M. after an unpleasant night in which I had to urinate frequently. Old age has its drawbacks. There are some pluses, such as free coffee at McDonald's, reduced fare on the Metro, and a monthly annuity check, but there are many minuses, including reduced energy, slower hiking speed, and regular trips to the pharmacy for pills which, in my youthful optimism, I thought I would never need, etc. Healthwise, I have lived a charmed life so it has been a bit difficult to adjust to a different type of living.

"I left the shelter while others were still asleep and walked back to the van, a mere 0.3 miles away. I heated water on my propane GAZ stove, and Sharon arrived shortly for the usual hot-cereal-and-coffee breakfast. We then drove to Big Island where we bought candy bars and bread and had a second breakfast at the little diner.

"We left Big Island and drove north on the Blue Ridge Parkway and parked the van at the overlook at mile 51.7. We hiked the one-half mile to Punchbowl shelter. I hid my Kelty pack behind the privy and then, carrying a day pack only, Sharon and I began hiking south on the Trail. Reached the summit of Bluff Mountain at 11:50 A.M., took a number of pictures from that excellent vantage point, then said good-bye to Sharon. I kept walking south; Sharon went back to the van, then to her home in Harpers Ferry. It was much fun being with her and hiking with her Thursday, Friday, Saturday, and a bit on Sunday.

"Pleasant walking. Met Mark Elliott and Sandra Bernoi within minutes after leaving Sharon. Later met Linda White, Tim Gfroerer, and three or four others including Fred Heath, who had been trying to catch up with me for days. He had planned to eat lunch at the Johns Hollow shelter, but it appeared to be some distance from the Trail, so I continued on to U.S. 501, arriving at 4 P.M.

"Rather than attempt to hitch a ride on U.S. 501, I walked north across the James River bridge and began walking and hitching on VA 130. Within a mile, I caught a ride with a Charlottesville, Virginia, family who took me right to my destination, mile 51.7 on the Parkway. The family had passed me by, but apparently after a quick conference, they decided that the white-haired old man looked harmless, and they turned around and returned to pick me up. As I wrote previously, there are a *few* advantages to being old!

"From the Parkway, I walked back to Punchbowl shelter and retrieved my Kelty pack from its hiding place. I then made my evening meal out of the lunch I had postponed eating earlier. Worked on notes and visited with a group of four men from Corydon, Indiana, a group that hikes together one week a year on the Trail. They started at Springer Mountain in Georgia in 1974. We had a big fire in the fireplace, since it was a very cool evening. To bed at 9:50 P.M.

Monday, June 25
Punch Bowl Shelter to Cow Camp Gap Shelter
14 miles

"Up at 6 A.M. Cereal and coffee for breakfast, but this time Grape Nuts instead of the instant oatmeal. First time on this trip for the Grape Nuts, but it was my daily standby in 1970. Left camp at 7:30 A.M., pleasant walk to Brown Mountain shelter. Missed my hiking partner, Sharon. Trail was certainly different. I hiked past the Lynchburg Dam, which was at high-water stage with water coming over the spillway, then continued hiking for almost two miles around and above the big reservoir created by the dam. Walked by and studied with interest the 4.5-acre virgin timber area marked with a U.S. Forest Service sign identifying the size of some of the mammoth trees on the site.

"Reached the shelter at 12:30 P.M., nine miles in five hours. Had lunch there and worked on notes, a good arrangement. Took off at 1:40 P.M., reached U.S. 60 at 2:30 P.M. Started walking to Hamms store and thumbing, but wound up walking the full mile to Hamms store. Had a cold beer, but no ice cream available!

"Began walking back to the Trail on U.S. 60. Stopped at a house to get some water from a Mrs. Ruth Duff of Duff's Place. Wound up getting ice cold water, two big dishes of ice cream, and lots of oatmeal cookies. Mrs. Duff helps many hikers, but ignores the bearded and roughly-dressed ones; she is scared of them! Hikers, take note!

"I reached the Trail at 4 P.M. and had a 4.4-mile hike ahead of me with a 2,000 foot climb. Made it to the summit at 6:30 P.M., then hiked another mile to the shelter trail. Reached the new Cow Camp Gap shelter at 7:20 P.M., much later than I like to hike. I had paid somewhat dearly for my jaunt to Hamms store, but that's part of the experience also.

"At the shelter, I met Jack and Dorothy Carlic, Mark Brokaw, and Fred Heath, all of whom had already eaten. They were building a fire in the steel fireplace circle. I ate a supper of Spam, cheese, and bread. Then, using hot water from the fire, I had coffee and Claxton fruitcake. Super. Postponed my paperwork and visited with the others. Much more pleasant. Visited until 9:30 P.M. with the fire blazing merrily. A most pleasant day and evening.

"On my daily log I made mention of some of the white paint blazes I had seen during the day. They had black borders painted on them. Shades of the late Dr. Jean Stephenson and the training she gave the good ladies of the Lynchburg club in its early years! I had also noted the occasional use of the offset double blaze, a most helpful device to aid the hiker."

Tuesday, June 26
Cow Camp Gap Shelter to Seeley-Woodworth Shelter
9 miles

"Up only once during the night, puzzling after all that coffee. First thing, I swept out the bathroom and later I washed the toilet seat with the remains of my soapy shaving water. Big improvement! Those seats do get a bit grimy after weeks of use.

"For breakfast, I had the rest of my Spam, plus Grape Nuts and coffee. The other hikers had all left by 7:45 A.M., some heading for the Priest shelter, others for Seeley-Woodworth. I worked on my notes and left at 9:30 A.M. A strenuous climb for the first half-mile, moderate rest of day. Excellent views from summit of Cole Mountain and another great view where I ate my lunch.

"My supposed easy day hike of 10 miles seemed rather long. Got into Seeley-Woodworth Shelter at 4:15 P.M. The Carlics were already there. I took a spit bath and washed underwear, hanging it on the line to dry.

"Again I performed the ritual of sweeping out the toilet and scrubbing the seat. Not the most pleasant job, but it makes such a tremendous improvement that it is well worth the effort.

"For supper, I cooked noodles and added a can of chicken—very filling. Coffee and fruitcake and half a candy bar for dessert. People kept coming into the shelter—H. Arnold, Andy Reece, J.P. McMullen; there were six of us in the shelter for the night. While eating supper, we were visited by Tommy Jamieson, a trail worker for the NBATC. Tommy's section runs from the Seeley-Woodworth shelter north for 2.3 miles to the Fish Hatchery Road.

"Enjoyed another fire in an iron fire ring, while water heated. All of us in bed by 9:30 P.M. A bit of excitement at 9:45 P.M. when a mouse got on Jack Carlic's hand, and in frantic haste to get it off, he knocked some equipment onto a sleeping hiker!

"On the Trail itself, we were still seeing evidence of Hugo's fury, but all the blowdowns had been cleaned up. Much recent trail work evident, including weeding, which was especially appreciated. Good sign program by U.S. Forest Service."

Wednesday, June 27
Seeley-Woodworth Shelter to Harpers Creek Shelter
14 miles

"Up at 5:30 A.M., cold breakfast. Got my stuff off the line, almost dry, and put the long-sleeved shirt on, damp as it was. Not uncomfortable, and it dried out shortly from the heat of my body.

"Left camp at 6:35 A.M., a six-mile hike with much climbing to The Priest Shelter. Arrived there at 11 A.M. Ate leisurely lunch with four to five others. Left the shelter at noon; almost all downhill for five miles to VA 56 in the Tye River Gap. Arrived at the road at 3 P.M. By 3:05 P.M., I had a ride to Bradley's store, 1.4 miles east.

"Bought $4.35 of snacks, including two pints of ice cream. Got a ride back to the Trail immediately, back on the Trail at 4 P.M. Began hiking out of the Tye River Gap, up, up, up until 5:15 P.M. where the Trail leveled out.

"Arrived at Harpers Creek shelter at 5:45 P.M. to find 13 members of the Hanover Camp of the Presbyterian Church of Richmond, Virginia, at the shelter and table. They made room for me at the shelter. I talked to the leader, informing him of the 10-person limit on group hikes on the Trail. A good day but rather hot.

Thursday, June 28
Harpers Creek Shelter to Maupin Field Shelter
6 miles

"Up at 5:35 A.M., cold breakfast. Left camp at 6:35 A.M., same as yesterday. Made steady progress up one of the most formidable sections of the Trail in the Pedlar District of the George Washington National Forest—three Ridges, the tallest of the three being just shy of 4,000 feet. I had already crossed the first ridge when the others caught up with me. We reached the summit of the highest at 9 A.M., and took one lengthy break on the way down at an overlook that permitted a view of all three ridges, with one of the ridges being much higher than the other two.

"I had predicted that we would reach Maupin Field shelter at 11 A.M.; actual time was 10:57 A.M. We had some discussion as to the route to follow to Rusty Nesbitt's Hard Time Hollow, but once that was settled we took off, Andy Reece and Gary Eanes ahead.

"They reached the Blue Ridge Parkway first and promptly got a ride. John McMullen and I walked the 1.4 miles to Rusty's domain in the hot midday sun. Quite a place, no electricity or telephone, but a bunkhouse plus two bunk beds in a separate living space, to which I was assigned. Total hiker capacity: 20.

"Although the place does not have electricity, it does have refrigeration of a sort, a covered spring house with a cold water spring bubbling within. At the time of my visit there were some 15 to 20 cans of beer floating around in the spring. Rusty informed me that at the beginning of the season he 'primes the pump' by tossing in a case of beer. From that time on, the hikers are expected to keep the spring supplied with beer.

"Around 1:30 P.M., eight of us piled into Rusty's 1966 Chevy van and drove into Waynesboro. First stop was the post office, where I picked up seven pieces of mail, but not the guidebook and map of Shenandoah National Park, which I had expected to receive from ATC.

"I cashed a $100 check at the bank adjoining the post office. The group made a number of other stops and finally reached the Western Sizzlin steak-house for an AYCE buffet meal. I had had only one candy bar since my light breakfast and was very hungry. We all ate gargantuan meals. I had a t-bone steak. The salad and food bars were fantastic.

"I walked out without paying. I called later and the cashier was well aware of my misdeed. I promptly mailed a check, but the cost of my oversight was time, a phone call, postage, and the inconvenience at both ends. Such things can happen to anybody, but it is a recognized fact that they happen more frequently to older people!

"I wrote up my notes for the day in the fading sunlight at Rusty's place. Later, I took a shower in the rainwater shower which was tolerably warm from solar heat. Very refreshing. To bed around 9:45 P.M. The others took a bath in the 'hot tub' out in the field some 60 to 70 yards from the house. The hot tub is a big tub with an inner and outer metal shell (Rusty, a professional welder, constructed it). A fire is built under the tub to heat the water. I was just too tired to participate. Another full day."

Friday, June 29
Maupin Shelter to Rockfish Gap
18 miles

"If Thursday was a full day, this was fuller. Up at 5:30 A.M. Breakfast eaten by 6:15 A.M. Misplaced my one belt, almost took the place apart trying to find it and even received help from others. Finally resorted to a piece of rope to hold up my pants. Then, when fastening my stuffsack onto my pack frame, I felt something at the bottom of the stuffsack that felt like a belt buckle. It was! Mystery solved.

"All of us were ready for the day's hike by 7:30 A.M. or so, but Rusty did not get up until 9:30 A.M.! We put our heavy packs in his van then walked to the Parkway, after which we were given a ride on the Parkway to the dirt road leading back to Maupin shelter. We walked that three-quarters of a mile, and at 10 A.M., we began hiking north on the Trail. I quickly fell to the rear (a situation to which I had become accustomed) and hiked by myself all day—18 miles from Maupin shelter to Rockfish Gap.

"Ran into the Carlics around 6 P.M. where they were tent camping at Mill Creek. When I hiked the Trail in 1970, the guidebook indicated that there was a shelter at Mill Creek. There wasn't! Someone anticipated something that didn't happen! Now in 1990, there is still no shelter, but one is badly needed because there is a 25-mile gap between shelters in this area. I visited very briefly with the Carlics because of the late hour.

"I, and the other hikers, had lost 15 minutes at Humpback Rocks because of inadequate blazing. After crossing Mill Creek, I crossed the Parkway again about two miles from Rockfish Gap, the third or fourth such crossing during the day. Reached Rockfish Gap and its tourist complex at 8:15 P.M. Obtained a ride immediately, along with a big drink of cold orange juice. Wow, was that appreciated. The young couple let me off at the Waynesboro fire station where I would spend the night. Linda White, Howard Arnold, and J.P. McMullen were already there. They had arrived at Rockfish Gap at 6 P.M. and promptly obtained rides.

"At the fire station, I visited with employee Tom Bellamy, then walked the eight blocks to the Kroger store with 24-hour service. I purchased a can of beer and a half-gallon of butter almond ice cream. Not a well-rounded meal, but one develops certain cravings on these long hikes, and these two purchases satisfied my cravings for that day.

"I drank half the beer on the lawn across from the fire station until I was informed by the city police that a city ordinance permits beer to be consumed only at bars or in private homes. I carried my beer to my 'home' for the night, the fire station, where I drank it and then sat down at the picnic table to eat the ice cream. I visited with another fire station employee, Tom Freling. My Kelty pack, and the packs of others, had been deposited at the station by Rusty Nesbitt some hours earlier.

"The 18 miles or so of hiking had left me mighty tired, but the beer and ice cream perked me up a bit. Made my bed on the lawn beside the station; beautiful night, half moon in clear sky; went to sleep promptly. Slept through two big emergency car accident calls, sirens screeching, etc. Howard, who slept inside beside the fire trucks, gave me the details in the morning. I slept straight through until 4:30 A.M. Great sleep. I phoned two of my friends in northern Virginia, Tom Simon and Ed Hanlon, to arrange a get-together farther north. As of this date, June 29, my cumulative expenses for the trip have gone over the $1,000 mark."

Saturday, June 30
Rockfish Gap to Calf Mountain Shelter
7 miles.

"Up at 5:30 A.M., showered (what a treat, nice big shower room, three or four shower heads), breakfast at Weasie's, lengthy, topped off with hot cherry pie. Ate with Linda White and Andy Reece. Read the *Washington Post*. Mayor Marion

Barry still in the headlines! Cincinnati still leading the baseball pack. Back to the station, then over to Kroger for grocery shopping ($17.85).

"Back at the fire station, I started to work on notes, at which point J. P. McMullin arrived sporting a new crew cut—$2.75! I hustled over to the Peoples Barber Shop and in about two minutes I was having my hair cut by the elderly and friendly George Cromer. Good haircut, and yes, the price was $2.75 and he would not accept a tip. Back to the fire station, stopping en route at the post office to check on the guidebook for the Shenandoah National Park. No luck.

"At the fire station, I was just getting started again on my notes and correspondence, when Ron Tipton and Dave Sherman, longtime friends from the Washington, D.C., area, arrived and sat down beside me at the picnic table! They had surmised that I would be in Waynesboro and headed straight for the fire station. Good calculating. What a surprise. Both of them had to be back in Washington that same night, but we did have half a day to visit and to get in some hiking.

"We drove up to the Parkway. Hiked the Trail from Rockfish Gap north through the Little Calf Mountain vista clearing, which Sherman and I had both worked on during the preceeding two years. We deviated from the present Trail route briefly to hike on the former Trail route, which is greatly superior to the present one. Regrettable that the National Park Service settled for the less desirable route.

"We walked past the trail leading to the Calf Mountain shelter down to Sherman's car in Jarmans Gap. From there, we drove to the Pizza Hut in Waynesboro and enjoyed one large 'super supreme' pizza. Delish! They then drove me up to the Parkway to Calf Mountain and I shouldered my pack, heavier with the $17.85 of groceries, and we said our good-byes.

"Again I hiked up and over Calf Mountain and this time into the Calf Mountain shelter. The group with which I had hiked south of Waynesboro was all there, plus one or two others. Too dark to do any writing. Visited a bit, then to bed. Skies very dark. I was awakened several times by the sound of rain on the metal roof of the shelter."

Sunday, July 1
Calf Mountain Shelter to Blackrock Hut
13 miles

"Up at 5:30 A.M., cold breakfast, and on my way at 7:10 A.M. Had to repack many of my recent grocery purchases. Made good time; the weather was cool. But I had one memory lapse that worries me. From the shelter, I headed first for the Jarmans Gap parking area, 1.4 miles. I could not understand why I did not reach it. Then I began to ascend rather steeply and I was going north and northeast when I should have been going generally west. Finally, I came to Skyline Drive some 1.9 miles north of Jarmans Gap at Sawmill overlook! I had walked right past Jarmans Gap and crossed Skyline Drive without making a mental note of it. I will make no more jokes about absent-minded professors!

"I proceeded with my hiking and crossed the Skyline Drive several times— a pleasant area in which to hike. A word of explanation is in order here Skyline Drive runs from Front Royal, Virginia, along the crest of the Blue Ridge Mountains for 105 miles south to U.S. 250 and I-64 near Waynesboro. South of Waynesboro, it is known as the Blue Ridge Parkway for 469 miles, and ends near the southern edge of the Great Smoky Mountains National Park in North Carolina. Together they total 574 miles of parkway through some of the most beautiful areas in the eastern United States.

"I ate my lunch at the Rip Rap parking area at milepost 90 on the Drive. Linda White and Janet joined me, and later others. I left at 1:45 P.M., more climbing and descending, very hot. There was almost no shade as the gypsy moth caterpillars are very active in this area.

"Reached Blackrock hut. Another word of explanation: the "huts" in Shenandoah National Park are the same as shelters north and south of the park, but because of an edict by a former park superintendent, they must be called huts! Reached the hut at 3:45 P.M., where the water was running freely from the pipe and was very cold. Super. I drank almost a quart.

"For my early supper, I cooked a Kraft Macaroni and Cheese dish. It worked out well cooked over an open fire. Put in seasoning sauce and a can of tuna. Very tasty, but I made much more than I needed and gave the extra half to H. Arnold, trail name Dapper Dan.

"After supper, heated water for a good shave, and combed my now very short hair. It had rained a bit during our early supper, but by 6 P.M. the sun was out.

"Finishing my diary notes shortly after 6 P.M., then to my daily logs for the past three days! Not good record keeping. I am traveling through the Shenandoah National Park without guidebook or maps, but of all the areas in the entire 2,144 miles of the Trail, the Shenandoah National Park is the one in which I am only barely inconvenienced. I have hiked the entire 94 miles of the Park on many occasions, especially the central, 34-mile section where I was a trail manager from 1981–85, and where I led many work trips and personally did much of the paint blazing."

Monday, July 2
Blackrock Hut to Pinefield Hut
13 miles

"Up at 5:30 A.M., left camp at 7 A.M., made good time. Reached Loft Mountain Campground at 10 A.M.; hiked the lengthy Trail circle around the campground, and did not reach the campground store until 11 A.M. The phone there was not working. Left my pack there and hitched a ride immediately with Park Service employee Sean Green to the wayside area.

"I called ATC in Harpers Ferry. No answer? Called PATC in Washington, D.C. Learned that Pocosin Cabin was booked solid for the entire ensuing week. So Hanlon and I will not be staying there as planned. Called Hanlon and left word on his answering machine. Obtained a ride immediately back to the camp store. Ate my lunch, got my dirty clothes in the washer. Got clothes all washed and dried. Bought more groceries, very expensive at the camp store.

"Began hiking around 2 P.M. Stopped at Ivy Creek maintenance hut, opening it with my key; very clean and inviting inside. I had spent some happy moments at this hut, especially during our overnight stays after working on the Little Calf Mountain vista clearing project to the south.

"Pushed on to Pinefield hut. Arrived at 6 P.M., again after walking in hot sun due to gypsy moth devastation. Found most of my hiking friends at the hut except for the two ladies, Linda and Janet, who had hiked on farther. Later joined by Thumper, Erik Matthias, of Minneapolis, Minnesota. Also, two ladies from Austin, Texas, showed up late; eight people in the hut.

"Had planned to cook milkweed pods I had picked at the overlook, but learned that Andy Reece had hitched a ride to the camp store. He arrived within minutes and I had beer, muffins, and cheese for supper. Fire in fireplace burned all night. Hut in very good shape. Larry Linebrink, the hut manager, is a PATC stalwart in trail work and in hut management. To bed at 10 P.M."

Tuesday, July 3
Pinefield Hut to Hightop Hut
8 miles

"Overslept a bit, up at 5:45 A.M. Hot and cold cereal breakfast. Stoked up fire from last night; boiled my six eggs. Ate the two eggs that had cracked in boiling. Much picture taking by my fellow hikers. The others left. Just Thumper and I are still here. Finished a letter to Marty Dominy, then brought my notes up to date. All finished by 9:30 A.M., and Thumper and I took off, some two-and-a-half hours later than yesterday. Made good time.

"Stopped at Simmons Gap Ranger Station. Called the Chuck Young residence near Warrenton, Virginia, and learned that Chuck was chauffering the English couple, the Carrs, around the northern section of Shenandoah Park. Left the ranger station at 11 A.M., much climbing. Ate our lunch just north of the Smith Roach Gap, hiking in bright sunlight again—gypsy moths. Reached Hightop hut at 3:15 P.M. Thumper had reached it ahead of me and he had put a can of Bud Dry beer in the cold spring. What a treat!

"Built a fire and heated water for shaving, but could not find my toiletry kit. Realized I had left it at Pinefield hut. Had carried that kit all up and down the Trail, in California, in Europe, even in Siberia, and had never misplaced it. Now this! I put a note in the shelter register as to my loss. Hope springs eternal in the human breast!

"Prepared an evening meal of hot soup, Spanish rice, and instant potatoes. Coffee and candy bar for dessert. At 6 P.M., Eddie Watson (Tennessee Walker) arrived from Blackrock hut. He had stopped briefly at Pinefield hut, saw my toiletry kit, found my name on my medicine vials, and brought the kit up here to Hightop. What a relief!

"After the evening meal, I brought my notes up to date. That done, the three of us visited and enjoyed the fire. All of us in the sack by 9:30 P.M., watching the fire flickering outside. Earlier we had enjoyed a gorgeous, brilliant red sunset; at 9:30 P.M., we likewise enjoyed an almost-full moon casting its light in the clearing. A most enjoyable day, and in retrospect, I should have planned more such short mileage days instead of trying to match my 1970 routine of two shelters per day.

"As to trail conditions, it was also a most successful day. First, no litter on the Trail. None. Second, trail workers had freshly weeded the entire eight miles. And third, we had seen some excellent waterbar work—earth and stone."

Wednesday, July 4, Independence Day
Hightop Hut to Bearfence Mountain Hut
12 miles

"Up at 5:15 A.M., barely light enough to see. Two packages of cold cereal plus hot coffee for breakfast, courtesy of Eddie. Left camp at 6:15 A.M., my earliest start of the trip. Pleasant hiking; made the six miles to South River picnic grounds by 9:30 A.M. Ate my full lunch there. I have two eggs left, no muffins. Wonderful day, sun shining, light breeze, low humidity.

"Left South River picnic grounds at 10:45 A.M. just as Erik was coming up the Trail. I left him there and proceeded north toward Pocosin. Erik caught up with me at Dean Mountain Road. I was very pleased to see the way the 60 to 70 check dams we installed in 1984 were effectively stabilizing a trail that had been badly gutted by extremely heavy rain. We visited the famous Pocosin spring, drank much of the good water, put more in our canteens. We then headed for Lewis Mountain Campground. Erik went on ahead.

"I arrived there at 3 P.M. to find Erik polishing off a pint of ice cream. I followed suit. First, I tried to contact Chuck Young by phone. Learned he was in Fredericksburg, Virginia, participating as a colonial soldier in the July 4 celebration. I then called Ed Hanlon. He has a room reserved for the two of us at Big Meadows Lodge Thursday night. First class tomorrow! Then I enjoyed a second ice cream with Erik. Made two more phone calls to Jerry Hyndman and Hugh O'Hara in northern Virginia, trying to line up rendezvous points for joint weekend hiking trips further north. While still near the phone booth, I was approached by Christopher and Melissa Cullen, brandishing the most recent issue of the *Appalachian Trailway News,* which contained an article about me.

Volunteers installing waterbars on an Appalachian Trail feeder trail near Salisbury, Connecticut.

They asked if I would autograph the article, which I cheerfully did. Later wondered how they knew I was in the area.

"I left Lewis Mountain at 3 P.M., and in half an hour I was at the Bearfence Mountain hut. Erik had arrived earlier and had gone on ahead, but not before depositing two cans of beer for me in the spring. For my evening meal, I heated up a can of corned beef hash. Put some of the hash aside for breakfast. A young couple arrived at 6:45 P.M., and the three of us were the only occupants of the hut.

"Another pleasant day, one in which I had seen one female deer with two fawns on the Trail. I would not see Erik again on my northbound trip. He had been a most pleasant and thoughtful hiking companion."

Thursday, July 5
Bearfence Mountain Hut to Hawksbill Mountain Parking Area
13 miles

"Up at 5:15 A.M. Used my wood stove for hot coffee, hot cereal, and the corned beef hash from the previous evening. Left camp at 6:35 A.M. and made very good time, for me at least, walking much of the time in 'gypsy moth sunlight.' It was delightful to occasionally walk into the cool havens provided by the big hemlock trees; the hemlock needles are not to the liking of the moths. I was again pleased to walk over areas where we had done intensive trail work from

1981–85. All check dams and waterbars are functioning well, although some of the bars atop Hazel Top need cleaning.

"I arrived at Big Meadows Lodge at 10:30 A.M., eight miles in four hours with my 40-pound pack. Walked non-stop the last six miles. Went to the room clerk at the lodge immediately. No record of a room being reserved by Ed Hanlon?! They did have cottages at $55 for two people, so I reserved one and moved in. I called Hanlon promptly—there was no misunderstanding, he had reserved the room for this date. Further, he was about to leave home and he would meet me on Skyline Drive at the Hawksbill Parking Area.

"I put on my light shoes, carried no pack, and headed north on the Trail. I was greatly impressed to see the excellent waterbar work on a two-mile stretch in the Rock Springs-Hawksbill area—both the installation of new waterbars and the cleaning of old ones. I have noted that in *Appalachian Trail Register* articles, trail managers are stressing more and more the need to not only install waterbars, but also to clean them on a regular basis. These bars had been cleaned nice and deep for perhaps 10 to 15 feet below the discharge point. This was the most impressive installation and cleaning job I was to see on my entire trip.

"I reached the Hawksbill parking area at 1:45 P.M., and Hanlon arrived one minute later. Such timing. He had driven 90 miles, I had walked about 6. We went back by car to Big Meadows for another visit with the room reservation people. No satisfaction whatever. They confirmed a $33 room for two, but we were stuck for the same room at $55.

"We rested a bit, then walked over to the dining room for dinner. Had a good night's sleep between sheets. Rained hard during the night. My log sheet shows that I have hiked exactly 900 miles from Springer Mountain in Georgia to Big Meadows here in Shenandoah National Park."

Friday, July 6
Hawksbill Parking Area to Pass Mountain Hut
14 miles

"Awake at 3:30 A.M., no sleep thereafter. Up at 6 A.M. and did some chores. Ed awoke around 7 A.M., and we walked over to the dining room for breakfast—buckwheat cakes and sausages, a bit more filling than my usual trail diet of cold instant oatmeal.

"Back at the cottage, I finished my notes on the Trail conditions, and around 9 A.M. we left for Luray. Arrived just at 10 A.M. for my appointment with Park Superintendent Bill Wade. Nice visit of about 20 minutes. After that I shopped for groceries ($11.88) while Ed visited the ARA office, which operates the lodge at Big Meadows. After hearing Ed's story, the ARA readily agreed to refund the difference in the price of the cottage we had rented. Good.

"I bought a fish sandwich at McDonald's and ate it on the drive back to Shenandoah National Park. Arrived at Hawksbill Gap at 11:45 A.M. I changed clothes and began hiking at noon, carrying no pack and wearing my blue running shoes. Ed met me at the three-mile mark and later at 3 P.M. at the Pinnacles picnic ground. At Pinnacles I discarded the lightweight shoes in favor of my Red Wing hiking boots.

"Reached the Panorama Restaurant at Thornton Gap at 5:20 P.M., U.S. 211. At that point, I said good-bye to my longtime friend, Ed Hanlon, shouldered my pack, and headed for the nearby Pass Mountain hut.

"After leaving Ed at 5:45 P.M., I found that both trailheads at U.S. 211 were badly obscured. Fairly easy going up to Pass Mountain hut. Arrived at 6:45 P.M., just 1.2 miles from U.S. 211. Jim Kitt, a retired U.S. Navy captain, was already at the hut. I got a fire going and heated the can of beef stew I had purchased at Luray. Built up the fire, warding off the insects.

"The Trail through which I passed today was a mixture of bad and excellent. First the bad—there had been no weed cutting or brushing out for the entire 14 miles. The Trail was almost impassable for a 300-yard stretch south of Hughes Gap, and again at a point a mile north of that gap. But there was some excellent paint blazing from the new relocation at Skyland and for two miles north, including a blue blaze trail. The new relocation through Skyland utilizing the Nature Trail is a big improvement."

For more than 20 years, Ed and I have provided support for one another in our Trail hiking. Ed has hiked some 1,500 miles of the Trail, including everything south of Virginia and everything north of New York, but it is doubtful he will ever finish his goal. He underwent a six-hour lower back operation in August 1991, which will require a long period of recuperation. Time will tell. (Ed Hanlon died suddenly of a heart attack on September 18, 1996.)

Saturday, July 7
Pass Mountain Hut to Gravel Spring Hut
13 miles

"Up at 5:30 A.M. On my way at 6:35 A.M. in cool, cloudy, good hiking weather. About 2.5 miles before reaching Elkwallow Wayside, I was surprised and pleased to meet Jerry Hyndman, a friend and neighbor in Falls Church, Virginia. His wife had dropped him off at the Wayside. We walked together, reaching the Wayside at 10:40 A.M. Jim Kitt joined us shortly, and in another 10 minutes, Chuck Young had joined us.

"I completed my daily log for the previous day, then we ate lunch: two eggs, muffins, a banana, then the Elkwallow special—blackberry milkshake.

"Around noon we put our packs in Chuck's truck and took off on foot for the Gravel Spring hut, reaching it around 4 P.M. Met Chuck Young at two crossings of the Skyline Drive. At the second crossing, he told us excitedly of seeing a baby cougar. Others had told him of a mother cougar and two cubs. Chuck went over to the sighting spot and saw just the one, but what a thrill!

"We said good-bye to Chuck on the Drive before shouldering our packs and hiking the remaining 1.2 miles to the hut. Wood very scarce at Gravel Springs and the area beset with nettles. After falling amongst them once, I put on my long-sleeved shirt and gloves.

"Used our two Sierra Zip Ztoves to cook dinner. I had Ramen noodles fortified with a can of chicken, and chocolate pudding and coffee for dessert. I then cleaned out the privy with a 'Russell Norton' brush before beginning work on my notes. Jerry and I are to meet his wife Joan at U.S. 522 tomorrow at 3:30 P.M. for a picnic dinner.

"Later, Frank Harrison showed up. He had begun hiking in Maine on May 3, reaching the Shenandoahs in only two months! He had many experiences to relate, such as hiking in one area where the snow was up to his chin when he broke through the crust! He hiked for 250 miles through Maine before he met anyone. He said he really learned the meaning of the word lonely.

"All of us pitched in on the wood-gathering project and got a big fire going. To bed at 9:30 P.M., another full moon showing."

Sunday, July 8
Gravel Spring Hut to Tom Floyd Wayside
10.4 miles

"Up at 5:30 A.M., hot cereal and coffee breakfast. Jerry and I left camp at 7:10 A.M., leaving Jim Kitt. Made good time all the way to Compton Mountain where we were surprised by Dave Sherman, who had a cooler with four cans of Stroh's beer. We consumed three of them, visited a bit, then walked to the Indian Run maintenance hut where we ate lunch.

"After lunch, we walked north out of the park to the Tom Floyd Wayside. Jerry left us at that point and began the 3.1-mile hike to U.S. 522 to meet his wife. Dave and I walked back south on the Trail to the road leading to the residence of Tom Floyd and walked up to it. It appeared not to have been used for weeks. Really remote! Tom, an ardent Trail worker, retired several years ago and is frequently gone from his home for weeks.

"After leaving the Floyd place, Dave headed back to his car. I went back to the Floyd Wayside. I retrieved Jerry's pack from its hiding place and headed for the 4-H center to meet the Hyndmans. Met neighbors Jeff and Kim Brown on the way down. Kim drove me all the way to the picnic pavillion, and the Hyndmans arrived in 10 minutes. It wasn't long before Jerry and I were consuming big pieces of fried chicken, German-fried potatoes, and fresh melon. What a meal. Later, we finished with chocolate brownie pie! They gave me all the leftovers. The party broke up around 5 P.M., and they gave me a ride on VA 604 and 601 to the Trail intersection. I had only half a mile to hike to the Floyd Wayside—uphill, naturally!

"Shortly after returning to the Wayside, I made the 20-minute round-trip to the spring and filled all water containers, including a half-gallon plastic one left at the shelter. Heated water on the very clever chest-high grill in front of the shelter. Enjoyed half a piece of that chocolate pie and several cups of coffee. Brought my notes mostly up-to-date, but with no table to write on it was painful to my back. Let the fire die down. To bed shortly after 9 P.M. I'm the only one here; don't know what happened to Jim Kitt."

Monday, July 9
Tom Floyd Wayside to Manassas Gap Shelter
14 miles

"Good night's sleep, up at 5:30 A.M. Took my time on the breakfast; heated up potatoes and chicken. That, and the remainder of the chocolate pie along with coffee, made a very substantial breakfast. Left camp at 7:40 A.M. Slow going, Trail very rocky.

"Reached U.S. 522 at 10 A.M. and pushed on through the National Zoo breeding ground, a.k.a. the 'Tick Farm.' I had no problem with the ticks, as the area along the fence had been recently mowed. Arrived at the Mosby campsite area, saw the sign and the blue blaze trail, but found no campsite. The area was a jungle, and the road that might have led to it was an impassable pond. I proceeded on to the Jim and Molly Denton shelter. Reached it at 1:10 P.M. after stopping first at the former homestead spring for delicious ice-cold water. It boasts a purifier and hose going to the shelter.

"Enjoyed my main meal there; heated up potatoes, onion slices, one plum tomato, pie, and coffee for dessert. Never had it so good. This shelter, popularly known as the Denton Palace, is definitely the 'Hilton' of the Appalachian Trail shelter chain! Enjoyed, really enjoyed, a not-so-cold shower at the solar-heated arrangement near the shelter. Washed my underwear, greased my hiking boots. Finished my notes on the outside table, and at 3:50 P.M., reluctantly began the five-mile hike to Manassas Gap shelter. I had a commitment to be at the Blackburn Trail Center on July 12; otherwise I would have stayed overnight at the Denton shelter.

"It was a long, hard five miles from the Denton Palace to the next shelter. Arrived there at 7:35 P.M. Ate a cold supper. Almost dark when I finished my meal. Too dark to write. Drank huge quantities of that good cold water from the spring. To bed at 9:15 P.M., to sleep in about one minute."

Tuesday, July 10
Manassas Gap Shelter to Rod Hollow Shelter
14 miles

"Awake at 3:30 A.M., almost a full moon shining. Up at 5:10 A.M. Hot coffee and one soft-boiled egg, plus cereal and one half of a Kay Garvey brownie. Brought my notes up-to-date. Left shelter at 7:25 A.M., overcast, sprinkling a bit. Put rain cover on my pack, and it rained briefly again around 9 A.M. Walked straight through to the signs indicating I was in Sky Meadows State Park—7.7 miles. Good. Took a short rest on the bench provided by the park. Very thoughtful. Pushed on, pleasant hiking as compared to yesterday, more shade, and the trail was not so rocky. Could hear the sound of trucks on U.S. 50 shortly after noon. By 1 P.M., I was at the Paris Restaurant on U.S. 50—10.6 miles in five-and-a-half hours.

"Trail well-blazed, but saw 35 blowdowns to U.S. 50—12 of them in the first mile north of Manassas Gap shelter. Scared up two small deer. Had the $3.50 special at the restaurant, plus two beers and ice cream. With the extras plus tax and tips, the $3.50 special eventually cost $13.60! Also, I had the use of the booth as my office for three hours.

"I left the restaurant at 4 P.M. for the final 3.6 miles of hiking for the day. Reached the Rod Hollow shelter at 6:20 P.M. just as I was beginning to think I had missed the side trail leading to it. It is only about six years old and it, too, was considered to be the 'Hilton' until later supplanted by Denton Palace. Rod Hollow was the first shelter to be built in the PATC domain that provided a separate building for cooking and eating. Only one other occupant, Bill Berthrong, who was just out of the U.S. Navy. Cooked two soft-boiled eggs with cheese, an onion slice, and coffee and a brownie for dessert. Visited with Bill until 9:20 P.M., when I retired for the night."

Wednesday, July 11
Rod Hollow Shelter to Bears Den American Youth Hostel
10 miles

"Up at 5:30 A.M. and had a leisurely breakfast before beginning what I had expected to be a rather easy 10-mile hike. Not so! And I should have known better, having hiked this route on three or four previous occasions. But one does forget. I left the shelter at 9:15 A.M., and experienced eight hours of steady up-and-down hiking. But if it was strenuous, it was also interesting terrain, with many stream crossings.

"At 11:30 A.M., I caught up with Bill, who was reading a book. I ate my lunch at that point, finishing up the last of my muffins and cheese. Resumed hiking at noon and hiked another five solid hours before reaching the Bears Den American Youth Hostel. I was very tired and my back was giving me much

The author. Note the white towel wrapped around pack frame to protect his back.

trouble. I wound a towel over the metal back supports on my pack to ease the rubbing on my back. I left the Trail at the interesting rock overlook, the Bears Den Rocks, and began walking up the road leading to the hostel. At that point, Peyton Robertson of Norfolk, Virginia, drove up in his van.

"Peyton is a 1989 hiker, and I had met him a year earlier at about this same point and hiked with him. He was now returning the favor. He recounted his experiences during the day trying to intercept me. As I contemplated my sore back, I wished he would have been successful in finding me so as to relieve me of that pack. After checking in at the hostel, I took a shower, changed clothes, and we sallied forth to eat an excellent roast beef dinner at Georges Restaurant in nearby Purcellville, and finished up the meal with pie and ice cream.

"Back to the hostel, after first buying some popcorn. Visited with other occupants at the hostel and with the very pleasant house parents, John and Jennifer Vasser. Popped corn. The hostel is only 45 miles from my home in Falls Church. I phoned my wife, Mary, and later my daughter in Harpers Ferry, both of whom I expected to meet the next night. Went to bed at the hostel shortly after midnight.

"In contemplating the events of the day, I could not help comparing today's hike, (tiring though it was) through the woods and across pretty streams, with the previous route, which involved hiking in the hot sun for some 12 to 13 miles on the nearby blacktopped VA 601. The Trail in this area is only about 50 miles from Washington, D.C., and yet I had hiked 10 miles without seeing a single house or car. The success of the National Park Service and the PATC in negotiating this off-road route has to be one of the big success stories (among many) in the land acquisition program."

Thursday, July 12
Bears Den Hostel to Keys Gap, WV 9
14 miles

"Awake at 4:30 A.M. and no sleep thereafter. Up at 5:30 A.M., brought journal notes up to date. Had a light breakfast at the hostel, where stove and cooking equipment is provided. Later, Peyton and I drove to the Round Hill Diner where we enjoyed a good ham and pancake breakfast. As we were leaving, Hugh O'Hara, a friend from Falls Church, came in the door. He had visited the two nearby McDonald's looking for me (someone must have clued him in on my preferences!), and then had visited the hostel, where they had directed him to the diner. We visited briefly and made plans for a weekend hike together to take place July 21–22. The weekend hike had been in the talking stage for more than a year, and now it seemed it definitely was going to happen.

"Back at the hostel, I prepared for the 14 miles to Keys Gap on WV 9 almost on the Virginia-West Virginia border. I carried no pack, but I did carry my light

Blackburn Trail Center.

rain jacket, and I wore lightweight running shoes. Left the hostel at 8:30 A.M., and lightly clad, I made very good time until I reached a very new and poorly marked relocation a mile or so south of the Blackburn Trail Center. I was not enthusiastic about the relocation, as it added mileage to the route and was over a steep and rocky area.

"Peyton walked in to meet me from the north, and we met at 11:30 A.M. It was 12:30 P.M. before we reached the center. Ate a quick lunch, then Peyton drove me north to Keys Gap, and at 2 P.M. I began hiking south. Made very good time, reaching the Trail center at 4:40 P.M., the exact time I had projected. It is rather easy to make those good predictions when you have hiked the same route on many previous occasions!

"It had rained slightly during the day and I had walked in wet areas the entire day. My lightweight shoes obviously were not colorfast, for when I took off my shoes and socks, I found that the socks and my toes were the same color—bright blue. I changed clothes, attempting to look as respectable as I could for the party that had been arranged by Ron Tipton and Dave Sherman.

"The skies had become very dark, and I was worried about my family and friends finding the way up the steep rocky road that leads to the center. It began to rain hard, but everyone made it up there, although parking was a real big problem. It is a problem anytime at the center, but in the dark of night with a hard rain pouring down, it became a real adventure. The guests were a mixture of PATC and ATC members, family, friends, and four Trail hikers who happened to be at the right place at the right time. I had not seen most of them since late March.

"The center is a turn-of-the-century rustic mansion made with logs. The very large living room-dining room area has a pitched ceiling some 25 feet high. The PATC purchased the building and adjacent land some 10 to 15 years ago, and members have been improving the buildings ever since. It is a steep, seven-minute walk from the center to the top of the mountain and the Trail.

"It was a great party with food and drink and wonderful visiting. The big event was a demonstration by Peyton Robertson of the proper way to make mint julep. The demonstration was the outgrowth of a heated discussion that had occurred some two years earlier between Peyton and Dave Sherman. It occurred at the Ivy Creek maintenance hut in the Shenandoahs after one of the work trips at the Little Calf Mountain vista clearing project. Peyton, a native Virginian of many generations, was describing the Virginia method; Dave, a native Georgian, likewise of many generations, was describing the Georgia method. There was no winner that night at Ivy Creek, but on this occasion, Peyton had brought all the proper 'fixins' for his demonstration. First, ice, which he crushed to just the proper size, six sterling silver drinking vessels with two handles, and bourbon—Kentucky bourbon that is, not Virginia bourbon or any other kind. It had to be Kentucky bourbon. And finally mint, not mint pulled from the garden and brought up in a paper sack. No indeed. There would be no shortcuts on this occasion. Peyton had brought with him mint plants still growing in potted soil. If the recipe called for fresh mint, then fresh mint it would be. I won't go into the step-by-step process, but Peyton demonstrated in his booming voice and gave each guest that desired some a small sample of the potent, but lip-smacking, concoction.

"All parties must end in time, and many of those present had to be at work the next day. I drove home with my family; it rained all the way home. Got my pack and other gear unloaded, showered and into bed. A great day. And having hiked slightly over 1,000 miles, I am roughly at the halfway point.

In the aforementioned demonstration of mint julep making, there was one very interested spectator, David M. Sherman of Albany, Georgia. While quite impressed with Peyton's demonstration, Sherman was not at all convinced that the Virginia method espoused by Peyton was superior to (or even as good as!) the method used in south Georgia.

Months after I finished my 1990 hike, Dave proudly displayed a small book only 5 x 8 inches in size and only 60 pages in length. It was entitled *The Mint Julep,* by Richard Barksdale Harwell, and it was printed especially for friends of the Beehive Press of Savannah, Georgia. Only 300 copies were printed, 100 for the author and 200 for the publisher.

Dave loaned the book to me, but only after extracting my most solemn promise that I would handle it with care and would return it promptly. I complied with both conditions. It was a fascinating little book. It describes in much detail the methods used in various parts of the country in making the mint julep. And while the differences and the details may seem slight to the casual reader, they obviously assume tremendous importance to the person or persons laying claim to the 'correct' way of making this popular concoction.

One little jewel in the book: 'Mint Julep is nectar to the Virginian, mother's milk to the Kentuckian, and ambrosia to Southerners anywhere.' And elsewhere in the book there is described a meeting of the Old Dominion Society that took place in New York City, on May 15, 1860. At the meeting, a 24-line poem was read to the members of the Society, ending in a toast. The meeting and the toast were described in the *Readers Digest* several years ago, and I memorized them because they seem so historically significant and even ironic when considered in light of the times and what was to happen shortly after they were uttered. Here are the words of the toast:

Here North and South and East and West
Are met in sweet communion-
Now drain this cup-this toast is best
VIRGINIA AND THE UNION!

Eleven months later on April 5, 1861, Virginia seceded from the Union!

I cannot leave the subject of trail-related parties without describing one of the most successful and unusual dinner parties ever held at the Trail center. The PATC holds many exciting affairs there, which attract anywhere from 50 to 100 people. There is the seafood festival in the spring, the barbecue in the summer, and the pig roast in October. But the party I am about to describe occurred in the afternoon and evening of July 25, 1984, and was held to honor Albie Pokrob and the coterie of six or seven hikers hiking with him from Georgia to Maine.

There were four of us who did the planning: Ron Tipton, who had hiked with Albie for several hundred miles on an earlier Trail thru-hike in 1978; Dave Sherman; Jean Cashin, of the ATC office in Harpers Ferry; and myself. It was not a surprise affair. Ron had kept in touch with Albie and had assured him we would have a dinner for him and his group. I am sure the hiking group was anticipating a dinner superior to the ordinary evening hikers fare, but I am also certain they were not expecting the formality of the dinner we had planned.

The script called for Jean to bring a catered dinner from Harpers Ferry, and she also agreed to bring linens, formal silverware, and candelabra. Ron would be dressed in his white wedding suit and would meet the group at the top of the mountain and escort them for the seven- to eight-minute walk down to the center. I was to be the chief waiter, and I would be wearing a tux and have a white towel over my arm.

In retrospect, and with no attempt at modesty, I think our planning was excellent. But in our wildest dreams, we could not have prepared and executed a script that was as exciting as what actually happened. Completely unknown to us, another series of events was taking place that would greatly affect our dinner.

Albie's parents and his sister had been vacationing in Florida, and on this day they were driving home to Connecticut. Hoping to meet Albie or to learn of his whereabouts, they had left the main south-north highway and journeyed through the Shenandoah National Park keeping their eyes open for Albie or other backpackers. No luck. They then headed for Harpers Ferry and inquired at the post office. No information on Albie. Disappointed, they headed back across the bridge that takes traffic over the Shenandoah River. Near the bridge, they spotted a lone backpacker. No, he did not know Albie but suggested they visit the office of the ATC. They arrived at the headquarters just as Jean was getting ready to depart on the 18-mile trip to the Blackburn Trail Center. The Pokrobs introduced themselves and asked Jean if she could supply any information as to Albie. Could she! She informed them that within minutes she was taking off for a dinner for Albie and his group, and if they would just follow her they would meet him.

After arriving at the center, Jean promptly decorated the guest table, which we had moved onto the front lawn. The Pokrobs were seated at the main table. Meanwhile, Ron had climbed to the Trail, an eight-minute walk up the mountain, and then walked south to meet the hikers. His timing was excellent. In his white suit, and carrying a poster board in hand with dinner menu in evidence, Ron formally welcomed them to the center, showed them the menu, and asked that they follow him. When they descended to the clearing in which the Center is located, they were met by Dave Sherman and Jean Cashin, who was wearing a full-length pink evening dress. For people who had been hiking in the woods for weeks, this was mighty heady stuff. As they approached the corner of the building, I met them and greeted them in the manner in which a head waiter courteously does. Then, as Albie came around the corner of the building and saw his parents and sister, he was absolutely speechless! It was a very moving family reunion.

The dinner was then served and enjoyed, and washed down with 'Wine du Garvey' as it was listed on the menu.

"There was a humorous aftermath to the dinner. Knowing that my waitering activities would demand my attention, I had given my camera with color film to one of the hikers to take pictures as he saw fit. One of the photos he took was of Jean Cashin in the formal evening dress with me beside her in the tux. I was not at home when the color prints were mailed to me from the lab, and my wife Mary opened the package. One of the first prints she saw was a 4- x 5-inch print of her husband in a tux with an attractive woman in pink evening dress! Yes, explanations were in order! I guess they were adequate, because after 59 years, I am still married to the same woman.

I was at home the five-day period between July 13 and July 17, and did no hiking. I had hiked as far north as Keys Gap on July 12 and I would begin hiking again on July 18 from Crampton Gap. So what about the 16 miles in between these two points? For two months prior to my 1990 hike, I had done some strenuous conditioning with a pack weighing anywhere from 35 to 42 pounds. On March 3, I had departed from Harpers Ferry for a round trip to Keys Gap, a distance of 16 miles. A fairly routine hike on a nice, spring-like day. I made several hikes in the Harpers Ferry-Virginia-Maryland area with Judy Jenner, longtime editor of *Appalachian Trailway News*, who was also getting in condition for her first real backpacking on the Trail. Earlier, on February 1, I had hiked from Crampton Gap to Harpers Ferry with two hiking companions, Ron Tipton and Dave Sherman, both of whom have hiked the entire Trail. And, if my hike to Keys Gap described above was 'routine,' the hike on February 1 was anything but routine.

It was a trip planned by Ron. We would rendezvous at Ron's home in Washington, D.C., drive to Crampton Gap, park the car, hike on the Trail south to the Harpers Ferry area, and return to the car at Crampton Gap via the Elk Ridge Trail. I agreed to go on the hike on the firm condition that I would be home by 5:30 P.M. for a family birthday party. I reiterated this several times. "No problem. No problem." Even so, when we reached Crampton Gap I asked Ron to let me see the map of our planned hike. "No map. Not necessary. I know the route!"

We proceeded south on the Trail on a brisk, sunny day. Upon reaching Weverton Heights, we stopped to look down at the Harpers Ferry area, the town itself, the two rivers (Shenandoah and Potomac), plus the three other modes of transportation, the highway (U.S. 340), the B&O Railroad, and the C&O Canal. It is one of the most spectacular views along the entire Trail.

From Weverton Heights, we walked slowly down the steep but well-graded Trail to the C&O towpath, and, still on the Trail, we hiked north to the tiny village of Sandy Hook, which is situated directly beside the Potomac and across the river from Harpers Ferry. We ate our lunch there at an outside table. It was 2 P.M. and I was getting uneasy about our schedule. Ron was still confident, "No problem." We climbed back up to the ridge via the Maryland Heights Trail; we passed the Civil War fortifications and then followed the Elk Ridge Trail north. At this point we were headed for Crampton Gap and our car.

At 3 P.M., with Dave about 50 yards in the lead, we came to a directional sign. Ron and I could read the big-lettered CRAMPTON GAP, but Dave had his arm and hand across the remainder of the sign. When he removed his arm, we were aghast. It read '10 Miles.' TEN MILES! Three hours minimum of hiking plus one hour minimum of car driving. That would get me home at 7:30 P.M. Nothing to do but make the best of it.

We pushed on rapidly, and at 4:30 P.M. we noticed a faint trail-road leading down to a house. We walked to the house, and I negotiated a ride to Crampton Gap which we reached shortly. In the fast-gathering darkness, I got out my billfold and extracted the money to pay the man. But in my haste to get home, I had left my billfold in the car of the man who gave us the ride! A comedy of errors. More time was lost as we drove back to the farmhouse and retrieved the billfold. Eventually I arrived home at 6:30 P.M. Not good, but not as bad as it might have been if we had not obtained that ride. And that is how I account for the 16 miles stretching from Keys Gap in West Virginia to Crampton Gap in Maryland.

■ ■ ■

My five days at home were hectic. I went through three-and-a-half months' accumulation of mail. I mowed the big lawn, weeded the garden, put cages around the tomato plants, and took my hiking boots to the cobbler to be resoled. I prepared a form letter apprising friends of my progress-to-date, and enclosed a revised itinerary. I duplicated more than 40 copies of the letter and itinerary, typed up envelopes and worked until 2 A.M. I spent July 18 getting envelopes typed and inserting letters with a personal note to each addressee.

Wednesday, July 18
Crampton Gap, Maryland, to Rocky Run Shelter
6 miles

"Up at 4 A.M., more frenzied packing. Went to 6:30 A.M. Mass. It would be my last opportunity to attend a church service until after the completion of my hike. I then went to McDonald's for a big breakfast with my usual early morning

McDonald's group. Mailed all my letters. At 10 A.M., I drove in my van with my daughter, Sharon, directly to the ATC headquarters in Harpers Ferry. I turned in the Virginia guidebook and my completed log forms for the period ending July 12.

"Afterwards, I had a big lunch at the home of my daughter, who lives in Harpers Ferry, took a much-needed 30-minute nap, and then the two of us drove to Crampton Gap State Park. Leaving the van there, we hiked in to the Crampton Gap shelter. The spring was dry and the place was not too inviting. Sharon continued walking with me for about a mile, after which she returned to the van and home.

"I continued hiking north, reaching at 5:30 P.M. the blue-blaze Bear Spring Trail, which leads right down the mountain to the PATC locked cabin. Continuing on, I passed at 6 P.M. the restricted U.S. government communications tower, and at 7:10 P.M., I reached the Rocky Run shelter. The Trail was well-blazed, free of litter, but suffered from 35 blowdowns, all four- to eight-inches in diameter. At the shelter, I met Jim Tidd, whom I had met further south over a week ago. At 8 P.M., another hiker arrived and that was it. Having had two substantial meals already, I ate a light supper, and being heavy-eyed from little sleep the previous night, I bedded down at 8:30 P.M."

Thursday, July 19
Rocky Run Shelter to Hemlock Hill Campground
15 miles

"Up at 5:40 A.M., cold breakfast, on my way at 7:06 A.M. Reached the Dahlgren Campground (hot showers) around 8:30 A.M.; walked through it and used the facilities. Then crossed U.S. Route Alt. 40. Minutes later into Washington Monument State Park. After walking for six miles, I crossed over Interstate 70, then under U.S. 40, and minutes later reached the Pine Knob shelter, where I ate lunch. This shelter is a rather dismal affair, poor location, and much litter, including food containers and beer bottles. Took a short, 20-minute nap, then pushed on. Counted 45 blowdowns between Rocky Run shelter and Pine Knob.

"I reached the Black Rock-Pojo area around 2 P.M. Took the blue blaze trail past the Pojo Memorial Campground primarily to get water. Continued on the blue blaze trail until it intersected with the Trail. No directional signs at intersection. I took a right turn—wrong! Met northbound hiker Tim Post, who convinced me I was going the wrong way! Turned around and followed him. Reached Hemlock Hill Campground at 7 P.M. Tim Post was already there, plus one other occupant. Later another couple arrived.

"Had a cold supper; too tired to gather wood and start my stove. Visited with Tim. Went to sleep on top of my sleeping bag about 8:30 P.M. I knew I would have one tough day getting to Pen Mar and this was the day. Now I have but 10 miles to reach County Park in Pen Mar for the rendezvous with Simon, O'Hara, and Longo."

Friday, July 20
Hemlock Hill Campground to Pen Mar County Park
10 miles

"Up at 6 A.M. Cold breakfast, but did make hot coffee. Left camp at 8 A.M. Very late for me, but it was an easy day ahead, or so I thought. Looked with interest at the large American chestnut tree described in the guidebook as being 'healthy.' Not so. It has many blossoms on it but the tree is diseased! Sad. Pleasant hike to Devils Racecourse shelter, especially in area of Little Antietam Creek and on top of the crest before reaching the shelter. Met two couples, the Katcows and Johnsons, making their first backpacking trip. They had stayed overnight at the Devils Racecourse shelter on their first night out, a bad choice, a poor location and not an inviting shelter. I cooked myself my meal of the day, a tomato-rice affair, which I planned to augment with canned chicken. A frantic search of my pack, no canned chicken! But the rice was filling. With some dried apple and a granola bar, my hunger pangs were satisfied. Took a 30-minute nap after lunch. Readers will have already detected the old age factor in this narrative—taking naps! A luxury to which the elderly are entitled.

"Resumed my hiking at 1:30 P.M. At 3:30 P.M., I left the Trail and followed the blue blaze trail to the popular High Rocks area. There were several cars there and I, along with others, climbed up the rocks to the flat rocky area that is used both for viewing and as a take-off platform for hang gliders. Leaving that area, I continued on the Trail and climbed slowly and carefully through an incredibly rocky jungle. Eventually, around 5 P.M., I reached the Pen Mar Campground and located the attendant, Emerson Bowman. No tent camping permitted, but I could sleep in the picnic pavillion. Much better.

I learned from Bowman that there was a restaurant a half-mile away, and at 6 P.M., he drove me over there for a sandwich. He gave me a brief car tour of the area, which was very popular during the early part of the century when trains brought people to the area for vacationing. It is still a most attractive area, with large homes and lodges, but the vacation trains have been supplanted by the automobile.

"Back at camp, I resumed my paperwork, but it became very dark and rain began falling suddenly and in sheets. A Frederick, Maryland, family picnicking nearby dashed to my section of the pavillion and provided me with another sandwich, chips, and peach cobbler. Great! At 8 P.M., both the family and Bowman left for the day, and I had the campground to myself. The rain stopped almost as suddenly as it began and it became quite chilly. I climbed into my sleeping bag and slept on top of the picnic table, really not much different from sleeping on the floor of a shelter except that one has to be a wee bit careful when turning over during the night. It had been a most pleasant day and it marked the end of my Maryland hiking."

Saturday, July 21
Pen Mar to Antietam Shelter, Pennsylvania
7 miles

"Awoke at 3:30 A.M.; up at 5:30 A.M. when it was barely light enough to see. Having serious intestinal trouble again. Drinking impure water? Quite possibly. In any event, I ate a quick cold breakfast, no hot coffee; did not think it advisable to start my wood burning stove in the confines of the pavilion!

"I was expecting three friends of mine to arrive at around 8:30 A.M., and I used the intervening time to work on my notes, as I was two days behind! At about the time I finished that work, a car arrived and out stepped, not my three friends, but a surprise—Ken Osterman of Towson, Maryland. Ken is one of three men in the Trail family with whom I share a special relationship regarding backpacking and the Trail.

"Sometime in the 1970s, each of the three was in the hospital, recovering from major surgery. Each was given reading material to while away the time, and in this reading material was an inexpensive paperback book bearing the title *Appalachian Hiker*. After finishing the book, each man vowed that if he emerged from the hospital a whole, healthy man, he would become a backpacker and hike on the Trail. Each emerged a healthy man. Each began backpacking. One, Dr. Kenneth McCoy of Syria, Virginia, hiked the entire Trail in 1978 and remains active to this day as a Trail maintainer. Ken Osterman, when I first met him in 1978, had hiked 1,200 miles on the Trail. Both had joined the PATC and ATC. Ken maintains the Antietam shelter in Pennsylvania, and in 1987, he became the treasurer of the ATC. The third man had identified himself to me on two occasions and I must confess I have forgotten his name. Now, back to Ken.

"Ken had ascertained through the Trail office in Harpers Ferry where I might be on Saturday morning, July 21, and there he was. He invited me to be his guest for the night at his summer home six miles from the Antietam shelter. I informed him that I was to be joined shortly by three other hikers. No problem. All of us were invited. I accepted the invitation with alacrity. Before Ken left, the other three arrived, and I introduced Ken and informed them of our change in plans.

"Long before my 1990 hike began, these three friends of mine in the Falls Church, Virginia area had stated their desire to hike with me on a weekend. This was the agreed upon time. They proceeded in two cars to Caledonia State

Park in Pennsylvania and parked Tom Simon's car at that point. Then Tom, plus Hugh O'Hara and Jim Longo, proceeded in Jim's car to meet me at Pen Mar where Jim parked his car. We began hiking north at 9:30 A.M. and within the first half-mile encountered a large number of wineberry bushes, perhaps the heaviest concentration I had ever seen. They were fully ripe and we took time to enjoy. Also within the first mile, we met PATC member Frank Moore hiking south.

"In short order, we crossed four hard-top highways including both the old and new PA 16. At 11:30 A.M., we reached the big, never-go-dry Bailey Spring, had lunch there and met Dave Parsons, caretaker of the Leroy Smith shelter farther north in Pennsylvania. Some 4.5 miles north of Pen Mar, we had a brief rest stop at the two very new Deer Lick shelters, each with a capacity of five to six people.

"In 1990, the state of Pennsylvania financed the construction of a number of these trailside shelters to replace or augment the shelter chain within the Michaux State Forest. The original shelters, many still in use, were made of logs and have seen the wear and tear of some 50 years. The new shelters are most attractive and of a design not seen elsewhere on the Trail. They are erected on pilings about 18 inches off the ground, which should minimize the rodent problem existing in many shelters. Hugh and I examined the spring about 100 yards from the shelter, a good flow of water. All in all, a most attractive and pleasant overnight facility.

"As we neared Antietam shelter, we were met on the Trail by Dave Sherman with four cans of cold beer. Deeply appreciated. The beer runs which Marty Dominy had performed in Georgia, North Carolina, Tennessee, and southwestern Virginia were being continued by Dave Sherman, who had pleasantly surprised me twice in northern Virginia and now in southern Pennsylvania. This was to be the last such surprise, but then, how many long-distance backpackers on the Trail have such a luxury? One could say 'What are friends for?' But the pleasant surprises I had had for almost 1,000 miles were definitely far beyond the norm.

"Reached the Antietam shelter at 3 P.M. and met Ken Osterman, who had arrived but five minutes earlier. We also met a very active PATC trail worker, Rex Looney, the overseer of the Tumbling Run shelters and installer of some impressive waterbars both north and south of the Antietam and Tumbling Run shelters. Driving in Dave Sherman's car and Ken's truck, we reached Ken's summer home, named 'Appalachian Dare,' some six to seven miles from the shelter. Ken was a great host, and provided us with a steak-and-baked-potato dinner. Dave left in a driving rain at 9 P.M. bound for home in Washington, D.C. The rest of us were in bed by 9:30 P.M. The end of the first day with my three friends, and a fine start it was."

Sunday, July 22
Antietam Shelter to Quarry Gap Shelters
13 miles

"Up at 6 A.M., cereal breakfast. Took a tub bath and washed underwear. Around 8 A.M., we all piled into Ken's truck and returned to Antietam shelter. Began hiking at 8:30 A.M. A steep, long climb for over an hour, but through very pretty forest, one huge stand of fern, then a big hemlock grove; all of us were impressed. The trail from Pen Mar to Quarry Gap shelters is mostly new since 1970, and ever so much nicer. Met Dave Parsons again; he is day hiking, filling in the gaps on his 2,000-mile quest.

"It was almost 1 P.M. when we ate lunch on the Trail. Continued to be impressed with waterbar work and expert paint blazing; the super blazing extended from Antietam five miles north. We reached U.S. 30 at 3:40 P.M. Tom then jogged the 0.6 mile to the parking lot and brought his station wagon back to where we were waiting. We promptly drove three miles east to Kemples Restaurant and ordered one large pizza with all the toppings. So good. Then out to the station wagon to sort through the extra food that Tom brought.

"I was put on the Trail crossing on U.S. 30. Said good-bye to three very nice guys and began the 2.6-mile hike to Quarry Gap shelters, arriving about 7:15 P.M. I prepared hot coffee and sampled the brownies that my daughter-in-law, Kay Garvey, had sent. Delish. Hung up my wet clothes to 'dry,' that is, to become less wet, overnight. To bed at 8:30 P.M. A very pleasant weekend."

Monday, July 23
Quarry Gap Shelters to Iron Masters Mansion American Youth Hostel
17 miles

"Up at 5:30 A.M. Hot breakfast using a Sterno can to heat water, having found the Sterno on the Trail. Got to work on two days of my notes and after that, the daily logs. While I was working, two thru-hikers stopped briefly. They were headed for the youth hostel and the nearby ice cream store some 17 miles to the north. Sounded like a good idea and I decided to give it a try.

"Took off at 8:40 A.M. and made good time all day. Pleasant walking. Reached the Potomac Appalachian Trail Club locked Milesburn cabin at 11:15 A.M. Ate my lunch at the inside table. Love these PATC locked cabins, a love affair I've had since I first joined the club in 1952. Left Milesburn and arrived shortly at the old Birch Run shelters to find a Boy Scout troop from Camp May, New Jersey, lunching there. At 2:40 P.M., I reached the side trail leading to another PATC locked cabin, the Anna Michener Cabin, one of PATC's finest. It was built from scratch with white oak logs in honor of Anna Michener, a PATC stalwart who was born and raised in the same county in which the cabin was built.

"Shortly after leaving the Michener area, I arrived at Toms Run with its four shelters, two of the very old, small ones plus two very new ones. Many shelters and cabins on this day! At 5:30 P.M., I reached the American Youth Hostel. The very likeable house parents, Joan and Bob Beard, had traded assignments with a New Zealand couple for the summer season, but I did not meet the New Zealand couple either. They were on a week's vacation, and Tom Martin, a house parent from Cape Cod, was filling in. He was reading a book when I walked in and he seemed somewhat incredulous when he saw me. He looked at me, then at the book cover, then back to me and nodded his head. He had just begun reading my book *Appalachian Hiker II* with my picture staring at him from the cover, and could hardly believe his eyes when he saw me. After we became acquainted, he took me to the store and bought me a pint of ice cream. Later I bought a half gallon and shared it with Tom and the two young hikers whom I had met earlier in the day.

"I used the very modern kitchen to cook a backpacker's meal—a Lipton's beef stroganoff sauce bolstered with a can of chicken and topped off with a quart of ice cream, the ice cream being a flourish not generally enjoyed by backpackers.

A pair of morels.

"This place is aptly named. It was a mansion occupied by the ironmaster, a very important person in the iron-making industry that flourished here in the late 19th and early 20th centuries. It has a fireplace (no longer in use) that is at least eight feet wide. I had stayed here many times, but this was my first time as a backpacker. After the evening meal, it was back to my paperwork. My back bothering me quite a bit, more from the writing than the hiking. Around midnight, I and the three others watched a videotape, *Five Million Steps,* relating to the Trail. Very well done. We ate more ice cream during the viewing. To bed at 1:15 A.M., not your usual backpacking bedtime. During the evening, I had called my daughter, Sharon, and made arrangements for her to meet me with my van at Duncannon, Pennsylvania, on Saturday morning."

Tuesday, July 24
Pine Grove Furnace State Park to Moyers Campground
(near Mt. Holly Springs)
11 miles

"Up at 6 A.M., breakfast in the kitchen, washed down with some excellent coffee brewed by Tom Martin. Each person using an American Youth Hostel is expected to perform chores as part of his payment, such as lawn mowing, vacuuming, whatever. My assignment this morning was to help clean up two bathrooms, which I cheerfully did. Then I made a number of phone calls and wrote cards and letters. At 10:45 A.M., I ate an early lunch of one cookie and a pint of ice cream. Said goodbye to Tom and began hiking at 11:10 A.M.

"Very pleasant hiking, but at 3 P.M., I had another attack of diarrhea, and I resolved to begin taking my medicine more regularly, something I should have been doing the past several days."

I presume I took the medicine, and it must have been effective, because I find no more mention in my notes about the intestinal problem. A year and a half later I'm still having mild problems, but nothing like I had in that three or four day stretch in Pennsylvania.

"At 5 P.M., I crossed PA 94, and at 5:40 P.M., I reached Moyers Campground. Made arrangements to sleep on the open air stage, which sports a well-worn rug. Rinsed off my filthy clothes and put them in the camp washing machine. Ate a sandwich and had a coke at the camp store. I visited a camping group of three couples. When they learned I was hiking the Trail, they invited me to join their group for a steak dinner—wonderful!

"I returned to the 'stage,' my shelter for the night. One other hiker also was there. To bed around 10 P.M., a full day. During the day I had passed a sign showing that it was the halfway point on the entire Trail."

Wednesday, July 25
Moyers Campground to the ATC Office, Boiling Springs, Pennsylvania
10 miles

For reasons I will explain, this was to be an exciting and pleasant day. Until 1990, the Trail through the Cumberland Valley followed a very busy highway. The effort to get it off the highway was one of the thorniest ever faced by the National Park Service in the Trail land acquisition program, which began in 1979. In the end, it was William Penn Mott, Director of the National Park Service, who ruled that the Trail should be removed from the highway and moved to a low-lying ridge.

Once the decision was made, the once violent opposition seemed to evaporate and land owners were quite willing to negotiate with the Park Service in either selling the land or in granting easements to permit the Trail relocation. As tracts were obtained, the Mountain Club of Maryland and the Cumberland Valley Appalachian Trail Management Committee began the nitty gritty job of getting the Trail on the ground, even going so far as to plant 12,000 tree seedlings in the spring of 1990. The new relocation had just been opened up a few weeks before I began hiking through it.

I had hiked the highway route in 1970, and again around 1980, and I was elated to hike through this new and, to me, vastly improved route. One of the blessings of the new route was the exciting Boiling Springs area where the Trail goes directly beside the lake and the pleasant office of the regional representative of the Conference.

"Up at 5:20 A.M. and on my way at 6:40 A.M. I finished my hiking for the day at noon when I reached the Boiling Springs office and the friendly volunteer on duty, Mrs. Frances DuBois. The regional ATC representative, Karen Lutz, was on leave and I was sorry to have missed her. I was permitted to use the ATC office as my own office for a few hours. I made arrangements to stay overnight at a bed and breakfast place operated by John Garman, which was situated just across the tiny lake from the ATC office.

"The cost was $25, which was a concession to a hiker from the usual $40 rate. I also called the John Scanlan residence in nearby Carlisle and made arrangements to have dinner at their home only four miles from Boiling Springs. John

(Jack) Scanlan picked me up at 5:30 P.M. and gave me a brief tour of the historic town of Carlisle, which has both a military and a football history. Prior to World War I, Jim Thorpe and his Carlisle Indians were one of the most prominent college football teams in the country. For reasons which remain somewhat obscure, the military establishment closed the school down during World War I. For the last quarter of a century, the Washington Redskins have used Carlisle as a base for their preseason football practices.

"At 10 P.M., Jack drove me back to my bed and breakfast home."

The Scanlans have an interesting life. John, a longtime State Department employee specializing in Middle East European countries, and his family were for many years fellow residents in Falls Church, Virginia. In the 1980s, they were transferred to Belgrade, Yugoslavia, where Jack was a staff employee and later served as the U.S. Ambassador. On two of my many hiking trips in Yugoslavia, I had met the Scanlans: once, in 1983, at the tiny village of Lipica (Lipizza) where for 400 years the world-renowned white Lipizzaner horses have been bred and trained; the second time in 1986, in the capital city of Slovenia, Ljubljana, when Jack was the Ambassador and was in Ljubljana on Embassy business.

It was therefore only natural that on this day in July 1990, our conversation would drift to Yugoslavia and the explosive situation that was rapidly developing. My last diary entry for July 25 reads as follows: 'Jack still working for State Department but considering a consulting job that would get him back to Eastern Europe.'

Imagine my surprise and pleasure in September 1991, while reading an English language version of the *International Weekly* issued in Belgrade, Yugoslavia, to see a full page devoted to an interview with John Scanlan and four excellent pictures of him. The interview centered on his transformation from Ambassador to his new role as vice president of the ICN GALENIKA Corporation. So his wishes to return to Eastern Europe have been granted, but he has returned to a country vastly different from the country that was still intact when he left in 1989.

Thursday, July 26
Boiling Springs to Darlington Shelter
13 miles

"Up at 6 A.M., and John Garman up within minutes after me to make me a pot of coffee. He was most grateful that I had slept on the floor of my bedroom rather than disturb the carefully made bed. He sat with me during my breakfast and kept plying me with fruit, juice, and a hot muffin, even a banana to carry for my lunch. An extremely nice chap.

Finally, I got away at 10:15 A.M.; made good time through some fields, some woods. I was really thrilled at the new relocation, such a vast improvement over that busy highway route. We have come so far so fast in these last 20 years. The Mountain Club of Maryland and the Cumberland Valley Appalachian Trail Management Committee have done a tremendous job, and I wrote to the MCM president to that effect.

I reached U.S. 11 at noon and ate lunch at Gino's Restaurant. After lunch, Gino took me outside on the busy highway and pointed to the framework of the new footbridge over U.S. 11, all done except for one large piece of steel. (The steel was installed a few weeks after my journey there and a big dedication of the new footbridge was held on September 22.)

"Pushed on after lunch and was offered a cold beer by landowner Maynard Myers on Bernhisel Road. Reached PA 944 at 6 P.M., but it then took me another hour and 25 minutes to hike the last 1.9 miles to the Darlington shelter. Contributing to my late arrival of 7:30 P.M. were the very sparse paint blazing and the abundance of blackberries and wineberries that I stopped to enjoy. The name Darlington is that of a deceased Methodist bishop who was a big supporter of the Trail. This is a new shelter replacing the one, at a different location, where I had stayed in 1970. The former shelter, which was in a low swampy area, showed a distinct lack of upkeep. It was one of the more dismal shelters I stayed in and I reflected at the time that it was a poor way to memorialize the good bishop for his support of the Trail.

"The new shelter is in a high, dry area and is four feet off the ground with no steps to help the hiker climb into it. Once inside, I decided to stay put, ate a cold supper and climbed into my sleeping bag. Too late to work on my notes; not good, but such is life on the Trail. And, I reflected that my accommodations tonight were not quite of the same quality as those of the previous night."

I worked out a deal with John Garman for hikers to use his backyard. The cost would be $1 to camp, $1 for a shower, $1 for laundry, and $2 for a continental breakfast with juice and a hot muffin. Most reasonable. I wrote up the terms and mailed them to Dan Bruce, and they were included in the 1991 *Thru-hiker's Handbook*. I also had them posted in the ATC office in Boiling Springs.

Friday, July 27
Darlington Shelter to Duncannon
11 miles

"Up at 5:25 A.M. and on my way at 6:17 A.M. Started with almost no water. The water is 0.25 mile from the shelter and I did not attempt to find it. I had one liter of water when I arrived the night before and I used that for both supper on Thursday and breakfast today. Pretty good! Or pretty sad!

"Pleasant hiking in mild weather. Impressed with the jungle-like effect one receives to the left of the Trail during the first mile. Vines cover the trees to such an extent as to make an impenetrable jungle. I reflected that I would hate to have to cut a trail through that maze! I had trouble with Miller Gap Road; the guidebook data was obsolete and the open-field blazing a bit incomplete. Understandable in view of the newness of the relocation. I picked up 15 pieces of litter, all placards reading 'NO DOE HUNTING.' At 11:15 A.M., I reached the turn-off trail that leads 100 yards steeply downhill to the Thelma Marks shelter. I decided not to waste the energy and I ate my lunch at the intersection."

I must relate a tragic incident that occurred at the Thelma Marks shelter on the night of September 13, 1990, just 48 days after I passed through. On that date, a young man and a young woman, Geoffrey Logan Hood and Molly LaRue, each age 26 and about to be married, had hiked southbound to there from Katahdin, Maine. At the point where I ate my lunch, they had probably stopped for a minute or two, then turned left and walked down to the Thelma Marks shelter. It would be their last hike. Each was killed during the night by a ne'er do well who either chanced upon them or had overheard their plans while they were at the Doyle Hotel where they had stayed overnight. The man had been shot, the young lady raped and mutilated with a knife.

There have been other murders on the Trail, but this one was so tragic it shook the Trail family as no other Trail murders had done. Memorial contributions on behalf of the two young people poured in from all over the country. The murderer was apprehended within days after the tragedy as he walked across the footbridge at Harpers Ferry, West Virginia. He was wearing some of the dead man's clothes and carrying some of his equipment. He was subsequently tried for and convicted of murder and sentenced to death in Pennsylvania. I am not a particularly emotional person, but reading about this tragedy, let alone writing about it, causes the tears to flow—some tears of grief, some of rage.

"After my lunch, I resumed my hike, reached the outskirts of Duncannon at 1:15 P.M., and reached the Doyle Hotel 30 minutes later. *The Philosophers Guide* had devoted quite a bit of space to this hotel, and following the advice of the Guide, I had phoned ahead from the Ironmasters Hostel to reserve Room 16.

"I registered, took my pack to Room 16 with its brass bed, showered, and put on clean clothes. Down to the nearby Sorrentis for a 'small' pizza. I realize that words like small, medium, and large are relative terms, but this 'small' pizza was 32 inches in circumference! I ate most of it at the pizza place, took the rest to my room for later consumption. In retrospect, I would have been better off to have skipped the pizza and eaten a dinner in the Doyle dining room. In any event, after finishing my pizza in my room, I went down to the dining room, and found a table in an out-of-the-way place to write up my last two days of activity. I spent two hours at that chore, then repaired to the bar and ordered a baked potato and a dish of coleslaw. I love baked potatoes and I hate to waste food, but this potato was so HUGE that I couldn't finish it.

"The person sitting next to me was a certain Glen Rusch, a permanent resident at Doyle whom I had met earlier. He insisted upon paying for my meal but also readily accepted the invitation to be my guest at breakfast.

"Later in the evening, I met two other thru-hikers from Micanopy, Florida, Frank Spirek and Dianne Ensminger, who invited me to have an ice cream sundae with them at a popular ice cream bar north of the hotel.

These two Floridians had a most interesting hike, and finished up at Katahdin in the fog on October 9, 1990. At roughly 200-mile intervals of their hike, they wrote a description in very vivid terms of what they had seen and experienced. These installments were sent to Florida, where they were reproduced and mailed to friends and acquaintances. I don't have Dan Bruce's *Thru-hiker's Handbook* before me as I write these words, but I do have the description of the Doyle Hotel provided in the *Philosophers Guide of 1990*. The conclusion I derive from the Guide is this—the Doyle is ROUGH around the edges; it is not very clean; but YES, the thru-hiker should stay there because it IS an EXPERIENCE! I would agree, but then I enjoyed the 'luxury' of room 16. Frank and Dianne had this to say of their experience:

'On July 27, we quickly hiked down into the town of Duncannon. We entered this rusty, old, former steel town with the intention of taking a day off. We headed straight to the Doyle Hotel, the only accommodation in town. From the outside, the Doyle looked like a gem—a four-story Victorian Inn said to be built by Anheuser-Busch. But the insides of this structure were a different story. The motel had definitely seen better days. Already, at 10 A.M., there was a fair-sized crowd drinking beer in the tavern. We were assigned Room 33 on the very top floor. As we ascended the stairs, things got worse. This once beautiful inn was now a pig sty. Our room had been recently sanded and painted. The remains of the old wallpaper and paint were just left on the floor. Our closet was filled with garbage! We found two old vacuum cleaners stuffed in front of the fire escape—neither worked. We finally found a dust mop, and worked for what seemed like hours to make the room a little more habitable. The bathroom was hopeless—a communal, co-ed affair with only a tub, no shower! The floor was covered by cigarette butts and ashes, the garbage was overflowing with coffee grounds, the tub and sink were filthy, and the toilet hadn't been flushed in ages. We pray that the half-bottle of bleach that we exhausted in that bathroom killed, or at least stunned, the critters living in the porcelain. That evening we had the pure pleasure of trying to sleep at the Doyle.

'We couldn't decide what was the worst part of our attempted night's sleep: the hot temperatures, the loud, nearby railyard, the noisy motel guests, the drunks stumbling down the hallway, or the mushy bed. Needless to say, we didn't spend another day in Duncannon.'

Would I stay there if I were hiking through? Yes, I would. Tim Yeoman, the proprietor and sometimes bartender is a most friendly and accommodating fellow, and the other hired help were equally friendly. However, I would try to get Room 16 again!

Saturday, July 28
Duncannon, Pennsylvania, to Wisecarver Summer Home, Otisfield, Maine

As I hiked through southern Pennsylvania, I realized that I was not making fast enough progress to complete the hike before the possible onset of seriously cold weather in Maine and New Hampshire. I decided it would be wise to go by car to Katahdin in Maine and hike south from there. So it was that on July 28th, my daughter Sharon drove my van north from Harpers Ferry to Duncannon to pick me up. She was accompanied by Eddie Watson, another Trail hiker who had likewise decided to flip-flop.

126

"Up at 6 A.M. and down to the bar at 7 A.M., sat beside Frank and Dianne. Waited for Glen—he did not show. Tim, the bartender, informed me that Glen had been up rather late at the bar and he doubted if Glen would be down for breakfast for some time. Those were not Tim's exact words but they convey the meaning. Accordingly, I ordered a man-sized breakfast of eggs, sausage, toast, hash browns, and coffee. Most enjoyable.

"Had finished eating, and was still visiting with my two Florida friends at 8:20 A.M., when who should appear but my darling daughter Sharon! Had not expected her (or Eddie Watson, the Tennessee Walker, who had driven with her from Harpers Ferry) until 9:30 or 10 A.M. As it turned out, the mileage from Harpers Ferry was only 130 miles, whereas I had made my estimate from Falls Church, some 50 miles further.

"I packed my gear quickly, got into the van, and we took off at 9 A.M. Sharon drove, though she had had only 45 minutes of sleep the previous night, but after a bit she surrendered the wheel to Eddie, who is an excellent driver and did most of the driving the rest of the day. It was uneventful driving via Interstates 81, 84, and 95 to Gray, Maine. Then Sharon took over for the final 30 minutes to the Wisecarver residence. Arrived at 9:15 P.M., 660 miles from Harpers Ferry. Beautiful scenery entire trip. Used a quart of oil every time we stopped for gas! I see a major overhaul or a new engine coming up.

"Sharon's husband, Tim, and his mother, Alice Wisecarver, quickly warmed up a chicken and rice dinner, and we made out famously. Sharon and Tim then took Eddie in the van to the cottage where he would sleep the next two nights. I was assigned to the attic, which Tim had cleaned up thoroughly, bed made, and a vase of fresh flowers! Never had it so good. To sleep promptly."

Sunday, July 29
Otisfield, Maine

"Up at 5:30 A.M. Came downstairs, shaved, and searched diligently, finally successfully, for coffee makings. Made three to four cups and enjoyed coffee and toast for breakfast number one. Went to 8:45 A.M. Mass some five miles away, did some grocery shopping, then back to the Wisecarvers' for breakfast number two—sausage and pancakes. Worked on notes, wrote cards, went over plans for rest of trip. Tim's aunt and uncle, Virginia and Marshall Sutton, have a vacation home adjacent to the Wisecarver home. I visited with them in the morning, and in the afternoon, Sharon and I enjoyed a swim with them in Lake Thompson. The weather and the water were perfect, a glorious day. Later, Sharon washed all my clothes and we assembled our food. Earlier, I had thoroughly greased my hiking boots. We tried out the miniature tape recorder that Hugh O'Hara had mailed to me from Falls Church. I am to mail the first tape or tapes to him when I reach Monson, Maine. Later, we assembled and labeled five packages and envelopes for mailing to such places as Monson, Maine, Gorham, New Hampshire, and Delaware Water Gap, Pennsylvania. All set for Monday's trip to Baxter State Park."

Monday, July 30
Otisfield to Baxter State Park

"Up at 5:30 A.M. to a world of fog. Made and consumed a pot of coffee and some cereal before others awoke. Later, had toast and scrambled egg breakfast with the family. Got our gear packed in the van. Marshall and Ginny Sutton over to say good-bye. Marshall plans to join me for a few days of hiking somewhere in Maine.

"Sharon, Eddie Watson, and I took off at 8:30 A.M. Stopped in Norway, Maine, for cash, gasoline, and to mail packages. Drove the 'back way' all day through Skowhegan and Monson. Stopped in Monson at the popular Shaw's Boarding House, visited with the Shaw family and some of the hikers, and took pictures. After that, it was slow driving over the horrible potholed roads of the Great Northern Paper Company (recently acquired by Georgia Pacific).

"Reached the Abol Bridge camp store on the Trail at 6:30 P.M. Bought gas there at $1.33 per gallon.

"Drove on to the entrance to Baxter Park. All campgrounds full! Retraced our route for seven miles and obtained a campsite at the Big Moose private campground. Selected a lean-to with screened doors! A wise choice as the mosquitos were out in force. Had a simple sandwich and fruit supper and then made two batches of popcorn. All of us in bed by 9:30 P.M., our screen doors very effective against the hordes of mosquitos."

Tuesday, July 31
Climbed the 'Big K,' Baxter Peak on Katahdin
10 miles

"Up at 5:20 A.M., breakfast at the campground, and on our way in the van at 7:30 A.M. Paid our $8 entry fee at Baxter Park, then drove to and parked at Katahdin Stream Campground. The three of us began hiking at 8:15 A.M., reached the 1.2 mileage marker at 9:00 A.M., the next mile marker at 9:50 A.M., and then it was almost two hours before we reached the last one. Finally reached the summit, Baxter Peak, at 5,267-foot elevation, at 1:30 P.M. The 13-foot stone cairn at the summit reaches up to exactly one mile. Sharon took many pictures, as she was traveling with two cameras, one color, one black and white. Some 15 to 18 people at the summit where we ate our noon lunch.

"A really spectacular climb on the Big K, my fourth such climb and the last. My other climbs were in 1969, 1970, and 1977. It had been about as perfect a

Ed and Sharon at the start of hike up Katahdin.

Rock climbing on Katahdin on the way to Baxter Peak.

The author climbing Katahdin with a helping hand from Eddie Watson.

day as one could ask for, low humidity, temperature in the 70s, clear and sunny all day long. We had enjoyed the wooded areas, the open rock areas, and the trail along the waterfall and the stream. Katahdin is indeed a fitting place to finish the 2,144 mile hike from Georgia to Maine.

"We began the descent at 2:00 P.M. and reached the campground and our van at 6:30 P.M. One mishap on the descent: while Sharon was standing on a high rock, her 15-year-old Petri camera case simply came apart, and the camera fell some 8 to 10 feet to the rocks below. The fall damaged the lens and the focusing apparatus, making it essentially worthless.

"From Baxter Park, we drove directly back to the Big Moose Campground and moved into the same screened lean-to we had used the previous night. We dined well on a two-and-a-half-pound can of beef stew with bread and fruit, along with a half-gallon of ice cream for dessert. All of us were very pleased with our day's achievement. After our evening meal, Sharon showered and changed clothes. With her wet hair and her freshly scrubbed face, flushed from all that sun, she looked pretty enough to hug, and I'm fairly certain I did just that.

"To bed early, Eddie and I now facing the 100-mile hike through the wilderness area of Maine with no resupply point until we reach Monson."

Wednesday, August 1
Katahdin Stream Campground, Baxter State Park, to Hurd Brook Lean-To
13 miles

"Up early and ate breakfast with coffee brewed on the two-burner Coleman stove that has been a fixture in the vans I have driven for some 20 years. Showered and shaved. Next job was to transfer all the groceries recently purchased into my pack, wincing each time I added those ounces to an already heavy pack.

"Left the campground at 8 A.M., drove to the Abol Bridge camp store and received permission to leave our packs there for pickup later in the day. Big help. Back to the entrance station at Baxter Park. We were getting low on gas, and there would be considerable driving to the starting point within the park. At that point, Eddie Watson suggested we ask the people in the van behind us if we could ride with them. Brilliant idea. I dashed back and talked to the young couple. Of course they would give us a ride! Sharon wheeled my van around, said hurried good-byes, and headed for Millinocket. We rode all the way, some 8 to 10 miles, to where both we and the young couple would begin our day's hiking at the Katahdin Stream Campground.

"Began hiking at 10 A.M. Reached the Daicey Pond Campground with its many lean-tos, some cabins, and even a library! Ate part of our lunch there, then began hiking on the Trail again; viewed Little Niagara Falls, and shortly after, Big Niagara Falls. We separated at that point. I went on ahead; Eddie remained to take pictures.

"Shortly, I reached a fast-flowing 30-foot-wide tributary of the Nesuntabunt River. No bridge. Spent 10 to 15 minutes cutting a small sapling to aid me in getting across; rock-hopped across barely getting one foot wet. Eddie caught up with me at 3 P.M., and at 3:30 P.M., we reached the Abol store and redeemed our backpacks. Ate a delayed lunch there, and I had a chance to work on my notes. I also made a purchase at the store—a head net. A very wise investment and I had occasion to use it almost immediately. Leaving the store, I encountered a sign erected by the Maine Appalachian Trail Club which informed hikers of the 100-Mile Wilderness ahead of them and the precautions they should take.

"Reached the Hurd Brook lean-to at 7 P.M. Eddie had a fire going and I heated the can of macaroni and tomato sauce Sharon had bought for me at the camp store. Not very appetizing but with two pieces of bread and a candy bar, it was sufficient. Fought off the mosquitos while eating. Mosquitos had been a problem all day and I had worn a long-sleeved shirt, not for warmth but for protection, and even a kerchief around my head. Got into my sleeping bag at 8 P.M. still wearing the long-sleeved shirt, my head net, and wool socks over my hands. In spite of the mosquitos, I got to sleep quickly and slept well."

132

Thursday, August 2
Hurd Brook Lean-To to Rainbow Stream Lean-To
11 miles

"On this day, no great elevation changes but walking along rocky paths. Within 2.5 miles, I reached the beautiful Rainbow Ledges, selected a good seat facing Katahdin to the north, and proceeded to bring my notes up to date. From the Ledge, I walked for another hour to Rainbow Lake and then followed the Trail around the lake at a distance of anywhere from 20 to 200 yards from its shores. I had hoped to eat my lunch at the sandy beach area where the former Rainbow Lake lean-to had been located when I made my 1970 hike.

"It had been in an ideal spot, but was so badly misused that the then property owners had requested it be moved. Somehow, I missed the turn-off and kept walking until I reached the west end of the lake and had lunch there. After lunch, the Trail led to the wooden overflow dam, then to a wooden dock where I had a brief but enjoyable swim. Come to think of it, I don't believe I had any swim in Maine that wasn't enjoyable! I passed the several overflow ponds south of the lake until 4:15 P.M., when I reached the Rainbow Stream lean-to.

"Eddie already had a fire going and I used it to cook a Kraft Macaroni and Cheese dinner with a 6.5-ounce can of tuna. Very tasty, and plenty left over for the next day. Had coffee and a candy bar for dessert. Regretted that I had not made some instant pudding.

"Somewhat later, I walked to a spot on the stream where the water had been dammed to create a small pond and had another brief swim. Did my paperwork, but there is no table at this lean-to and my back hurts like the devil when I try to write without a table. No mosquito problem here at Rainbow Stream; how different from last night! Sleeping tonight on the 'baseball bat' floor of the lean-to; the term 'baseball bat' refers to the two-inch round saplings with which, at one time, all lean-tos in Maine were floored. One hiker described them as a type of medieval torture! Newer shelters being built by the Maine club use the conventional flooring, which in some cases has been placed atop the saplings. I fervently hope, however, that the Maine club retains a few of the baseball bat shelters so that upcoming generations of hikers will know what it was like to backpack in Maine in 'the good ole days!'"

My meals for the next 10 days through Maine would generally be exactly the same for breakfast and lunch: cold cereal (usually instant oatmeal) and coffee for breakfast, and for lunch, one hard-boiled egg, and one-half muffin. Note the one-half muffin! In the earlier part of my hike, I had a whole muffin, but during the 100-Mile-Wilderness hike to Monson I had to retrench a bit to make things last. So be it.

Friday, August 3
Rainbow Stream Lean-To to Wadleigh Stream Lean-To
8 miles

"Up early and on my way at 6:55 A.M., while the other three were still in the sack. A gorgeous day. The trail led along Rainbow Stream. In about 1¹/₂ hours, I came to the point where the stream narrows and becomes a gorge. I missed the 'emerald pool' shown on the map, as did the other three who followed me. We had all planned to go for a dip there.

"I reached, and walked around, the pleasant Crescent Pond, one-half mile long and about 200 to 300 yards wide, a real jewel. The Trail began ascending and at 11:30 A.M., I reached a rock overlook high above the Nahmakanta Lake, which provides an excellent view of the north end of the lake. I met Eddie Watson at that point, and shortly we were joined by a boy and a young lady who had hiked up from the private campground at the north end of the lake. In 1970, the Trail led directly by the campground, which is operated by Paul and Fran Nevel, but they had been absent at the time I walked through. I was tempted now to visit them, but that one mile hike down the mountain and then back up deterred me.

"My friend Ron Tipton from the Washington, D.C., area and his family were due to arrive at the campground the following week, and we had hoped to rendezvous at that point, but it was not to be. Continuing on the Trail, I reached the north summit of Nesuntabunt Mountain. (Those Indian names bewilder me. I find it necessary to refer to the guidebook on every occasion to spell them correctly!) I signed the register book, and then proceeded another 250 feet to a viewpoint that takes in the entire lake. What a sight! Another one of the relocations in Maine that has made the Trail in that state really breathtaking.

"I pushed on slowly to the Wadleigh Stream lean-to, learning that Eddie had been there earlier and had hiked the additional 0.4 mile to the beach to set up his tent. The other two hikers, Chris Monroe and Chris Gibson, with whom I was to hike through much of Maine, arrived shortly and they too continued on to the beach to set up their tent.

"I found considerable camping gear upon my arrival at the lean-to, but assumed correctly that the owners of that gear were down at the beach. I, too, proceeded to do the same, but before leaving I noticed a newspaper amongst the camping gear. I picked it up. It was a daily paper and it was dated Friday, August 3—TODAY! How could that be? Very puzzling.

"I walked the short distance to the beach, meeting the Don Morrison family of Gray, Maine, in the process. The mystery of the newspaper was solved. The Morrisons had purchased the paper that morning in town, then flown in a bush plane to the lean-to! I took a short swim, noting the loons on the lake close to

LOG FOR EDWARD B. GARVEY

1. Date __Friday, August 3, 1990__   2. Log No. __104__

3. Travel From __Rainbow Stream Shelter__

   To __Wadleigh Stream Shelter__

   Beginning __6:55__ a.m. Finishing __2:20__ p.m.

4. Number of Miles Hiked

   (a) By Trail __8__   (b) Other __1__

   (c) Cum. Miles by Trail __37__ (d) Other __6__

5. Weather __Excellent - low humidity - nice breeze__

6. Food __cold cereal / 1 apple, 1 pc bread - raisins /__
   left-over maccaroni + cheeze

7. Condition of Trail __Excellent - 2 blowdowns, excellent blazing__

   Section No. __2__   excellent sign program

   Section No. _____

8. Shelter and Bed __Wood floor - flat wood, Wadleigh Shelter__

9. People __4 on Trail, 4 at shelter - corrected 3 more arrived in pouring rain at 7 p.m__

10. Plants _____

11. Money Spent __None__

12. Lean-Tos Inspected (see reverse)

    Section No. __2__ no Broom, no table - does have toilet
    Lean-To Name __Wadleigh Spring__

    Section No. _____   Lean-To Name _____

    Section No. _____   Lean-To Name _____

13. Incidents __(1) Seeing Nahmakanta lake in all its beauty from the two view points__
    __high above the lake on Nesuntabunt Mtn. (2) Taking a swim at the sand beach just__
    __0.4 m from Wadleigh Shelter (3) The commotion caused when 3 hikers from Acton MA__
    __arrived in a torrential downpour at 7 p.m. We made room - 8 in the shelter - "always__
    room for one more
14. Trash Pick Up __2 pieces - trail extremely clean__   when it's
    raining !"

    Maine sign program is excellent so far -- esp. good at shelters
    where distances and direction signs are given both to north and
    south of the shelter. Every sign so far looks as though it just
    came out of the sign shop yesterday. Very artistic, routed signs
    white on light brown.

Daily log maintained by the author during trip.

shore with Eddie trying to get close enough for a picture. It was clouding up rather ominously and I returned shortly to the lean-to. In doing so, I noticed a National Park Service Appalachian Trail aluminum survey marker imbedded in the ground. Love to see those markers. It indicates the Park Service has surveyed the land and intends to or has already purchased it.

"At the lean-to, I worked on my notes until 5 P.M., then put them aside to cook another supper of the 1990 hikers' standby, the Kraft Macaroni and Cheese dinner, plus a candy bar, a few raisins, and much coffee. Then back to my notes until the skies became extremely dark and the rains came—in torrents. I was so thankful to be in that shelter and I thought of my three friends camping on the beach!

"At 7 P.M., three men, drenched to the skin, arrived at the shelter. All three were from Acton, Massachusetts. They spent 2½ hours under the overhang of the roof, changing into dry clothes and making their evening meal. At about 9:30 P.M., they came into the sleeping area and bedded down. It was a tight squeeze with eight of us in the lean-to, but we made out okay."

Saturday, August 4
Wadleigh Stream Lean-To to Potaywadjo Spring Lean-To
10 miles

"Finished my instant coffee, but begged some off one of the Acton men who had more than he needed. I now have enough to reach Monson. I reached the sand beach on the lake. Learned that Eddie had left at 5 A.M. Chris and Chris were drying out a bit after last night's heavy rain. I had a 10-minute swim. Truly delightful. OH! This Nahmakanta Lake. Would love to come up here for a week, stay at the Nevel Camp and swim, canoe, and enjoy day hikes. Hiked along the lake until after 8:30 A.M.

"Stopped briefly at the spot where Gus Crews, Norm Greist, and Steve Clark had stopped in 1969 and had found the Narragansett beer in the spring. Had lunch around 11 A.M. on the bank of the Nahmakanta stream. At 12:20 P.M., I met Jim (age 62) and Nell Froning from Cincinnati, Ohio, who were using my *Appalachian Hiker I* as their guide. They were enjoying their hike, but 'you didn't say in your book how hard it would be!' Nell said reprovingly.

"Continuing my hiking, I suffered a bad fall, the second of the day. The first one earlier in the day jarred me but did no damage. On the second one at 1:20 P.M., I slipped on a log going over a muddy area and fell face down into the soft sticky mud. Opening my eyes I saw blood on my glasses. With a 40-pound pack on my back it was most difficult to extricate myself from that mud, but I did. And since I was walking beside a stream I was able to wash the mud off my face and my clothes. I had four contusions on my right hand and wrist; without a mirror I could not see how badly the area around my left eye had been cut, but it did not appear to be too serious.

"I began hiking again and shortly met three northbound hikers. One of them, Mark Di Miceli, on his fifth hike of the Trail, washed my cuts and applied iodine. Bless him! I continued my hike and reached the Potaywadjo Spring lean-to at 3:30 P.M. Potaywadjo is one of the biggest springs in Maine.

It has a tremendous flow of water, making an instant stream. I got a fire going promptly and made a beef stroganoff mix plus a can of tuna. It made for a very tasty dish, with much left over for Sunday. Shortly after, four other men arrived as a group; nice group, enjoyed visiting with them. They cooked as a group and had their own tent. There were three or four others who stayed in the lean-to."

When I started hiking in Maine, I began to use a tiny tape recorder to help out with my day-to-day journals. I have alluded, briefly, on earlier pages, to the recorder given to me by Hugh O'Hara and Jim Longo. Not only did they give me the recorder, but they also assured me they would have the material transcribed. Their thought was that, through this device, I would be spared much of my laborious record keeping. I was somewhat dubious about the effectiveness of the process they suggested, but I did use the recorder. It is very small, about 4.5 inches long, two inches wide, and about three-quarters of an inch thick. It operates on two size AA batteries. I would play the tape back sometimes when writing my notes to check names, times, places.

I have on tape my interview with Keith Shaw on August 15, when he described in his unmistakable Maine accent the account of the fellow who ate 18 jumbo-size eggs at one sitting at Shaw's Boarding House. On the same night, I taped an interview with an Englishman who described his hike through a hostile part of North Carolina (where the Don Nelan shelter had been burned by arsonists), where he observed and proceeded to gather some 100 1.5-inch-long fishing hooks strung across the Trail at various points to injure hikers.

When I completed my first tape, I mailed it to Hugh and Jim, and when I returned home after the completion of my hike, there was the typed account of every minute on the tape. The person doing the typing had absolutely no knowledge of place names, and some of the spellings were a bit garbled, especially those Indian names such as Nahmakanta, Katahdin, Piscataquis, but they were close enough for me to recognize them. Not only had the tape been transcribed, but Hugh had loaned it to some of his friends, who had received both a vivid account of my fall on August 4 and a description of some of the beautiful scenery I was enjoying—vivid accounts of lakes, mountains, rivers. In retrospect, I think I could have made better use of the tapes than I did. I describe the tape episode so that future hikers may take advantage of the possibilities.

Sunday, August 5
Potaywadjo Spring Lean-To to Cooper Brook Falls Lean-To
11 miles

"This was to be one of the more enjoyable days of my entire hike, which says a lot because I had many, many days after which I could revel in feelings of appreciation, joy, and success with respect to the areas through which I had hiked that had been or would be protected for this and future generations. I had been hiking for well over three months, and it had been an experience of hiking on Cloud Nine, hiking over a trail that was vastly more beautiful and more satisfying than the one I hiked in 1970.

"Now, on this day in August of 1990, I began hiking at 6:50 A.M. and reached the shore of Lower Jo-Mary Lake at 8 A.M. At 8:15 A.M., I came upon a sign reading 'Sand Beach.' It was the same spot my friends and I had visited in 1969 on my first hike in this part of Maine. I enjoyed one of the nicest swims ever, the lake so quiet and serene; the beach, about 30 yards long, was comprised more of tiny pebbles than sand and had an abrupt descent where one could push off into deep water within a few feet of shore. The water, having been warmed by the suns of June and July, was just the right temperature. And to think that this area is now owned by the U.S. government and managed by the MATC! Can you fault me for being more than a little exuberant?!

"At 10 A.M., I reached the site of the former Antlers Camp, one of the many sporting camps that operated in Maine during the earlier part of the century. As far as I know, all of them are now closed, an era that faded into history. On my 1970 hike, on September 22, I was saddened to learn that I was to be one of the last paying guests at the West Carry Pond Camp, as the camp was closing after 75 years of operation. The Antlers Camp had closed even before my 1970 hike, but there were three buildings still standing, one of them used frequently by hikers. As acquisition by the National Park Service of the Antlers property became imminent, Dave Sherman and I, greatly interested in that one good building, each made a substantial contribution to the MATC to have the building spruced up a bit for overnight use by Trail hikers. The money was accepted with the assurance that it would be used for the purpose intended. Approaching the former Antlers Camp, I looked for the building for which I had donated my money. All three buildings were gone! What had happened? Where were they?

"As I left the Trail and walked toward the lake, I saw a large canvas wall tent. Some 30 to 40 feet from the tent there was a masonry outdoor fireplace with a small fire burning. Beside the fire, sitting in an easy chair, sat a man sipping occasionally from a bottle of Jim Beam whiskey. An ice cooler was next to him. He greeted me as I approached and bade me sit down in a chair nearby. I accepted his invitation. The man's name was Charlie Sweet; probably in his 50s or 60s, a carpenter by trade.

"During the immediately preceding years, he had worked intermittently on the three buildings that had been there. He worked for a man who held a lease on the property on which the former Antlers Camp had operated. He (the lessee) had visions of restoring the old Antlers Camp to its former glory and having a road built into the area so that tourists in large numbers would have ready access to the camp. One of the three buildings on the property had almost no foundation, and over the years it had sunk into the ground. Charlie's principal assignment was to get that one building restored to its former height and standard of occupancy. He had spent about nine months on that job. When he finished his assignment, the lessee learned that either the State of Maine or the National Park Service was determined to acquire rights to the land, to have it remain in its present secluded state, and that no road would be built. As a result, the buildings were removed to another part of the lake.

"I gathered that Charlie had no particular love for the lessee as an individual, but he did respect the man's right to establish a camp and to attempt to make a profit on his investment. After Charlie finished his narrative he looked expectantly at me and it was my turn.

"I told him of my 40-year association with the Trail movement, and of my strenuous activities during the past two decades in attempting to get the federal and state agencies to acquire a right-of-way of sufficient width to protect the Trail in perpetuity for its entire length of over 2,100 miles. After I finished my statement, Charlie leaned back in his chair, took another sip of the Jim Beam and said, somewhat reflectively, 'So, you are the enemy!'

"'Yes,' I said, 'I am the enemy!' He did not seem too disturbed and shortly offered me a cold beer from his cooler. Then he located a small glass and gave me a tiny portion of his dwindling supply of bourbon.

"There were two younger men with Charlie who had been swimming in the lake when I arrived, Larry Young and Bowdoin Neally. Neally is a third-generation member of the Snow-Neally Corporation that manufactures metal products, including the axes sold by L.L. Bean. They returned from the lakeshore and prepared a midday meal of ribeye steak, bacon, and pieces of venison. As this was a Sunday, I suspected they were running out of supplies. Near the end of the meal, Charlie turned to me and said, 'It is a mark of respect for a friend that he be given the last ounce of bourbon in the bottle,' and he then handed me the bottle.

"I accepted it with the demeanor that such an offer dictated and I slowly consumed the last ounce. We said our good-byes and I then walked slowly along the lakeshore to the place where the buildings had formerly stood. Nothing left but an unsightly pile of building remains. I stood for a few minutes looking out at this beautiful lake with its population of hauntingly beautiful birds, the loons, and reflected again that there just had to be a trailside shelter at this spot.

"I thought of Jim and Hertha Flack, and of their book *Ambling and Scrambling on the Appalachian Trail,* and of their story describing how they had been forced to stay in one of the buildings for four days while Mrs. Flack recovered from a badly sprained ankle. And I thought of the picture taken by Albie Pokrob of the early morning sun just peeping over the horizon and flooding the cabin with sunlight. It was with deep regret that I left the Lower Jo-Mary Lake area, knowing that my chances of ever getting back there again were very slim, and hoping that future hikers would derive as much pleasure from the lake area as I had.

"During my afternoon hike, I had to revert to the head net and wear a long-sleeved shirt to ward off the mosquitos. Pleasant hiking past a pond or two and past the outlet stream from Cooper Brook. Reached the Cooper Brook Falls lean-to at 4:30 P.M. Eddie Watson and one other hiker were already there. I was furious to find a huge amount of Richmore Food trash left there earlier in the day by 24 Boy Scouts and their leaders! Eddie Watson had seen them deposit the trash there.

"I had been active in the Scouting movement for many years, and it really hurt me to see that trash. I could not blame the scouts, but I did blame the leaders. I asked Eddie, who would be leaving earlier, to obtain identification if he ran into the group again. Had I obtained identification, I would have written to the BSA Council headquarters as to the flagrant violation of camping principles.

"By the time darkness arrived, there were some seven to eight people at the lean-to. I collected wood and started a fire, and heated water for coffee. Kept the fire going until bedtime. Among the hikers was one Jeff Walker, who was just back on the Trail after a bout with giardia. I had been suffering for some weeks from what I suspected might be a mild form of giardia, and I queried Jeff closely as to the symptoms he experienced. I had some of the same symptoms but not all of them so I am still puzzled as to what my problem might be.

"The lean-to at Cooper Brook Falls is unique among the 240 odd shelters on the Trail. The water coming over the falls has formed a deep pond, which has overhanging rocks to make ideal diving platforms. On my 1969 hike through this area with five other men, we stopped overnight at this shelter. I have in my files a picture taken by Steve Clark, of the MATC, of me in mid-air (nude, of course) diving off one of those rocks into the pond. I did get in a brief swim on this day, also at the same spot, but the swim of the day was that one at Lower Jo-Mary Lake.

"Everyday on the Trail is an adventure. It just happened that on this day, Sunday, August 5, I met more people and found the day more adventure-filled than on most other days."

Who is Albie Pokrob?

The name Albie Pokrob appears in several places in this book, to the point that the publisher asked if Albie was just a friend of mine or someone special. He is both . . . a longtime friend and a rugged outdoorsman who seems to revel in activities during the colder months of the year. He has hiked the entire Appalachian Trail on three occasions. During the period between 1980 to 1983, he worked as a weather observer at the Mount Washington weather station in New Hampshire. Mount Washington is over 6,000 feet high, and has the dubious distinction of having the strongest winds in the country . . . once recorded at 231 miles per hour. Between 1987 and 1995, Albie worked in Antarctica during their summer months. In 1995-96, Albie and his wife Kacy spent an entire year in Antarctica. The coldest temperature? Minus 108 degrees Fahrenheit! But Albie stoutly maintains that the winters atop Mount Washington are more severe than those in Antarctica, mostly because of the wind-chill factor.

Monday, August 6
Cooper Brooks Falls Lean-To to Logan Brook Lean-To
12 miles

"Arose at 5:45 A.M., but did not get away until 8 A.M. Talked at length to a middle-aged lady, Roseanne Tallentire, a grandmother of four, who was getting off the Trail at that point. Getting homesick for her grandchildren back in Ohio. She gave me her unneeded food, which was greatly appreciated because I was getting a bit low and it would be another five days before I would reach Monson, Maine, my next resupply point.

"She planned to backtrack north on the Appalachian Trail to the road crossing, then hitch a ride to Monson where her car was parked. I checked on her when I arrived at Monson on August 11, and found that she made it safely and took off in her car for Mansfield, Ohio.

"After leaving the lean-to, I promptly encountered an area which must have been a type of convention center for the moose population. I found moose droppings in 25 places in the first 15 minutes! It was an overcast day with intermittent rain. Encountered a rather unusual Trail condition: huge three-by-twelve-inch paint blazings for two miles west of Cooper Brook. At one point, I could see five of these blazes from one spot on the Trail.

"I ate lunch at the Mountain View Pond, and on leaving it, I found myself in a tangle of blowdowns, some 50 in 1.5 miles. Made for very slow hiking. I surmised that a freak storm had leveled the trees in this area. I was obliged to ford the East Branch of the Pleasant River, a rather strenuous affair performed in a steady rain. With the rain and the fording, I was wet from the waist down, and I was chilled by the time I reached the Logan Brook lean-to at 5:15 P.M.

"Mike Callahan had arrived before me, and was comfortably ensconced in his sleeping bag. I peeled down to the skin, put on my polypropylene pajamas, and crawled in my sleeping bag. At 6:30 P.M., Mike fired up his stove, and I had hot soup and hot coffee, but an otherwise cold meal. Hung up my wet clothes, hoping the strong wind would dry them out a bit overnight! At 7 P.M., two honeymooners (nine days) arrived after a 15-mile hike from Chairback lean-to. Very pleasant couple, and we all visited until 8:30 P.M. when, by common consent, we all drifted off to sleep."

Tuesday, August 7
Logan Brook Lean-To to Carl Newhall Lean-To
7 miles

"On my way with Mike at 7:30 A.M. He quickly forged ahead. The first order of business was to climb White Cap Mountain, an elevation gain of 1,900 feet over a very steep '3R' (Rocks, Roots, and eRosion) trail. Raining with a heavy fog. Stone cairns in place to aid the hiker. Reached the summit, elevation 3,844 feet, at 9:05 A.M. Lost 10 minutes trying to find the route south; no cairns, and blazes almost non-existent.

"In another 45 minutes, I reached the summit of Hay Mountain, and then the fun began! The Trail was badly overgrown with thick-foliaged balsam trees from four to six feet high. Could see neither my feet nor the Trail much of the time. Many blowdowns, tough ones. I could not detour around them because of the thickness of the foliage. Had to get on hands and knees some of the time and pull my pack underneath the blowdown. The jungle-like situation lasted up and over West Peak. The balsam trees were dripping wet and every time I brushed against them I received a cold shower. Took two spills, injuring my right knee on one of them.

"Met four northbound hikers. Reached Carl Newhall lean-to at 1:30 P.M., soaked to the skin. Took off all my clothes, put on the warm pajamas. Ate a good lunch with hot coffee, courtesy of Mike. Wrote my notes while stretched out full-length on my sleeping bag.

"It is 42 miles from the Carl Newhall lean-to to Monson, Maine, and I made an inventory of my remaining food. I had two hard-boiled eggs, two muffins, one can of tuna, and two packages of Lipton Pasta and Sauce. Should be enough to get me to Monson. Cooked a Lipton beef sauce dinner, ate all I could and gave some of it to Mike. Dennis Shockley let me use his GAZ propane stove. All of us in the sack by 8:30 P.M. Still raining and dripping."

142

The injury to my right knee plagued me the rest of my hike, and will probably bother me the rest of my life. An orthopedic doctor X-rayed the knee, finding a cartilage problem aggravated by two things—the fall against the rock and the fact that I'm almost as bowlegged as a pair of ice tongs. Orthopedic shoes were prescribed, and I wear them but don't detect any improvement. And at age 82, I think I will skip surgery and live with the discomfort.

Wednesday, August 8
Carl Newhall Lean-To to Chairback Gap Lean-To
10 miles

"Up at 5:15 A.M. The usual, somewhat-uninteresting breakfast, but enough to sustain me until noon. Much more pleasant hiking than yesterday. I met a northbound hiker, Trail name 'Bubba,' who hailed me by name. I had met a number of northbounders since leaving Katahdin, but Bubba was the first whom I remembered having hiked with in the south.

"Mike Callahan caught up with me at 9 A.M., and at 9:30 A.M., we stopped to study the signboard showing the layout of the side trails leading to the Gulf Hagas area. It was raining, as it had the previous two days. Mike and I had agreed that we would take the Gulf Hagas loop trail, an additional five miles of hiking, if the weather was decent. It was raining steadily so we regretfully passed it up, but we did take the much shorter hike into Screw Augur Falls. That in itself was spectacular, and even standing in a steady rain we could appreciate its beauty. We could only speculate on what we missed by not taking the longer route through Gulf Hagas, which is described by some as the Grand Canyon of the East, a title also claimed by an area in north central Pennsylvania.

"A mile past the Gulf Hagas side trail, we came to an area called the Hermitage, a virgin stand of giant pines owned and protected by the Nature Conservancy. This area, too, is well worth visiting. In another mile or so, after walking the pine needle area of the Hermitage, we forded the West Branch of the Pleasant River. The Trail had been particularly pleasant to walk on, up to the river crossing. For some distance, it had widened out to four to six feet and had led along the interesting Gulf Hagas brook.

"Shortly after crossing the Pleasant River, we saw a sign reading 'Parking Place 2 Miles.' So, a day trip could be easily arranged by driving to the area. I later learned that the Hermitage-Gulf Hagas areas can also be reached by driving through the Katahdin Iron Works, then through a gate controlled by the St. Regis Paper Company. A future trip, perhaps. Hope springs eternal in the human breast!

"In the early afternoon we began climbing the three peaks of the Chairback Range, all of them difficult, the last one, really strenuous, over one huge rock pile. About 2:30 P.M. before we reached the summit, and 3:30 P.M. before we reached the Chairback lean-to. Four people had reached the shelter before we did. Small shelter, very crowded, everything wet! My meal for the night: one hard-boiled egg, half of a muffin, and a few peanuts. All in all not a particularly pleasant day, but then nobody ever guaranteed that hiking the entire Trail would be pleasant and sunny everyday!"

Thursday, August 9
Chairback Gap Lean-To to Long Pond Stream Lean-To
11 miles

"Beautiful day for a change! First order of the day was to climb Columbus Mountain, then Third mountain, then Fourth! Then, early in the afternoon, we climbed Barren Mountain, elevation 2,600 feet. Really strenuous hiking. Ate a couple of light snacks during the day; finally ate lunch atop Barren Mountain near the fire tower. Excellent views of Long and Cloud Ponds during the day from Third and Fourth mountains. Good views in a number of places during the day. The clear, sunny weather is a big plus.

"Left Barren Mountain in mid-afternoon. Shortly, at 5:30 P.M., we reached the blue blaze trail leading to the Long Pond Stream lean-to. We forded the knee-high Long Pond Stream, getting wet from the knees down. Obtained water from the very good spring some 200 yards from the lean-to, also scrounged up a good supply of wood and got a good fire going. Heated up much water, using part of it to rehydrate the package of freeze-dried beef stew Mike had given me; also used the hot water to shave, my first shave since Sunday night. Can't remember when I've gone that long without a shave, even on the Trail. Watched the fire die down; it made huge amounts of smoke, which kept the mosquitos away. In addition, the smell of that pine wood smoke was pleasant.

"A sign seen earlier in the day on Third Mountain: 'Monument Cliffs. First blaze placed here in 1932 by Walter D. Greene.' Greene was a Broadway actor and one of the pioneer Trail workers in Maine.

"Embarrassing incident for the day: as dusk was approaching at the lean-to, we were joined by a young couple who managed to ford the stream without getting wet. Mike and I, two experienced hikers, had plunged across in knee-deep water! Experience does not always denote wisdom!"

It had been pleasant hiking except that it was so-o-o strenuous, grades of 20 percent or more over Third and Fourth mountains. At the fire tower, I tripped over a projecting piece of heavy cable while trying

---

to get into position to take Mike's picture. In doing so, I severely jammed the big toe on my left foot, an injury that was to bother me the rest of my hike and for many months thereafter. From an injury standpoint, this was NOT a good week for me, a lifelong injury to my right knee and a painful injury to my left foot. So be it.

Friday, August 10
Long Pond Stream Lean-To to Leeman Brook Lean-To
12 miles

"Up with the chickens as usual. Left shelter at 6:55 A.M., waited for Mike at the road south of the shelter. It began raining at 7:15 A.M., four days of the last five! Turned out to be a rough day. They *all* are! Reached Big Wilson Stream around noon and forded it, knee high. Ate lunch on the far side. Mike, and Walt Haltell, whom I had met earlier, were already there.

"After lunch, took off boots, wrung the water from my socks, proceeded hiking. Minutes later, I repeated the process at another ford! (Thompson Brook) In mid-afternoon, crossed Little Wilson Stream. Intermittent rain all day. Passed the Little Wilson Falls (very spectacular), which Steve Clark and I visited in 1970. Had a devil of a time finding the Trail near North Pond. Mike, and others, had the same trouble earlier. It seemed that the person who had done the blazing was suggesting that we walk directly into the pond?! Wasted a good 15 minutes there. Finally got on the Trail, but it was so late (6:30 P.M.) I was convinced I had passed the Leeman Brook lean-to. Left a note on tree for Mike just in case.

"The lean-to area was a muddy mess. Four other short term hikers there; nice group, very courteous. This was another night that I took off my boots, got into the lean-to and stayed for the night, not emerging once. Mike had one two-man freeze-dried beef stew available and we shared it. Ate all the rest of my raisins and peanuts. So, I finish this 100-Mile Wilderness experience with all my food gone except one can of tuna, enough cereal and dry milk for breakfast, and two or three tablespoons of peanut butter. Good planning.

"All of us in bed around 7:30 or 8 P.M. I lay awake for perhaps 30 minutes thinking over aspects of the trip. Weather has been demoralizing. But it was thus in 1970, and again in 1977, when Ed Hanlon, Bill Husic, and I hiked from Katahdin to Monson."

Saturday, August 11
Leeman Brook Lean-To to Monson, Maine
4 miles

"Up at 5:25 A.M., cold cereal breakfast, no coffee. Raining—five days of last six. Mike hustled off at 6:05 A.M., I at 6:15 A.M. Very rough going, slippery and sloppy, mud, mud. Reached ME 15 around 8:30 A.M. and received a ride immediately with Anne Brown, a friend of the Shaws in Monson, who called me by name and informed me that Dave Startzell and his wife, Judy Jenner, were also staying at Shaw's Boarding House.

"Within minutes I was at Shaw's, a big 'WELCOME ED GARVEY' sign in the living room. So good to see the Shaws again and to visit with Dave and Judy. Dave brought me up-to-date on some of the Trail news. Seems that the House of Representatives Interior Sub-committee had inserted a $14 million figure in the appropriation bill for Trail acquisition in fiscal year 1991. Also, it appears likely that the National Park Service will acquire the entire shoreline around Nahmakanta Lake, and that the county will acquire land outside the corridor. Great news!

"Mike brought back 14 pieces of mail for me from the post office. Pat Shaw made pancakes for Mike and me to augment our scanty breakfast. Then I went through my mail. Around 1 P.M., Mike and I visited the local restaurant for sandwiches and coffee. Put all clothes in the washer, then the dryer. Rained off and on all day. Made a number of long-distance phone calls to my wife, relatives, and friends. Shopped for groceries in late afternoon ($22.50). At 6 P.M., enjoyed a turkey dinner with boiled potatoes, cranberries, and beans. What a difference from my Trail meals of the last 10 days!

"The Shaws presented me with a birthday card signed by them and the nine other guests, then a chocolate birthday cake. My birthday is in November but what the hell! This was not the time to quibble about dates! I weighed 134 pounds stripped on the Shaw scale, almost 25 pounds lighter than when I began my hike on April 14, and the lightest I've weighed since I finished high school in 1931!

"Dave Startzell and Judy Jenner began hiking at midday, bound for Katahdin. Yes, it was raining!

"Later in the evening, Keith Shaw and I sipped on some wine in his living room. I phoned Ed Hanlon in Oakton, Virginia, to remind him of our visit here on August 27, 1977, shortly after the Shaws first opened their boarding house."

Sunday, August 12
Shaw's Boarding House in Monson, Maine

"Breakfast at 6:45 A.M., with Keith performing the honors. No cold instant oatmeal for me today or the next several days! Today, it would be two jumbo eggs, two thick slices of bacon, three pieces French toast, plus orange juice and that good Hills coffee.

"Some picture-taking of Mike and me with the 'Welcome Ed Garvey' sign in the background. I had grown very fond of Mike, and we hated to part company, but he was still in the work force and had a rather tight schedule to keep. He planned for a 14.5-mile hike on this date, which would take him to Moxie Bald

Mike Callahan and Ed at Shaw's Boarding House.

Mountain lean-to. I had discovered that the sole of one of my boots was coming loose, and it would be another day or more before I left the Shaws.

"Met a fellow hiker, Bob Rhoades of Ramona, California, age 67, who was resting for a day at Shaw's before resuming his hike. He had given much thought to the condition of the Trail over which he had already hiked, the excessive steepness, the erosion, the seeming tendency of some of the clubs to make a reputation by making trail relocations excessively steep. The two of us received permission from Pat Shaw to use her kitchen to prepare our lunch. Washed our dishes later. All the comforts of home. Spent the afternoon writing up my trail reports. All completed. Bought groceries. Wrote cards and letters. A typical rest up day.

"I received a call from Sharon in the evening. My van, which she had driven south from Katahdin, had suffered a broken water pump and had to be towed into Oxford, Maine. I authorized a host of repairs that were overdue, a lube job, tune-up, the works. Ah, the joys of owning an ancient van that has a history of frequent breakdowns!"

Monday, August 13
Shaw's Boarding House, Monson, Maine

"Up at 4:30 A.M. Down to the kitchen early and had sausage, egg, and pancake breakfast with Bob Rhoades. No one goes hungry at Shaw's! I weighed 138 pounds, a gain of four pounds since arriving at Shaw's two days ago. Drove with

Keith and Bob to where Bob would begin the day's hike to Moxie Bald Mountain lean-to. Had my boots been in good shape I would have gone with him. At 10 A.M., I drove to Dover-Foxcroft to have a cobbler repair my boots. No luck, but we did, after much effort, obtain the name of a cobbler who operates from his home near Blanchard. Keith bought a huge supply of groceries for his boarding house operation and I, a few for my limited needs.

"Back at Shaw's, I had lunch, and at 3 P.M., we made contact with the cobbler, Bob McCarter, and drove to his home. I was informed that my ancient and precious Red Wing Irish Setter boots could not be repaired! Sob! Back to Monson as Keith showed me the former route of the Trail, which is now a jungle in part. At Shaw's, I immediately called my wife, Mary, and asked her to mail, via priority mail, my well-worn Danner hiking boots.

"Arriving at Shaw's later in the day were the two Chris's, Monroe and Gibson, with whom we had hiked the previous week. Very pleasant and considerate young men who had recently graduated from the University of Western North Carolina. I was to hike with them the rest of the way through Maine. There were six or seven of us at the Shaw table that night, eating a dinner of baked potatoes and meat loaf, and later in the evening, cake, coffee, and ice cream."

Tuesday, August 14
Shaw's Boarding House in Monson, Maine

"Up four to five times during the night—too much coffee. Up for good at 5:40 A.M. Breakfast with Jack Mortick and his wife, the two Chris's, and Nelson Peterson, an employee of the state of Maine. The Morticks are driving back to Maryland today. Jack, like Bob Rhoades, is disturbed by the steepness of the Trail and the erosion. A pleasant day at Shaw's, visiting with the Chris's and others who arrived during the day. Mailed a recorded tape to Hugh O'Hara in Virginia, and wrote a number of cards. Worked on the outline of my book.

"One of the hikers arriving during the day was an Englishman, Colin Cotton. He has been mailing all his personal records, passport, money, etc., from mail stop to mail stop. This time, Monson, the envelope did not arrive! It did not rain during the entire day, a good hiking day wasted! Another super Shaw dinner—roast chicken! I'm getting spoiled."

Wednesday, August 15
Shaw's Boarding House in Monson, Maine

"Up at 5:30 A.M. House very quiet; nobody is getting off early to hike, so Keith can sleep a bit longer and serve a later breakfast! I was down in the kitchen early and made some instant coffee using the extremely hot tap water. Breakfast at 7 A.M.—pancakes, one jumbo egg, and sausage. Checked my weight after breakfast—144, up from 134 the previous Saturday morning when I arrived.

After breakfast, I proposed to the other three hikers that we hike without packs from ME 15 to the blue blaze trail going into Shaw's; it was agreed to by all. Keith left us off at ME 15 at 8:15 A.M. It was 10:15 A.M. when we reached the blue blaze trail, and 11:00 A.M. when we arrived at Shaw's.

"Had a light lunch at Shaw's, then at 3:30 P.M., I walked uptown and bought cheese and one half-gallon of ice cream, which I shared with 63-year-old Jim Hamilton. This was his first year of retirement, and he had hiked all the way from Georgia. Another 115 miles to Katahdin and he would be a 2,000-Miler.

"My final dinner at Shaw's was spaghetti with wine that Keith had bought for me. Near the close of the dinner, I assembled the eight other hikers, and then with Keith and his wife Pat, I tape-recorded the incident of the thru-hiker who had bragged up and down the Trail that when he got to Monson he would 'eat the Shaws out of house and home!' The tape is a riot. I have played it before a number of audiences, and it arouses reactions of humor or revulsion, or both.

"On the morning of the eating extravaganza, the bragging hiker had come down to the kitchen and eaten an entire package of doughnuts. The menu that morning was bacon, eggs, and toast. After the hiker had eaten the doughnuts, Keith asked him how many eggs he wanted and how he wanted them cooked. The answer: 'I'll take six, over easy.' So Keith fried the six jumbo-size eggs and served them with four pieces of toast and four slices of thick bacon. The man ate the entire quantity in reasonable time, washed it down with coffee, and then announced, 'Now I'll take six more, sunny-side up!' So Keith proceeded to cook six more eggs, and served them with four more pieces of toast and four thick slices of bacon. This second batch went down more slowly, and was accompanied by much squirming and shifting of weight. When the fellow had finished, Keith announced, 'Well, you've eaten 12 eggs and broken the previous record of 11 eggs at one sitting.'

"The big eater cogitated a bit and then announced, 'I think I'll set a record that no one will ever break. Cook me six more, scrambled!' Keith cooked the additional six eggs. In his Maine accent, he related, 'I added a whole quart of milk and really beat the hell out of the mixture. When I served them along with the bacon and toast it made a huge mound on his plate! Oh yes, of the last six eggs, two had double yolks! And these were jumbo eggs.' The man finally, after much more squirming, cleaned his plate. Incredible. He sat in his chair for several minutes, then moved his chair back quickly. As Keith related it, all the others at the table promptly moved their chairs back also, fearing the man was going to vomit. But he didn't. After some time, he got slowly to his feet and then collapsed on the floor, lying there and groaning. He finally crawled to the stairway and up the stairs, collapsed on the bed, and remained in bed for four days, during which time he ate nothing. At the end of the four days, he arose and asked to be taken to a doctor. The doctor, after examining him and being apprised of what he had eaten, looked him square in the eyes, and said, 'You're a fool. You could have easily ruptured your stomach or had a cholesterol seizure.' The braggart eventually left Monson and to my knowledge was not heard from again.

"Later in the evening I recorded another conversation, this one with Colin Cotton, the Englishman, who described his experience in Tennessee while hiking in the area where locals had burned down the Don Nelan shelter. While hiking, he noticed something glistening in the sunlight. The 'something' was a 1.5-inch, deep sea-type fish hook, and it was one of about 100 Cotton found over a distance of several hundred yards. The fish hooks were hung in such a fashion as to tear into the flesh of the hiker at the face and crotch level. This was in an area where the locals had become incensed over the efforts of the U.S. Forest Service to acquire an Appalachian Trail right-of-way there."

Tuesday, August 16
Monson, Maine, to Moxie Bald Mountain Lean-To
15 miles

"Up early. French toast, bacon, one egg breakfast. My last such breakfast for many a day. Over to the post office at 8 A.M., my hiking boots had arrived! Hustled back to Shaw's, put on the boots, after which Keith drove me to the trailhead. Began hiking at 9 A.M. Pleasant day. Walked for a good part of the day on the recent Trail relocation that follows the Piscataquis River, a wonderful relocation. Made slow time; tremendous amount of mud walking and four or five fords of the river. The hike to the shelter seemingly without end and daylight time getting shorter. Realized it would be almost dark when I arrived at the shelter, with an excellent chance I would have to camp on the Trail.

"At exactly 7:30 P.M., I made out the sign to the shelter and walked to it. Had a cold supper that was preceded by hot coffee and soup courtesy of the two Chris's. Into bed promptly, no time or daylight for writing trail notes. I had thoroughly enjoyed my five-day stay with the Shaws, but I was glad to get back on the Trail."

Friday, August 17
Moxie Bald Mountain Lean-To to Pleasant Pond Lean-To
12 miles

"A rough day. Began hiking at 6:15 A.M. and finished some 14 hours later! Four of us hiking together at the outset. Reached the cut-off trail to the summit of Moxie Mountain. Left our packs there and walked the 0.3 mile to the summit, which has a long-abandoned fire tower. Spectacular views of the lake country from the summit.

"I hiked alone most of the rest of the day, hiking west to Pleasant Pond. Caught up with the Chris's at noon, when I took a dip in Moxie Pond beside Bingham Road. Began the long 4.74-mile climb to Pleasant Mountain (elevation 2,274 feet) at 2 P.M. A long, tedious climb with many ups and downs. Forded a couple of rivers. Just about 7 P.M. when I reached the summit. Part of the delay, perhaps 30 minutes, was due to my own stupidity. I had left the Trail briefly to visit a viewpoint, and when I returned I did not know whether to go right or left! After about 30 minutes of trial and error, I got on the right trail. Getting dark when I came down the very steep, dangerous trail, 1.2 miles from summit to the lean-to. Used my flashlight toward the end on former blue blaze trail that was converted into the AT. A brutally steep, eroded, and dangerous trail.

"Chris and Chris met me at 8:30 P.M. with flashlights on the blue blaze trail to the lean-to. It was just by chance that I had noted the blue blaze trail. There was no sign posted there, and a northbound hiker I met earlier had missed the lean-to. But it was wonderful to reach that shelter, and the two young men heated up their stove to provide me with hot soup and coffee. Bless them! A muffin and some peanut butter finished off the meal. Into my sleeping bag at 9:30 P.M. Two nights in a row getting in at dark or after dark. Not good."

Saturday, August 18
Pleasant Pond Lean-To to Caratunk, Maine
6 miles

"Up at 5:20 A.M. Took a 7 A.M. dip in the crystal clear waters of Pleasant Pond. What a pleasure! Back at the shelter to see Chris and Chris off at 8 A.M.; they were planning on taking the 10 A.M. canoe ferry across the Kennebec River. I spent a leisurely morning at camp working on trail notes that had been neglected for the previous two days because of the dawn-to-darkness hiking. Cooked an early lunch—a Lipton rice dish, which I fortified with a can of chicken.

"Left the shelter at 11 A.M. A pleasant walking trail to Caratunk replaced the boring five-mile road walk I had hiked in 1970. Met seven people on the Trail during the short six-mile hike. Arrived at the little town of Caratunk at 3 P.M., and went directly to the general store operated by Dan and Marie Beane. Obtained the room over the store. They provide the room and beds; the hikers provide their own sleeping bags. Good arrangement for $5 a night.

"Had one cold beer on arrival, later a half gallon of ice cream; a strange combination I admit, a repeat of my menu on arriving at Waynesboro, Virginia, on June 29. So good to get into camp early and have time for relaxing. Wrote a few cards. Called Marshall Sutton in Otisfield, Maine. Gave him my itinerary for the next five to six days, as he plans to meet me somewhere along the Trail. It had been a delightful, warm day, temperature in the 70s, and I went to bed at

8 P.M., lightly clad. Put on more clothes during the night; still later, I dug out my sleeping bag from my pack and climbed into it as it had turned quite cold. Had the big room over the store all to myself."

Sunday, August 19
Caratunk to West Carry Pond Lean-To
14 miles

"Up at 5:30 A.M. Cereal breakfast, but no hot coffee! Miss my two buddies and their stove. Really chilly in the room above the store. Put on my nylon jacket and trousers over my warm sleeping gear. Walked across the street to the Beane residence to shave and brush my teeth. No running water in the room, but it does have a toilet, which must be flushed by pouring water into it. The Beanes make improvements as money and time become available. Having built my own home from footings to roof, I can empathize completely with the Beane situation.

"Writing my diary notes at 7:15 A.M.; have almost three hours to kill before the canoe ferry is available. Wrote a number of cards, my principal means of communication on long backpacking trips. I can remember when post cards cost one cent! It was a devastating blow to my pocketbook when the price doubled to two cents! It is now 19¢, still a bargain, and a great convenience.

"Called Steve Clark, a longtime friend who lives in Sanford, Maine. He is a stalwart in the Maine ATC going back to his high school days, when he assisted in building the shelter chain through parts of Maine. Steve informed me that he had returned very recently from a strenuous work trip in the White Cap Mountain area, cleaning out the heavy growth of balsam on the Trail from Hay Mountain up and over West Peak, the same area over which I had experienced a nightmare on August 7. How I wished they had performed that work trip some two weeks earlier. It would have saved me much misery and the fall during which I had severely injured my right knee.

"Had a second breakfast in the store, hot coffee and a piece of pie—really living it up today! Walked to the Kennebec River at 10 A.M. Met three National Park Service employees, David Hurst, Chuck Blauser, and Skip Staffel, who are headquartered at Martinsburg, West Virginia, and making arrangements for a boundary survey of the corridor. On a Sunday yet! Faithful employees. We have had so many over the years, federal, state, and others who have been willing to put in extra effort to provide for a completely protected Appalachian Trail from Maine to Georgia.

"It was a delight to get the canoe ride across the Kennebec on a clear, brisk, sunny day. The canoeist was Steve Langley. Uneventful crossing. The operation was put into effect fairly recently after the drowning of a thru-hiker who was attempting to swim across the river.

"Pleasant hiking weather, sunny, breezy, and crisp. Tried to find the Carrying Place, a privately-operated eatery off the Trail, but I found the signs a bit confusing and gave it up. I crossed the dam across the pond and stopped a few minutes at the Pierce Pond lean-to. Had stayed overnight here in 1970 and remembered the experience with fondness, an evening on which the pond was totally calm and I had enjoyed an early evening swim with the trees and the mountains mirrored in the pond. This time, however, I rather hurriedly checked the log book and learned that Chris and Chris would be staying at the new West Carry Pond lean-to some 9 miles further south.

"It was 2 P.M. when I read the entry, and I realized I would have to hustle to make it before darkness. Pushed hard the rest of the day, much better hiking from Pierce Pond south. Reached East Carry Pond, then set sail for West Carry. Reached it at 7 P.M. Good. Sun still shining. I took the Trail around the pond and met my two friends at 7:25 P.M. Stopped hiking and went with them to the lakeshore to watch a glorious sunset, which ended at 7:30 P.M. Proceeded to the new shelter, very nice, large, two skylights. Stoked up the fire that the men had started earlier. Cooked a Lipton rice and sauce dish, much coffee. Sat around the fire until 9:30 P.M. on a perfect August evening. A feeling of autumn in the air, excellent campfire, bright stars overhead. One other occupant in the shelter who was not very communicative. All of us in bed by 9:45 P.M."

> In my daily log under the caption 'INCIDENTS,' I wrote the following: "Getting into the shelter at or after 7:30 P.M. for the third day in four! Crossing the Kennebec by ferry, meeting three NPS survey people, Hurst, Staffel, Blauser. Hiking for 1.8 miles on the Benedict Arnold route of 1775." And under the caption 'TRASH PICK UP,' I wrote: "one piece, burned it in campfire. Maine trails exceptionally clean."

Monday, August 20
West Carry Pond Lean-To to Little Bigelow Lean-To
7 miles

"Up at 5 A.M. to stoke the fire, which had unexpectedly flared up, lighting the area in front of the shelter. Got a good fire going and heated water for cereal and coffee. Took a morning dip in the pond at 7 A.M. The water seemed warm, perhaps because of the contrast with the air, which was a chilly 46 degrees.

"Left camp at 8:20 A.M. Pleasant day; met two Canadians from Quebec. Their English was a bit halting, but they informed me that a friend of mine was waiting for me in his car on Long Pond Highway. It turned out to be Marshall Sutton, who would hike with me for two days. Shortly after Marshall joined me, we reached Flagstaff Lake. Chris and Chris were already there. Ate our lunch there on the beach, then another delightful swim. Proceeded toward Little Bigelow lean-to, and while taking a short rest, we were joined by Russell Norton of New Haven, Connecticut.

"Norton is the man who, in 1989, offered to provide free brushes to any trail club needing them, so they would be placed in the shelters to provide a means of keeping them clean. He was somewhat disappointed that he was finding so few of them in the shelters. I had thought that Norton had obtained brushes free of charge from some brush manufacturer. Not so—he had purchased them with his own funds.

"I, too, had looked for these brushes all the way from Georgia, and was puzzled that I found so few of them. Where were they? In the homes or cars of the shelter overseers? But Russ Norton's generosity in making these brushes available is just one example of the affection so many people have for the Trail and for the people who use it. Let's hope that more and more of these brushes find their way into the shelters. I did use some of them to sweep out the shelter floor and to sweep out the privies, where they were more convenient to use than conventional brooms.

"Marshall and I reached the Little Bigelow lean-to at 3:30 P.M. to find a big group there from the Student Conservation Association. There was a mild dispute as to territorial rights, but Marshall and I wound up in the shelter with another couple, Lillian White and her companion, Paul Lucarelli. Lillian was in

Typical cairn in the Bigelow Range, Maine. Flagstaff Lake is in the distance.

a state of exultation. She had been trying for 20 years to complete the entire Trail, and on this day she was just two days from achieving her goal.

"A number of others arrived at the shelter who were close to the 2,000-miler goal—Craig Davis and his wife, Dave Patrick, Jim Bodmer, Gerry Roctore. I did not get the names of all, nor am I sure of the spelling. I had gotten to work immediately on my notes when we reached the shelter, but because of the confusion of people milling around it became very difficult. Another group not planning to stay at the shelter, left the Trail to come over and meet me and take pictures. This was Marshall's first night at a shelter on the Trail and I think he was a bit overwhelmed at the amount of activity. It WAS a bit unusual, and completely different from my hike of 20 years ago when it was exciting just to meet two or three people on the Trail in Maine.

"Back to Lillian White and her almost completed hike. She told me that she was only a few days behind me through parts of New England in 1970, but never could catch up. That was 20 years ago! In 1990, almost anybody could catch up with me and speed by me!"

Tuesday, August 21
Little Bigelow Lean-To to Avery Memorial Lean-To
7 miles

"Marshall and I up at 5:30 A.M., used his Svea stove to provide hot coffee and hot cereal. Left at 7 A.M. and began the all-day trek of getting first to Little Bigelow Peak, and finally to Avery Peak. The Trail extremely rocky, every step an adventure. During the day, we met the Warren Doyle group, whom I had last seen at Damascus, Virginia. Reached the Avery lean-to around 4 P.M., only to find it fully occupied by senior boy scouts from Quebec.

"Marshall and I selected a big tent platform perhaps 100 feet from the lean-to. Within minutes, Lillian White and Paul Lucarelli arrived and erected their tent on one side of the same platform. Marshall and I had considered going to the next lean-to at Horns Pond, only three miles further south, but luckily decided against it. At 6 P.M., who should arrive but my daughter Sharon and her husband Tim. Great! Marshall and I cooked an evening meal of Lipton Rice and Sauce plus a can of tuna, adding flour and milk to thicken it. Very satisfactory with muffins and Citadel spread, which Sharon had brought.

"I visited the nearby caretaker's cabin hoping to find Phil Pepin, but the cabin was locked. Later, we made sleeping arrangements, putting down my ground cloth on the tent platform and putting my 8 x 10 tarp over Sharon, Tim, and me. Marshall slept in the tent with Lillian and Paul. Cold night. I slept with trousers over my warm pajamas, plus my nylon jacket and shirt. Did not sleep too well. Paul, making a tour of the various tent platforms and campsites, counted 24 people in all.

"The spring at Avery Shelter was dry, so we obtained water some 300 yards north on the Trail from a boxed spring containing ice cold water. I made two trips there over big boulders. An adventure in itself. On the second trip, one of the young men from Quebec carried the heavy water bag back to our tent platform."

Wednesday, August 22
Avery Memorial Lean-To to ME 27, Stratton, Maine
8 miles

"Up at 5:30 A.M. Marshall's stove was not working, so we used Paul's butane stove. Hot cereal and coffee, plus more of Sharon's Citadel Spread. Left camp at 7:45 A.M. Weather absolutely wonderful and beautiful views. Slow going, trail steep and rocky. The Bigelow Range is tough. Maine is tough!

"Made it to the Horns Pond lean-tos before lunch. Enjoyable hiking in spite of the steepness. Only four people at Horns Pond Tuesday night, 24 at Avery! Met many people in small and large groups, probably 40 in all, including a group of 15 freshman from Bowdoin College. Reached my van at 4 P.M., where Sharon and Tim had left it. I left my pack there with Tim, and I walked the 25 minutes on the Trail to ME 27, arriving there at 4:25 P.M. just as the other three arrived in the van.

"Drove into Stratton and went directly to the Widows Walk and met the proprietors, Mary and Jerry; their last year in the bed and breakfast routine. Great people. Drove to Cathy's restaurant. Sharon and I put in a phone call to my wife, Mary, to wish her a happy birthday; sang the happy birthday song to her when she answered the phone. Then I dashed over to Potter's Market for groceries ($22.50), and met my roommate, Nick Palmer, a fellow Virginian who lives only five to six miles from me. Also, I was surprised to run into Phil Pepin, who had sent me a letter at Hanover, New Hampshire, inviting me to stay at his home, and at his caretaker's cabin atop Avery Peak. My change in plans, going up to Maine and hiking south, had thwarted his plans.

"A bit later, I rejoined my group and we had a wonderful dinner, courtesy of Marshall. Back to the Widows Walk, did some last-minute transferring of food, and then said good-bye to my 'family.' Then, a quick and much-needed shower, my first since Shaw's at Monson. Then over to the laundry. Met Phil Pepin there and enjoyed a beer with him. Arranged to meet him Thursday at the end of my day's hike and stay overnight with him. Then back to my room; Nick was already in bed, so I quietly got into mine at 10:45 P.M. A very, very full day."

Thursday, August 23
ME 27 to Caribou Valley Road
8 miles

"Up at 5 A.M.; shaved, first time since Monday morning. Worked on notes; over to diner at 6:15 A.M. Had excellent breakfast with the two Chris's, who joined me. Really like those two young men! Back to my room, where Nick

Palmer was eating breakfast. Took all my grocery purchases and fit them into my pack. A real chore. Am afraid to guess what the pack now weighs, 43 pounds, perhaps. I put a few articles in my day pack and left my heavy pack in the office of Widows Walk.

"Took off and caught a ride in 15 minutes at the far end of town. Not sure exactly where I should have gotten off; elected a spot that proved to be too soon. Finally picked up at 9:45 A.M. by Mary of Widows Walk, who had Nick Palmer with her. Drove me to the Trailhead. Nick lives in Arlington, Virginia. Very respectful of me, because of my age I suspect; he seemed to be very pleased that I was his roommate.

"Began hiking at 10 A.M.; moderate grade for perhaps two to three miles, then got steeper. Ate lunch at noon; reached the summit of North Crocker at 1:30 P.M., elevation 4,168 feet. Reached South Crocker at 2:17 P.M., elevation 4,010. Slow progress from there to Caribou Valley Road; left note for Chris and Chris at Crocker Cirque Trail. Reached Caribou Valley Road at 3:54 P.M. Walked on the road perhaps 10 minutes, when Phil Pepin arrived. He had been there earlier and had walked into Crocker Cirque campground, but found no sign of Chris and Chris. Phil took me on a sight-seeing trip, then back into town. Bought batteries for my tape recorder and then checked with the Hotel Plaza, where the two young men had stayed. They had checked out at 7:30 A.M.? Where are they?"

"Out to Phil's very nice rural home. Phil cooked a steak and corn supper, plus made garden salad. Excellent. After supper we drove back into town, 1.5 miles, for ice cream. Phil's home is filled with Trail memorabilia, a beautiful Clyde Smith routed sign that was never erected, a Katahdin summit sign that endured 13 seasons on Baxter Peak! To bed at 10 P.M."

Friday, August 24
Caribou Valley Road to Spaulding Mountain Lean-To
4 miles

"Up at 4:30 A.M. Phil had gotten away earlier, but so quietly that I had not heard him. Made myself a two fried eggs and muffin breakfast with some very soft ice cream to top it off. Then worked on trail reports. Drank lots of coffee. Great to have Phil's home to spread out.

"Called Mary, of Widows Walk, to postpone my pick-up time until 10 A.M. I wrote a short letter to Dave Brownlie in Falls Church, Virginia, recounting the floor-laying job at the Avery lean-to, which he had engineered in 1979. Left with Mary at 10 A.M. Stopped at post office and then at grocery store for bagels. Mary left me off at Caribou Valley Road where I had discontinued my hiking the previous day. She would accept no money for her taxi service. Within five minutes, I had to ford the Carabasset River—wet feet for the rest of the day. Slow, slow climbing, one hour and 20 minutes to cover 0.8 mile. Borrowed some drinking water from Phil Wrightson. It was 12:37 P.M. when I began hiking around the 500-foot-deep bowl. At 1:15 P.M., I met Chris and Chris descending from the blue blaze trail that leads to the top of Sugar Loaf Ski Resort. Very pleased to see them.

"I pushed on; one more hard climb and then the long descent to Spaulding Mountain lean-to, a new roomy one with three skylights and space for eight people. Had some snacks, then the Lipton Alfredo noodle dish. Made half a batch with a can of tuna—excellent. Gave a third of it to Chris Monroe. Had coffee and a Hershey bar for dessert. Another nice day. It had taken me 5.5 hours to hike 4 miles!"

Saturday, August 25
Spaulding Mountain Lean-To to Poplar Ridge Lean-To
8 miles

"Up at 5:30 A.M. Left camp at 6:50 A.M., climbed steadily; trails steep but could hike them standing up, except in a few instances when I had to resort to all fours. Reached Orbeton Stream at 11:15 A.M., 5.7 miles. Ate lunch near the sluice. The two Chris's had joined me as I was eating. Crossed Orbeton at 11:45 A.M., figured it would take three hours to climb to the summit of Poplar Ridge. Reached the ridge at 2:30 P.M., and reached the Poplar Ridge lean-to at 2:40 P.M. Rested for an hour, studied maps and *The Philosophers Guide*. Doubtful if we will stay in Rangely overnight, but we will definitely plan to eat a meal at Doc Grant's Restaurant where I had eaten on two previous occasions.

"Chris and Chris arrived at 3:30 P.M., later, Trevor Mildren, then John Weinberg, Pacer Bryan and his wife, then Dave and Vivian Bradley. Finished the other half of the Alfredo dinner with Spam chunks. Visited with the Bradleys. Poplar Ridge lean-to is OLD, probably 40 years; still has the 'baseball bat' flooring. Wood for a fire very scarce."

Sunday, August 26
Poplar Ridge Lean-To to Piazza Rock Lean-To
9 miles

"Left camp at 6:50 A.M., arrived at the base of Saddleback Junior at 7:50 A.M. Filled my canteen with water. No water supply until summit of Saddleback, and the spring there is intermittent. Trail to Saddleback Junior is a '3R' trail, very discouraging. Reached summit of Saddleback Junior at 8:30 A.M. Clear view of The Horn and Saddleback. Very steep descent from Saddleback Junior, '3R' all the way, hand over hand. Reached summit of The Horn at 11 A.M., elevation 4,023 feet. Had a snack there.

"Began my descent from The Horn. Marked with both orange and white blazes, the orange blazes marking the boundary of Madrid County. Reached the summit of Saddleback, elevation 4,116 feet, at 1 P.M. All of us had lunch there. The sky temporarily overcast, cool breeze; put on a long-sleeved shirt. Very pleasant resting on top of the mountain with a good view of all the other mountain peaks, plus the ski village of Saddleback directly below us to the north.

"Around 1:45 P.M., when I began the four-hour, four-mile descent of Saddleback—'3R' almost all the way. Went past three ponds, Eddy, Mud, and Ethel. My two friends had caught up with me, but they elected to stay at Eddy Pond for an hour or so to see a moose. I reached Piazza Rock lean-to at 5:45 P.M., very tired. My knees are aching and the left toe area is very sore from the fall atop Barren Mountain on August 9. A young man from Ohio, the volunteer caretaker, checked me in—no charge.

"For supper, the three of us pooled two packages of Kraft Macaroni and Cheese and my can of tuna and made one big pot. Very satisfactory. For dessert, a cup of blueberries, courtesy of Chris Monroe who picked them atop Saddleback Junior. How thoughtful. I have finished almost all my food, the bagels, peanuts, raisins, dinners, and vegetable oil are all gone. Chris Monroe made two batches of popcorn—excellent.

"Five of us in the shelter. In bed by 8:30 P.M. Met Steve Pinkham, an active member of the MATC from Portland, Maine. Very knowledgeable on the land ownership situation on the Trail corridor. Have 60 miles left to hike in Maine. Will be both glad and sad to get it behind me, but will never forget the experience!"

And on the plus side, from my daily log under the caption 'CONDITION OF TRAIL,' I had written: "excessively steep grades, rocks, roots, and erosion, most of the day. Excellent paint blazing. Only one or two small blowdowns on nine miles of trail. Excellent sign work. Much low bridge work in muddy areas. Good stair steps in steep areas." So! The Trail may be steep and eroded, and muddy, BUT there are people out there working on it! Ah, the volunteers again. May we never lose that aspect of the Trail project.

Monday, August 27
Piazza Rock Lean-To to Rangeley, Maine
11 miles

"Up early as usual, ate a hot breakfast and then walked the 1.4 miles to ME 4. Tried for 30 minutes to a catch ride. No luck, so I began walking. After about a mile, I stopped at Potters Wheel, a private campground. The owner, at that moment, was about to drive into Rangeley and so gave me a ride into town. At 10 A.M., I was in Doc Grant's Restaurant, just as I was 20 years ago.

The two Chris's were already there. They had caught a ride at the Potters Wheel spot also.

"Had an excellent breakfast, two big blueberry pancakes with sausages and coffee. Parted company temporarily with my two friends. I used Doc Grant's restaurant as my office for the next two hours, writing up my notes and visiting with the waitress, a local gal with a good sense of humor who filled me in on the history of Doc Grant and his restaurant. I had last eaten at this restaurant in 1979 after a number of us put in a new wood floor in the Myron Avery Memorial lean-to. Peggy, the waitress, gave me a small quantity of vegetable oil and sugar to replenish my stock, and a small spoon to replace the one I had lost.

"At 1:15 P.M., I sallied forth to buy my groceries ($20.20). Can't believe some of the prices—$2.79 for a three-quart package of powdered milk! Someone reading this entry 10 years from now will comment, '*only* $2.79, that's cheap.' Such is inflation. Like many in my age group, we tend to think of prices in bygone years and find it difficult to adjust to inflated prices.

"After grocery shopping, I went back to Doc Grant's where I had my pack and proceeded to repack it with the new groceries. Then over to the pizzeria to meet my friends for pizza and beer. A most pleasant lunch. I had earlier visited the local Chamber of Commerce to seek help in obtaining rooms or some type of shelter. No luck. August is a VERY popular vacation month in Maine and accommodations are difficult to obtain.

"Earlier in the day, the two Chris's had met and talked to Nancy Kettle, the proprietor of the Alpine Shop. After our lunch, they chanced to meet her again in the city park, and she readily agreed to let us stay overnight in her quarters above the ski shop. Not only that, but she also invited us to join her and her family for a spaghetti supper. It turned out to be a most pleasant affair. I begged off at 9:30 P.M. or so and went to bed. The Chris's settled down later, after visiting with Nancy and family. It turned out that Nancy had done a bit of backpacking herself, and had hiked most of the 100-mile trip to Katahdin the previous year, but she regretfully gave it up after four consecutive days of rain.

Tuesday, August 28
Rangeley to Sabbath Day Pond Lean-To
9 miles

"Arose at 5:30 A.M., went downstairs to shave. Left the Kettle house at 6:25 A.M. and walked to Doc Grant's Restaurant. It was locked, and I had to knock to be admitted. Had two of the huge raspberry pancakes and coffee. Wrote a few cards and phoned my wife to advise her of my whereabouts. Then it was out to the highway to hitch a ride back to the Trail. The two Chris's and I got a ride in the same van with a man-and-wife team from Manhattan, New York.

160

She, Patty Juntow, works with the Arthur Frommer travel channel in New York City. She also has an uncle and aunt in the Falls Church, Virginia, area and I made it a point to meet them later.

"We were back on the Trail by 8:30 A.M., the two young men quickly forging ahead. At 10:15 A.M., after 2.2 miles of hiking, I reached the first pond, and at 12:30 P.M., the second one, the Little Swift River Pond and campsite. Ate my lunch there on top of an overturned metal boat down at the lakeshore, and wrote my notes there. Pleasant hiking all day, only two climbs—one of 750 feet, the other 500 feet and gentle grades. Reached the powerline at 4 P.M., and the Sabbath Day Pond lean-to at 5 P.M.

"A group of Colby College students on a get-acquainted hiking trip were camping just above the lean-to. The Chris's had gone ahead for a swim at Long Pond and they returned shortly after I arrived. Using their stove, I cooked up hot soup and the contents of a can of chunky beef stew for supper. More than adequate. The Chris's left for Long Pond again to see the sunset, and while they were gone I collected wood and made a large fire. The two young men returned shortly and Chris Monroe made popcorn.

"It was a wonderful evening, very quiet, a half-moon shining over the pond, and three of the Colby girls conversing quietly down by the shore of the pond. The flames of the fire provided pleasant illumination. I lay on top of my sleeping bag in the lean-to enjoying the scene and reflecting on events of the day and of the previous day at Rangeley."

Wednesday, August 29
Sabbath Day Pond Lean-To to Bemis Lean-To
9 miles

"Up at 5:25 A.M. Chris M. mumbled that I should go on ahead, as they would sleep until 8 A.M. We had planned for a swim at Long Pond first thing, then breakfast there, but it had rained during the night and the skies were overcast. I had cereal, one muffin, and much hot coffee. Took off at 6:45 A.M.; sign read '2.4 miles to Route 17.' I walked more than three hours before reaching ME 17. A newer sign there read 3.8 miles to Sabbath Day Pond. Very difficult descending from ME 17 south to where I would begin the Bemis climb, big rocks, steep grade. It was 11:17 A.M. before I began climbing; reached first peak about 1:30 P.M. Had eaten a good lunch at noon. Reached second peak at 2:15 P.M., and reached Bemis lean-to at 3:20 P.M. No one was there. A young lady, Holly Leeds, arrived around 4:30 P.M. I had a snack upon arrival. Time now is 5 P.M. No sign yet of the Chris's. Very cool, feeling of fall in the air, very much! Am very glad I flip-flopped. Will be glad to get into south Vermont and Massachusetts in September or early October."

Thursday, August 30
Bemis Lean-To to South Arm Road (Andover, Maine)
9 miles

"Left shelter at 6:40 A.M. after a day's hike to the privy (170 steps each way!). Made steady progress. Did not see any sign at third peak, or at summit of Bemis Mountain, although I was informed that one was there. Walked right on through until I reached the blue blaze trail to Elephant Mountain lean-to—had walked about three miles at that point.

"Discovered I had lost my lightweight Yugoslavian day pack with my clean clothes in it. Met and talked at length with Alice Gmuer, a Swiss-born lady with a thick German accent. She had hiked the Pacific Crest Trail, and had some very pronounced views on the undesirability and shame of the steep, eroded trails in Maine. She had hiked also in Alaska and described the very old Chilkott Trail, which had been built to an acceptable grade and was still in use without evidence of erosion.

"I reached the summit of Old Blue at 12:20 P.M.; ate lunch there with Steve Visser, a young man with a guitar, who had entertained us the previous evening at the Bemis lean-to. We were joined shortly by the Chris's, who presented me with my missing day pack. Sunny day, beautiful view from the summit.

"Took off at 1:20 P.M.; a steep, treacherous descent. Only 2.8 miles, but it was 4 P.M. when I reached South Arm Road. Caught a ride in a pickup truck, the first vehicle that came by, then picked up the Chris's a half-mile ahead. The driver, a young 23-year-old, who had picked up many hikers, took us directly to the Andover Arms Bed and Breakfast place. Cost, $8.50 to sleep in the barn, showers included. Patty and Larry Wyman are the proprietors.

"Took a shower, then bought a chicken dinner at Dave's Grocery-Restaurant. Ate outside, but it was a bit on the chilly side. Worked on my notes a bit and visited with Dan Bruce (Wingfoot) and listened as he described his plan for the annual book he will write to replace *The Philosophers Guide*. Met Joe Wolff, with whom I had hiked in Georgia and Tennessee. Visited around the kitchen table until 11 P.M. Bought and consumed most of a half-gallon of ice cream, with various fellow hikers digging in for a few spoonfuls. This is a great place. Making plans to stay here another night. To bed at 11:30 P.M., rather late for a thru-hiker!

Friday, August 31
South Arm Road to East B-Hill Road, Andover, Maine
10 miles

"Awakened at 5 A.M. by village clock. Did not hear any of the others during the night. Up at 5:30 A.M., shaved, worked on notes. Big breakfast at 7 A.M., creamed eggs on muffins preceded by fruit cups and cereals. Six of us at the breakfast table. After breakfast, I put my dirty clothes plus those of the two Chris's into the washer.

From left to right: Chris Monroe, author, and Chris Gibson. Also pictured are David and Deshawon, foster children of Pat and Larry Wyman.

"At 10 A.M., Pat Wyman drove the Chris's and me back to the point where we had discontinued hiking the previous day. I carried nothing, the other two shared carrying my few things. Began hiking at 10:30 A.M.

"Climbed Moody Mountain in 45 minutes. Then made the very slow and steep descent to the river, Sawyer's Notch, one of the more strenuous climbs and descents in Maine. Leaving the river, I climbed up to the Hall Mountain lean-to, reaching it at 2:20 P.M. The two Chris's related with great excitement their sighting of a huge 16-point bull moose at the shelter. They had gotten to within 10 yards of him and had taken pictures. Resumed my hiking, and at 5:15 P.M., I reached Surplus Pond where the Chris's were having a breather. They took off shortly and reached East B-Hill road at 6 P.M., then caught a ride immediately back to Andover Arms. I made the 1.9 miles to East B-Hill Road by 6:30 P.M. No traffic. Began walking, and at 7 P.M., I was picked up by Larry Wyman and his brother Greg, who had driven out to meet me.

"Upon my return to Andover Arms, the corn bread casserole and boiled corn were reheated. So the day ended well, but very late. Found that my 28-year-old ground cloth was missing! Perhaps it had gotten mixed up with someone else's gear or lost on the Trail. Had I taken the simple step of using a marker to write my name on it, I'm certain it would have been returned to me. Hindsight, great stuff!"

Saturday, September 1
East B-Hill Road to Frye Notch Lean-To
5 miles

"Awakened again at 5 A.M. by the village clock. Over to the house to shave. Pat was already up and the coffee was ready. Took a cup with me back to the barn to enjoy while packing up my gear for the day's hike. Another substantial breakfast of cereal, French toast, bacon, and more good coffee. Settled up with Pat and bought from her three large plastic trash sacks to substitute for my missing ground cloth.

"Felt badly about the ground cloth. It had no value, but I had purchased it at the REI (Recreational Equipment Inc.) store in Seattle, Washington, in 1962, on a one-day visit to the World's Fair. It had served me well for 28 years, and I was confident it would see me through to the end of my backpacking activities, which, as it turned out, was to be much sooner than I anticipated. After breakfast, I hurried over to the two grocery stores to resupply ($12.30). Not much to choose from, and I did a poor job, which I was to regret later.

"At 9:30 A.M., the Chris's and I put our packs in Pat Wyman's car and she drove us the 8.5 miles to the East B-Hill Road where we had finished the day before. Said our good-byes to Pat, and got a hug from her, a very warm person. One of the many, many along the Trail, from bed and breakfast owners to friendly post office employees, who make hiking the Trail such a pleasant experience.

"Began hiking at 10:30 A.M., an easy day ahead of us. Stopped briefly at noon to visit with the Chris's, who were taking a breather. Reached summit of Surplus Mountain at 2 P.M. Then the steep descent to Frye Notch lean-to, reaching it at 2:30 P.M. Ate a late and hearty lunch there, to be followed later by a very light supper. So good to get into the shelter early. Steve Visser resewed my Appalachian Trail patch on my pack. This shelter had no table, but did have a privy, which was in desperate need of a good sweeping. I looked in vain for one of the 'Russell Norton' brushes.

"Another Steve, Steve Woodward of Hartford, Connecticut, tenting a few feet from the shelter, loaned us his folding saw, which I used to cut much dead firewood. We had a wonderful fire. Steve Visser played his guitar, and four other people from a nearby tent site came over to enjoy the music. A very pleasant evening, bright moonlight.

"A couple of unpleasant episodes at the Wyman home, which are painful to relate. The February 1987 issue of *National Geographic* contained an excellent article about the Appalachian Trail. Pat had put the magazine out for hikers staying overnight to read. Within a few days it disappeared. More recently, a 1990 spring issue of the *Appalachian Trailway News* had disappeared within a day or two after being made available to hikers. I sent a note to Jean Cashin of the ATC, and the missing issue of the ATN was promptly supplied. Later, I sent the Wymans a copy of the missing *National Geographic* from a supply that was given to me for my services in reviewing the article while it was still in the draft stage. But these petty thefts give the Trail hikers a bad name, and it seems such a shabby way to treat those who are attempting to make the lot of the hikers a little more pleasant when they are away from home."

Sunday, September 2
Frye Notch Lean-To to Speck Pond Lean-To
10 miles

"Up at 5:20 A.M. Cold cereal breakfast and no coffee! Puzzling. On my way at 6:30 A.M.; pounded away all morning, meeting many hikers, including a group of 13 to 14 from Harvard. The Chris's and Steve caught up with me in mid-morning after I had climbed East Bald pate and West Bald pate. We met on a side trail going to the Grafton Notch lean-to, but we did not take the time to go there. Steep, eroded trail until the last mile or so before Grafton Notch.

"Ate our lunch on the side trail. Reached ME 26 at Grafton Notch at 1 P.M. The three young men forged ahead, and I hiked by myself the rest of the day. Began hiking up the trail to Old Spec at 1:30 P.M. I was now on trails maintained by the Appalachian Mountain Club (AMC), and the trail markings were not up to the standard I had encountered previously in Maine.

"Hiking toward Old Spec, the Trail began *descending*—very strange. I became more and more uneasy, but I WAS following white paint blazes. At 2:30 P.M., I found myself right back at a Trail junction where I had been one hour previously! I'm making too many of these kinds of mistakes. Resumed my hiking, but the error was to cost me dearly. Trail not well-blazed. Around 7 P.M., I reached a steep rock face where I could see Spec Pond far below me. No paint blazes. Had to scramble down the sharp rock face, hoping I was on the right trail. Halfway down I found a white blaze! Finally, got off the rock and onto a dirt trail. Found a sign pointing to Spec Pond. Found another sign reading Old Spec shelter, but no distance given. It became VERY dark. Finally I heard voices. I hailed, got a response, then a light, as the caretaker, Jonathan, came up to me. He guided me to the shelter, where space was available for one more person— ME! With the aid of Jonathan's flashlight, I paid the $4.00 fee and provided name, address, etc. Ate a bit of food from my pack and crawled into my sleeping bag. VERY THANKFUL to be off that steep rocky trail. Asleep in minutes. All's well that ends well, but I deplore these late arrivals."

Monday, September 3
Speck Pond Lean-To to Full Goose Shelter
5 miles

"Only five miles today but believe me, they were five tough miles. The Mahoosuc Notch is the most dreaded or most bragged about section of the entire Trail. It is a freak of nature in the form of a very sharp 'V,' hundreds of feet high and into which huge rocks have fallen from the sides down into the bottom. The result is a tortuous rock scramble of gigantic proportions.

"I arose at 5:30 A.M. and ate a cold breakfast in the shelter. Just before leaving, I discovered that the fellow sleeping next to me was Tom Thwaites, of Penn State University, a fellow I had known for more than 20 years. Why he did not make himself known to me is still a mystery. Perhaps he did not want anyone else in the shelter to know that he was in any way, shape, or manner acquainted with a man who was stupid enough to be hiking in these rough mountains in total darkness!

"In any event, I began hiking at 7 A.M., following the Trail which winds around part of Old Spec Pond. I stopped to rinse off my face and hands in the pond, and the water felt warm, perhaps because the air temperature was in the low 40s. In 1970, I had gone for a dip in the pond, but on that occasion the water temperature was 54 degrees and my swim was unbelievably short! Continuing with my hike, I shortly came upon Chris, Chris and Steve who had camped on a fairly flat rocky outcropping. They had set up their tents, anchoring them to large rocks, of which there is no shortage in Maine! They had also enjoyed a glorious sunset and a moonlit night. I ate another breakfast and we then proceeded to hike on the Mahoosuc Arm leading to Mahoosuc Notch.

"Eventually, we arrived at Mahoosuc Notch (east end), descended through it, then began hiking through the infamous Mahoosuc Notch itself (west end). It was my third journey through the Notch, and probably because of my age it seemed even tougher than on the previous occasions. The three young men gave me much help; Chris Monroe even carried my pack part of the way.

"At one point, a man coming from the south passed us, remarking: 'I'm sure Mr. Garvey has other friends to help him!' What an unkind remark and how pointless. I had met the fellow hiker earlier in my hike down in Georgia, and he had seemingly gone out of his way to insult or demean almost everyone with whom he came in contact. In hundreds of days of hiking on the Trail, and over 40 years of hiking, this was the most objectionable person I had met. I'm sure I will never know just what his motive was in his approach to life.

"We ate our lunch in the Notch, and I think I left behind my container that included my mixture of salt, pepper, and curry powder. Leaving the Notch, we began hiking the steep, rocky, eroded trail leading to Full Goose shelter. Arrived there around 5 P.M. The three young men decided to continue on to Carlo Col shelter. Having no desire for a late night arrival at a shelter, I chose to stay at Full Goose with the two men who were already there, John Smilanski and Eric Chukowski (two good Polish names!) of the Washington, D.C., area. They had collected a goodly supply of wood and built a fire, which was to last all night.

"I did some clean-up work on the privy. Swept it out, then used warm, soapy water to clean the enamel toilet seat and cover. Big improvement. Almost a full moon shining over the area. So pleasant to lie on top of my sleeping bag and enjoy the fire lighting up the inside of the big, 16-person-capacity shelter. Woke up around 10 P.M.; the fire still burning brightly.

"Late in the afternoon, before reaching Full Goose shelter, we had met 78-year-old Ken Carpenter and a companion, who were hiking from Delaware Water Gap in Pennsylvania to Katahdin in Maine. I think he was the only person I met in my entire hike who was older than I."

Tuesday, September 4
Full Goose Shelter to Gentian Pond Shelter
9 miles

"Up at daybreak. Hot breakfast, courtesy of John Smilanski with his Peak 1 stove. On my way at 6:45 A.M.; a long tiring day. I reached the side trail to Carlo Col shelter at noon and ate my lunch at the Trail junction, not wishing to waste the time and energy in going to the lean-to. Am writing these notes without the benefit of my tape recorder, on which I had recorded observations. It is not repeating the information I recorded. Will try to get it fixed in town.

"I reached the Gentian Pond lean-to at 7 P.M., a shelter and tent site combination, the shelter had double-deck bunks. However, there were only two occupants, Matt Wolfe and I. He fired up his Svea stove, enabling me to cook a Kraft Macaroni and Cheese dinner, plus a cup or two of coffee. It was getting very dark as I finished eating. Left much of my gear on the shelter floor and crawled into my sleeping bag completely exhausted. Visited with Matt until 9 P.M., then fell into a deep sleep. No time to work on notes. Not good. The open side of the shelter faced west, enabling us to get our full share of daylight."

I think Tuesday, September 4, when I reached Gentian Pond, was the point on the entire trip at which I was the most exhausted and my knees, feet, and entire body were the most sore. I clearly recall the pain of just moving the eight to ten feet from the stove to my pack and sleeping bag.

Wednesday, September 5
Gentian Pond Lean-To to Gorham, New Hampshire
11 miles on the Appalachian Trail, 4 miles off the Trail

"Up at 5:30 A.M. Hot breakfast, courtesy of Matt Wolfe, of Dayton, Ohio, with his Svea stove. On my way at 6:45 A.M. for an all day grind until 7 P.M. due partly to bad advice I had received as to the best route into Gorham. It was a pleasant route, taking me past three ponds. The first two were uninviting, but at noon I reached the third pond, which had a very inviting approach and a place to eat lunch and take a swim. After lunch I toyed with the idea of taking a swim, but as it had become overcast and windy I abandoned the idea.

"During the afternoon hike, I met a number of old friends, including Tim Osman and Melanie Dean, the Brits known as Thatcher's Children. Had a nice visit with them and expect to meet them later in Harpers Ferry, West Virginia. Also met a young man, last name Tripp, whom I had met in Damascus, Virginia, in late May. Later, it was Dapper Dan, whom I had met several times beginning down in Georgia. At 2 P.M., I climbed a high spot and had my first glimpse of the Androscoggin River far below me, which flows into Gorham, New Hampshire.

"In mid-afternoon, I found an expensive jacket with a Delta Airlines ticket stub showing the owner to be a Nicholas McCorkle. I carried the jacket out and later delivered it to Delta Airlines for return to the owner. Also in the afternoon, I took a nasty spill, hitting my head on a rock. It raised a welt and really jarred me. I came to a junction where the Trail and the Mahoosuc Trail separate. I took the Mahoosuc Trail, a blue blaze trail that would involve more hiking mileage, but would take me right into Gorham without the need to hitchhike in on U.S. 2. It proved to be a bad choice.

"The trail led me over Mt. Hayes, and later I reached a road where the trail seemed to end. I wandered around an unmanned electrical generating plant trying first one road, then another. It was getting late and the sky had become overcast. Finally, I did find a road that took me out of the area, and I promptly got a ride into Gorham, New Hampshire, right to the Gorham House, my destination for the night. I was pleased to find Chris, Chris, and Steve Visser eating burritos on the front porch. There was enough left for me—most welcome.

"Found a note from my friend, Albie Pokrob—had just missed him by hours. He and his wife, Kacy, had left for Grafton Notch, from which point they would hike to Katahdin. He left a box for me, which included brownies and two bottles of Heinekin beer, also a $10 gift certificate for my favorite restaurant, Welch's. Took a much-needed shower, removing five days of grime. The three young men and I enjoyed the brownies, plus Steve's ice cream and a pot of coffee in the dining room of the Gorham House. I telephoned Phil Pepin at Stratton, Maine, and arranged for him to pick me up on Friday, September 7, at 3 P.M. for a trip into Augusta, Maine.

"The Gorham House is a bed and breakfast, but it also has a big barn for use by hikers. I had stayed there on previous occasions when the place was under different management. All of the mattresses in the barn were occupied, so I slept on the floor on my own sleeping pad. Went to sleep immediately but awakened in early hours."

Thursday, September 6
Gorham, New Hampshire

"I was awake much of the night. It was not due to the fact that there were 16 other hikers in the barn, nor because I was sleeping on the floor, since I had been doing that for days (nights!). It was just one of those nights when I woke up and could not get back to sleep. I arose at 5:30 A.M. and walked a mile down to the McDonald's restaurant, where I lived it up a bit. No instant oatmeal this day; I enjoyed McDonald's big breakfast! Read the paper to find out what was happening in the world, checked out a laundry, and then called the Appalachian Mountain Club at Pinkham Notch. I talked first to the Trailmaster, Pete Williams, then to Don Aarons, the Hutmaster.

"The purpose of my call was to arrange for the three young men hiking with me to work their way through the hut system. All three were getting a bit low on cash, and the Appalachian Mountain Club people have always been sympathetic to such situations and have tried to provide work for hikers in exchange for room and board. I made tentative arrangements, and learned later that they had worked out satisfactorily.

"The three young men worked today at the Gorham House, painting the front porch. Big improvement. Later in the day, they used up a sizeable portion of their remaining cash to purchase huge quantities of groceries, which they mailed to themselves at such places as Glencliffe and Hanover, New Hampshire, and to Cheshire, Massachusetts.

"This was my R & R day. I took my dirty clothes to the laundry. Then to the post office to pick up some 15 pieces of mail. Back to the laundry to read part of my mail while keeping an eye on the washer and dryer. Letters from all over, some of them dated back in June and early August, forwarded to me from various places. Even one card from my two young Yugoslavian friends who were vacationing in the Benelux countries. Such letters are really appreciated when you have been out of circulation on a long distance hike.

"Finished reading the mail in the dining room of the Gorham House. Ate my lunch in the barn, but in the evening I repaired to the excellent Welch's Restaurant where I had eaten on previous occasions. One can get an idea of the cleanliness of a restaurant by examining either the kitchen or the restrooms. I can't speak for the ladies' restroom, but the one provided for the men has always sparkled with its cleanliness. I thoroughly enjoyed the dinner, and paid for it with the gift certificate left for me by Albie Pokrob. Bless him!"

I would meet up with the two Chris's and Steve later; on October 3, I would be at the post office in Cheshire, Massachusetts, to meet them as they arrived to pick up their grocery packages!

Friday, September 7
Gorham, New Hampshire

"Up at 6 A.M. and walked 20 minutes to McDonald's. After breakfast, I bought new batteries for the tiny recorder I had been using for my trail observations. Turned out the batteries were not the problem. Finally got the recorder working, however, and concluded that either the recorder was a bit temperamental or the person using it was inept, probably the latter. I also got a haircut and greased my hiking boots.

"One of the other hikers using the barn, Irv Winkler (Trail name Pockets), presented me with a huge sub sandwich at lunchtime. He had purchased two at a two for one sale, and one was all he could handle.

"At 2:45 P.M., Phil Pepin arrived and we took off for Augusta, Maine, on a very rainy afternoon. We stopped at Lewiston, Maine, to visit the factory from which Phil operates, then continued on to Auburn for an excellent fish dinner at a huge restaurant there.

"We arrived at Augusta and the meeting place at 6:45 P.M. for a meeting of the elected officers and others who direct the operations of the Maine Appalachian Trail Club (MATC). I was pleased to meet and visit briefly with some longtime friends, Steve and Barbara Clark, Dave Field, and Lester Kenway, and I met the president, John Morgan, for the first time. I spoke to the group of perhaps 20 people for seven or eight minutes. I congratulated them on the tremendous job they were doing in construction of both trails and shelters with their small membership of barely 300 people. I also addressed the problem of the many miles of the Trail that have excessively steep grades making hiking difficult and dangerous and resulting in serious erosion. I finished up and got a good laugh by stating that I had never encountered a hiking club that was so insistent that the privies they built *had* to be in a different county from the shelters which they served! My statement was a gross exaggeration of course, but it was a subject that had been discussed by hikers as we visited around the shelters at night. One hiker reported counting 172 steps to a privy! I am afraid the distances in Maine, for whatever reason, would not meet the standards expressed in that very humorous but practical little booklet written by Chic Sales many years ago.

"The meeting lasted more than three hours and I was having great difficulty keeping awake. I was very much awake, however, when a discussion ensued on a forthcoming meeting involving land purchase and the degree of protection that would be provided for the Trail as it coursed beside the beautiful Lake Nahmakanta. The meeting would be attended by representatives of the current landowner, the state of Maine, the National Park Service, and the MATC. Dave Field was to represent MATC, and he desired guidance as to what recommendations he should make.

"The meeting broke up shortly after 10 P.M. Phil and I departed Augusta at 10:20 P.M. and got back to Gorham after 1 A.M. A long day. I got to bed at 1:30 A.M., and Phil still had that long drive back to his home in Stratton, Maine. I was very pleased to have attended the MATC meeting and to have listened to them discuss their problems. The treasurer's report, which they handed out, showed total financial assets of $98,000. They do a super job with few people and not much money."

> Greasing my hiking boots and getting my hair cut seemed to be the actions of one who was planning on continuing his hike. However, I am fairly certain that I considered discontinuing the hike during my approach to Gorham.

Saturday, September 8
Gorham, New Hampshire

"Up at 7 A.M., somewhat late for me. Sun shining. Down to McDonald's for two breakfasts! My appetite is still good even if the rest of me may not be. Back to the barn; had made my decision. I had decided to discontinue my hike at Gorham. Called Delta Airlines, made arrangements to fly home from Boston on

Tuesday, September 11. Will take bus from Gorham to Boston. It was a difficult decision to make, but I had informed everyone who was interested that I would try to hike the entire Trail, but if I found it was beyond my physical capacity OR if it ceased to be fun, I would terminate the hike. It turned out to be a bit of both.

"Hiking through Maine was a wonderful experience but it had taken a lot out of me physically. If I had continued I would have faced about 100 miles of strenuous hiking in the White Mountains of New Hampshire. Furthermore, beginning in 1965 on an Appalachian Mountain Club Range Walk, I had hiked all through or most of the way through the Whites on six different occasions and the prospect of doing it again just for the sake of having done it was not too alluring.

"Having made my decision, I called my wife to inform her of my plans. Later, I had lunch at the Gorham House and had an opportunity to visit at length with Ron Orso, who operates the bed and breakfast place. The last issue of *The Philosopher's Guide,* which I used during my hike, devoted quite a bit of space to Ron and the trials and tribulations of dealing with the large groups of hikers who stay at 'the barn.'

"During my visit with him, he browsed through some of the yearly journals he maintains and he recounted stories of the incidents mentioned in them. He

A cluster of Indian pipe.

told of the Jewish Rabbi, who, fearful of what he referred to as the Jewish mafia, conducted religious ceremonies at 2 to 3 A.M. The Rabbi was asked to leave after five days. He also told of the two British hikers who had started at Katahdin with almost no hiking equipment and little food, and who had arrived at Gorham living on 250 calories a day—one of the two men was in bad shape; and the man who ran up a $46 phone bill on Ron and left without paying.

"When I hear about some of these incidents, I experience a bit of guilt. It harks back to a weird letter and a tainted box of candy that were sent to me a year or so after my first *Appalachian Hiker* was published in late 1972. The letter was from a couple in New England. It was polite, a 'Dear Mr. Garvey' thing, but it went on to say they were sending me a box of candy that I would not find acceptable because they had put lime in it! They had done this, they stated, because they did not find 'Acceptable' the large number of hikers who were appearing on the Appalachian Trail because of my book, robbing them of the solitude and enjoyment they had formerly experienced on the Trail. Henceforth, they would do their hiking on other trails. The candy did arrive, and a tiny taste revealed that yes, it did have lime in it! I had to concede that the couple had used a dramatic method for making their point. However, the taxpayers have paid almost $100 million to-date for the Trail and its surrounding corridor, and we have several thousand volunteers who maintain and protect it. We cannot put forth all this money and effort, then restrict the Trail for those whose love of solitude is ruined if they meet other hikers.

"Now that my decision to return had been made, it was time to enjoy the town of Gorham, with its friendly people and good restaurants. I had precious few opportunities to go to church during this trip. I went to a Saturday night Mass with a young lady, Lynn Propke, who was spending a few extra days for a very good reason, waiting for money from home! After Mass, a meal at Wilfred's Place, another one of Gorham's good places to eat. Back at the barn, I was afforded a chance to visit with some of the northbound hikers I had hiked with earlier—Mark Elliott and Sandy Bernoi, J.P. McMullin, Ed Seibert. To bed at 9:30 P.M. A late arriving hiker came in and I spoke to him briefly but did not realize who he was until the next day."

Sunday, September 9
Gorham, New Hampshire, to Laurel, Maryland
649 miles by car!

"Up at 6 A.M., no longer adhering to hiking schedule! Learned that the man who had arrived late Saturday night was Ed Talone, whom I had sponsored for membership in the PATC some years earlier. We walked to McDonald's together, and had a long breakfast, after which Ed showed me where the bus station was located. I inquired as to the time they opened; 6:30 A.M. and yes, I would have time for breakfast before the bus left for Boston Tuesday morning.

"Back to the barn, where I met a big bearded guy by the name of Lin Price. He had finished a week of hiking in the White Mountains and was now heading back in his pick-up truck to Washington, D.C. He was leaving very shortly and I was welcome to go with him. Great. Packed my gear in a hurry, had my bill calculated for four days—shower privileges, use of the dining room, all for $22. I wrote a check for $30, a little extra to Ron for the very few who walk out on him! Put my pack in Lin's truck and we left Gorham at 10:30 A.M. What a dramatic change in plans. Just a few minutes after I had made plans to return home by bus and air on Tuesday, I find myself driving home on Sunday in a pickup truck!

"We headed west on U.S. 2, then south on various interstates to I-95, which we followed directly to Laurel, Maryland, near the Washington, D.C., metro area. We drove directly to the home of Greg Goulding and his wife, friends of Lin's. They had been expecting us, and we had a midnight snack of beef stew topped off with cinnamon rolls. To bed at 1:20 A.M.; I slept on the couch, Lin on the floor. Age has certain privileges!

"One unpleasant development. During our drive to Laurel, I began to experience the symptoms of a common cold—runny nose, sore throat. Five months of hiking, sleeping on floors or on the ground, and not even a sniffle; now this!"

Monday, September 10
Laurel, Maryland, to Falls Church, Virginia
HOME!

"Awake at 4:30 A.M. after only three hours sleep. Up at 5:30 A.M. Greg left for work at 6:30 A.M., and shortly thereafter Lin, Greg's wife, and I had a bacon and pancake breakfast. We left the Goulding home at 8:45 A.M. and later drove to my home in Falls Church, Virginia. Lin visited with us briefly before he was on his way to Charlotte, North Carolina. After Lin left, I had a chance to examine our 'new' home, as Mary had taken advantage of my absence to have new flooring installed in our kitchen and family room, and to have other rooms either painted or papered. A tremendous improvement and a tremendous amount of work by my wife and my son Dan in moving furniture and doing the cleanup work. Weighed myself before taking a shower—146 pounds. About what I expected. I'm certain I put on one pound per day during my four days in Gorham.

"And a direct quote from the last paragraph of my hike diary: "My cold is hitting me with full force, constant drip, drip, drip. Also, I am still sore all over. Those last two days (hiking towards Gorham) especially tough on me. I can't remember a night when I was so exhausted and my entire body so sore as the night I reached the Gentian Pond Shelter.""

Oddly enough, the day I hiked into Gorham with my trusty Kelty pack and its contents of 40 pounds would turn out to be my last day of backpacking ever! I have not had the pack on my back since I ended my 1990 hike, and in view of a heart condition that has developed, it seems very doubtful that I will ever again be able to engage in such strenuous activity.

3

Finding And Hiking
The Trail

If you have read Chapters 1 and 2, you have a pretty good idea of *what* the Appalachian Trail is. You may now appreciate a word of information as to just *where* the Trail is and how you can find it. A quick study of the map will give you a rough idea of where the Trail passes through each of the 14 states. The next step, if you desire more precise information, is to obtain a road map. The road maps issued by each state's highway department show fairly accurately where the Trail intersects each primary highway. Futhermore, the highway departments of all the states involved have erected highway crossing signs identifying intersections of the Trail and primary highways. These signs range in size from the modest 24-inch ovals in Connecticut to the much larger signs in Pennsylvania. At secondary highways, the Trail is frequently identified by signs erected by trail clubs.

If at this point your interest has been aroused to the extent that you desire to locate the Trail and see what it looks like, you have a good chance of doing so. By using the road map and your car, and by keeping a sharp eye for road signs, you should be able to spot a point where the Trail crosses a highway. Once you have located a Trail crossing, you can park your car and hike on the Trail in either direction to find out what it is like. While hiking on the Trail, you may find a wooden directional sign giving distances to points of interest in either direction, e.g., distances to an overnight shelter or to another highway intersection.

You may, however, be an individual who desires to have more complete information before hiking the first step. Or you may not like the idea of exploring a strange trail all by yourself. There are a number of ways you can obtain additional information. You might telephone your local newspaper's sports department and ask one of the editors for information on hiking clubs in your area. Or you might check whether your local library has available one of the guidebooks issued by the ATC. Yet another possibility is to contact one of the eight national forests or the two national parks through which the Trail passes. But the surest way is to write to the organization that coordinates the activities of the clubs and individuals who maintain the 2,000-plus-mile Trail. This organization is the Appalachian Trail Conference, P.O. Box 807, Harpers Ferry, West Virginia, 25425. Ask for the information packet and a list of hiking clubs in your area.

The ATC consists of 33 hiking clubs, which share responsibility for maintaining the Trail (see appendix A). Most of these clubs schedule weekend or Sunday hiking trips on an almost year-round basis. If one of these clubs is located near you, you may (1) telephone the club office, (2) contact a club member, or (3) scan the leisure sports section of the newspaper to ascertain the date, locale, and other particulars for forthcoming hikes. In this way you can arrange to hike with a group of people; the more experienced hikers will be glad to answer your questions regarding maps and equipment, overnight shelter accommodations, and so on.

If you live in a location where there are no hiking clubs, the ATC information packet should suffice. In the packet, among other things, is the very informative, 30-page publication, *Walking the Appalachian Trail . . . Step by Step*. There is no charge for the packet but donations are gratefully accepted.

Far and away, the best and most detailed information is available through the ATC's guidebooks. Each five-by-six-inch guidebook contains detailed data on some 200 to 300 miles of the Trail, and describes interesting side trails. Guidebooks frequently contain interesting historical information concerning features found along the Trail, or about the country through which the Trail passes.

Every book is divided into a number of chapters, each containing detailed information on a length of the Trail that extends anywhere from 5 to 20 miles. Each section of the book first prints the summary information for that particular section of Trail and then lists the detailed trail data. The Trail is described twice in the book—once from north to south, and again from south to north. On the following page is a reproduction of a complete page of one such guidebook, the *Appalachian Trail Guide to Central and Southwest Virginia*, 11th edition.

I would advise any hiker to buy the guidebook. Half the fun of a trip is to study the book before the trip begins and then go through it afterwards and make annotations in the margins about things personal to you; the date you hiked a particular trail, the place you saw a hen turkey with her young, the place you saw a fox or a bear. Since most hiking is done within a 100-mile radius of the hiker's home, it follows that a single guidebook will serve the average hiker for years. Certain trails will carry a special fascination for the hiker, and these will be revisited from time to time.

I have already mentioned road maps as being of assistance to a person who desires to locate the Trail. Once on the Trail, the hiker will desire more detailed maps that will show the location of each overnight shelter, each source of water,

Tobacco Row Mountain. During very dry seasons, expect Forest Service personnel with binoculars and a radio to be on top. For circuit hike here, see section introduction.

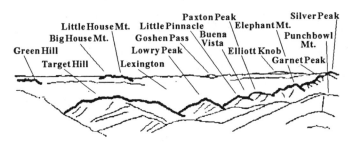

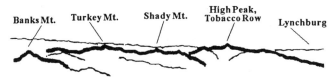

2.2   Switch back left. Old trail on right.
      From here to Saddle Gap is original 1930 A.T.
2.8   Passing view of Little Apple Mountain to east and Silas Knob, Rocky Row, and Apple Orchard Mountain ahead to southwest, cross buried pipeline in small, cleared sag.
3.0   Cross small knoll with glimpses of Bluff Mountain behind, and, in 200 yards, bear left through tight saddle.
3.3   At large rock, switch back right.
3.5   Reach Salt Log Gap (2,573 feet).
      Not to be confused with Salt Log Gap between Rocky Mountain and Tar Jacket Ridge, 21.7 miles north. Blue-blazed Belle Cove Trail in gap leads right 5 miles to U.S. 501. Belle Cove Branch water is normally available 0.5 mile down this trail. To left, unblazed White Oak Flats Trail leads 3 miles to White Oak Flats and 4 miles to parkway mile 55.2. The term "salt log" comes from notches cut in a fallen log where handfuls of salt were placed for livestock—the forerunner of the modern salt block. Ahead, look for spleenwort, a fern.
3.7   Pass rock overhang on left.
4.6   Skirt the natural amphitheater on the west side of Silas Knob and pass view to west of Maury River Valley and Allegheny Mountains, southwest of Three Sisters Knobs,

Page from the Appalachian Trail Conference's Appalachian Trail Guide to Central Virginia.

each intersecting trail, road, and stream. Fortunately such maps are available for almost the entire length of the Trail. Each of the ATC's guidebooks include maps, which for the most part are on the scale of one or one-half inch to the mile. The beginning of each chapter also lists the names of any other maps that pertain to the section of Trail being described.

More than 850 miles of the Trail pass through eight national forests. In addition to the guidebook maps, many hikers like to carry with them the U.S. Forest Service maps that show the route of the Trail through each of the eight forests. If you desire these maps, write to the U.S. Forest Service, 1720 Peachtree Road, Atlanta, Georgia, 30309, and ask to receive the maps showing the Appalachian Trail in the six national forests in the southern region. You may also write to the U.S. Forest Service, 3103 West Wisconsin Avenue, Milwaukee, Wisconsin, 53203, and ask to receive the Appalachian Trail maps for the White Mountains and Green Mountains national forests.

Those who desire to have the ultimate in detailed map information may write to the U.S. Geological Survey, Map Sales, Box 25286, Denver, Colorado, 80225, and ask to receive the index of topographic maps that pertain to the Appalachian Trail. The index will be mailed to you free of charge, along with an order blank and a booklet entitled "Topographic Maps." This booklet has copious illustrations in color using the same colors and symbols that are used on the topographic maps (topos).

Many hikers planning trips of short duration on the Trail either remove from their guidebook or otherwise reproduce only those pages that pertain to the area being hiked. These pages, plus the pertinent maps, are then placed in a clear plastic map case. Such practice cuts down on both weight and bulk in the pack. Furthermore, the map, with its contents clearly visible through the case, can be referred to even in wet weather without being damaged.

Most of the information in this book relates to the Georgia to Maine hiker and there is no question that hikers going all the way need all the advance information they can get. But perhaps 98 percent of all Trail hiking is done by those who are to be on the Trail for a single day (day hiking) or on short backpacking trips of two days to two weeks. There seems to be a feeling in some circles that the person who hikes the entire Trail in one year is just a cut above the person who is tied to a job and must squeeze in hikes on weekends and on one- and two-week vacations in order to complete the entire Trail. I personally feel that it requires more perseverance, and much more money, to do it over a period of years. Which method results in the greater satisfaction is debatable. Thru-hikers have the thrill of walking through all or parts of three seasons—spring, summer, and autumn. They become lean and hard from the day-after-day hiking up and down and along mountains. They learn to sustain themselves and to come up smiling through fair and foul weather. They become attuned to the mountains and to the hiking routine, and develop a rhythm the short-distance hiker seldom experiences. And yet, except for the Trail itself, thru-hikers learn precious little about the country through which they pass and the people who inhabit that country. They leave the Trail only to replenish their food supply and to pick up and dispatch mail.

Instead of having one, long, five-month experience in a single year, the short distance hiker has many, many experiences over a period of many years. The planning, the picture-taking, the reminiscing, even the automobile trips themselves, each becomes a separate excursion to be enjoyed in full measure before getting ready for the next trip to complete additional mileage on the Trail. One family in Ohio completed the Trail over a period of years, driving some 90,000 miles in the process. What a series of rich experiences about which to reminisce at family get-togethers in the years to come.

Two hiking friends, Gus Crews and Norm Greist, mentioned elsewhere in this book, are among the 2,000-Milers who accomplished the task (enjoyed the experience!) over a period of years—Gus hiked his last mile in 1972 at the age of 70, and Norm in 1975 at the age of 65. How long did it take them? For Gus it was a 15-year experience, and for Norm a mere 45! Each of these men developed a much better knowledge of the Trail than I, because they did so much more planning for each trip, and because they began and terminated short hikes from so many more approach points than I did. And in doing so, they became acquainted with the small towns and villages along the Trail and with the local people.

Those using the short hike approach will make much more use of road maps, Forest Service maps, and Park Service maps than will the thru-hiker. The maps in the guidebooks generally show only the Trail and perhaps two or three miles to either side (adequate for the hiker on the Trail, but not of much help to the hiker trying to reach an approach point via an automobile). If you are a small group and can get all your members and their gear into one car, then by all means use one car. You may think that having more than one vehicle would give you greater mobility. It doesn't. It restricts your mobility because you have additional vehicles that must be moved from place to place. I've been involved in hikes that involve much car shuttling, and I find it extremely frustrating. You begin to wonder if the purpose of the trip was to enjoy the mountains and to hike or to shuttle cars for long distances over poor roads each morning and afternoon.

If you have one car and you wish to day hike for several days, it can be done by spotting part of the group each morning at one point on the Trail and the remainder at another point. The two groups hike in opposite directions and exchange the car keys at the meeting point for the midday lunch. If you have one car and you wish to backpack rather than day hike, it is best to drive to the point where you will complete your hike and arrange for a local person to drive your group to the starting point of the hike and then to drive the car back to his or her home. In that way, you are always hiking toward your car, and regardless of what time you finish the hike, the car is there waiting for you, having been in a protected place during the course of your hike. It is becoming increasingly risky to leave a vehicle unattended for several days or a week alongside a public road while hiking the Trail.

So far in this chapter I have provided general information, which probably would be of more value to one having no previous knowledge of the Trail than to one already having some experience of it. Now let's return to the central theme of this book, the long-distance hike on the Trail—either mine or someone else's.

While the short-distance hiker needs but one guidebook, hikers going all the way through need all 10 guidebooks. Or do they? Do hikers *have* to have all the guidebooks to hike the Trail? The answer is that they do not. But without the guidebooks, hikers will miss so much. Many, many points of interest will not be seen because hikers will not know they exist; even if they did know, they would frequently not know where to look for them. Not all points of interest, trailside shelters, or sources of water along the Trail are marked. They should be, but they are not. I think of the first young man I met down in Georgia who had spent his first night on the Trail a mere half mile from the shelter where I stayed overnight. Why didn't he walk the additional half mile to the shelter? Because he did not know it was there. He was traveling without a guidebook. In the May, 1970, issue of *Appalachian Trailway News*, Andrew J. Giger tells of his end-to-end hike on the Trail. He tells of catching up with a couple who had been on the Trail for 55 days. He mentions that the couple was "carrying no guidebook, a severe disadvantage."

Let us assume that you purchased all 10 guidebooks and you wish to use them to the maximum advantage. If you plan to hike from south to north, you will find it advantageous to remove the north to south description from each guidebook. Next, combine the south to north descriptions into five guidebooks. Following that, go through each of your five consolidated books and highlight points of maximum importance, particularly sources of water and locations of overnight shelters.

An additional precaution that will pay dividends is to obtain copies of *Appalachian Trailway News* for the past two or three years. Study each issue carefully and mark in the margin of your guidebook any information that would be pertinent to your hike. Such information might be the location of new trailside shelters built since the last edition of the guidebook, the locations of old shelters that have been torn down, burned, or otherwise abandoned, and listings of areas where the Trail has been rerouted.

Everett and Nell Skinner, who made their leisurely traverse of the entire Trail in 1968, documented the locations of eating places and grocery stores, and provided other valuable bits of information. Much of this information was published in the January, 1970, issue of *ATN*. Some of the parenthetical notes provided by the Skinners in their article are gems; for example, "we ate at every restaurant we passed in order to shop less and eat heartily without carrying surplus food." In describing the Dodson South Mountain Inn in Maryland, the Skinners said, ". . . restaurant, wonderful chicken Maryland! Waitress told us anybody would know we weren't bums. She meant it so sincerely we couldn't take offense. We still chuckle over it. Just off Appalachian Trail crossing U.S. alternate Route 40."

The Appalachian Trail Data Book, compiled by Daniel D. Chazin of the New York-New Jersey Trail Conference, is provided as an adjunct to the guidebooks. *The Appalachian Trail Data Book*, which is revised annually, will be useful in planning a trip of a few days or a few weeks, or a hike of the entire Trail. For details on locations of water sources, nearby points of interest off the Trail, and many other things, the hiker will need to use the guidebooks or *The Thru-hiker's Handbook* published by Dan Bruce.

The history of *The Appalachian Trail Data Book* is interesting. Early in 1970, the late Maurice A. Crews reviewed the 10 Appalachian Trail guidebooks and typed up copies of a list of significant points along the Trail (trailside shelters, grocery resupply points, and highway crossings). The mileage points were listed in cumulative fashion, beginning with a zero point at Springer Mountain in Georgia, and reaching a mileage of slightly over 2,000 at Baxter Peak on Katahdin in Maine. These sheets were made in preparation for the scheduled 1970 Crews-Garvey hike of the Trail. Mr. Crews was unable to make the hike, but I used his fact sheets extensively throughout my hike, making many corrections and additions to them based on my on-the-Trail observations.

After the completion of my hike in October, 1970, Mr. Crews and I further revised the fact sheets, and early in 1971, we made them available to Col. Lester L. Holmes, then executive director of the ATC. The mileage fact sheets were made available to the public in 1971, both as a separate publication of the conference and by Appalachian Books as an appendix to the book *Appalachian Hiker*.

From 1971 through June 1975, the demanding and laborious task of correcting and reissuing the fact sheets became a personal project for Colonel Holmes. Had it not been for his perseverance and championing of the fact sheets concept, they would probably have ceased to exist. After 1975, the Publications Committee of the ATC assumed the responsibility, and in 1977 issued a completely new book entitled *The Appalachian Trail Data Book*.

I have included a photo of one page of this book to give you an idea of the information provided. For those of you planning to do any long-distance hiking of the Trail, you should know that the book is compact, measuring only 7 x 5 inches, and may be ordered from the ATC. Likewise, I have included a page from *The Thru-hiker's Handbook*, which contains a wealth of other information for almost every mile of the Trail, and can also be ordered from the ATC, or from the Center for Appalachian Studies, P.O. Box 525, Hot Springs, NC 28743.

CENTRAL VIRGINIA

G B S	North to South	FEATURES	Facilities (See page xv for codes)	South to North	G B S
	Miles from Rockfish Gap, Va.			*Miles from New River, Va.*	
◆	36.3	Fish Hatchery Road; **Montebello, Va., P.O. 24464** (P.O.,C,G,L 1.9m W)	RCGL	184.3	◆
	37.5	Porters Field		183.1	
Va. 18	38.4	Twin Springs	w	182.2	Va. 18
	38.7	Seeley-Woodworth Shelter	Sw	181.9	
	39.4	Elk Pond Branch	Cw	181.2	
	40.6	North Fork of Piney River	Cw	180.0	
	42.5	Greasy Spring Road		178.1	
	43.0	USFS 246		177.6	
◆	44.2	Salt Log Gap (north), USFS 63	R	176.4	◆
	45.5	Tar Jacket Ridge		175.1	
Va. 19	46.4	Hog Camp Gap, USFS 48	RCw	174.2	Va. 19
	47.7	Cold Mountain		172.9	
	48.5	Cow Camp Gap Shelter (S,w 0.6m E)	Sw	172.1	
	49.5	Bald Knob		171.1	
◆	52.3	U.S. 60; **Buena Vista, Va., P.O. 24416** (P.O.,G,L,M 9.3m W; G 1m W)	RGLM	168.3	◆
	54.1	Brown Mountain Creek Shelter	Sw	166.5	
Va. 20	56.1	Pedlar Lake Road (USFS 38)	R	164.5	Va. 20
	58.2	Pedlar Dam		162.4	
	58.5	USFS 39, Little Irish Creek	RCw	162.1	
	60.3	Rice Mountain		160.3	
	62.2	Robinson Gap Road (Va. 607)	R	158.4	
◆	62.5	Blue Ridge Parkway, mile 51.7; Punchbowl Mountain Crossing	Rw	158.1	◆
Va. 21	62.9	Punchbowl Shelter (S,w 0.2m W)	Sw	157.7	Va. 21
	63.4	Punchbowl Mountain		157.2	
	64.5	Bluff Mountain		156.1	
	66.0	Salt Log Gap (south) (w 0.5m W)	w	154.6	

Page from The Appalachian Trail Data Book.

Once you have chosen to thru-hike the Trail, you must decide whether you will hike from south to north or vice versa. An equally important decision is whether you plan to hike alone or with one or more companions. Most books on hiking urge strongly that you not travel alone. And yet many people do. If safety were the only factor to be considered there would be no solo hikes. Danger is always present in mountain hiking. There is the danger of bad falls, when bones can be broken, or severe cuts sustained from the thousands of knife-edged rocks that dot the Trail. A heart attack, stroke, or sudden severe illness could occur. There is a slight danger of a poisonous snakebite or an attack by a vicious or rabid animal. All of these things could occur whether you are alone or in the company of others, but the possibility of getting help is greatly increased if you have one or more companions. Again, why so many solo hikes? The answer is that it is very difficult to find someone who is free to hike at the same time you are free to hike, who wishes to or is able to hike at the same speed you wish to hike, and who has a personality compatible with yours. It is one thing to hike with a companion or several companions for a few days or even a week. It is an entirely different matter if you plan to hike with the same person or people for a five- or six-month trip.

Two of those who hiked the entire Trail together in 1960, Owen F. Allen and Lochlen L. Gregory, in describing their hike (*ATN* January, 1961), had this to say: "It may be worth mentioning that the warning given us by Earl Shaffer against hiking together has solid foundations. On the Trail, 'mole-hills' can become 'mountains,' and on more than one occasion we found ourselves acting stupidly childish, although we had worked together for two years. It bears consideration by any who plan to hike together for very long."

Two other men who hiked together, Murray S. Chism and Edward N. Little, required (or permitted themselves the luxury of) eight months in 1959 to complete the Trail from Georgia to Maine. Of all those who have hiked the entire Trail in a single year, I have always felt that these two men obtained the full measure of enjoyment. They hiked through three seasons (spring, summer, fall), and finished up amid winter conditions in snow and ice on Mt. Katahdin on November 8, 1959.

For my first thru-hike, I had planned to do most of my hiking with Maurice A. (Gus) Crews of Bethesda, Maryland. We took two conditioning hikes in February and March of 1970, and on the second of these, Gus developed an infection. His doctor advised him against taking the long hike, and Gus heeded the advice. Despite this, it seemed that I would have plenty of companionship. After I announced in the January 1970 issue of *ATN* that I planned to begin the hike at Springer Mountain during the first week of April and that I would welcome company for a few days or a few weeks, I received about 12 to 15 inquiries. However, for various reasons I hiked with only one person of that group, and then only for part of one day.

tain, 30 feet to the left at the point where the Trail crosses an old rutted and overgrown jeep road. (1170) ←19.0m/7.3m→

The next 10 miles into Duncannon will give you a good idea of what the A.T. is like in the remainder of Pennsylvania. Note that this portion of Trail is not all rocks. Neither is the rest of Pennsylvania. In the next hundred or so miles, you will have plenty of relatively easy treadway between the rocky parts, so do not get spooked by all the warnings you have heard.

Cove Mountain: route from Blue Mountain to Cove Mountain was selected and blazed by Earl Shaffer himself in 1956.

Thelma Marks Shelter: built by Earl Shaffer; water down steep, blue-blazed trail in front of the shelter. Take a cup or water bottle for dipping, since the spring source is nestled in rocks. (980) ←7.3m/8.9m→

Memorial trees: planted beside the Trail in memory of 1990 thru-hikers Geoff Hood and Molly LaRue.

Hawk Rock: overlook with view of Duncannon and the Susquehanna River valley for many miles north. Products from frontier farms and many of the communities you see once flowed into Duncannon, to be shipped all over the world. Prior to 1736, all of what you see was the domain of the Iroquois, some of whom no doubt stood gazing from this spot in ages past. An unofficial campsite 0.1 mile south of the overlook has no water.

DUNCANNON, PA. (pop. 2,445): once called "the jewel of the Susquehanna," but considered by many of its residents to be a town that has seen better days. From a thru-hiker standpoint, however, it provides basic services and is also fairly convenient, since everything is located within fairly easy walking distance. Hiking is not of major interest to the town's people, though they are quite friendly to A.T. hikers that pass through their community. **Doyle Hotel**—legendary in thru-hiking circles. Built around the turn of the century by Anheuser-Busch, the hotel was run by the Doyle family for more than four decades. Now under new ownership, the hotel is being renovated. Most of the early thru-hiking pioneers stayed here (check the old registers if they are still around), and many a hiking tale has been told around the bar on the ground floor. Today, the hotel caters to short-term renters and to hikers during the summer months. Rooms are inexpensive ($15S $20D $5EAP, 3 max) and bathrooms, two per floor, have only tubs, and the toilets are vintage (notice the name on the front of some of the older toilet bowls, perhaps the inspiration for the phrase, "going to the John"). Pets are allowed, and a public telephone is available in the lobby. The bar features television, air conditioning, and beer on tap for 60¢ a glass, and offers a full menu for breakfast, lunch, and dinner. Patrons begin arriving around eight in the morning, and you will never see the bar without at least one regular holding down the fort. The bar and hotel are closed Sunday, though you can check in on Sunday (manager lives on premises). The Doyle is obviously not 5-star, but the folks who run it are, and they make thru-hikers feel at home. **Other lodging**—Clark's Ferry Plaza Motel: recently renovated clean rooms for $25S $30D $33 (3 persons or more), 4 max; a/c, cable, washer/dryer, no pets (MC, Visa, AE, Dis); family-style restaurant in motel for $4 per tentsite, pay showers; railroad tracks quite close, and trains pass often. **Meals**—Sorrento's Italian Restaurant: L/D, casual and take-out, pizza, subs, cheese steaks, stromboli (Can anyone eat a whole one?), all considered excellent by

thru-hikers of past years; open Mon-Thur 11am-11pm, Fri-Sat until midnight, Sun 4pm-11pm. • 3B's Ice Cream Shop: located about 0.6 mile north of the Doyle, open daily 11am-10pm. **Groceries**—Mutzabaugh's Market: large supermarket, good for long-term resupply; open Mon-Sat 6am-10pm, Sun 7am-9pm (now located in new facility on Route 274, old store you pass on A.T coming into town boarded up) • 24-hour convenience store behind the Doyle. **Laundromat**—F.W, centrifugal water extractor, good place to wash a synthetic sleeping bag; open 7 days, 8am-9pm. **Stove fuel**—Coleman by the pint at True Value Hardware Store. **Other services**—bank w/ATM • pharmacy • newstand • doctor • dentist • health clinic. ✪ Post-office hours: Mon-Fri 8am-4:30pm (Wed until 5:30pm), Sat 8am-noon; 717-834-3332. **Nearby town**—Harrisburg (about 15 miles southeast).

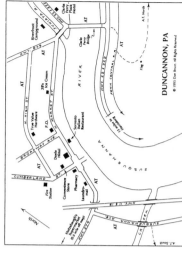

DUNCANNON, PA

✪ **Harrisburg, Pa.** (pop. 53,264): a large city with all major services, including a large backpacking store, Wildware Outfitters (717-564-8008) with JanSport, Kelty, Camp Trails, Gregory, Mountainsmith, Lowe, North Face, Sierra Designs, Eureka!, Moss, Hi-Tec Sports, Danner, Merrell, Vasque, MSR, Optimus/Svea, Camping Gaz, Peak 1, Trangia, Caribou, Marmot, Thermarest, Thorlo, Wigwam, repair services; open Mon-Fri 10am-9pm, Sat 10am-6pm (MC, Visa, AE); Camp Hill store open Sun noon-5pm.

Clark's Ferry Bridge: named for Daniel Clark, who operated a ferry service here in 1785. It spans the Susquehanna River, longest river crossed by the Trail at 444 miles in length. The Connecticut River is second at 411; the Potomac, third at 383; the James, fourth at 340; and the Hudson, fifth at 315.

The next 8 miles are maintained by York Hiking Club volunteers. Earl Shaffer was one of the founders of this club, and was active for many years. A recent major project of this club was the building of the Clarks Ferry Shelter in 1987.

Pages from The Thru-hiker's Handbook.

I therefore found myself traveling alone for about two-thirds of the entire hike. Sometimes I met friends by prior arrangement and hiked with them for a few days to two weeks. Sometimes I met people on the Trail who were hiking north, and I joined them for short periods of time. I thoroughly enjoyed the company of all those I met, and it has been enjoyable through the years to reminisce with these people about areas hiked and experiences shared. And yet, even though I am naturally a gregarious individual, I did enjoy those days when I had the solitude of my own company. No one, unless he is a total recluse, can live his life exactly as he pleases. Each day of a man's life is a series of compromises and accommodations with members of his family, his coworkers, his boss, his neighbors, and others. It was pleasant, therefore, to have some days on which all the options were mine: the time of arising and the time of going to bed, the food to be eaten at each meal, the speed at which to hike, and the side trails to be explored.

In 1970, I found myself hiking and sleeping alone about two-thirds of the time. That was when 10 people hiked the entire Trail. But in 1997, more than 200 people will complete the Trail…at least 21 times the number in 1970. And if 21 times as many finished in 1997, it follows that there were about 21 times as many who were trying to finish. For my 1990 hike, I had made plans for two friends to hike with me from Springer Mountain in Georgia to the northern-most part of the Smoky Mountains National Park, but I had no fear of being alone much of the time after those two men returned to their homes. I was confident that I would have plenty of company all the way to Maine. So, I would say to those contemplating a hike of the entire Trail not to worry about hiking alone. Unless you are starting at an unusual time of the year, you will have companionship. The makeups of the little groups hiking the Trail are fascinating. Sometimes just two people, sometimes three or more, and always with some people dropping out for various reasons; others rejoining after a day in town or a quick trip home to visit family. Likewise, the caring attitude that the hikers develop for each other is both interesting and impressive.

You will also be surprised at the number of people who have long harbored a desire to hike the entire Trail. An 18-year-old high school senior, Richard Vogt, writing from New Jersey in 1975, commented that: "I first hiked on the AT in 1971 from Bear Mountain, New York, to the Delaware Water Gap. I met and talked to many people and it's kind of sad how many expressed a wish to hike the entire Trail at one point in life, and let it pass by." (Vogt didn't let the idea pass him by—he hiked the whole Trail in 1975.)

Probably 90 percent of the thru-hikers start in Georgia rather than in Maine. There is a reason for this, especially if the hiker plans to begin his hike in the early spring. Spring comes early in Georgia but very late in Maine. There is frequently snow on the ground in Maine until June 1. Even after the snows melt, the ground is still soggy until well into summer. In addition, the mosquitos, flies, midges, no-see-ums, etc., make life miserable for the hiker until almost the first of August. Early spring in the southern Appalachians is beautiful in the extreme. Spring flowers are already in evidence by April 1, and as the hiker walks north, it is like hiking in eternal spring. The hikers cannot hike north quite as fast as spring advances, but it is a fact that one who begins his hike in Georgia around April 1 will probably see and enjoy more of the spring season than ever before in his life. As I review my daily diary notes for those delightful April and May days, the entries describing the trillium, bluets, spring beauties, rhododendron, the beauty and fragrance of the wild azalea, the birds I heard and saw, I get the urge to revisit that beautiful area. For those planning to hike the entire Trail in five or six months, I would strongly recommend the south to north route. In that way, you can enjoy the best of both seasons, spring in the southern Appalachians, autumn in Maine.

TRAIL MARKINGS

This chapter would not be complete without describing the manner in which the Trail is marked. In order of importance (to me, at least) these markings are: (1) white paint blazes, (2) four-inch diamond-shaped metal markers, (3) wooden directional and informational signs, (4) blue paint blazes, (5) cairns, and (6) mileage markers. Readers desiring a thorough knowledge of trail markings and the methods of applying them may obtain the *ATC Field Book, A Self Help Guide for Trail Maintainers*.

White Paint Blazes

Without a doubt, the white paint blaze is the most important and infallible method of marking the Trail. The blaze is two inches wide and six inches high. Blazes are painted on trees, rocks, and other objects along the Trail, and face the hiker like highway markers. When placed on trees, they should be at eye level. Blazes are supposed to be within sight of each other on narrow woods trails and at somewhat greater distances in more traveled sections. Hikers should always have a blaze in sight, either by looking forward or backward along the Trail. Occasionally a double blaze is used to alert hikers to potentially confusing changes in the direction of the Trail. There are currently two types of double blazes in use: the conventional double blaze and the offset blaze. With the conventional double blaze, one blaze is painted directly above the other and simply conveys a warning to be alert. Where the offset blazing is used, the top blaze is moved two inches to the left to indicate a left turn and two inches to the right for a right turn. At its biennial meeting in 1995, the ATC authorized (but did not require) the use of the offset blaze to replace the conventional double blaze. The offset blaze requires no more work to install, and it provides the hiker with twice as much information as does the conventional blaze.

Theoretically, the hiker should be able to find the Trail from Georgia to Maine by reference only to the white paint blazes. There are several reasons why it doesn't quite work out this way. For one thing, such occurances as lumbering operations, road widenings, and fires can destroy all evidence of blazing over a considerable area. More recently, ski slope development and mountain-home construction have done the same. A second reason is that those doing the paint blazing sometimes get a little careless. Trail maintenance crews know the Trail so well, they assume that all others should likewise know it. They do not try to see the Trail

Example of old Axe-blazed marker now painted with contemporary white blaze.

through the eyes of a stranger. Therefore, they omit blazes, particularly at trail and road intersections. The hiker must perforce stop and reconnoiter. To say that these interruptions to your hiking schedule are irritating and frustrating is to state it too mildly. Words like maddening and infuriating are much more suitable. If you find areas like this on the Trail, you will be doing your fellow hikers a great favor if you promptly drop a postcard to the ATC describing the area that is inadequately blazed. The ATC will correct the situation through its Trail Standards Committee, developed in 1971, an effective means for alerting maintaining organizations of any areas that were inadequately blazed.

Another reason that one cannot rely entirely upon the white blazes is that the organization responsible for maintaining a trail section sometimes has been unable to properly blaze the trail. For example, the 70 miles that lie within the boundaries of the Great Smoky Mountains National Park are blazed so sparsely that most hikers do not realize they are blazed at all. For years, I had thought that the omission of such blazing was because park officials were reluctant to permit it. I learned in October, 1978, that the real reason is that the maintaining organization—the Smoky Mountains Hiking Club—had been unable to perform the blazing. When I hiked through the Smokies in 1977, I found that *some* excellent blazing had been done, but it was so sparse that many of the thruhikers were unaware of the blazing.

Diamond-shaped Markers

These four-inch markers with the familiar joined *A* and *T* are used sporadically along the length of the Trail. At the time of my hike, it was used very frequently and effectively in Maine, and to a lesser extent elsewhere. Unfortunately, the metal marker seems to have high value as a souvenir; in a few areas of heavy traffic, the markers seem to disappear almost as fast as they are erected.

Directional and Informational Signs

These wooden signs are a great help. They tell hikers the distance to the next shelter or to a spring, or inform hikers when they have reached the summit of a mountain; these signs also tell the name of the mountaintop and its elevation. I found some sections of the Trail to be very well-marked with these signs. Maine was outstanding. Other sections of the Trail were almost devoid of such signs. See page 37 for an example.

Blue Paint Blazes

These blazes, which are the same size as the white ones (two-by-six inches), are used to identify side trails leading off the Appalachian Trail. The blue blaze trails lead to such things as overnight shelters, springs, and viewpoints. To be of maximum value, the blue blaze trails should be further identified by signs

Appalachian Trail diamond-shaped metal marker.

The National Scenic Trail marker.

informing the hiker where the blue blaze trail goes and how far it is to the shelter, spring, viewpoint, or whatever it is that lies at the end of that particular trail.

Sometimes signs are not erected, and sometimes they are destroyed or stolen. It is in such situations that the guidebooks prove of value. If the guidebook indicates that there is a shelter 200 yards to the right of the Trail at milepoint 13.52, for example, and you find a blue blaze trail leading off to the right at a point in the general area where you think milepoint 13.52 should be, then it is a safe bet that the blue blaze trail will lead you directly to the shelter.

Cairns

The Trail route across open fields and over mountaintops where no trees exist is marked by piles of stones, called cairns, or by blazes painted on rocks, or by both such devices. As hikers proceed from Georgia to Maine, they will find many spots where cairns could be used effectively, but they will find precious few cairns until New Hampshire. In that state, and in Maine, the cairns are used frequently and effectively. See page 154 for an example.

Mileage Markers

These are another seldom-used trail marking device. I found them used extensively only in Maine, plus in one other seven-mile stretch in eastern Pennsylvania. I found them to be extremely useful. The Board of Managers of the ATC in a November 1970 meeting made a provision for extending the mileage marker concept throughout the entire length of the Trail.

To understand the mileage marker concept, you must realize that the entire Trail is divided into a number of sections. These sections are generally delineated by road intersections. That is, if the Trail is intersected by two roads that are three miles apart, you then have a "section" that is only three miles. On the other hand, in some areas, such as Great Smoky Mountain National Park, there is only one intersecting road in some 70 miles. In such areas you might have a "section" that is 35 to 40 miles in length. Unfortunately, hikers are seldom certain of their exact location within a given "section."

The guidebook, for example, may state that "at 13.82 miles, Trail to right leads 200 yards to Jones Pond shelter." As nighttime approaches, the hiker begins to wonder how much farther he must walk before reaching "13.82," and after he has walked a considerable distance, he will wonder if perchance he has missed the side trail at "13.82." The mileage markers, located at one-mile intervals, give the hiker some reassurance and permit him to orient himself with respect to the various points of interest described in the guidebook. The distances used on mileage markers are always reckoned from the *north* end of the section, and the mileages used are keyed to the guidebook mileages. The mileage marker is a painted arrow pointing to the north end of the section plus a figure, e.g., *3.0*, and the word *miles* or more frequently just the abbreviation, *m*. The markers in Maine are usually painted on large rocks beside the Trail.

Rock mile-marker.

National Scenic Trail Marker

The last marker that I shall describe in this chapter is the National Scenic Trail marker. The National Trails System Act directs the Secretary of Interior and Secretary of Agriculture to establish a uniform marker with a distinctive symbol for each National Scenic Trail. Such a marker has been established for the Appalachian Trail. The Department of Interior is manufacturing these markers in only one size—nine inches. The markers will be used at points where the Trail intersects a road and where the intersection is not already marked with a highway crossing sign. These signs are very attractive and are located in particularly vulnerable areas—along roadsides. As a result, these markers also quickly disappear.

4

Food

Hikers who have hiked long distances on the Trail have used three principal methods of supplying themselves with food:

METHOD 1

Buy your entire supply of dehydrated food in advance of the trip, pack it in watertight containers, and bury it in food caches at various points along the Trail. This method was used successfully by Howie Bassett in 1968 and again in 1969 by Jeff Hancock.

METHOD 2

Buy your entire supply of dehydrated food in advance of the trip, repack it in boxes suitable for mailing, and have these boxes mailed to you at prearranged mail stops along the Trail. This method is used by many thru-hikers.

METHOD 3

Buy all of your groceries from rural and small-town grocery shops along the Trail. This is the method I used on my 1970 trip. Most of the thru-hikers in 1976 also followed this procedure, and, with only two or three exceptions, this was the method I used on my 1990 hike.

If the hiker's principal goal is to hike, hike, hike, with the least amount of lost time, then he would do well to use Method 1. Its disadvantage is that it requires a substantial amount of automobile travel prior to the trip in order to bury the food containers. And, of course, there is always the possibility that one or more of the caches will be disturbed or stolen, though this possibility is perhaps somewhat remote. Of the 100 caches buried by the Hancock family, only one was found to have been disturbed, and about half of the contents of one gallon–plastic jar had been damaged. But from the standpoint of speed, it is hard to argue against Method 1. The hiker checks his notes, locates the food cache, removes the food, which has been repackaged into meal-size plastic sacks, and he is on his way. Just one disturbing thought occurs to me as I describe this method. What happens to all those one-gallon plastic jars after the food has been removed? Litter! Tsk! Tsk!

Method 2 is somewhat like Method 1 except that the food caches consist of boxes which, hopefully, are waiting for you at the previously selected post office stops. It is more time-consuming because the hiker must leave the Trail and either walk or hitch a ride into town. But most hikers desire an occasional break in town anyway. There they can get a square meal, have their clothes laundered, and receive mail. And, since few places along the Trail have the variety of dehydrated foods required, hikers would do well to consider Method 2 if planning to eat dehydrated foods.

Method 3 is for hikers who have sufficient time to hike the Trail in a more relaxed manner, or for those who do not care for dehydrated foods as a steady diet. I fit into both these categories. I also found that shelf items in the grocery store are generally much cheaper than their dehydrated counterparts. I frankly enjoyed the sashays into town to buy food, visit with the townspeople, receive mail, write a few quick letters, launder my clothes, get a shower, and eat a couple of good meals that I did not have to cook myself. On the average, I found I could buy groceries every four or five days without having to travel too far off the Trail.

But suppose you have decided to go the dehydrated food route. Where does one buy enough dehydrated food for a five- or six-month trip extending for more than 2,000 miles? Fortunately, there are a number of suppliers from which such quantities can be obtained. Their names and addresses are listed in Appendix B. A word of caution here. If there will be only one or two people in your party, be certain to choose a supplier that prepares dehydrated food in packages for one or two people. I remember two young ladies I met on the Trail in April 1970. Before embarking on a three-month backpacking trip, they had purchased $170 worth of dehydrated food, only to find upon its receipt that all the packages were packed for parties of four people. This meant that before beginning their hike they had to open every package and repackage its contents.

A word of definition is in order as to the term "dehydrated foods." Most of us tend to think of dehydrated foods (including freeze-dried foods) as those available only at backpacking, camping, or mountaineering supply houses. But Webster defines dehydration as "the artificial drying of food products to reduce weight and preserve them for future use." If this definition is strictly adhered to, all grocery stores carry a number of dehydrated items on their shelves; for example, raisins, apricots, and dried soups, to name a few. And some hikers have taken to dehydrating their own food. For the purposes of this chapter, I shall consider dehydrated foods (including freeze-dried food) to be those foods put up in packets of one, two, or four servings and available at supply houses catering to campers, hikers, and mountaineers.

Your choice of food, then, will be determined first by your decision to go either the dehydrated food route or the grocery store route; and second, by your decision as to whether you plan to cook one, two, or three meals per day, or perhaps no meals per day. And lastly, your decision will be governed largely by your personal preferences in food.

Many hikers I met during my five-month Trail hike who were aware that I planned to write this book urged that I include particular foods I found most satisfactory, as well as recipes for dishes I used most often. This I will do. But first I must quote a passage from the book *Appalachian Trail,* by Ann and Myron Sutton, published by J.B. Lippincott, Philadelphia, Pennsylvania. You will enjoy reading this, if for no other reason than that it will make you happy you are buying your trail food in the 1990s rather than in the early 1800s. The Suttons, after describing some of the tremendous walking feats accomplished by the English in the early 1800s, describe the diets followed by these hardy hikers of 180 years ago:

"And what kind of diet were these feats performed on? If a man walked thirty-six miles to breakfast and thirty farther to dinner, what did he eat? The reply concerned more what walkers should not eat. 'Vegetables,' went the answer, 'such as turnips, carrots, or potatoes, are never given as they are watery, and of difficult digestion. On the same principle, fish must be avoided, and besides, they are not sufficiently nutritious. Neither butter nor cheese is allowed; the one being very indigestible, and the other apt to turn rancid on the stomach. Eggs are also forbidden, excepting the yolk taken raw in the morning. And it must be remarked that salt, spiceries, and all kinds of seasonings, with the exception of vinegar, are prohibited. . . .

"With respect to liquors, they must be always taken cold; and home brewed beer, old but not bottled, is the best. A little red wine, however, may be given to those who are not fond of malt liquor; but never more than half a pint after dinner. Too much liquor swells the abdomen, and of course injures the breath. The quantity of beer, therefore, should not exceed three pints during the whole day, and it must be taken with breakfast, and dinner, no supper being allowed. Water is never given alone, and ardent spirits are strictly prohibited, however diluted.

"It is an established rule to avoid liquids as much as possible, and no more liquor of any kind is allowed to be taken than what is merely requisite to quench he thirst. Milk is never allowed, as it curdles on the stomach. Soups are not u.ed; nor is anything liquid taken warm, but gruel or broth, to promote the operation of the physic."

There you have it, fellow hikers! Right out of the *Hikers' Manual* of 1810 or thereabouts. I found the list of "don'ts" to be impressive and almost all-inclusive. I find the section giving advice on the eating of eggs to be especially repulsive. Imagine, if you can, on a cold raw morning, swallowing a raw egg yolk and then washing it down with a little vinegar! But let's get back to the 1990s and see what is now acceptable. I suggest that beginners consult *The Thru-hikers' Handbook, The Appalachian Trail Backpacker,* or *The Thru-hiker's Planning Guide* (Workbook Edition).

One of the more thoughtful reviews of my first book appeared in the June 15, 1972, issue of *Appalachia,* the publication of the Appalachian Mountain Club of Boston. The reviewer was Edward N. Little, who had hiked the entire Trail in 1959. While he gave me high scores on most points, he pointed out, quite correctly, that I had failed to adequately discuss the need for a balanced diet for a trip of five or six months duration. I still have not done so! I describe the foods that I ate and the method of cooking them, but the development of a really balanced diet from the foods generally available to the long-distance backpacker is another project.

And now, before I describe some of the meals you might prepare, let me discourse a bit on what the long-distance hikers really eat—not what they should eat. The articles you have read or will read will tell you the amount of energy used while backpacking. They will tell you that you consume or burn up something like 4,000 to 6,000 calories a day; that to compensate for that, one must eat a well-balanced diet; and the experts will then proceed to tell you of what that diet must consist. I have absolutely no quarrel with this line of reasoning. And there are a few 2,000-milers who actually do take the time to prepare well-rounded meals. The vast majority, about four out of five hikers, eat the simplest foods they can on the Trail, regardless of nutrition, and then try to make up for it when they buy a meal in town or at a bed and breakfast. And in 1990, I was just as guilty as the rest of the hikers in taking the easy way out on food preparation, instead of taking the extra time to prepare a better balanced meal as I did in 1970.

There may be a few long-distance hikers that stick to the three meals a day routine they have at home. I found it most advantageous to have three or four light meals and snacks during the day, and then a full cooked meal at night. The great majority of the 1976 2,000-Milers also ate one hot meal per day, a few had two hot meals, and a very, very few opted for three. I ate a light breakfast about 6:00 A.M., a snack about 9:30 A.M., a light lunch around noon, frequently another snack about 3:00 P.M., and a hearty, cooked meal around 6:00 P.M. To each his own.

About three-fourths of the time, my breakfast consisted of dry cereal only. For those meals, I measured out a generous-size portion of the cereal, then added dry milk and sugar. All such meals were prepared in advance; that is, at the time I bought the boxed cereal during my hike, I measured out meal-size portions of the cereal, milk, and sugar, and packed this into plastic bags. Then each morning it was necessary to pour the contents of one bag into a container, add water, stir, and eat. I varied this by occasionally eating a slice of Claxton fruitcake, by drinking a cup of one of the instant powdered breakfasts, or by eating one of the many varieties of fruit tarts that have become popular in recent years. Early in the hike, however, I discontinued the instant powdered breakfasts, as I felt they cost too much for the food value delivered. The same reasoning applied to the tarts. They made a good combination with a cup of hot coffee, but I felt I was eating mostly pastry dough with only a tiny amount of sweetened fruit thrown in.

Near the end of my hike, in September and early October up in Maine, I frequently heated water for breakfast and enjoyed the luxury of hot coffee (instant coffee). This practice proved so pleasant that I seriously toyed with the idea of buying a small coffeepot at Monson, Maine, to make fresh-brewed coffee on each of the last 10 days of my hike. But reason prevailed over appetite, and I contented myself with the instant coffee. Later I discovered (*Consumer Reports* magazine, January 1971) that expert coffee tasters believe the better instant coffees to be fully as tasty as the brewed coffees. This explodes my long-held conviction on this subject and bears out my wife's contention that my preference for brewed coffees "is all in the mind." So be it.

If cold cereals were my most frequently eaten breakfasts, which particular cereals did I use? I found the combination of General Mills' Total and Kellogg's Concentrate to be very good. I bought these two cereals frequently and mixed them together before putting them in plastic bags. Unfortunately, Concentrate is no longer being produced. The hiker may develop his or her own combination, or may wish to use Quaker Oats instant oatmeal envelopes as described below. I also used Post Grape Nuts frequently. I bought Kellogg's Corn Flakes once when I could not buy the others. Before opening a package of Total or Corn Flakes, I would put the package on the floor and stamp it to reduce the volume. As might be imagined, this action required a hasty explanation to the grocery store proprietor and any other patrons. It was somewhat disconcerting at times to go through the stamping process on a large box of flaked cereal and then discover what a small amount of food was left. From the standpoint of weight versus volume, I vote for Grape Nuts. Its large box contains 24 ounces of food. Some of the other cereals, in boxes half again or twice as big, would contain only 8 to 12 ounces of food. Don't be deceived by the size of the box.

During my 1990 hike, I departed from the "Grape Nuts, powdered milk, sugar" packages I prepared myself, to a somewhat newer product on the market with the packaging already done. I'm referring to Quaker Oats instant oatmeal.

Quaker's Fruit and Cream variety comes in boxes of 10 individual envelopes. Eight of the envelopes contain flavored and lightly sugared oatmeal, two of them are plain with no sugar and no flavor. Guess which ones were the last to be eaten! Add hot water if you have it, or use cold water. I used this product throughout my hike, sometimes using one envelope for breakfast, sometimes two. I observed one of my fellow hikers who consumed three each morning.

During the course of my 1970 hike, the breakfast cereal industry came into heavy criticism—being scored for valuable nutrients, which they lacked, and for undesirable elements, principally heavy concentrations of sugar, which they contained. The criticism continues to this day, and the cereal companies continue to manufacture many junk cereals. The breakfast cereal I used most frequently, Post Grape Nuts, emerged from this bombardment with a relatively high score—being mildly criticized for somewhat low protein, but scoring well on most other factors. Also, since 1970, a number of granola products have entered the market. Some of these are subject to the same criticism as other cereals, that is, much too much sugar. In recent years, I have made much of my own granola from a recipe devised by Darwin and Eileen Lambert, two professional outdoor writers who live in a pre-Civil War house on the edge of the Shenandoah National Park. Here is the recipe:

CRUNCHY GRANOLA

1/4 lb. melted margarine	7 to 8 cups uncooked oatmeal
1/2 cup brown sugar	1 cup wheat germ
1 tsp. salt	1 cup coconut
1 tsp. vanilla	1/4 cup sesame seeds (optional)
1/2 cup water	1/2 cup chopped nuts(optional)

In Dutch oven, combine margarine, sugar, salt, vanilla, and water. Stir over low heat until dissolved. Add remaining ingredients and stir until moistened. Spread on two ungreased cookie sheets. Bake 2 hours at 275 degrees, stirring occasionally with a fork. Or bake at a higher temperature for less time—but be careful not to scorch.

Comments by the Lamberts: "We sometimes substitute honey or molasses for brown sugar and use a little less water. And we sometimes use sunflower seeds instead of nuts, just for variety. We never seem to tire of this. We add raisins or bananas when we serve it, but backpackers could add dry fruit."

When I make the Lamberts' granola, I mix it in a heavy aluminum pot of 8- to 10-quart capacity instead of a Dutch oven. In lieu of measuring out 8 cups of oatmeal, use the full 18-ounce package you buy at the store—it equals 8 cups. I have made many batches of this—sometimes doubling the recipe. Excellent stuff!

For snacks and lunches, I ate such foods as peanuts, mixed nuts, raisins, apricots, dates, candy bars, cheese, bread, and several types of pemmican (Citadel spread, Nonesuch Mincemeat, and Claxton fruitcake). When I could find them along the Trail, I also ate strawberries, raspberries, blueberries, blackberries, cherries, and apples.

When I mention bread, I do not mean the loaves of bread available at grocery stores, as these are too big and soft for backpacking. Something smaller and firmer is in order in the bread department. I found English muffins to be particularly good. Bagels are also excellent. Small packages of hamburger buns or hotdog buns are satisfactory, but they are somewhat softer than the muffins.

Occasionally in 1970, I ate French bread rolls flown over from Paris by Air France. I boasted that I was probably the only hiker on the Appalachian Trail who enjoyed the luxury of bread rolls baked in Paris and flown to this country. It just happened that my daughter Kathleen worked part time for Air France at nearby Dulles International Airport. On incoming flights from Paris there would frequently be sizeable quantities of these delicious long-keeping French rolls left over from the flight. These would be given to any Air France employees on duty at the time. Some found their way into our freezer and later into my Trail-food supply. I never ate one of these French rolls without marveling at the miracles of present day transportation. It seemed incredible that I could be sitting at a remote spot on the Trail eating a bread roll that had been baked in Paris, France.

One other "bread" product that has come on the market bears the trade name "STOVE TOP," which is labeled as a 15-minute stuffing mix. It comes in various flavors—chicken, cornbread, and pork chop, to name three. It could easily be called dehydrated stuffing. One box makes six, half-cup servings. Inside each box are two packages. One contains a concentrated, heavily seasoned, soup-like mix. You pour this in water, bring it to a boil, and simmer five minutes. From the other package, you pour into your "soup" mix the required amount of dry bread crumbs, stir them thoroughly into the soup, wait five minutes, and that's it. The stuffing, still hot and giving forth a delicious aroma, is ready to eat. It satisfies your craving for bread in a most delightful way. I've made the mix several times; it is very simple. If you wish to add the gourmet touch, after the stuffing is cooked lift it slightly off the skillet bottom and put it in a little margarine. Spread the dressing out so it forms a loose patty, and cook it a bit longer until the bottom is lightly browned and crisp. Serve with the crust side up.

A certain backpacker, who did his hiking about 100 years before most of us, stoutly maintained that for food he desired nothing more than bread, bread, bread, and more bread. I am speaking of John Muir, who did his hiking and exploring in the Sierra Nevada Mountains in the latter part of the 19 century.

Author's Sierra stove.

In the book *The Wilderness World of John Muir* (Houghton Mifflin Co., Boston), Muir, in his journal of July 7, 1869, wrote:

"Bread without flesh is a good diet, as on many botanical excursions I have proved. Tea also may be easily ignored. Just bread and water and delightful toil is all I need . . . not unreasonable much, yet one ought to be trained and tempered to enjoy life in these brave wilds in full independence of any particular kind of nourishment."

But in reading elsewhere in the book, I noted that where Muir described a particular meal he frequently mentioned other items in addition to bread. The bread-only diet I would find about as uninteresting as the rice-only diet described elsewhere in this book.

Before leaving the muffin and bread subject, let me describe an excellent luncheon combination which I used extensively in 1976, and all the time in 1990, that is, buttered muffins and hard-boiled eggs. In 1974, fellow PATCers Bill Husic, Ed Hanlon, and I hiked for six weeks in the Alps of northwestern Yugoslavia and in the mountains of nearby Italy and southern Austria. Stopping each night at the dorms, rifugios, and huts (the names given by the respective countries to their mountaintop inns), we noticed the almost universal practice of using small rectangular tins, which were used to transport such foods as luncheon meats, breads, crackers, jam, etc. Husic promptly bought one and has used it extensively on his long hikes on the Trail. On our 1976 hike in the southern Appalachians, Hanlon came upon the ingenious idea of packing six well-buttered English muffins in a one-pound coffee tin with a plastic top. In a separate plastic egg container, he carried six hard-boiled eggs. That was lunch for six days. Margarine is better than butter for this purpose as it keeps much better before turning rancid.

For my 1990 thru-hike, I cooked up a half dozen eggs at almost every resupply point along the Trail. When it wasn't feasible for me to boil the eggs I would ask the lady of the B&B place or hostel where I was staying to perform the chore. With eggs and muffins plus (always) a plastic jar of peanut butter, I felt secure. Eggs are somewhat bland so I used a single condiment shaker containing salt, pepper, and curry powder. Use any condiment combination you can concoct. It adds much to the enjoyment of the meal.

How long do the eggs keep? Ray Baker, who hiked the entire Trail in 1964, would frequently purchase a dozen eggs at a time, and leave them in the original carton. He had no problems with spoilage. In June 1976, while hiking on the Laurel Ridge Trail in Pennsylvania, I too carried the six eggs and six muffins and ate the last of them eight days after the hike began—this was in hot, humid weather. Even fresh eggs keep without refrigeration much longer than generally supposed.

I can't leave the subject of eggs without passing on a method of keeping eggs fresh for incredible lengths of time without refrigeration. Here's how: immerse a fresh egg in boiling water for just five seconds—not five minutes but five seconds. It will then keep for weeks without refrigeration. When I first read of this little trick, it seemed hard to believe so I conducted my own test. On May 31, 1976, I put three fresh eggs in boiling water for five seconds. I then put them up in my attic, which is 10–15 degrees warmer than the other rooms in the house. On June 14, two weeks later, I fried one for breakfast. Just like a fresh egg. On June 28, I fried another one, which tasted just like a fresh egg but the yolk was somewhat flatter when first put into the griddle. On July 21, some seven weeks after the five-second boiling, I fried the last one. It too tasted just like a fresh egg, but the yolk appeared almost flat when put into the griddle. Eggs, which can be poached, soft-boiled, hard-boiled, fried, or scrambled, are high in protein, and, when you think of it, the hen that lays them is really most considerate in providing the hiker with a bio-degradable container in which the egg can be carried.

Another lunch staple you should NEVER be without—peanut butter. It's a marvelous all-purpose food. I have stopped at the Hot Springs Hikers' Hostel in North Carolina on a number of occasions since that 1970 hike, and on one occasion I witnessed a peanut butter episode that remains clearly in my mind. In one of the bedrooms there were four thru-hikers sitting on the floor in a compact circle. A large pail of peanut butter was positioned in the middle of the circle. Each hiker was armed with a tablespoon and they proceeded to dig in— restoring a calorie deficit from those many miles of hiking! William Buckley, the syndicated columnist, wrote a humorous article some years ago in which he extolled the virtues of peanut butter and in which he also described his own life-long love affair with peanut butter and jelly sandwiches.

And now for the explanation in regard to Citadel spread, Nonesuch Mincemeat, and Claxton fruitcake. All three of these might be considered to be pemmican. American Indians, frontiersmen, and Arctic explorers were known to rely on pemmican on long overland trips. Webster defines pemmican as lean, dried meat pounded into paste with fat and dried fruit and then pressed into cakes. Two of the three foods I describe contain no meat, but they certainly qualify on the other counts. The third, Nonesuch Mincemeat, qualifies on all counts. Consider first Citadel spread, a name rather jokingly given to a concoction devised by Bill and Beth Oscanyan, members of PATC, who live in northern Virginia near VA 7. When my nephew, Shannon Garvey, and I arrived at the Oscanyan residence on June 16, 1970, I had covered 880 miles from Springer Mountain. Within minutes we were treated to hot coffee and a generous chunk of Citadel spread fresh out of the refrigerator. The spread was delicious, and I was very seldom without it during the remaining 1,100 miles of my hike. I hastened to obtain the recipe from Beth Oscanyan; here it is as it appears in my diary for June 16:

CITADEL SPREAD

18 oz. jar Skippy Creamy Peanut Butter
2-4 oz. bacon grease (residue from 6-8 slices)
1/2 cup honey
2-4 cups granular powdered milk (Carnation)

Add milk and stir until mix gets crunchy. Put in pint plastic freezer containers. It will keep in refrigerator indefinitely; it keeps for at least three weeks unrefrigerated.

That's the recipe as given to me. I made the mix a number of times during the rest of the trip and made some alterations. I used any kind of peanut butter or powdered milk I could get. I love bacon grease, but sometimes I had to use vegetable oil. Also, I added to the mix such things as mixed nuts, dates, and raisins. I never did use it as a spread because I kept adding milk during the mixing process until I achieved a consistency as firm as soft fudge candy. I ate the Citadel spread at various meals and between meals. If I had hot coffee for breakfast, I would finish off my cereal breakfast with a chunk of the spread with more hot coffee. From northern Virginia to Mount Katahdin I gave little samples of this spread to many people. Almost invariably I was then asked to furnish the recipe, which I did. I recommend it highly.

Since the Citadel spread recipe first appeared in my book in 1971, I have received comments on it from many sources. One was from Beth Oscanyan, who concocted it. She wrote that peanut butter, while high in proteins, is not a complete protein, since it lacks some of the essential elements found in animal proteins. However, the addition of the powdered milk in the recipe overcomes the deficiency, so that the final product is indeed a complete protein.

A most interesting series of comments came from John Shores in a sequence of letters to his parents in January, 1973. Writing from Columbia, South America, where he was working in the national parks of that country, and living with and eating his meals with a Columbian family, the younger Shores related:

"Jan. 5: Going to bus to the park tomorrow. Plan to make some Citadel Spread to carry with me. . . . I'm off to buy some peanut butter, honey, and dry milk, plus a container for it.

"Jan. 12: I ate another mixture of Citadel Spread, almost. I may mix up some more so that we can eat some in Cali this weekend. I really enjoy nibbling, which is probably indicative of my slightly undernourishing diet. But eight tablespoons of peanut butter are supposed to supply protein necessary for one day (two servings of four tablespoons each, or two servings of two eggs).

"Jan. 17: What scares me about making Citadel Spread is that I can eat all 8 oz. at a sitting, without looking up once. Something about mild forms of starvation that is disturbing. It's so slow I can't get fired up enough to do much about it except watch. I mean this can't really be happening to me! I have Citadel Spread on hand not to build my weight up, but to maintain it!"

And now the Claxton fruitcake, made by Claxton Bakeries of Claxton, Georgia, 30417. These cakes are individually wrapped, and measure eight inches long by approximately two inches square. It is sold in three-pound boxes (each box containing three one pound cakes), and can be mailed anywhere. I mailed Claxton Bakeries a check and informed them where I wanted box number two sent, and later where I wanted box number three sent, etc. At each point, the box was waiting for me. Well, almost. I arrived at Glencliffe, New Hampshire, at 8:20 A.M. on August 15, 1970, expecting to find a three-pound package of Claxton fruitcake at the post office. No such luck. But my disappointment was short lived. Five minutes later, a mail truck arrived; the postmistress promptly handed me my precious fruitcake. This fruitcake is easy to pack, keeps well, and is delicious to eat. What more could one ask? It contains flour, raisins, cherries, pecans, shortenings, and pineapple, among other things.

On my 1990 hike I had it easy. Van Hill, a member of the Georgia Club, wishing to participate in my hike, made arrangements with Claxton Bakery. They shipped Van a five-pound package, and he mailed me a pound at a time as I would request by postcard. It was much appreciated. Long after I finished my hike in 1990, one of the one-pound packages was forwarded to me from a post office somewhere along the Trail. And to be certain I did not lose my taste for this unusual cake, Van Hill personally delivered a two-pound package of the cakes to me at my home in 1991!

While working on my book, I wrote to Claxton Bakery to inquire about current prices. The most interesting reply is dated August 4, 1992, from Albert Parker, president of Claxton Bakery:

"Dear Mr. Garvey: Your card arrived this week and it was good to hear from you. Baking isn't as strenuous as hiking . . . so at 76 years old I am still at it! We haven't received our new fall literature from the printer, so I have marked new prices on an old form and enclosed it in this letter. Would you believe we still occasionally hear from folks that have just read your book in anticipation of hiking the Appalachian Trail. I'm sure folks will be looking forward to your revised book. My wish for you is to enjoy many more happy and useful years. Sincerely . . . Albert Parker."

Two days after I received the letter, a box arrived from Claxton containing three one-pound fruitcakes! I already had Claxton fruitcake coming out of my ears, so I took the three-pound box to ATC headquarters in Harpers Ferry, placed the cakes and a cutting board in the reception room, and made them available to ATC employees and visiting hikers. Long live Claxton Bakery! Long live Albert Parker!

The prices were $10 for a two-pound box, $13 for a three-pound box in 1990. State your preference—light or dark. My suggestion—order either the two-pound or three-pound box, keep one pound for immediate consumption, and mail the rest to yourself at a point farther up the Trail.

The mincemeat that I recommend for backpacking is sold in small dried cubes approximately $1^1/_2$ x $2^1/_2$ x $3^1/_2$ inches in size, but is also available in 9-ounce packets. The cubes and packets cost $3.40 in 1996. They are prepared and sold by Borden's and possibly by others, and are available in stores during Thanksgiving and Christmas; so, if you are planning a long-distance hike, you will need to stock up ahead of time. Each cube when cooked in water makes enough filling for an eight-inch pie. This give you an idea of how much food is concentrated in that little cube. I nibbled on the cubes occasionally for daytime snacks. At the evening meal, I would cook up part of one cube and use it as a sauce over cooked rice.

A word of warning on the mincemeat cubes. Don't go overboard on them, as did one young hiker who had read my description of their food value. He bought a large supply of them, feeling that he could get by on the mincemeat and nothing else. In a very short time he became heartily sick of them and wound up giving them away to fellow hikers.

And now to dinners. My evening meal was my most enjoyable meal, as you might expect. I tried to arrive at a trailside shelter about three hours before darkness was due to set in. This would give me about one hour to make my shelter inspection and to complete my paperwork for the day. I would then have about two hours to gather firewood, prepare my evening meal, clean dishes, shave, and bathe.

Occasionally my routine upon reaching camp varied. If mealtime was a good two hours away, I might have heated up a pot of water and enjoyed a cup of bouillon or some other light pick-me-up before my shelter inspection and paperwork. A second variation was to stop at the shelter at about 4 P.M., promptly cook the evening meal, then begin hiking again during the cooler part of the day. I used that routine to permit me to watch a sunset or sunrise from the top of the ridge, to sleep in a cooler spot, to seek solitude away from an already crowded shelter, or simply to get an earlier start the next day to reach a particular destination.

What dinner dishes are available to the backpacker traversing the entire Trail or large segments of it? If you are using the dehydrated foods, there is almost no limit to the variety of vegetable, meat, and dessert dishes available. But since I followed the grocery store method, I list only those dishes made from ingredients generally available from such stores.

Before I begin listing these foods and giving recipes, I must confess that I did eat some dehydrated foods during my hike. Several times, fellow hikers pressed upon me a package of their favorite dehydrated or freeze-dried foods with the request that I "give it a try."

During the first week of my 1970 hike, at the Addis Gap shelter in northern Georgia, I found a bonanza—six packages of freeze-dried food, each carrying a price tag of $1.55 and containing portions for two people. This meant 12 dinners, two of chili con carne, 10 of chicken and rice. I should have been content to take one or two packages and leave the rest. But you become possessive about food when you are on a long hike of this nature, and dependent upon the food you have in your pack. Accordingly, I took all six packages and alternated those freeze-dried dinners with my more conventional ones for the next several weeks. Many a time, as I lugged those rather hefty packages of freeze-dried foods up and down the mountains of Georgia, North Carolina, Tennessee, and Virginia, I had reason to reflect on my greediness in taking all six packages. I ate the last half-portion of the sixth package on May 16 at Niday shelter in the Jefferson National Forest in Virginia. That was five weeks and 500 miles after I had picked it up! The question arises, "How stupid can you get?" And the answer comes back, "Pretty stupid!"

And what did I cook in 1970? There were four items that I listed in my previous book, but two of them were Lipton products that are no longer available. The other two I heartily recommend follow, as well as two additional items:

1. Creamed tuna or creamed chicken over either rice or instant potatoes.
2. Appalachian Trail Mix.
3. Betty Crocker Tuna Helper and Betty Crocker Chicken Helper.

I had tried these dishes on hikes prior to my 1970 thru-hike, but without much success. But before I began my thru-hike in April, my wife gave me some extra tutoring, which paid handsome dividends. The creamed tuna and creamed chicken became my old reliable standbys. I never tired of either one. Both of these dishes are inexpensive, nourishing, and delicious.

CREAMED TUNA OR CHICKEN

When I could get them, I bought the small three-ounce cans of tuna and chicken. At many stores, only the larger six-ounce cans were available, so I bought them. For rice, I preferred Uncle Ben's Five Minute Rice, but I used any of the quick-cook rices if Uncle Ben's was not available. Usually, I used the two-pot method, cooking the rice in one pot and all other ingredients in the other. When time was short, I cooked everything in one pot.

Two-pot method

Light up your stove or have a fire going with enough wood beside it for your entire evening meal. Nearby (hopefully on a table), put all the items you will need for the meal: a can of tuna, rice, cooking oil, seasonings, etc. In one sauce-pan (use pans of three- or four-cup capacity), pour enough water to cook the amount of rice you plan to use. Add margarine or vegetable oil plus salt. Measure out the proper amount of rice and put it to one side. All the proportions are on the rice box cover. Put the saucepan on the fire so water begins to heat.

Now let's proceed to the other saucepan and the remaining ingredients. Using a can opener, cut all around the top of the tuna can except for one inch. Then, using the top of the can as a squeezer and using both hands, squeeze out all excess tuna oil into the second saucepan. Then add one tablespoon vegetable oil or margarine, followed by one-quarter cup of water, one tablespoon of flour, and three tablespoons of dried milk. Put all these ingredients into the second saucepan, put it over the fire and stir vigorously. Bring the contents slowly to a light boil, stirring frequently. Keep an eye on saucepan number one, so that the rice doesn't stick or burn.

Back to pan number two. Keep this pan over low heat and stir until you have a thick sauce. If it's too thin, add more flour. If it's too thick, add more water. You can't lose on this dish. When you have it the way you want it, spoon in the tuna chunks from the can and work them into the sauce. Then remove both pans from the fire and pour the cream sauce and tuna chunks over the rice. It will be too hot to eat immediately, so you will have a few precious minutes to immediately rinse out pan number two and fill it with water for your beverage or dishwater.

So far, I've said nothing about the seasoning for the sauce. At the time you begin making the sauce in pan number two, add salt, pepper, basil leaves, and oregano, in any combination you please. After you have mixed in the tuna chunks, taste the concoction and add more of any spice you think is needed. I suggest you practice making this dish at home until you get the process letter-perfect.

One-pot method

From a taste standpoint, the end result is not as good as the two pot method, but you dirty only one cooking utensil. Use the same ingredients. Proceed to make the cream sauce first; when it has cooked slowly for a minute or two, you simply add the tuna and rice and additional water for the amount of rice you have measured out. Bring to a boil and simmer slowly until the rice is tender. It's as simple as that.

For simplicity, I have furnished directions only for tuna and rice. Follow the same directions for canned chicken. Occasionally, you will desire to use instant potato mix instead of rice. Use the two-pot method and pour the cream sauce and tuna chunks (or chicken) over the potatoes.

In the preceding paragraphs, I have explained how to make cream sauce starting from scratch. Here is a quicker way to make the sauce. Squeeze the oil out of the tuna can into a saucepan. Add one packet of instant cream of mushroom soup. Add about one-quarter cup water—hot or cold. Stir and heat over fire. As mixture thickens, keep adding water until you have a thick cream sauce. One packet of instant soup makes enough cream sauce for one six-and-a-half-ounce can of tuna.

APPALACHIAN TRAIL MIX

This is a terrific trail food. I became acquainted with it in 1970 while hiking through Vermont with three young hikers, one of them Craig Bumgarner. Craig had eaten at the home of some friends a week before his brief hike and had become captivated with a one-pot meal he had been served. He promptly obtained the recipe and the ingredients. He brought about five pounds of the mix on his hike, and cooked it almost every evening, sharing it with us occasionally. During a break in my 1970 hike, I purchased four pounds of the mix—two pounds of short grain whole rice, one pound each of lentils and barley. The stuff keeps forever. The one drawback to this dish is that it takes one hour of cooking over a slow fire. But does it? A much-traveled hiker from Waco, Texas, Ms. Emma Parrish, writing to me in 1991, said that she and a friend used the Appalachian Trail Mix frequently and "at noon, we would stop and boil water, put the Appalachian Trail Mix and water in a wide-mouth plastic water bottle, put it in the middle of the pack, and by evening with just a little cooking it was ready to eat. What a treat!"

On April 25, 1990, my friends and I ate our evening meal at the renowned dining room of the Nantahala Outdoor Center in Wesser, North Carolina. Our main dish was an item called Sherpa Rice. It was basically the Appalachian Trail Mix plus some excellent seasoning and with cheddar cheese and small sausages added. Here's the recipe without the cheese and sausage:

Mix two parts short grain whole rice to one part lentils and one part barley. Mix two cups water to one cup of the mix. Add seasoning. Cook one hour over low heat in a covered container.

Before writing about my most successful experience with the Appalachian Trail Mix, let me discourse a bit on one of its principle ingredients, short grain whole rice. During the first week of my 1970 hike, down in Georgia, I met by chance a young college student, and I hiked with him almost a week. He had embraced an Eastern religious diet that dictated he exist on a diet composed chiefly of short grain whole rice, one-half cup each day. Occasionally, at lunch time, he would cook up a small batch of buckwheat groats. During the last two or three days of our hike together, he accepted some raisins from me to supplement that rather uninteresting rice diet, but he accepted nothing else. I admired him for his self discipline, and I listened carefully to his discourses on the value of the short grain whole rice diet. This young man was carrying a 15 pound sack of rice. At the rate of a half-cup each day, he had enough food for 75 days, or 2¹/₂ months. It seems doubtful if any one will ever try such a feat, but it makes for impressive speculation.

At the time the young man left me, he had been on the rice diet for nine days. He appeared to be in excellent health but had lost considerable weight. He had not had a bowel movement in those entire nine days. Apparently his body was absorbing all of the little amount of food he was eating.

Frankly I was impressed with the short grain whole rice idea, not as a steady diet but as the principal part of an occasional main meal. Even though I carried some of the rice with me for several hundred miles, I never did use it during the first four months of my hike, primarily because of the long cooking time required. Whole rice (as distinguished from the polished partially cooked rice) requires a solid hour of simmering over low heat in a tightly covered container.

One other story on the short grain whole rice, with which I was captivated when I first read it. During the Russo-Japanese War of 1906, the officer corps in the Japanese navy became afflicted with a devastating disease called scurvy. It is caused by a lack of Vitamin C in the diet. But why just the officer corps? Why were not the able seamen of the navy likewise affected? Because the poor seamen were restricted to the brown short grain whole rice, while the more privileged officer corps ate the polished white rice from which the Vitamin C had been removed!

In 1970, I had set an easy 10-day schedule for myself for the 100-plus miles from Monson, Maine, to Katahdin. I arrived at each of the shelters around 2 or 3 P.M. Great. I should have done more such scheduling in 1990. On the 1970, hike I arrived at the Potaywadjo Spring shelter in northern Maine on October 2, at 2:45 P.M., found plenty of firewood, and placed the following ingredients into the only large cooking pot I had:

1 1/2 cups A.T. Mix (all I had left)
1 pkg. dehydrated diced potatoes
1 pkg. dehydrated green beans
2 Tbl. Buttery Flavor Oil
6 1/2 ounces canned flaked tuna
4 cups water

For seasoning, I added salt and pepper plus all of the basil leaves and krauterbutter I had left. I cooked this for one hour at low heat over a "V" type fire. I had no cover for my large cooking pot, but I fitted a piece of aluminum foil over the pot. This served very creditably. When it finished cooking, I had almost two quarts of tender, well-seasoned mix. I ate more than half of it for my evening meal and finished the rest the following evening. The Appalachian Trail Mix cost about $1.10 in 1970, $4.71 in 1988, and $5.50 per pound in 1992. The inflation is obvious. Each pound provides 2¹/₃ cups of the mix.

One reader, Sandra Koojer, was captivated by the Appalachian Trail Mix recipe and began doing some experimenting using the basic Mix but adding other things. She came up with three additional recipes which she named: (1) Herbed Tomato Blend, (2) Mushroom Curry In-The-Pines, and (3) Syrian Salad. A description of the basic mix and the additional dishes was published in the *Mother Earth News,* Issue No. 570.

A FEW OTHER EASY MEALS

Here are two more dishes that provide a tasty meal—Betty Crocker Tuna Helper with Cheesy Noodles and Betty Crocker Chicken Helper. Both of these are very practical for backpackers because you can readily buy the canned tuna or canned chicken. The directions provide for a 10-inch skillet, but backpackers don't carry 10-inch skillets. Not to worry. Use a saucepan. The recipe also calls for a small amount of milk. If you have it, use it. Otherwise just use a bit more water. The recipe for the full package provides five servings. A hungry backpacker could cut the recipe in half and get a full meal. Add any of your own seasonings. I have used this on a number of occasions. Highly recommended.

And now to the Lipton pastas which I observed in such quantities on my 1990 hike. I heard a radio discourse recently in which a man groused about the term, pasta. "All I hear these days is pasta. What happened to macaroni and noodles?" Good question. Macaroni and noodles are still with us, but the "in" word is now "pasta." Another of life's whims. In the course of writing this chapter of the book, I visited our local supermarket. Lipton does have an imposing array of pastas—beef, chicken, parmesan, stroganoff, Romanoff, and Alfredo, to name six. They vary in weight from 4 to 4.5 ounces and cost about $1.35 per package in 1992. Each package makes about two servings. While backpacking, one could make a huge meal from one package or an average meal with a bit left over for breakfast. Whenever possible, I added a can of tuna or chicken to the recipe.

And, as a final pasta, I switch to the Trail standby, the Kraft Macaroni and Cheese dinner. This is a favorite among backpackers and has been a favorite within the Garvey family for many years, primarily as the key component of a macaroni, cheese, and tuna casserole dish. On the Trail it is eaten as is, with a can of tuna added if available. One 7¹/₄-ounce package makes four servings which means that a hungry backpacker can get two generous meals from it.

Chuck Young, of Warrenton, Virginia, who works frequently as a volunteer at ATC headquarters in Harpers Ferry, tells of the two young ladies who visited ATC while Chuck was working there. They expressed a need to find a place where they could get cleaned up and get a good meal. Chuck took them to his home, where it developed that the two ladies had existed on macaroni and cheese dinners every night on the Trail from Georgia to Harpers Ferry! Mrs. Young cooked them a good, non-macaroni and cheese dinner, after which Chuck took them to a supermarket where they bought food for the next six days of hiking. And what did they buy for their dinner? You guessed it, six more packages of macaroni and cheese!

For all of the pasta dishes there is one basic rule to remember—bring the water to the boiling point before adding the pasta!

The above is not intended to be an exhaustive treatise on evening meal dishes, but merely on the ones I have used most frequently and know to be good. I have already mentioned two of the desserts I used frequently, namely Claxton fruit-cake and Citadel spread. My most frequent dessert for my evening meal, however, was instant pudding. My favorite brand was Royal, with A&P brand a close second. Each package of Royal pudding weighs $4^1/_2$ ounces and makes $4^1/_2$-cup servings. For Trail hikers, it would be more accurate to say that each package makes two meal-size servings.

At each point where I purchased groceries, it was my practice to retire to my motel room, to a booth in a nearby restaurant, or to the front porch of the grocery store and repackage my groceries. For the instant puddings, this meant opening each package and pouring the contents into two plastic bags. Into each plastic bag I added $^1/_3$ cup of powdered milk. I secured the top of each bag with a twist tie and put all the bags into a large plastic bag. Upon reaching my shelter each afternoon, one of the first orders of business was to make the instant pudding. For this I used a one-pint plastic shaker. Into the shaker I poured one cup of water and then poured in the contents of one of the plastic pudding sacks. I would shake vigorously for perhaps 60 seconds and then put it aside. My dessert would be ready for me an hour or so later when I had finished my main dish.

Since I have already alluded to some of the spices such as salt, pepper, etc., this may be a good time to discuss the subject of condiments. In the earlier part of this chapter, we read what the English hikers of the 19th century thought about condiments, that is, no salt, spiceries, or seasonings of any kind except vinegar. Let's dismiss that philosophy as a bad dream. Writing about a hundred years later, George W. Sears, under the pen name Nessmuk, wrote his famous book, *Woodcraft*. Nessmuk advised his readers to carry a single container of spice, including both fine white salt and white pepper, mixed at a ratio of 10 parts salt to one part pepper. Not bad advice, not bad at all, even in this day and age. Nessmuk further advised, rather emphatically, not to carry any of the other numerous condiments such as oregano, thyme, etc.

Now let's consider what a more "recent" expert on condiments advises. In the January 1956 issue of *Appalachian Trailway News* appears the excellent article "Gormandize the Trail," by Ellen H. Connelly, an experienced nutritionist. Miss Connelly strongly recommended the addition of a few spices to your pack so that a little change and adventure can be achieved in your trail cooking. I quote a few sentences from that article: "Granting that some things can't be improved on—fresh spring water, the first cup of morning coffee, wild strawberries—nearly everything else you cook on the trail can be given new and different flavor with the addition of a bit of herb and spice. The wonderful thing about herbs and spices is that they pack so much flavor into so little bulky, weighable matter. A little of them goes a long way." And later in the article, "You don't need to take a wide selection; pick the three or four that will do the most for your cooking, and plan to alternate them."

I am a strong advocate of the Connelly philosophy. When I began my hike in 1970, I was carrying salt, pepper, sugar, and cinnamon. Six weeks later, on May 22, near the James River in Virginia, I was joined by two hiking companions from the Washington, D.C., area—Gus Crews and Charlie Burroughs. If Ellen Connelly was enthusiastic about the use of spices, Charlie Burroughs was even more so. During each of three days he hiked with me, he gave me pep talks on the use of his favorite herbs and spices, concluding each talk with "and it really doesn't weigh anything!"

I was a receptive listener. On May 25, I left the Trail and returned home for a 12-day break. When I resumed hiking on June 6, I was carrying three additional items in my condiment bag: oregano, basil leaves, and instant minced onion. Shortly thereafter, at one of the post office stops along the Trail, I received a letter from Burroughs containing two things: typewritten instructions on the use of his favorite herbs and spices plus a small packet of one such herb, Krauterbutter. (Krauterbutter—an herb-butter seasoning made by McCormick & Co.). It seems doubtful if any of the end-to-end hikers of the Trail could boast such a wide variety of condiments. And did I regret carrying this wide assortment? Not at all. They made my meals ever so much more enjoyable; before reaching Katahdin, I had used up all of the condiments and had to resupply for a few of them.

I urge you to give some of these spices a try. Try them out at home or on short backpacking trips. You may decide that the simple salt and pepper condiments are all you need. Or you may be one of those (like me) for whom cooking and eating is one of the real pleasures to be enjoyed on a long traverse of the Trail. If so, you will probably wind up carrying a few of these extra herbs and spices.

One other item I will mention at this time, although it is not a condiment, is butter or margarine. Backpacking these items in their solid form is a messy proposition. I carried liquid shortening in a one-pint plastic bottle inside a plastic sack and secured it with a wire twist top—this to prevent unsightly grease stains on my Kelty pack. And what specific liquid shortening do I recommend? I started out using plain vegetable oil, any kind that was available. Near the end of my 1990 hike, and since then, I have used a very good product called Parkay Squeeze Spread made by Kraft. The spread is yellow as butter and the plastic container the same color . . . all designed to make you think butter. Each container holds 16 ounces of spread. It keeps for months even in warm weather and appears to be leakproof. It has a retractable pouring spout.

Now that we have considered things to eat, let's consider cooking utensils. This seems to be an appropriate place to quote an article that appeared in the July-September 1970, issue of the Bulletin issued by the PATC of Washington, D.C. This article seems to have been reprinted from a number of previously issued outdoor publications. It was originally written in 1966 by a Mr. John Echo. I quote it because it does contains some good ides for simple cooking and even simpler ideas for pot cleaning the cooking utensils. If you think the techniques advanced by the author take you back too far toward the Stone Age, you may settle for some modifications I will suggest later in this chapter. Here is the article, entitled "Courageous Cookery" or "Why Not Enjoy Backpacking?"

Courageous Cookery or Why Not Enjoy Backpacking?

By John Echo

Once the convert backpacker has accepted the subtle gustatory nuances associated with sustained operations beyond the chrome, he should try the advantages of ultra fringe living so that he will realize what he is paying for his nested pots and pretty pans carried so diligently and brought home so dirty after every "wilderness experience."

The following system works. It is dependable and functional. It works on the big rock. It even works when the weather has gone to hell, you are wet and cold, and the wind is blowing a Dirty Degan right down the back of your hairy neck. It is not for the timid. It consists of a six-inch sauce pan, a Primus stove, a plastic cup, and a soup spoon. If you insist on the metal cup, you must never fail to mutter, "I'm having fun, I'm having fun," every time you burn your lips and spill the soup in your sleeping bag.

Breakfast: Instant wheat cereal—sugar and powdered milk added— ready 2 minutes after water boils. Eat from the pot. Do not wash the pot. Add water, boil, add powdered eggs and ham. You'll never taste the cereal anyway. In 3 minutes, eat eggs. Do not wash pot. Add water or snow and boil for tea. Do not wash pot. Most of the residue eggs will come off in the tea water. Make it strong and add sugar. Tastes like tea. Do not wash pot. With reasonable technique, it should be clean. Pack pot in rucksack and enjoy last cup of tea while others are dirtying entire series of nested cookware. Enjoy sunrise or take morning stroll while others are washing, in cold water, entire series of nested cookware.

Lunch: Boil pot of tea. Have snack of rye bread, cheese, and dried beef. Continue journey in 10 minutes if necessary.

Dinner: Boil pot of water. Add Wyler's dry vegetable soup and a beef bar. Eat from pot. Do not wash pot. Add water and make potatoes from dry potato powder. Add dry gravy mix to taste. Eat potatoes and gravy from pot. Do not wash pot. Add water and boil for tea. Fortuitous fish or meat can be cooked easily. You do not need oil or fat. Put half-inch water in pot. Add clean, salted fish. Do not let water boil away. Eat from pot when done. Process can be repeated very rapidly. Fish can even be browned somewhat by a masterful hand. Do not change the menu. Variation only recedes from the optimum. Beginners may be allowed to wash the pot once a day for three consecutive days only. It is obvious that burning or sticking food destroys the beauty of this technique.

If you insist on carrying a heavy pack, make up the weight you save with extra food. Stay three days longer.

Reprinted from the *Rambler* (Wasatch Mountain Club, Salt Lake City, Utah), which reprinted from the *I.A.C. News,* Idaho Falls, Idaho, which reprinted from the 1966 *Peaks and Trails.*

I love such fried dishes as bacon and eggs, pancakes, and hamburgers, but when I began my Trail hike in Georgia, I did not carry a frying pan. There is a definite place for such foods in some types of camping, but they are not practical dishes for backpacking. Instead I carried two small, nested aluminum sauce-pans. These saucepans were five inches in diameter and about $2^1/2$ inches deep. One cover served both pans. The total weight was seven ounces. A light-weight pot holder weighed another ounce. Cleaning pads and a plastic bag to carry them in added one more ounce. Already I had violated some of the "Courageous Cookery" concepts. I had also violated another one: I cleaned the pots—not after each dish, but after each meal. But, more importantly, I never, not even once during the whole trip, cleaned the outside of the pots—just the inside.

I fully intend to wash the outside of those pots someday; but even as I re-write this chapter, some 24 years later, I have not done so. I used to give occasional talks on my 2,000 mile hike. During those talks I demonstrated the equipment I used. It was important that those pots had that blackened look that comes only from repeated use over countless cooking fires.

In addition to the two cooking pots, I started out with two stainless steel cups and two stainless steel soup spoons. Although I did use them, a single cup and spoon would have been sufficient. Contrary to the comments of the Courageous Cookery author, the metal cups gave me no trouble in drinking hot liquids. The cups I had were made for the Sierra Club, and I could drink hot liquids from them just as safely as from plastic or china cups.

At the 700-mile mark of my hike, I changed my cooking equipment. I kept the two saucepans, got rid of one steel cup, and added a larger aluminum cooking pot, which weighed seven ounces and was $6^1/_2$ inches in diameter and $3^1/_2$ inches deep. It held seven cups. I had more weight, but I had more cooking capacity and a larger container in which to carry and heat water. I also exchanged my one-ounce pot holder for a sturdier one weighing three ounces. For the last 1,300 miles of my hike, my cooking equipment plus cup, spoon, and carrying sack weighed 20 ounces. The equipment I was carrying would have been sufficient for a two- or three-man party; it was a bit elaborate for a single hiker.

On my 1990 hike, I carried essentially the same equipment except that I eliminated the larger cooking pot in an effort to reduce weight. I made the decision reluctantly as it would, to some extent, eliminate the cooking of some of the one-pot meals.

On my 1970 hike, I carried no stove for the first 700 miles. I did carry a stove for the last 1,300 miles, but used it only occasionally at first. Up in Maine, where I experienced a number of cold, rainy days, I began to use the stove regularly to enjoy a hot breakfast. By 1990, because of the increasing number of hikers and the decreasing wood supply, the trend was almost entirely moving to gasoline stoves. I, too, carried a stove, but a tiny wood-burning one called a Sierra Zip Ztove. I ran into perhaps three or four others who were also using this little wood stove. It had a battery powered fan that produced total consumption of the one-inch to two-inch twigs I used for fuel. It had its limitations on those nights when I got into a shelter during the rain.

As indicated elsewhere in this book, on May 9, with the weather looking very ominous, I did break up and carry with me a supply of dry wood chips, which I used later in the Roaring Fork shelter while the rain fell steadily outside. And on another occasion in the Smoky Mountains National Park, during a pouring rain, I found enough wood inside the shelter to keep the little stove going for about 45 minutes. It provided hot beverages for some nine women who kept coming in from that driving rain. But there were a number of other nights when I enjoyed a hot meal through the courtesy of others who had gasoline stoves, whereas if I had been eating there by myself it would have been a cold meal.

The Swedish stoves—Optimus, Primus, Svea—dominated the small camping stove field for many years, but in more recent years, the Coleman Company of Wichita, Kansas, has produced some excellent lightweight stoves, mostly gasoline-fueled but also one that is multi-fueled. The Coleman stoves have two advantages over the Swedish stoves: (1) they require almost no priming time; (2) they simmer foods, whereas the Swedish stoves are really only efficient when operating at full power. The small outdoor stoves fascinate me, and I have a collection of over a dozen—alcohol, butane gas, gasoline, and wood burning.

We now approach the other part of Chapter 4—water. I had long rather dreaded the rewriting on this subject. On my 1970 hike, the rules were rather simple—one drank from a spring without any treatment, but drank from an open stream only after treating it. Treating it meant boiling it (the safest) or purifying it by adding iodine or other substances.

When I wrote the update of the *Appalachian Hiker* book in 1978, the situation had changed little. But in 1990 it was a new ball game. It seemed that every second or third backpacker was carrying a filter—a filter being a water bag with a filtering device to prevent bacteria or viruses from getting into the water bag. I had no such device, and I relied upon the two medicines my doctor had supplied me with—Lomotil and Pepto-bismol. He assured me that if I did become ill because of tainted water the combination of those two medicines would take care of the situation. As I related in an earlier chapter, I experienced a number of bowel problems, but never did have a case of diarrhea like the one on my 1970 hike. Nor did I pick up Giardia which can be incapacitating, and whose symptoms include stomach cramps, belching, gas, diarrhea, and exhaustion. I did use some of the Lomotil pills, plus one or two of the Pepto-bismol, but I did not use them in the manner prescribed. Had I done so I might have recovered more quickly. I did not add substances to the water I drank, but I did boil it occasionally as the situation seemed to demand.

The ATC carries a small brochure prepared by the National Park Service, entitled "Is the Water Safe?" and the *Appalachian Trailway News* has published a number of articles dealing with the treatment of water. One of the contributors on water treatment is Roland Muesser, who supplied and received questionnaires from 136 thru-hikers. I quote from a letter he wrote on the subject: ". . . And a real surprise, diarrhea and Giardia rates are the same for those who always purify their water as those who never do." I am relating to the reader the situation as it exists, but I do not feel competent to give advice on the subject.

5

Evaluating Equipment

In the next four chapters, I will discuss equipment needed on a long hike—that which I used and that which is available on the market today. But first, I want to make some general observations on evaluating backpacking equipment, before getting into detailed descriptions in the succeeding sections.

In addition to extensive hiking experience in the United States, several other opportunities have enabled me to test equipment. In December 1971, at about the same time that my first *Appalachian Hiker* was published, I began working on a part-time basis at Appalachian Outfitters of Oakton, Virginia, and I continued in that affiliation until 1982. (One of the last customers I waited on was a certain Newt Gingrich, who came in with his wife and two daughters. I told them about the Appalachian Trail and talked Newt into filling out an application to join the Potomac Appalachian Trail Club. His membership was for two years. He did not renew it!) This store specializes in equipment and supplies for backpackers, mountain climbers, cavers, canoeists, and cross-country skiers. My work permitted me to acquire firsthand knowledge of new equipment coming into the market and I received feedback from knowledgeable customers and fellow employees.

During the years 1972-74, I participated in five outdoor recreation exhibits sponsored by the U.S. Information Agency in Yugoslavia, in Moscow, in eastern Siberia of the former U.S.S.R., and in Hungary. In these exhibits, I demonstrated various backpacking and camping equipment. I concentrated on the erection of a backpacking tent and the cooking of freeze-dried foods, primarily because they proved to be attention-getters and crowd-pleasers. In one city alone (Irkutsk in eastern Siberia), during a $5^{1}/_{2}$-week period, I put up the backpacking tent 441 times, always within the three-minute period I had allotted myself, and cooked 174 casseroles of chunk chicken! (Yes, I can still eat chunk chicken.)

Those two trips to Yugoslavia turned out to be forerunners of six more trips from 1974 to 1989 that I took at my own expense, during which I led small groups of hikers (14 in 1983, 12 in 1986) on hiking trips over the beautiful mountains of Slovenia and Croatia in what is now a horribly war-torn country.

Over the years I have written many articles on backpacking equipment. One such article appeared in the *Shoppers Guide,* the 1974 Yearbook of the Department of Agriculture. The article was reprinted by the tens of thousands and distributed for years by the Consumer Information Center of Pueblo, Colorado. Almost everything I wrote in that concise article more than 20 years ago is pertinent today, except, of course, for the prices. I have now had many years of using, selling, testing, demonstrating, and writing about backpacking equipment.

Although I have formed some very definite opinions on many aspects of shopping for such equipment, the longer I have been involved in equipment evaluation, the less opinionated I have become about specific brands and models. I have learned that there is very keen competition in the manufacture and distribution of such equipment, and there are a variety of hiking boots, packs, sleeping bags, tents, and stoves that will do the job for you. If I had any doubts on this score, they were removed in 1976 when I got in touch with 47 members of the 2,000-Miler class that year. I asked each of them to fill out a questionnaire for me on various aspects of their trip, including the make and model of the equipment used. Near the end of the questionnaire appeared this question:

"Regardless of what equipment you actually used on your 1976 hike of the AT, if you were to completely re-outfit yourself for another complete hike of the AT, what equipment would you buy (list make and model)?"

Most 2,000-Milers take from 120 to 150 days to complete the hike, and they have ample opportunity on the trail itself and during evenings spent at shelters to discuss and observe the performance of various makes of equipment. I had half suspected that, by consensus, one type of backpack might have emerged as the best pack; one particular type of tent might have emerged as the best tent, etc. Not so! Almost without exception, these long-distance hikers indicated that if they were to rehike the entire Trail, they would purchase exactly the same make and model of hiking boot, tent, stove, or whatever. It made little difference as to what make or model was involved or how much or how little they had paid for it. The attitude seems to be that if a particular hiking boot or backpack has served them well for 2,000 miles, they would buy exactly that same boot or pack for another long hike. One develops a certain loyalty to a piece of equipment that performs well through both good and bad weather during a 2,000-mile hike. And in my own case, I have to be careful that my loyalty to certain pieces of equipment does not bias my judgement against other makes and models of equipment that perform equally well.

These days, endorsement of products by the prominent, and by the not-so-prominent, is a common type of sales pitch; the would-be purchaser should be extremely wary of these. If you are a potential purchaser of outdoor equipment, you would be wise to ignore the advertisements that appear in outdoor magazines. They tell you merely that the person making the endorsement has either (1) been paid hard cash to lend his prominent name to endorsing that particular product, or (2) been provided with free equipment and supplies for his group's expedition with the proviso that there be product endorsements lauding the particular equipment that was furnished free. This way of financing a trip has been quite popular.

While still working at Appalachian Outfitters, I received a letter from two people in Colorado who were planning to hike the Trail the following year. They were looking for sponsors to provide them with free, lightweight hiking, backpacking, or camping equipment. In return, they would provide advertising or endorsement for Appalachian Outfitters in whatever form desired. The same letter was undoubtedly written to scores of other dealers and manufacturers.

The late Barry Bishop, of the National Geographic Society of Washington, D.C., is one of the few Americans to have climbed to the summit of Mt. Everest. He, and his wife Lila, at one time designed and produced high-quality expedition tents, and they were approached by groups seeking free tents for upcoming expeditions. On one occasion, they were approached by three different groups within a six-day period. Of this general practice, Bishop had this to say:

"Many groups think they can get free equipment but usually they are wasting valuable time in their attempts to do so. Their chances are about one in a thousand. Expeditions to far off places or long distance hikes are no longer extraordinary events but have become commonplace. Furthermore no one gets something for nothing. If equipment and supplies are accepted, then the enjoyment factor of the trip is lessened . . . there are pictures that must be taken, articles that must be written, or endorsements that must be made. But the person who goes on an expedition with responsibility to no one reaps the full measure of the enjoyment factor. He is beholden to no one."

So much for product endorsement. What about equipment evaluations? They are certainly better than product endorsements, but the evaluations have pitfalls too. How many times have you heard radio or TV commercials in which it is said that "a nationally recognized testing agency found the XYZ aspirin (or whatever) to be 44 percent faster acting than any other brand tested!" *What* testing agency? How many brands were tested? In what publication were the results of the tests published? On the other hand, if it is reported that the National Bureau of Standards has made laboratory tests to determine the relative efficiency of goose and duck down as compared to certain synthetic fills, it becomes a different matter, because the Bureau of Standards is a U.S. Government-financed testing agency whose testing would be thorough and impartial.

On balance, I'm skeptical of evaluations made by magazines, especially if any of the products tested are made by corporations that regularly advertise in that particular magazine. There is always the suspicion that the magazine would be very reluctant to downgrade any product tested if such downgrading would result in the loss of regular advertising.

One publication that earned tremendous respect was the *Equipment Bulletin* published by the PATC. The Equipment Committee was composed of a number of very knowledgeable outdoorsmen with a preponderance of rock climbers. They really did a thorough job of checking out equipment, evaluating the results, and publishing the information in the easy-to-understand *Bulletin*.

Unfortunately, the *Bulletin* was discontinued years ago because of the tremendous increase in the amount of equipment to be tested and the time limitations of the volunteers who did the testing. But it is that type of evaluation (non-profit organization, no advertising) that I would be much more inclined to accept.

A magazine that *is* still in business, one that has always seemed impartial, is *Consumer Reports.* I like the way the tests are made—products are bought in the marketplace so no free samples are submitted by the manufacturer. After the tests are made and the results analyzed, the products are resold. The magazine does not accept advertising. Unfortunately, this magazine does not tackle backpacking equipment. Perhaps one day it will.

Even though the evaluations of magazines may be suspect, feel free to use these as a starting point. Look at what equipment is new on the market (or which has staying power), and choose some options that might suit you. Instead of investing a lot of money, try renting the equipment from a store. Valuable information can also be obtained simply by going out on weekend hikes with any of the various hiking groups in metropolitan areas. Experienced hikers are only too glad to discourse on their equipment and to disclose where they bought it. Another method is to look in the yellow pages of the telephone book under Camping Equipment listings. You will know you're in the right place if you see yellow page ads that feature backpacks with names like Kelty, Camp Trails, or Jansport; hiking boots with names like Vasque, Danner, Fabiano, or Raichle; and sleeping bags with names like Marmot, Moonstone, Sierra Design, or North Face.

Visit one of the outdoor stores listed and talk to the salespeople. You will know in a short time if the salesperson is merely a purveyor of merchandise or if he or she is an outdoors person who has actually used the types of equipment you wish to buy. If you do not have access to an outdoor store you must resort to catalogs, of which there are many.

There are a number of books that discuss backpacking equipment in general. A good reference book for equipment is *The Appalachian Trail Backpacker* by

Victoria and Frank Logue, published by Menasha Ridge Press. The Logues not only discuss the use and merits of different kinds of equipment, they also list and sometimes offer comparative descriptions of the various brands currently available.

Another book, Dan Bruce's *The Thru-hiker's Planning Guide,* published by the Center for Appalachian Trail Studies, conveys much practical information about equipment, footwear, clothing, etc., and also contains a product guide section that lists currently popular brands and models of gear. Dan has also designed a homepage (http://trailplace.com) full of material that is interesting and useful to the long-distance hiker. His plans are to further develop his homepage into an online equipment evaluation guide based on surveys of the 1997 thru-hikers. This information will be constantly updated and will be linked to other sources of information such as magazines and manufacturers.

The authors of both of these books have hiked the entire Trail one or more times, and they are very knowledgeable about equipment.

The author giving a haircut to fellow hiker Gary Eanes at Rusty's Hard Time Hollow.

6

The Pack

Sometime around the year 1950, a carpenter and backpacker in southern California by the name of Dick Kelty began experimenting with the design and construction of a better backpack. In the 1950s, and perhaps for a hundred or more years before, packs for expeditions or long-term hikes were made from heavy canvas with wide web shoulder straps. All of the material to be taken on the trip was placed in one large opening, which I refer to as "the hold," as in the hold of a ship. The pack cover would then be brought over the opening and buckled into place. All of the weight was carried on the shoulders and the pack clung tight to the back, making for instant perspiration.

Kelty devised an aluminum frame with a gentle curve to follow the slope of the body's back. The frame was constructed in such a manner as to permit the passage of air between the body and the pack. Kelty also provided a hip belt so that much of the pack weight would rest upon the sturdy hip bone instead of the more fragile shoulder bones. His packs, when placed on the market, were an instant success; the general design has been copied by many other pack makers. When the Kelty literature first appeared, I was greatly impressed and ordered one without ever actually having seen one. It replaced one of the heavy canvas packs described above.

My first Kelty pack, called the A4, had three compartments plus two side pockets. I used mine on backpacking trips totaling about 700 miles, mostly on the Trail in Virginia, Maryland, and Pennsylvania. It was a tremendous improvement over my previous pack. I used it so extensively that I wore out and replaced one set of shoulder straps, as well as the waist strap. I added two large pockets on the back of the pack. I started my 1970 Appalachian Trail hike with that 16-year-old Kelty.

As if age were not enough, I inflicted an almost mortal wound to that faithful pack during the automobile trip down to Georgia to begin the hike. While traveling on Interstate 95 near Richmond, Virginia, my luggage rack tore loose from my car. When it did, my fully-loaded Kelty pack also came loose and splattered over the pavement at 60 miles per hour. The fabric was torn here and there, but the metal frame was undamaged, and the pack served me well for much of the trip.

As I neared the 1,000-mile mark in my hike, I noticed that the shoulder straps were wearing badly. I was also having trouble finding enough space for supplies, so I ordered by phone the big BB5 expedition-size Kelty pack and frame from Appalachian Outfitters in Oakton, Virginia.

Less than three days after I placed my order, the new pack and frame were waiting for me at the post office in Delaware Water Gap, Pennsylvania. The new pack boasted almost 900 cubic inches of additional space (3,680 cubic inches total capacity), and weighed 63 ounces (3.94 pounds). It had no interior compartments, which meant that it was necessary for me to buy additional carrying bags of various colors and sizes. (I mailed my original 1954 pack back to Virginia, where it hung for many years like a revered Civil War relic on the walls of Appalachian Outfitters at Oakton, Virginia.)

I do not wish to convey the impression that Kelty is the only packframe available on the market. Far from it. It's just that it is the one with which I have had the most experience. The biggest chunk of the backpack market has been captured by Camp Trails, which makes a variety of packs and frames within a wide price range. Most of the Camp Trails frames will accommodate a number of different packs, and the literature provides information on possible combinations. The Jansport pack also has made significant inroads into the market, and in my 1992 survey I found that an internal pack frame, the Osprey, had become very popular. Other pack brands include Gregory, North Face, and Mountainsmith, among others.

It is an important decision as to what type of pack should be carried for a 2,000-mile hike. One has to choose not only the pack itself, but the selection of articles to be carried in it as well as a cover to be placed around it in rainy weather. Today, there are a variety of packframes and packbags on the market that are suitable, and durable enough, for an extended hike.

Except for hiking boots, there is no item of your equipment for which good fit is as important as the pack. The better packs come in small, medium, large, and extra large sizes. And there are devices provided with which each of these sizes can be adjusted a bit. In the fitting process, knowledgeable and helpful salespeople will insert weights in the pack so that the fitting can be done under more realistic conditions. Many items needed by the backpacker can be ordered by catalog, but hiking boots and the pack should, if at all possible, be fitted by an experienced salesperson.

Elsewhere in this book I describe the various items you may carry in your pack and their uses. Chapter 4 details food supplies, cooking equipment, and stoves. Chapter 7 treats sleeping equipment, ground cloths, mattresses, etc. How do you fit all this equipment and supplies in your pack? When you are on a long hike, it's important to keep the items you carry organized. This practice helps you keep track of your belongings and saves time when you are hunting for a specific item. The following paragraphs indicate what articles I carried in each part of the packbag:

Area 1 is the area I refer to as "the hold" because it is such a big area in relation to the other six areas. In this area, I carried eight sacks, each sack containing items similar or related to other items in that particular sack. To the extent possible, I used sacks of different colors so that I could readily identify and remove any needed item. The contents of each sack were as follows:

Sack 1. Extra clothes: underwear, socks, shirt, trousers, parka, my all-purpose deerskin mittens, pajamas, and (in cold weather) wool cap. Also included were my rain parka and rain chaps.

Sack 2. Condiments.

Sack 3. Food for dinners.

Sack 4. Food for breakfasts and lunches.

Sack 5. Cooking equipment, pot holder, cleaning pads.

Sack 6. Gasoline stove, eye dropper, alternate cover.

Sack 7. Toilet articles.

Sack 8. Miscellaneous: First aid kit, newspapers, towel paper, plastic sacks, litter bags, nylon cord, string, clothespins.

Loose Item 1. One quart aluminum gas container.

Loose Item 2. One pint shaker, which doubled as an extra canteen.

Area 2 is the large back pocket in which I carried guidebooks, maps, trip diary book, sewing kit, extra clevis pins, beer can opener, whistle, and two plastic envelopes containing stationery, pencils, stamps, address book, and postcards.

Area 3 is one of two upper side pockets. In this pocket I carried two plastic bottles plus an aerosol container of Off insect repellent. The two plastic bottles had a total capacity of about five cups. I used them for carrying water except for a few rare, occasions when I used them to carry table wine! The larger of the two plastic bottles was green in color, and its original white label was still very clear and prominent. The label read Liquid Car Wash, and whenever I took a copious drink from that container, eyebrows were raised and questions asked.

Area 4 is one of the two lower side pockets. In it I carried a rain cover for the pack, a tube of liquid soap, and a small flashlight.

Area 5 is the second of two upper side pockets. In it I carried a thermometer and a 14-ounce capacity plastic bottle containing liquid vegetable oil. The thermometer was a Taylor instrument with metal carrying case.

Area 6 is the second of two lower pockets. In it I carried a waterproof match case, candles, fire starters, and a small camera.

Ed's pack.

Area 7, at the bottom of the pack frame, was used to carry a three-pound sleeping bag, ground cloth, and a short, foam-pad mattress. All three were carried in a large stuffsack.

Area 8 was myself and the things I carried on my person—my pocketknife, compass, watch, and metal cup, etc.

The BB5 pack served me well for the remainder of my 1970 hike and for many short-term Trail hikes thereafter. It also accompanied me on three extended hikes in the rugged mountains of Croatia and Slovenia. For later trips to Yugoslavia, I used an internal frame pack that could be quickly converted from pack to traveling bag with handle.

When I began making plans for my 1990 hike of the Trail, there was no question as to what pack I would use. The BB5 pack with which I had finished my 1970 hike looked as though it had enough mileage left in it to go the route once more. Two of my friends made the not-too-gentle recommendation that I replace the Appalachian Trail patch. I had to concede that after twenty years of use and three overseas trips, the patch was beginning to look a bit ratty, so I did replace it.

Before leaving the Kelty pack entirely, I will share with you a 1992 letter regarding the BB5 Kelty pack's being used in Eastern Siberia.

Mr. Neil Sampson, Ex. Director
American Forestry Assoc.
1516 P St NW
Washington, D.C.

Dear Neil:

This is a follow up on my phone conversation with you on Wednesday, July 15, 1992, in which I made a request that the American Forestry Assoc. write a check for $100 payable to me to replace one written in 1974 payable to one Alexander A. Koshelev of Irkutsk in Eastern Siberia. I thought I was making a very routine request but from your general reaction I gathered that you had serious doubts as to my credibility if not even my sanity! After much explanation on my part and much laughter on the part of both of us you agreed to write the check if (1) I would return the 1974 check and (2) if I would write an explanation that you could print in American Forests for the enjoyment of AFA readers. Here's the story.

In September, 1973, I found myself in Irkutsk in Eastern Siberia after a four-day and night rail trip from Moscow on the Trans Siberian railway. At Irkutsk, I joined some 20 other Americans, many of them bi-lingual (Russian-American) participating in an Outdoor Recreation exhibit sponsored by the U.S. Information Agency. I had had a long career in hiking and backpacking, had hiked the entire Appalachian Trail in 1970, had written a popular book on the experience, and in 1973, I was president of the Potomac Appalachian Trail Club. All of these activities were factors leading to my selection to participate in the exhibit. On October 14, 1973, a week before the six-week exhibit was to close, the director of the exhibit permitted three of us from the exhibit to accompany two Russians on a hike into the Chersky Mountain range south of Lake Baikal, the famous body of water that comprises 20 percent of the world's fresh water! My American companions were James Torrence of the U.S. Forest Service, and Julie Bubul, one of the Russian-speaking American guides in the exhibit. Both of them were experienced outdoors people. The two Russians were Alexander Koshelev of the Siberian Power Institute and a young Russian woman by the name of Ludmila Timonova. This was mid-October, but in the mountains in which we were to hike, a heavy snow had already fallen. We had to ford the icy Sludyanka River on seven or eight occasions. The hike itself was exciting enough with the snow and the fording, in which both Alex and I suffered missteps with the ice cold water going up to our knees. We started a fire in the heavy snow and cooked a late breakfast. Later, an outdoor lunch beside a tent of a Russian work camp, and still later, the long trudge up the mountains in 9-degree weather to a station in a clearing named Cossack Meadow where we spent the night with two Russian weather observers. On our return the next day, we obtained a truck ride from the work camp all the way to Sludyanka where we boarded a local train that lumbered slowly over the Trans Siberian railway taking us back to Irkutsk. Torrence complained of illness on the train ride and during the following week, as the exhibit came to a close, his life hung by the slimmest of threads as he hovered between life and death. Finally, the Russian government permitted an Air Force cargo plane converted to a hospital to proceed from Frankfurt, Germany, all the way to eastern Siberia to evacuate Torrence and then continue east all the way to the Air Force hospital at Kyoto, Japan. Readers of the *American Forests* with long memories may recall the article that I co-authored with Alex Koshelev and which appeared with color pictures in the July 1974 issue of the magazine.

For that article, the AFA sent me two checks, each in the amount of $100—one for me and one for Alex. But what was I to do with Alex's check? Remember this was 1974, the U.S.S.R. had an iron-fisted Communist government, censorship of mail, the KGB, and the whole bit. I discreetly raised the question with Alex in a letter but he never referred to my letter in subsequent correspondence so I surmised that my letter had been intercepted. I concocted a very brilliant plan. A friend, Orville Crowder, a resident of Harpers Ferry, West Virginia, and well up in his years, was taking another of his around-the-world tours, which would take him to Irkutsk. I gave him forms from a Washington, D.C., bank which he would have Alex sign so I could establish a bank account for him. But alas, Crowder suffered a severe heart attack on the day of his scheduled flight and died shortly thereafter. So much for Plan B. My correspondence with Alex dwindled to a stop in 1983 and for 18 long years the check remained in my safe. Then I was electrified to see in the June, 1992, issue of the *National Geographic* an exciting story about Lake Baikal even showing the small city of Sludyanka from which our hike had begun. I promptly wrote to Alex, again told him about his check and requested his advice as to the disposition of the check. His reply was most interesting. Actually, I had gone on two hikes with Alex during my stay in Siberia and I had carried a Kelty backpack from the exhibit, very similar to the one I had used on my long hike of the Appalachian Trail in 1970. I noted that Alex was a great admirer of that pack and I had let him carry mine for considerable distances.

After I returned from Siberia in 1973, I purchased one such pack from Appalachian Outfitters where I worked part time after my retirement and sent it to Alex via an American who was participating in a later exhibit being held in Odessa near the Black Sea. Therefore, the pack would be mailed to Alex from within the country and hopefully would not be subjected to a customs search and the imposition of customs duties, which would approximate the value of the pack. That plan, unlike my Crowder plan, had worked and Alex received the pack. He informed me recently that he had carried tremendous weights in it, especially on some 30 expeditions crossing Lake Baikal in the ice and snow of winter; that the aluminum frame had cracked on several occasions, and that while welding jobs had provided temporary relief, he really needed a new Kelty aluminum frame. So, if AFA comes through with that check, I will again be faced with the problem of getting that pack frame to Alex.

But that's not all. Russia is now operating under a free economy. Alex and friends have organized a guide and travel enterprise and are looking for business. If you are intrigued with the idea of an air or rail trip to Irkutsk and the opportunity to hike in the Baikal mountain range, or cruise around the ports of call on the fabulous Lake Baikal, get in touch with:

Alexander Koshelev
P.O. Box 1241
Irkutsk 33
Russia 664033.

Don't call me. I'll have enough problems getting that Kelty pack frame to eastern Siberia!

Sincerely,
Edward B. Garvey
Enclosure . . . One check for $100

Oh yes . . . Jim Torrence. After two successful blood transfusions aboard the evacuation plane, he made a dramatic recovery and went on to become the Regional Forester at Portland, Oregon, before retiring.

PPS. My phone call to you was placed from Harpers Ferry. Upon arriving home in Falls Church, Virginia, I did, after a long search, find the check with a letter of transmittal from James Craig, former editor of *American Forests*. In a rare moment of foresight, I had written a note in the margins of the letter, to wit: "Called AFA 7/14/75, talked to Mrs. Galvins, who informed me the check would be voided 12/31/75. Can be reissued later if Alex's situation changes."

How much should your pack weigh? This is most difficult to answer. I have come to the conclusion that there is no one correct answer. You would be surprised at how much weight people carry.

For those who desire to hike the entire 2,000-plus miles in the shortest possible time, pack weight of between 18 and 25 pounds without food seems to be the norm. For those who desire to hike in a more leisurely fashion, a pack weight of between 25 and 35 pounds seems to be the average. The 47 hikers in 1976 who answered my questionnaire carried packs averaging 30 pounds (pack weight without food). And then there are those super-strong hikers who carry packs in the 50- to 60-pound range.

On June 17, 1970, I was surprised to meet a 16-year-old boy who had started out at Katahdin on June 14 carrying a 70-pound pack; he had twisted his knee badly on top of the mountain. He had flown home and was hiking with a much lighter pack and trying to condition himself for another try.

Over the years, I have counseled many people before they began their hikes, sometimes in small groups, sometimes on a one-to-one basis. One of those who surprised me greatly was 72-year-old Laud Pitt, now deceased. He had done much hiking over the years but not really any serious backpacking. He had read and reread my book and brought it with him when we had our meeting. He showed me the pages of his book. It seemed that about every fourth word was underlined. I'm certain that I warned him about keeping his pack to a reasonable weight. Yet, when he started out at Springer Mountain in Georgia, his pack weighed 47 to 49 pounds! Not only that, but in a day or so he met another hiker almost as old as he whose pack weight was 58 pounds. They both gave up on the hike after only three days. All the weeks and months of planning, of buying food and equipment, came to naught because they had not followed two cardinal rules—they had not kept the pack weights low and they had not taken preliminary hikes. In defense of Laud, I should mention that he did have the courage to write an article about the danger of overly laden packs and failure to take preliminary hikes. The article appeared in the June 1980 issue of *The Potomac Appalachian,* published by the Potomac Appalachian Trail Club.

At the other end of the weight scale, two hikers come to mind—Emma (Grandma) Gatewood and a 1990 hiker I met very briefly in Maine. Grandma did not carry a typical pack. She carried all her belongings in a small denim bag that she had made herself, and it never weighed more than 17 pounds. I met the other hiker in 1990, at the Spaulding Mountain lean-to in Maine, just as darkness was setting in. He was so lightly equipped that my snap observation convinced me he was a day hiker. Not so. One of the other hikers talked to the late arriver and learned that he was a thru-hiker carrying a pack weighing about 12 pounds. In the course of writing this book, I wrote to the fellow asking for details as to the items he was carrying and their weight but he politely declined, stating that each hiker should do his own experimenting. Regrettable. The information would have been valuable. Each hiker must make his or her own decision, but I suggest that a final decision not be made until the preliminary hikes have been taken with the fully-loaded pack.

Rhododendron.

I started my 1970 hike with a pack weighing 26 pounds without food, and gradually began adding more weight, including a stove, fuel, and heavier cooking gear. When I left Monson, Maine, on that 1970 hike, I was carrying a hefty 52 to 54 pounds, but then I had set a very slow schedule for those last 10 days, wishing to savor each day before finishing up at Katahdin. On my 1990 hike, I averaged about 40 pounds with food, which is not bad, but considering my age I probably should have pared the weight down a bit. I note that in reviewing my diary I was exasperated with myself on one occasion when my pack weight had reached 46 pounds.

In the remainder of this chapter I shall say a few words about the rain cover for the pack.

A good rain cover is a must even for hikes of short duration. Most packs are made of water repellant nylon that permits the passage of air (and also water!) for ventilation. So more protection is needed. There are a variety of rain garments available; some cover the pack only, some cover the hiker only, and some cover both the hiker and his pack.

The garments known as ponchos fulfill a number of wet-weather purposes. A poncho will protect the hiker and his pack, will serve as a ground cloth, and will serve as an emergency shelter. In my assortment of camping gear there are two ponchos, but I haven't used them for years. I feel that while they do a passable job of performing many functions, they are not ideally suited for any one function.

On my own hike, I carried rain gear for myself, a ground cloth, and a form-fitting rain cover for my pack. Kelty came out with one of the first good rain covers, but they can now be obtained from a number of suppliers. The better ones fit snugly all around and underneath the pack and use various types of fasteners to keep them tight. Covers weigh about four ounces and come in several sizes so as to fit the particular size pack you own. When not in use, they can be folded into compact packets and inserted into one of the outside pockets of the pack. Keep this item handy! I used the rain cover extensively not only during rains, but also when the woods were still wet from previous rains. Tom Lundberg, a 1976 2,000-Miler, stated that the Kelty rain cover was "the most valuable and most used item I carried."

7

Sleeping

When hiking, one-third of the backpacker's hours are spent within the confines of a sleeping bag. It follows, then, that such things as the sleeping bag, ground cloth, and mattress deserve attention. During the late September and early October days of my 1970 hike, when I was hiking alone up in Maine, I was spending almost half of the 24 hours in the sack. It was almost totally dark by 6:30 P.M. during some of those overcast rainy days, and it was 6:30 A.M. the next morning before it was light enough to distinguish objects.

You have already seen the sketch of my pack. Area 7, the sleeping area of the pack, includes:

Stuffsack	4 ounces
Ground cloth	13 ounces
Mattress (foam pad)	20 ounces
Sleeping bag	51 ounces
Total	88 ounces

The total weight of 88 ounces (5½ pounds) does not tell the complete story. Additional items such as pajamas (i.e. sleeping garments), if you use them, and a tent or tarp in which to sleep must also be included. More on that later. Now, let's discuss one item at time.

Stuffsacks

My stuffsack was the biggest one I could find, a Camp Trails bag 22 inches long and 10 inches in diameter. The following is the method I used to pack my sleeping gear into the stuff bag. There may be a better way, but this way is quick and practical. Step 1: Roll up the mattress tightly, insert it in the stuffsack, and then fluff it out so it leaves an open space in the middle. Step 2: Stuff your sleeping bag into the open space inside the mattress. Step 3: Fold the ground cloth carefully until you have a compact, envelope-size package about 18 inches by 4 inches. This can be slipped just inside the stuff bag between the stuff bag and the foam mattress. Simple.

Ground Cloth

The next item is the ground cloth, which is a lightweight, waterproof sheet that is placed on the ground either as the base for a tent or to protect the sleeping bag from moisture and dirt. The one I carried on both the 1970 and 1990 hikes was the same coated nylon ground cloth I had purchased from Recreational Equipment Inc. (REI) in Seattle in 1962. It is 72 inches long and 56 inches wide. It has grommets at each corner, which would indicate that it may have been intended for an emergency shelter, but I used it only as a ground cloth. I had used it for some 28 years and it was still functional, but it turned up missing during my 1990 hike in Andover, Maine, at the barn where we slept. Either I lost it on the Trail or it became mixed up with someone else's gear at the barn. If I had but taken a few minutes to write my name on that ground cloth with an indelible ink pen, I would probably still have the trusty ground cloth today! If backpacking is to be a very occasional hobby, an inexpensive piece of plastic will serve as a ground cloth. But for extended use, I would definitely recommend the coated nylon.

Mattress

Now for the foam mattress. For years prior to 1970, I had used rubber air mattresses. They were reasonably satisfactory, but the nuisance of inflating the mattress each night was exceeded only by the greater nuisance of attempting to deflate it the next morning. Foam mattresses have become increasingly popular within the past few years. They are bulkier than a deflated air mattress but also much lighter. I purchased one such mattress a month before my hike. Its size is 20 x 36 inches. I used the foam pad on two of my many conditioning hikes and found it satisfactory. That 20 x 36 size may seem small but I found that it was adequate for my hips and shoulders.

There are a few hardy souls who carry no mattress, but I am not in that category. Allen and Gregory began their hike in 1960 without mattresses, but early in their hike they made arrangements to have mattresses mailed to them. Unless you *know* that you can make out satisfactorily without a mattress, I would suggest giving the foam pad a try. The one that I have was made by Colorado Outdoor Sports Corporation. A similar pad made by Foam Design costs $12 in 1997.

In the years since 1970, another product—closed-cell insulation—has become very popular. Trade names of some of the closed-cell products include Ensolite, Superlite, and Valera. Closed-cell products do not absorb water, and some are used as fillers for life jackets. The closed-cell products are much less bulky than the foam pad, somewhat lighter, and much firmer. They are not as comfortable but they have terrific insulating qualities. I keep a piece of Ensolite on the seat of my camper vehicle the year round—no one enjoys the shock of sitting down on the icy cold plastic seat of a car when the vehicle has been sitting overnight in winter weather. And in the summer, I find the Ensolite more comfortable than the smooth plastic car seat. The cost of these ranges from $12 to $20.

In my backpacking, I alternated between Ensolite and the foam pad (*open cell insulation*) bought in 1970. In summer time, I used a piece of Ensolite that is ¼-inch thick and 20 x 40 inches in size. In cold weather, I used a piece that is ⅜-inch thick, and is 21 x 56 inches. The Ensolite can also be purchased in one-half-inch thickness for those who desire even more insulation.

Another type of mattress that has become very popular is ThermaRest. One carries this mattress uninflated with the valve closed. When making camp one opens the valve and the ThermaRest inflates itself. Simply close the valve when the ThermaRest reaches the desired amount of inflation. The ThermaRest mattress is somewhat heavier and more expensive than the other mattresses, but in convenience and comfort it gets a high rating.

Sleepwear

I always wear pajamas and socks when using a sleeping bag. They protect the sleeping bag from perspiration, provide additional warmth, and can be used as undergarments in very cold weather. The use of warm pajamas also permits me to carry a lighter weight sleeping bag than would otherwise be the case.

I advise against sleeping naked in the bag unless you plan to be hiking by yourself the entire trip. One hiker rather ruefully related the story of hiking with two other hikers, one of whom slept naked. The latter perspired heavily, and within short order the bag acquired a very objectionable stench, so much so that the other two would wait to see where the naked sleeper would stake out his position for the night. Then, and only then, would they select *their* sites so as not to be downwind from the naked sleeper!

For pajamas, I selected the extra thick polyethylene shirt and drawers for my 1990 hike. A friend of mine, Ken McCoy, played it a little smarter. He bought two pairs of the lighter weight item, using only one pair in warm weather, and both pairs in cold weather. If you can find those with a roll collar, you would be wise to buy that type. Mine are the crew-neck type and I was very conscious of my uncovered neck on really cold nights. In warm weather, I frequently slept on top of the bag, crawling partway into it in the early morning hours when it becomes cool.

Many backpackers do not use pajamas, per se, but carry two-piece thermal underwear. While they are not as warm as the pajamas described above, they are much less bulky, less expensive, and serve effectively both as undergarments and as sleeping garments. There are others who prefer to protect their sleeping bags from perspiration by using a thin, lightweight, cotton inner liner. This would be lighter weight than the pajamas I used, but it does not give additional warmth and could not be used as an extra undergarment as can the pajamas. However, if hiking is to be done in the warm summer months only, the cotton inner liner may be the more practical of the two items. The point I am trying to make is that you should use something to keep the sleeping bag clean. Pajamas, underwear, or liners can be easily washed; sleeping bags are *most* difficult to wash.

Sleeping Bags

The last item to be discussed in this chapter is the sleeping bag. There are few areas in which I have done more studying. Over the years, I have spent hours reading about baffle construction, tube type constructions, insulation, loft, compressibility, loss of heat from radiation, convection, etc., etc., etc. From my own experience and observations, from the reading I have done, and from conversations with people knowledgeable in this field, I think I can reduce the great bulk of information on this subject to the following four statements:

1. Down-filled bags are superior to bags filled with other materials.
2. Mummy-type bags offer the most warmth for weight and bulk involved.
3. You need not buy the most expensive bags offered by the various manufacturers.
4. For hiking on the Trail during the period April 1 to September 30 (when perhaps 90 percent of the backpacking is done), a down mummy bag weighing around three pounds is adequate.

If you are in the market for a sleeping bag, what brand should you buy and what price should you pay? The sleeping bag, your packframe and your shoes will probably be the most expensive items on your entire list of backpacking equipment. Buying any of these items is somewhat like buying jewelry, and the axiom, "if you don't know your jewels, know your jeweler," certainly applies to these more expensive backpacking items. If there is a specialty backpacking store in your locality, visit it and become acquainted with the proprietor and/or the salesperson. Find one who seems to know the merchandise and whose opinion you think can be relied upon. Don't rush into the purchase of a sleeping bag. It costs too much for hasty action, and once it is bought, you will have it long time. Don't get yourself in the position of buying a bag that is too expensive to discard, yet with which you are dissatisfied. If there is no outdoor store in your locality, I suggest you send for catalogs from the suppliers. A backpacking or outdoors magazine often provides phone numbers and addresses.

Good bags in the three-pound weight range were selling for $100 to $200 in 1995. If money is no object, you can spend another $25 to $50 and get a better-built bag weighing a few ounces less, but this is certainly not necessary for conditions you will encounter on the Trail. Be sure the bag you buy will fit you. Most quality down sleeping bags are made in regular and extra-long lengths. Some are made in children's and extra-wide sizes.

The sleeping bag I used on my 1990 hike was an Arete model made by Camp 7. It is a down-filled bag, rated to be comfortable down to 20 degrees, and whose total weight was approximately two pounds. It was more than adequate for the time of year in which I did my hiking—April 14 to September 4.

I have described the sleeping gear arrangement that I used on my 1990 hike, and now I will describe another sleeping bag arrangement, one of the lightest and most compact I have seen. It belonged to Ed Hanlon, a longtime hiking friend going back to the 1950s. Hanlon hiked with me for a week on my 1970 hike and provided some welcome shuttle service on my 1990 hike. For some years, Hanlon carried a very warm and very, very heavy (nine pounds!) sleeping bag issued to him when he served in the U.S. Marines. In 1975, I prevailed upon him to purchase the Camp 7 "Arete" model extra-long bag. When stuffed into a lightweight stuffsack, it measures seven inches in diameter and 15 inches in length. The total weight of the bag and stuffsack was two pounds. The sleeping bag was then placed in a much larger Camp Trails sack along with the rest of Hanlon's sleeping gear: one tube tent, which doubled as a tent or ground cloth, thermal underwear (two pieces that served as pajamas), wool socks, wool cap, Ensolite pad, and an air pillow. Total weight of all his sleeping gear, including the tube tent, was $6^3/4$ pounds. The size of the stuffsack with all gear inside was 10 inches by 20 inches.

8

Clothing

With the exception of rain gear, I did not purchase any additional clothing for either my 1970 or my 1990 hike. I used what I already owned. Most of it consisted of items which could be purchased at any nearby department store. In saying this, I wish to discourage no one from visiting the specialty stores that cater primarily to outdoor equipment and supplies. I do wish to make the point, however, that hikers planning a long-distance hike on the Trail may be able to use clothes already in their possession, or that they can buy inexpensive articles of clothing at department stores or even mail order houses.

Shirts and Trousers

My requirements for shirts and trousers perhaps slightly more demanding than most hikers. On my 1970 hike, I was still a member of the Board of Managers of the ATC, and I desired to meet with representatives of the eight national forests and the three national parks through which the Trail passes. On my 1990 hike, the ATC had informed all maintaining clubs and some of our Trail partners that I was hiking the entire Trail again and making detailed observations of Trail conditions. Also on the 1990 hike, I had the pleasure of giving a short talk at Appalachian Trail Days in Damascus, Virginia, and in early September, I had the pleasure of meeting with the board of directors of the Maine Appalachian Trail Club at Augusta, Maine. I desired, therefore, to look reasonably presentable for each of these occasions.

No one expects the Trail hiker to wear a business suit and shiny shoes. On the other hand, hikers need not and should not look like bums. We have an obligation to landowners and to our neighbors along the Trail to look reasonably presentable, and I maintain that this can be done without sacrificing one iota of comfort. If readers of this book remember nothing else about it, I would hope that they would remember that personal appearance and courtesy to others are never out of style, even on the Appalachian Trail.

I may seem a little oversensitive on this issue, but I point out that in February, 1971, I had the privilege of testifying on two occasions at committee hearings at a special session of the General Assembly of Virginia. These were hearings on bills to protect the Trail in Virginia. At both hearings, I listened to landowners from northern Virginia describe the disreputable characters using the Trail. I had already given my testimony, and with my 56 years, white hair, and business suit, I did not in any way resemble the rough-looking characters being described. That fact was not lost on the landowners either, for two of them amended their statements by saying, "Now we're not referring to people like Mr. Garvey!"

During the five-and-a-half months I was on the Trail in 1970, and the four months in 1990, I used four sets of trousers and four shirts. Two trousers were of medium to heavy weight and the other two were lightweight. Of the shirts, two were long-sleeved and two were short-sleeved. With one exception, all shirts and trousers were purchased at Sears or Montgomery Ward.

In selecting trousers or slacks for backpacking, it should be remembered that any pack with a waist strap renders almost totally useless the four pockets on a conventional pair of trousers or slacks. Had I foreseen the difficulty this was to cause me I would have either (1) purchased slacks with pockets in a lower position, or (2) purchased extra pockets and sewn them on my existing slacks.

On my 1990 hike, I stopped for a day at Daleview, just north of Roanoke, and succeeded in finding and purchasing a pair of trousers with additional pockets at a lower, easily accessible area.

I wore one set and carried one set at all times. I did not alternate from day to day, but wore one outfit day after day, no matter how grubby it became. I could, when I visited civilization, get a shower, shave, and don clean clothes. I could then saunter forth looking (and even smelling) like a gentleman. People living in cities and towns along the Trail know deep down inside that the Trail hiker lives in a hot, sweaty world, but somehow you have the feeling they would rather not come into too close contact with hot, sweaty individuals. I tried to please, and I felt that I succeeded reasonably well.

On the shoulder of each shirt, I wore a trail patch. On two shirts, I wore the blue, white, and gold AT Maine-to-Georgia patch issued to all members of the ATC. On the other two shirts, I wore the green, black, red, and gold patch issued to members of the PATC of Washington, D.C. (now Vienna, Virginia). With my advanced years, my white hair, hat, matching shirt and trousers outfit, and with that prominent gold patch, I looked sort of "official." People might not have known to what organization I belonged, but I at least gave the impression that I belonged to *some* organization. I know for a fact this impression was responsible for my getting rides into town on a number of occasions when it was necessary for me to leave the Trail.

If you are a member of an outdoor organization that issues an identifying patch, by all means wear the patch on your shirt, jacket, and pack. If you are hiking as a member of an organization such as the Boy Scouts, wear the uniform. I've always been puzzled at the attitude of Boy Scouts toward their uniforms. Few garments are made that are more suitable for the hard wear of outdoor living than the Boy Scout uniform. Members of that organization will wear the uniform religiously to indoor meetings throughout the year. Then, when going on a 50-mile hike, for example, they wear everything except the uniform. Strange!

Pants versus Shorts

No discussion of hiking clothes could be complete without the issue of whether shorts should or should not be worn while hiking the Trail. An early ATC publication contains a rather positive statement that shorts are just not suitable for Trail use. It then goes on to provide some pretty convincing reasons why they are unsuitable. Nevertheless, some hikers have worn shorts for all or most of their hikes. While I enjoy hiking in shorts during the proper conditions, I almost never wear them while hiking on the Trail. There are a number of places on the Trail where you are forced to walk through stinging nettles. These sting even through trousers; it would be much worse on bare legs. I am allergic to poison ivy. If properly clothed, I can walk through acres of the stuff. With bare legs, it would be suicide. I know! It happened once in 1947, requiring me to be absent from work for two weeks, the only extended sick leave I took in almost 35 years of government service. There are many places along the Trail where poison ivy grows thick and lush. If you're allergic to the stuff, don't wear shorts.

Despite the efforts of trail maintenance crews, briars and underbrush make inroads on the Trail. It is impossible to walk through these areas in shorts without getting badly scratched. In addition to these factors, I felt that trousers protected me from insects, lessened the dangers of cuts and lacerations from rocks and trees, and afforded some protection from snake bites. If, in spite of these things, you prefer to wear shorts, more power to you. I would suggest though, that you carry along one pair of trousers for cool nights and other situations for which shorts are not suitable. Trail hikers of 1995 who preferred to walk in shorts used gaiters when the situation demanded, thereby having the best of both worlds—leg protection but no long trousers.

Outer Garments

Now, let's consider outer garments: windbreakers, parkas, and rain gear. Because I began my 1970 hike in Georgia on April 4, I knew that I might have a few nights when temperatures would drop below freezing. Chuck and Johnny Ebersole, who began their hike on March 30, 1964, reported a temperature of 16 degrees their first morning out. I deliberated as to whether I should take my 4-ounce windbreaker or my 25-ounce parka. I gambled a bit and opted for the lighter garment—it turned out to be the correct decision. On no occasion did the temperature ever drop below freezing on my 1970 hike. I did exchange the lighter garment for my 25-ounce parka for the last four weeks of my hike up in Maine. There seemed to be more of a chill in those long autumn nights up in Maine than there were in the early spring nights of northern Georgia. Moreover, I had a healthy respect for the temperatures and winds I might encounter on top of Katahdin. On my 1990 hike, I used the 4-ounce windbreaker as my outer garment for the entire trip.

On the basis of what I experienced, I would say those beginning their hike in Georgia in early spring would be quite comfortable in a windbreaker with a hood weighing somewhere in the 6- to 10-ounce range. A word of warning for those beginning their hike in Georgia in the early spring: Do not send your cold weather clothing home until after you have hiked through the Smokies. One year in the 1970s, hikers in Georgia experienced an unusual warm spell and promptly mailed home their cold-weather gear. When they neared the Great

Smoky Mountain National Park, a cold snap with heavy snows descended. Many hikers were in dire straits as they plowed through the snow in inadequate clothing.

Two other outer garments are a cap, and mittens or gloves. I wore a hat with a brim in warm weather, and a cap, either wool or orlon, in cold weather. The warmth of the cap was welcome not only during the daytime, but also while sleeping at night. On the other hand, my all-purpose, loose-fitting deerskin mittens were among the most practical and frequently used items in my pack. I carried them with me on my entire 1970 trip. They served not only for warmth, but also protected my hands when I was climbing in rough rock areas as well as when I was gathering and breaking wood for fires. Moreover, I used them at many meals as hot pad holders. Unable to find a replacement for them on my 1990 hike, I used cloth gloves—good, but not as functional as the deerskin mittens.

Rain Gear

Rain Gear presented problems. I've had many discussions and much experience concerning this item. Without going into the history of my 1970 trip, I will simply state that for my 1990 trip, I purchased an inexpensive rain jacket made by Kelty. It is coated nylon, loose-fitting and well-ventilated. It weighs just a few ounces and takes up very little room in the pack when not in use.

Early in my Trail hiking, I worked out a procedure to deal with the rain that proved quite satisfactory. If the temperature was 45 degrees or above, and if I was hiking, I wore no rain gear. At those temperatures I knew I would be wet, either from perspiration if I wore the rain gear, or from the rain if I did not. I therefore chose the rain. I reasoned that the rain would have a more salubrious effect both upon me and upon my clothes than would the perspiration. At temperatures below 45 degrees, the chill factor enters in. Then I was glad to don the rain parka.

I also had a set of rain chaps. I despised them, even though they did their job. Each chap weighed only two ounces. At the top of each there was a tie string, which could be fastened to your belt loop. I never wore the chaps except in cool weather. This meant that my fingers and thumbs were cold and clumsy, not the best situation for tying knots, especially when those knots must be tied over on the right side and the left side of your body. The tie strings themselves compounded the problem, as they were thin, sleazy affairs that were difficult to tie and had a pronounced tendency to become untied after a few minutes of wear. Even when I wore the chaps for brief periods of time, I could feel the moist heat building up in my crotch area, and I began to understand why so many babies (wearing rubber protective garments over their diapers) are afflicted with diaper rash. So much for rain chaps, a must for bone-chilling rains in temperatures from 32 degrees to 45 degrees, a nuisance at temperatures above 45.

I also suggest two other types of rain gear for consideration—items I did not cover in my original book; one is ages old, the other has just come on the market. The first of these is the umbrella. That's right, the umbrella. Before you scoff and write the umbrella off as a sissy approach to the rugged outdoor sport of backpacking, consider the journals of the Lewis and Clark expedition of 1804-1806, which I have read with great interest. The journals throw little light on the day-to-day routines of cooking, making camp, etc., but occasionally a tidbit of information will appear. Lewis describes an experience in which Clark and a small body of men camped overnight in a cave near a river. Heavy rains caused the river to rise rapidly during the night and the cave began flooding. Lewis describes the hasty middle-of-the-night evacuation and remarks, "In the excitement, Clark forgot his umbrella." Aha! So the expedition carried umbrellas, at least one!

George F. Miller, the super hiker who was hiking seriously before most of us were born, hiked the entire Trail in 1952 when he was 72 years old. He carried a huge umbrella, both for protection while hiking and for nighttime protection. If you still have doubts, I suggest you read the excellent and humorous article "VIVA LES UMBRELLA" that appears in the Winter 1975 issue of *Wilderness Camping*. In the article, the author, Jim Lockyer, describes his own experiences with the umbrella and the alternate expressions of ridicule and envy from other hikers.

The other item—a material called Gore-Tex—is the most recent of a number of fabrics to appear on the market that claim to be both breathable and waterproof. Gore-Tex rain garments are available, as are other items (sleeping bag covers, gaiters, etc.). I have heard and read the comments of both scoffers and enthusiastic endorsers of the new product. I have not yet used it myself and I offer no comment other than to provide the information that it is available.

Bandannas

Another useful article I consider indispensable is a jumbo-sized bandanna handkerchief. L.L. Bean sells one that is 22 x 23 inches. However, any size, 18-inch square or larger, will suffice. They can be tied around the forehead to serve as a sweatband, worn around the neck as a kerchief, or tied in a triangular fashion to protect ears and necks from insects. I found the kerchief to be particularly effective against gnats. Those little insects are especially fond of hikers' ears, and the kerchief provided more effective protection than insect repellent.

Undergarments

Now let's proceed to underwear—both the lightweight variety and long johns for colder weather. As to underwear pants, that's entirely a matter of preference and I do not discuss the topic. As to underwear tops, the t-shirt is the most commonly used. I recommend dark colors. The light-colored ones show soil quickly, and in a short time, an impression of the strap from the backpack clearly reflects the color of whatever outer shirt you may have been wearing. I used a light-colored one on my 1970 hike, and I still have the yellow colored t-shirt. I keep it for sentimental purposes! It is easily identified by the wide colored band across the shoulders.

One disadvantage to the t-shirts with their short sleeves and low neck cut — they leave much exposed skin surface, which is a hazard in mosquito and fly country. A lightweight knit shirt with long sleeves and a collar gives more protection without being too warm.

If you plan to begin your hike in Georgia before April 1, or if you plan to finish at Katahdin after September 30, it is advisable either to carry long-handled underwear (full length drawers, long-sleeved upper garment) or warm pajamas that can double as undergarments in the event of sudden cold weather with high winds.

The January 1964 issue of the *Appalachian Trailways News* contains the story of two women who hiked up to Katahdin one late October day. What started out as a pleasant hike on a fair, warm October day turned into a nightmare when winds of Arctic gale proportions arose, accompanied by rain, then sleet, then 16 inches of snow. One of the two women lost her life, and a park ranger attempting to rescue the women also lost his life. Their bodies were not recovered until that May. It was probably knowledge of this tragedy that convinced Elmer Onstott (after hiking all the way from Georgia) to turn back after getting within a few thousand feet of Baxter Peak on October 25, 1986. A severe storm was raging on the crest of the mountain at the time.

It is well, therefore, to carry warm clothes when climbing Katahdin in October, even if the weather is mild when you start out. For cold weather hiking, I have found that lightweight Duofold underwear is very satisfactory. The Duofold products have a light layer of cotton next to the skin and a light outer layer of wool; however, most experts advocate synthetics such as polypropylene or Thermax as the more desirable fabric to be next to the skin.

9

Footwear

Boots can be a controversial subject, as I found out in 1969. I had the audacity to write an article entitled "How High the Boot, How Heavy the Shoe?" which appeared in the July-September 1969 issue of the *Potomac Appalachian Trail Club Bulletin*. In my article, I poked a little fun at the trend toward the very heavy hiking boots. I even mentioned that pro-football players had switched from the high-top shoe to the low-cuts, and I suggested that sturdy, low-cut shoes might be suitable for hiking on the Trail. I received many comments on that article, some good, a few bad. Many people, quite probably knowing more about the subject than I, have graciously contributed to my store of information on the subject. My article produced so much reaction that Jim Shores, the editor of the *Bulletin*, felt compelled to print another article on hiking shoes in the next issue. That article, written by William A. Turnage, made some very effective arguments for the heavier weight hiking shoe.

And it hasn't gotten any easier over time. It isn't just leather boots the hiker must pick from, but also the types of lightweight fabric boots now produced.

During my 1990 hike, I noticed that a number of hikers were wearing boots with fabric tops, either partially fabric or all fabric. I did not make a foot count, but I knew there were quite a few who had abandoned the traditional leather boot. I wanted to know if this trend was continuing.

While writing this book, I frequently visited the ATC in Harpers Ferry, West Virginia. There I would chat with the one person in the ATC organization who knew what the long-distance Trail hiker was wearing, eating, and thinking— Jean Cashin. Jean is an attractive, outgoing, friendly gal in her 60s who used to greet every hiker coming through the portals of the ATC building. She was hired in 1972 by Col. Lester Holmes, the first executive director of the ATC. Her principal assignment over the years was to provide information on the Trail, and to help the long-distance hiker in any manner she could. From time to time, I touched base with her on various aspects of the book.

When I asked her about the trend toward lighter-weight boots, her answer truly amazed me: "Ed, you won't believe this but most of the hikers are now using shoes with fabric tops." To confirm Jean's suspicions, we studied photographs of recent thru-hikers and concluded that in 1994, approximately half of the thru-hikers were wearing hiking boots with the conventional leather uppers, the other half were wearing the lighter-weight boot with fabric uppers. I asked, why the trend? She said that the hikers "figure on using either two or three pairs for the entire hike and they simply throw one pair away when it's badly worn and begin using another!"

Sobering information—the American 'throw-away' philosophy. I am 82 years old as I finish this book and was raised in an era when you threw away almost nothing. I thought of a time not too many years ago when the iron wedge I was using to split wood became dull and deformed. I called the Department of Public Works in my hometown and asked the department head where they took wedges, mattocks, and other tools that needed to be reshaped. His reply was amazing, "Well, Ed, we used to take such tools to an old blacksmith in Fairfax County, but he's 90-years-old now and can't do that work any more." "Well, what do you do now?" "Well, I uh, uh, hate to say this, but we just throw away the old tools and buy new ones!" Damn, I thought, that's almost sinful. And now the Trail hikers were doing it.

Those who wore the boots with partially fabric uppers were resigned to the fact that they would throw away one pair, possibly two, during the course of their 2,144-mile hike. The cost of the throw-away boots—approximately $75 to $150 per pair. My all-leather boots, Red Wing Irish Setters, would have taken me all the way through for the cost of a resole job at a midway point of my hike.

Five Million Steps! That's what it takes from Georgia to Maine on the Appalachian Trail. And for each one of those five million steps, the pressure on your feet is intensified by a pack that may weigh from 25 to 50 pounds.

Be kind to your feet. Buy a good pair of socks and a pair of shoes big enough to allow for the swelling that comes from constant hiking day after day and from the added weight of your pack.

Never start a hike with new shoes. To do so is to invite misery. Break in new shoes *thoroughly* on short jaunts. Hike in them for at least 50 miles. Half of that distance should be with a pack on your back.

I have seen so many hikers suffer so much needless misery from sore and blistered feet that I long ago vowed this book would contain this warning for all.

MY 1970 HIKE

I began my 1970 hike with a pair of Red Wing Irish Setter shoes (so named because of their color). I had purchased them in 1967 and had hiked in them for perhaps 150 miles of trail walking, so they were thoroughly broken in. They were six-inches high, weighed three pounds, nine ounces, and had a light-colored composition sole with a rather shallow tread. They were very comfortable. On my thru-hike, I wore them for over 700 miles (about two months) before I returned home for a two-week break from hiking. The tread was nearly gone, but the composition soles were still three-eighths of an inch thick at their thinnest point. I felt that the shoes still had several hundred miles of comfortable wear without resoling. Had I planned to use those shoes for the entire trip, I would have had them resoled during that break, and I am certain they would have made it all the way to Katahdin without need of any further repairs. That was not to be.

In my *Bulletin* article on hiking shoes, I speculated that L.L. Bean's Ranger Moccasins might be suitable for Trail hiking, and stated that I planned to give them a thorough testing. This boot is low cut (less than four inches) and weighs only two pounds, two ounces. Little did I realize when I made that statement, what a wonderful testing opportunity I was soon to have. When I returned to the Trail on June 6, 1970, I was wearing a pair of Ranger Moccasins I had bought in 1968.

I wore them through part of the George Washington National Forest, all of the Shenandoah National Park, through northern Virginia and Maryland, and through all of Pennsylvania, about as tough a 200-mile stretch of walking as there is to be found. Pennsylvania is not tough because of its strenuousness or altitude (the mountains range from 1,000 to 2,000 feet), but because of the ever-present rocks on the Trail that hour after hour punish feet, legs, and shoes.

Midway through Pennsylvania, I realized that my moccasins had had it. Neither the sole nor the heel had any tread whatsoever. They were slippery on wet inclined surfaces. They lost their shape badly, so that near the end I seemed to be walking almost as much on the inside part of the leather uppers as I was on the sole of the shoe. Yet I did enjoy the lightness of those shoes, and the fact that I could get in or out of them in seconds. Also, in defense of that shoe, I must again point out that they served me for more than 400 miles of tough Trail hiking with a 35- to 40-pound pack. Would I wear them again for this type of hiking? No, I would not. For casual weekend hiking, with no pack or a light-weight pack, they would be quite adequate. But for just a few more ounces of weight and with a few more dollars, one can purchase a six-inch, sturdier shoe with ankle support and thicker sole that provides better traction and gives much more protection against the bone-bruising capabilities of ever-present rocks. So much for the lightweight, low-cut shoe. It was a noble experiment; and while one *could* hike the entire Trail in such shoes, I am now convinced that there are better ways of getting the job done.

I wrote my wife asking her to mail me the Red Wing shoes. My wife is not quite so familiar with my hiking shoes as I am (I wear them, she doesn't!). When I checked in at the post office in Delaware Water Gap, Pennsylvania, a box of shoes was waiting for me. When I opened the box, I found that instead of the Red Wing shoes, my wife had mailed my six-year-old Pathfinder shoes, sold by L.L. Bean.

The Pathfinders are six-inch high shoes that weigh three pounds, eight ounces. I had them resoled once by a local cobbler who replaced them with materials on hand, namely a composition heel and sole that had no tread whatever. I used them as work shoes around my home, but for seven weeks, they were my hiking shoes through New Jersey, New York, Connecticut, Massachusetts, the Green Mountains of Vermont, and the White Mountains of New Hampshire. Although they provided very little traction, these shoes performed admirably; figuratively giving up their lives for the cause. By the time I reached Gorham, New Hampshire, the soles had worn through to the leather inner sole, the leather uppers had burst, and one heel was almost off. They were not worth repairing, so I use them and the Ranger Moccasins as Exhibits A and B in some of my talks to hiking groups in order to show what the Trail can do to a pair of shoes.

At this point I took my second two-week hiking break to return home for my daughter's wedding. I returned to the Trail on September 11 for the final 300-mile-stretch to Katahdin. I couldn't decide whether to resume wearing my Red Wing shoes or to hike in my nine-inch-high Bean Hunting Shoes. I had hiked in Maine on two previous occasions and knew that the trail can be pretty wet. I did not relish the idea of having wet feet for long periods of time during some of those cold, damp days of late September and early October. I therefore chose the Bean Hunting Shoes.

The Hunting Shoes have rubber bottoms and leather tops and are a lightweight shoe (even the nine-inch-high boots weigh just three pounds per pair). However, the soles are rather thin, there is very little arch support, and all rubber-bottom-shoes can be uncomfortably warm on even mildly warm days, and can be uncomfortably cold on cold days. Still, I reasoned that the comfort of dry feet would more than compensate for the other recognized shortcomings of the Hunting Shoes.

Even though my reasoning may have been logical, my choice was a mistake. The thin, soft, rubber soles with their rather shallow chain-tread provided me with almost no traction, and I suffered more falls in Maine than in the previous 13 states. The thin soles also afforded little protection against sharp rocks; for several months after I completed my hike, my left foot was still sensitive from the bruises received from stones. But the most revolting feature of the Hunting Shoes was that my feet became wet and stayed that way for days. Near the end of my hike, it rained for eight days out of nine. On the one day it did not rain, the woods and underbrush were saturated from the three-day rain. The leather-upper part of the shoes became water-soaked and the water ran down inside the shoe into the rubber bottoms. Once that happened, I was doomed. It was next to impossible to dry out socks during the short, late summer and early autumn days. At one point, I washed two pairs of socks and hung them from my pack with clothespins for two days. At the end of that time, they were still wet.

When I reached Rangeley, Maine, some 200 miles short of Katahdin, I purchased a pair of lightweight, fleece-lined shoes called "after ski" boots. They added two pounds more to my pack and were very bulky, but they were more than worth these minor inconveniences. Each day thereafter, promptly upon reaching the shelter, I took off the wet soggy boots, donned dry socks, and put on those warm fleece-lined "after ski" boots. What pure unadulterated pleasure. The only fly in the ointment was the knowledge that sometime the following morning I would have to reverse the procedure. How I dreaded those moments.

In defense of the Bean Hunting Shoes, I should state that I probably could have avoided some of my miseries if I had done a thorough job of waterproofing the uppers. Even so, I doubt if any leather shoes, no matter how well waterproofed, could have withstood the day-in and day-out soaking to which those shoes were subjected.

I dreaded the thought of slipping and sliding up and down Katahdin in those shoes, so I sent an S.O.S. home for my Red Wing Shoes. The Red Wings were waiting for me at the ranger's office at the Katahdin Stream campground, and I wore them on the final day of my hike to the summit of Baxter Peak.

OTHER BOOT STORIES

Though I wore my Hunting Shoes for only a short period, one pair of hikers, Murray Chism and Edward N. Little, in their 1959 eight-month traverse of the Trail, wore Bean Hunting Shoes the entire distance. They wore the 10-inch height in the cooler weather, the six-inch in the hot weather. In commenting on the Bean Hunting Shoe, Chism and Little wrote, (*A. T. News*, May, 1960): "The soles are flexible and not very thick, so many persons use a separate insole in them. Without such insoles (we used none), the feet must be conditioned to stand travel over rough and stony trail."

One of those who seemed to have the least trouble with shoes was 69-year-old Elmer Onstott, who hiked the Trail in 1968. In his January 1969 article in *Trailway News*, Elmer wrote as follows:

"The shoes I wore were the best grade of nine-inch boots sold by Sears. The Goodyear soles went all the way and have several miles of hiking left in them. I

Ed's Red Wing Irish Setter boots after 4,000 miles of use.

wore from two to four pairs of socks, one nylon pair next to the skin and three pairs of medium-weight wool socks to fill my shoes after I lost 32 pounds in weight. I had no blisters."

One could go on and on as to the types of shoes worn by different thru-hikers. Let me describe just three more that justify inclusion, primarily because they are so different. Allen and Gregory, on their 1960 hike, wore the light-weight (approximately 2.5 pounds) Maine Guide Shoe, which is six inches high. Mrs. Emma Gatewood (Grandma Gatewood) hiked the entire Trail in 1955 and again in 1957, and again over a five-year stretch from 1960 to 1964. And what kind of shoes did she wear? Sneakers. That's right, sneakers! I don't know whether they were the low-cuts or the six-inch variety, but I have it on the word of many people living on or near the Trail that Grandma Gatewood wore sneakers. George F. Miller, at age 72, hiked the entire Trail in 1952. Miller may have been one of the most experienced hikers ever to hike the entire Trail. He had hiked regularly since his youth. In 1913, he walked the highways from Farmington, Missouri, to New York City, an estimated 1,000 miles in 26 days and three hours. He had performed other noteworthy hiking feats. For his 1952 hike, he fashioned his own pack, part of it resting on his chest, part of it on his back, perfectly balanced. What kind of shoes did he wear? The article describing his hike (*PATC Bulletin*, January-March 1953) says this:

"Two pairs of Bean's high-topped shoes headed Mr. Miller's list. Walks over Washington's streets, aggregating 100 miles or more, were sufficient for the 'breaking in.' When pair No. 1 became muddy, cold, and damp, he switched to No. 2, and he was prepared to visit a cobbler when soles or heels became worn."

Miller was the twelfth hiker to have completed the entire Trail. The article on his hike was the first I ever read about one of the thru-hikes. I often pondered the wisdom of carrying the extra pair of shoes. It seemed as though Miller was adding a needless three pounds to his pack load. Had Miller been an inexperienced hiker, I probably would have dismissed the idea as a novice's overcautious approach to the subject. But Miller was anything but inexperienced. He had made painstaking preparations for every aspect of his hike, even to a printed daily log form. He kept his pack weight under 30 pounds. He carried no camera or field glasses. Considering all the facts, one must ascribe considerable significance to his decision to carry that extra pair of shoes. I make no recommendations on this point. I merely recite the facts for what they are worth. Even though it has been 40 years since I first read the Miller article, I am still "pondering" the issue of that second pair of shoes.

For my 1990 hike, I had a choice between four pairs of hiking boots, which I had purchased and used over the years. I had a lightweight and a medium-weight pair of Fabiano boots, and a lightweight pair of Danner boots. I also had a pair of 12-year-old Red Wing Irish Setter boots. I selected the Red Wing boots and promptly ordered two sets of resoles. I had my cobbler put on one pair of the resoles shortly before I began my hike, and the other pair of soles during my five-day break in mid-July. The cobbler did a good job of resoling the boots on the first try but unfortunately, not on the second. See Chapter 2 and my four-day layover in Monson, Maine, waiting for a replacement pair of boots from home. The Red Wing boots were brought back to my home by another northern Virginia hiker, and I belatedly had the cobbler finish his repair job. I am still using them.

WHAT TO LOOK FOR IN A BOOT

The hiking boot is the most important part of the backpacker's equipment. In the 1970s, when I was affiliated with Appalachian Outfitters, I specialized in boots—the fitting, the waterproofing and general care, the breaking-in process, and the type of socks to be worn with the boot. It was particularly enjoyable to deal with people who were just getting into the hiking game because I knew the questions that were going through their minds and the doubts they were assailed with as they viewed and sometimes hefted the many weights, sizes, and styles of hiking boots on the display shelf.

Experienced hikers will already have established preferences for the weight of the boot, the brand name, the model, and the price. In the preceding paragraphs, we have seen that thru-hikers of the Trail have worn everything from sneakers to 10-inch-high boots. Now let's examine what is available on the market, and move into the delicate area of recommending a type and price of shoe for the person who has had little previous experience with hiking. We will discuss such things as the boot height, weight, sole, and cost.

The first recommendation comes easy: the height of the boot. A six-inch-high boot is high enough for the walking you will do along the Trail, and for most other trails for that matter.

You will want to consider weight next. And what weights are there? I've had to revise my thinking on this, but, for a size 10, a lightweight boot would weigh from 3 to 3.5 pounds, a medium-weight from 3.5 to 4.5 pounds. Anything over 4.5 pounds is getting into the heavy-weight category. The weights given are for a *pair* of boots, not a single boot.

For the person venturing into the hiking game, I would suggest a lightweight boot. The lightweight boot is especially suitable for those who do not weigh more than 160 or 170 pounds and who plan to use the boots primarily for day hiking with only occasional backpacking. I am a 160-pounder; I have used a pair of these lightweight boots for the past 15 years, both for day hiking and extensive backpacking, and I find them quite satisfactory.

The medium-weight boot is better suited for heavier people or those who expect to do extensive backpacking, particularly in rocky areas. They are generally stiffer in the ankle area and thus provide more protection. Generally, they also have one or two extra midsoles, which build up the overall thickness of the sole. This in turn provides more protection from stone bruises in rocky trail areas.

Since 1975, I have either bought or experimented with four different pairs of medium-weight boots. They *do* provide more ankle support, they *do* provide more protection from stones, and after four or five hours of continuous hiking, you *do* become painfully aware of the fact that you have an extra pound or so of weight on your feet!

I rarely recommend or sell heavy-weight boots to backpackers.

One December, a 16-year-old girl and her parents came into Appalachian Outfitters to buy some boots. She weighed no more than 100 pounds and was perfect for lightweight boots. I explained the merits of the lightweight Fabiano boots, and the parents liked what they heard—lightweight boots, extremely durable, could be resoled, easy to break in, and the cost, only $35. Daughter expressed neither enthusiasm nor indifference and allowed herself to be fitted. After the fitting process, she was silent for a long moment and then said somewhat apologetically, "Sir, these are a good fit but could I just try on those Vasque Hiker II boots," referring to a pair of boots that were 1.5 pounds heavier and $15 more expensive. Papa became angry, questioning his daughter as to the need for the heavier boots. I fitted her with the Vasque boots, at which point she became even more apologetic and asked if I could fit her with the still heavier Vasque Whitney model. If Papa was angry before, he was now furious. Nevertheless, I fitted her with the heavier $60 Whitneys, and for the first time she began to show enthusiasm. When she looked at herself in the full-length mirror, she was ecstatic. Expressions like, "These are cool . . . these really look cool. These are exactly what I want," poured forth. As she took the boots and headed for the check-out counter, I explained to her parents what they already knew, that I hadn't really *sold* her the heavy boots, she had *bought* them. They weren't happy but they understood.

Heavy weights are ideal for those involved in expedition-type, mountain activities, especially where snow and ice are involved. They are also very suitable for people like the AMC hut workers, who carry tremendously heavy supply loads up and down the mountains, day in and day out. But for the backpacker, these extra-heavy weights are overkill and are really not necessary. There are times, though, when logic or functional use is excluded from the transaction in favor of looks, prestige, elitism, or whatever you wish to call it.

Fit and Breaking In

Of equal importance as the brand of shoe, its weight and its price, is the fit of the shoe and the breaking-in period required before embarking on a hiking trip of extended duration. If you plan to wear two heavy pairs of socks for your hiking, then you should be wearing two pairs of heavy socks when you are being fitted for your hiking shoes. If you plan to hike (as I do) with a thin pair of inner socks and a heavier pair of outer socks, then you should be wearing such socks when you are fitted for shoes. Take plenty of time with the shoe fitting until you are certain you have the fit you want. Put your full weight on the shoes. Be sure there is a half-inch of wiggle space between the end of your toes and the shoes. Be sure they are loose across the instep. Remember that the addition of a 30-pound pack will cause your feet to spread slightly. Remember, also, that the hour after hour pounding of carrying that same pack will cause them to swell a bit. So be certain you have a roomy fit.

It has been many years since I wrote the preceding paragraph, and experiences of others and my own have come to make me almost a fanatic about insisting on a roomy fit in hiking boots. In 1976, Roger Leavitt of New Vernon, New Jersey, hiked the entire Trail. He began with a well-broken-in pair of Raichles which he stated, "fit fine at the start of the trip, but after three or four weeks of continuous hiking they were tight with only one pair of socks and my

Deformed tree on the Appalachian Trail.

toes were getting sore." He left the Trail in southwestern Virginia, thumbed a ride to the Appalachian Outfitters store in Salem, and purchased a bigger pair of boots, which were long enough and wide enough to be comfortable even when wearing two pairs of socks.

Again in 1976, three of us hiked the 140 miles from Wesser, North Carolina, to Springer Mountain, Georgia, and on into Amicalola Falls, in nine days. After about the third day, my feet had swelled so much that by mid-afternoon of each day the little toe on each foot became very painful. The swelling and pain would disappear overnight, only to reappear by mid-afternoon of the following day.

I cannot overemphasize the importance of thoroughly breaking in a new pair of hiking shoes before embarking on a long hike. Even a two-day weekend hike can be torture if you are wearing new shoes that have not been well broken in. I took my first overnight Boy Scout hike in the spring of 1927. To this day, I can remember the name of the boy, the appearance of his new black shoes, and the misery he endured for two days on that first overnighter. Don't let it happen to you. On my 1970 hike, I hiked with companions, and I met others on the Trail, who were suffering the tortures of the damned because of ill-fitting or inadequately broken-in shoes.

How much breaking in is required? I would say a minimum of 50 miles. And, if you are planning on a long-distance hike on the Trail, then half of that 50 miles should be with a pack on your back, a pack of the weight you plan to carry on your hike.

Waterproofing

Before embarking on a long-distance hike, you will wish to make your leather shoes water repellent. The Hiking, Camping, and Mountaineering Equipment Committee of the PATC has been testing boots, shoes, and waterproofing products for years. The Committee has this to say on the subject:

"For waterproofing leather—and leather should never be fully waterproofed—a good treatment is to apply 3 coats of silicones in volatile solvent, spacing the treatments 24 hours apart, followed by routine rubbing in of a wax-type boot grease. The leather should be re-siliconed about once a season."

Don't be confused by that term, "volatile solvent." If you ask a shoe store for a silicone waterproofing compound such as "Shoe Saver" or "Gard," to name two, the product you will receive will already have been diluted in a volatile solvent.

Socks

There have been so many opinions expressed on socks that I have come to the conclusion there is no "right" method or combination of socks that is superior to all others. Over the years, I have found it very satisfactory to wear a thin pair of socks next to the foot plus a heavier pair of outer socks. There are those who stoutly maintain that the outer sock should be wool. I have worn wool, cotton, and nylon, and all have been very satisfactory. My only objection to the heavy cotton socks is that it takes forever to dry them if you try to wash them on the trail during your hike.

Allen and Gregory, on their 1960 hike, each carried three pairs of Ward's cushion-sole 100 percent nylon outer socks. I promptly purchased two pairs of such socks. That was 20 years ago. I used those socks extensively over the years, and wore them well over 1,000 miles on my 1970 hike. They are still in good shape and seem to be almost indestructible. In more recent years, I have been wearing Norwegian Rag Wool socks as the outer sock, and on some occasions the WickDry heavy duty sock, which is 50 percent cotton-50 percent synthetic.

For inner socks, I have generally worn cotton, but on my 1970 hike, I purchased two pairs of WickDry Inner socks as manufactured by Rockford Textile Mills. These proved very satisfactory and very durable. The manufacturer suggests they be worn under wool or cotton, which would seem to exclude nylon. I wore them under wool, cotton, and nylon, and they proved satisfactory for all three fabrics. These socks are machine washable-machine dryable, and almost indestructible.

VIBRAM

Since my first book was published in 1972, the number of retailers and manufacturers of backpacking equipment has increased at a phenomenal rate. Competition is keen and, with one exception, no one product has dominated the field. That one exception is VIBRAM, the heel and sole product that adorns most backpacking boots now sold in the United States.

Mr. William A. Kamper wrote a most interesting article, "How Vibram Came to the U.S.," which appeared in the July-September 1970 issue of the *Potomac Appalachian Trail Club Bulletin*. It seems that sometime around 1942, an Italian bootmaker named Bramani developed a new type of boot with molded rubber lugs on the soles and heels. After the war, the bootmaker VItale BRAMani began marketing the boot under the name VIBRAM.

Vibram has become the most prominent of the composition soles and heels used by hikers and backpackers in the post-World War II decades. The success of the Vibram product resulted in widespread promotion of other composition-type soles and heels, usually dark-colored, fairly hard, and long-wearing, in which the lugs are in the form of crosses about an inch long. Two of the other post-World War II composition soles and heels with which I am familiar are Galibier and Patons. Vibram itself comes in various qualities, thicknesses, degrees of hardness, and price. There were other composition soles and heels on the market long before Vibram. The earlier ones were softer and more comfortable, but they did not have the long-wearing or gripping qualities of Vibram.

The backpacking fraternity is generally familiar with only one of the Vibram soles, the conventional lug sole with its eight, one-half-inch crosses in the sole and one in the heel. However, even the conventional lug sole comes in six models—Montagna, Montagnabloc, Roccia, Rocciabloc, Lacima, and Kletter lift. Domestically, Vibram soles are manufactured by Quabaug Rubber Co. of North Brookfield, MA 01535.

With the huge increase in the number of people using the existing hiking trails, and the erosion that is taking place on some of those trails, it was inevitable that someone would attempt to determine whether some or most of the trail damage might be attributable to the hard Vibram lug sole. Actually it was two someones, Dr. E.H. Ketchledge and Dr. Ray E. Leonard, of the State University College of Forestry at Syracuse University. Their research was conducted over a four-year period in the Adirondack High Country of New York. The results of their research were published in the October-November 1970 issue of the *New York State Conservationist* and I will quote just a few sentences of the article to illustrate the point I wish to make:

". . . but after studying three trails for days on end, in all kinds of weather, and at all times of year, we believe the greatest share of disturbance is due to the pounding from the hikers' boots, particularly those with the cleated Vibram-type soles. The constant cutting-in of boots roughens the surface, thereby creating an essentially eroded topography. With each step of the hiker, soil is depressed further into the bottom of the cut, where the stream flowing downhill in the trail during and after a rainstorm carries it off the slopes."

While the Ketchledge-Leonard research shows that lug type soles are responsible for *some* of the trail damage, my own observations lead me to believe that the greatest damage is caused by (1) improper trail design (i.e., trails installed at too steep a grade), (2) inadequate maintenance (i.e., failure to install water bars or other devices to divert the flow of water off the trail bed), and (3) the utterly indefensible practice of some hikers in taking short cuts on graded trails.

If we accept the premise that sharp lug soles do more damage that a smoother sole, what can we do about it? Vibram (i.e., Quabaug Rubber Co.) is not insensitive to the problem. When I wrote them on this issue, I promptly received a letter from Herbert M. Varnum, the president. He furnished me with one pair of each of two other Vibram soles, the Security sole and the Sestogrado sole. Each type would, I believe, be quite acceptable for backpacking purposes and would do less damage than the conventional lug sole. The problem now is to convince boot manufacturers that the hiking public will settle for, or actually prefer, a somewhat softer hiking sole with less prominent cleats and lugs than what's presently being furnished. Furthermore, some of the professional forest and park manager types have begun switching back to the composition soles that were in use prior to the advent of Vibram soles. Even one of the 1976 thru-hikers of the Trail, Jim Gardner of Union City, Pennsylvania, wrote that he had a pair of heavy-duty hiking boots with lug soles gathering dust in his closet, and that he found it more expedient to use the industrial-type boots with smoother tread soles on his 2,000-mile hike.

It is regrettable that the Vibram sole, which is such a superior product for technical rock climbing and other high mountain activities, is coming under fire because it is being used in situations for which it was not primarily designed. John Kettlewell, writing in the Washington, D.C., *Speleograph* (Feb. 1977), states that:

"After many years of caving, thousands of hours underground, and introducing considerable numbers of amateurs to caving, I have seen massive evidence that a standard hiking or climbing boot with Vibram soles is *extremely hazardous for caving* . . . for two reasons: (1) the hard rubber becomes extremely slick when wet, and (2) the 'waffle' pattern collects mud, reducing the traction of the boot to nothing."

I will terminate the Vibram issue with a quote from a letter written by Dr. Ray Leonard to Herbert M. Varnum of Quabaug Rubber in January 1977. Leonard wrote:

"There is certainly a place for Vibram soles among the climbing public. It is unfortunate in terms of trail degradation that the lug-type sole became such a fad. Its use by the casual hiker on lower slopes is probably not necessary and injures trails in these locations."

All the comments I have made in this chapter with respect to hiking shoes relate only to shoes with leather uppers. I have not addressed the phenomenon of the recent switch to fabric-type boots, which exists at least among hikers of the Trail. I do not know at this time whether the switch is nationwide, or if it is a temporary or permanent switch in preference. If it is a permanent change, many of the comments with respect to damage by Vibram soles will no longer be relevant.

In July, 1995, while finishing up work on this manuscript, I made a final survey of the shoe situation by checking with Lila Johns, the very knowledgeable manager of Appalachian Outfitters in Oakton, Virginia. The 1995 trend is back to the leather boot, particularly the lightweight one-piece (no seams!) boot, which is definitely a throw away boot because it can't be resoled.

10

Not Necessary But Nice

This chapter is about those things which are not necessary, but nice to have along on a long-distance hike. Items such as a camera, binoculars, books, a thermometer, an altimeter, a radio, a diary, and that most wondrous camping article—the Swiss Army Knife—are among those things you might wish to carry. Before buying, borrowing, or carrying any of these articles on a long hike, you should reread Chapter 5 and consider carefully the maximum pack weight you intend to set for yourself. You must consider how often you will use some of these articles and how much enjoyment you will derive from them; you must weigh these benefits against the energy and sweat of carrying them for days on end, in hot weather and cold, in drought, and in a slogging rain.

No two backpackers think alike in their preparations for a long hike or in the particular type of enjoyment they expect to obtain. There are those who desire nothing more than to hike, hike, hike, and who consider as wasted time any interruption to study and identify a flower, to listen to the song of a bird, or even to stop for a few minutes to enjoy a beautiful view. There are others who have a hobby in a particular field, such as photography or bird study. Such persons will stop occasionally to indulge in these hobbies, and will carry equipment and supplies for these purposes.

There are some thru-hikers of the Trail who have carried no camera whatsoever, feeling that a camera was excess baggage. At the other extreme was Elmer Onstott (1968), a 69-year-old man who carried a tremendous amount of camera equipment. Elmer believes he is the only thru-hiker to have carried a tripod the entire distance. I don't know exactly how much his camera equipment and supplies weighed, but it was probably in the 10-15 pound range. But photography was a big thing for Onstott, and he obtained some of the most complete and expert photographic coverage of the Trail at that time. And, since Onstott ate uncooked foods on his trip, he did not have the weight of cooking equipment, a stove or fuel.

View of the James River.

I carried a small camera on my 1970 trip, but if I could have foreseen the mishaps I was to have with it and how I would not obtain any acceptable pictures, I would not have carried it at all. My camera was a compact little six-ounce, 16 mm Minolta with a built-in light meter and a built-in close-up lens. I knew it had limitations for distance shots, but I was not too concerned about that. I was, however, anxious to document by color slides such things as the word content of signs and to obtain pictures of flowers, people, and grouse chicks (if I could catch them). I had two things operating against me: my general incompetence as a photographer, and the fact that I dropped the camera in the water twice during the first week! But even later in the trip, after I had the camera checked over at a camera shop, I was unable to get any clear, sharp pictures.

Somewhere in between the Garveys and the Onstotts are those who have carried other cameras, not too heavy in weight, and who have obtained some very good, clear slides. Garnett Martin in 1964 and the Skinners in 1968 obtained some very acceptable slides. Reproductions of Martin's slides appear in Ray Baker's delightful book, *Campfires Along the Appalachian Trail.* Another 1964 hiker, Chuck Ebersole, obtained color slides of high enough quality to be accepted by the National Geographic Society for some of their publications. Since an end-to-end trip on the Trail is usually a once-in-a-lifetime experience, I would advise hikers to carry a camera. You may not get professional quality pictures, but if you have just a little more skill than I have, you will be able to obtain pictures good enough for home consumption and for illustrating a lecture.

On my 1990 trip, I carried a Minolta XG-7 camera that I had purchased expressly for a 1978 trip to the mountains of Yugoslavia. It had provided me with some excellent pictures over the years, but as 1990 approached, I noted that the camera had become a wee bit balky, and shortly after my hike began, the camera ceased being balky and became downright defiant! It also weighed three pounds. I sent the camera home. A later inspection at a camera shop disclosed that it was not worth repairing.

Since the publication of my *Appalachian Hiker II* book in 1978, a whole new generation of cameras—lightweight, completely automatic—has appeared on the market. All the more reason why you should carry a camera for your once-in-a-lifetime hike! During the course of my 1990 hike, I met one young man, John Garesche, of Chappoqua, New York, who was taking a picture of each and every shelter along the entire Trail.

I have an excellent pair of compact, lightweight binoculars. They weigh 11 ounces, including their leather carrying case. I did not carry them on this trip, although I have carried them on a number of trips of shorter duration. There were times on my hike when I would have liked to have them, but all things considered, I think I made the right decision. If you are one of those who derive much pleasure from bird watching, then by all means carry binoculars and forego something else.

On my 1970 hike, I carried only one book—the ATC guidebook for whatever section of the Trail I was hiking. I carried a mountain of other paper in the form of daily log sheets, green calling cards, ATC literature, and writing materials. But I carried only one book. As of 1997, there are a number of additional books, all issued by the Trail Conference, from which the hiker may choose.

11

Trail Etiquette

Until recently, the Appalachian Trail crossed over much private property and many public roads, occasionally causing friction between the landowners and hikers. The aggressive land acquisition program, carried out by the National Park Service, the U.S. Forest Service, and the states, has taken the Trail off of almost 200 miles of road and relocated it on mountain ridges. The hiker of the 1990s crosses fewer privately-owned holdings and meets fewer landowners than was previously the case. Even so, the Trail still goes through three national parks, eight national forests, and a number of state and county parks where the general public and hikers will meet. Furthermore, hikers generally make sashays into town to restock with groceries. There is an obligation, therefore, to wear presentable clothing.

In Chapter 8, I alluded to the desirability of wearing presentable looking clothing. The hiker can look presentable without sacrificing one iota of comfort. However, there is a segment of the hiking community whose clothes look as though they had been rescued from rag bags. Many of these people are impeccably attired in their day-to-day business activities, yet they feel the need, when preparing for a hiking trip, to seek out the most disreputable clothes they own as being most appropriate for an outing.

When I was hiking in Maine in the 1980s with Ed Hanlon of Virginia and Cletus Quick of Los Angeles, California, we stopped overnight at the Long Pond lean-to. We talked to a young man who had hiked all the way from Georgia. He proudly displayed a dirty looking t-shirt and exclaimed, "Look at that t-shirt—it hasn't been washed since I left Georgia!" The three of us looked at one another, each thinking the same thought—Big Deal! Another time I hiked an entire week with a well-to-do corporate executive whose clothes were so ragged I felt they should be burned. Apparently I made my point, because on the last night of our trip, with a good fire burning, the clothes, after a sad farewell, were consigned to the fire. Some weeks later, I received a letter from the man's wife thanking me for convincing her husband to take a course of action she had been advocating for years!

GARBAGE

On the Trail itself, away from homes, roads, and stores, there is a certain code of ethics the hiker is expected to observe. One aspect of the code relates to litter. The hiker will see signs reading: "Pack it in . . . pack it out" or "Take nothing but pictures . . . leave nothing but footprints." Carry a supply of litter bags. Dispose of trash at any suitable trash receptacle point, such as a highway litter barrel, picnic area, or U.S. Forest Service Recreation Area. Even though you may see piles of trash at a shelter or even a covered garbage dump, do not add to them. Carry out everything you bring in. Don't bury anything! Be able to say at the end of your 2,000-mile hike that you did not leave a single item of trash at any point along the entire 2,000-mile Trail.

If you have the strength and determination to do it, you are urged to pick up any litter you find on the Trail. On my 1970 hike, I picked up all litter. It proved to be a backbreaking job at times, especially the area around New York City. On my 1990 hike, I had set a goal of picking up five pieces of litter a day. At age 75, I knew that I did not have the strength to do a number of things I had done 20 years earlier. In addition, there was much less litter in 1990 than in 1970, probably because hikers are becoming more litter-conscious and are more willing to pick up litter. The following incident illustrates a practice which I have tried to inculcate in those hiking the Trail or any other trail.

On June 5, 1990, I was hiking with two individuals, Bill Miller and Ed Seibert. Our destination for the day was Jenkins shelter near Bastian, Virginia. We reached the shelter late in the day, after 20 miles of hiking, and met Judy Jenner, whom I had been trying for several days to meet. The fireplace conversation drifted to the Trail conditions, and I mentioned how clean the Trail had been the previous few days. I further added that on that day I had picked up only three pieces. Judy commented that she had picked up four or five pieces. Then both Bill and Ed chimed in to state that they likewise had each picked up four or five pieces. The litter pickup had certainly been no strain on any of us, but collectively we had left the Trail ultra clean. The point I have tried to make is that if each person would pick up just a few pieces of litter each day, it would be no burden to anyone, and overall it would have a terrific impact on the appearance of the Trail—or in your own community.

I do not wish to leave the litter subject without recognizing the activities of some of the clubs who do acknowledge the problem. The New York-New Jersey Trail Conference annually conducts a well-publicized, well-organized campaign to remove all litter from all shelters under their jurisdiction. Dump trucks are arranged, and the participation of many individuals and organizations is obtained. Litter, almost by the cubic acre, is removed each year. The Green Mountain Club of Vermont has an ongoing program to provide trash collection receptacles at reasonable intervals and to erect signs at shelters indicating where these receptacles can be found. The U.S. Forest Service has placed animal-proof trash receptacles at strategic points along the Trail in the Chattahoochee National Forest in Georgia, and has erected signs to inform hikers of the precise mileage in either direction where the trash receptacles are located. I am sure other clubs are likewise engaged in similar activities. I have described only those whose programs have come to my attention.

Litterbugs do not enjoy an enviable reputation in any country. In 1972, two Russian correspondents traveled the length and breadth of the United States, visiting our parks and forests in particular, and writing a series of articles that were printed in Russian (and later in U.S.) newspapers. They were very interested in the Trail, and the State Department arranged for them to walk on part of it in the Shenandoah National Park, and later to meet with me at the downtown Washington, D.C., PATC headquarters. One of the two, Vasily Peskov, a noted writer of outdoor books, is an avid outdoorsman and a dedicated conservationist. I showed slides of my Trail hike, answered many questions about the role of the hiking clubs in the Trail program, and then served them the standard Garvey PATC lunch—grilled cheese sandwiches washed down with wine, followed by ice cream and coffee.

One year later, it was Peskov's turn to be the host during my six-week tour in Moscow participating in the Outdoor Recreation Exhibit. On a beautiful June day, he took Roy Feuchter, of the U.S. Forest Service, and me on a hike through the huge green belt that surrounds Moscow, an area so vast that all of the city's seven million people could visit it at one time without getting in each other's hair. We walked through miles of spotlessly clean wooded areas—clean, that is, except at one point where a large sign requested people not to litter. Beside the sign were the remains of a discarded broken bicycle and about two bushels of other household trash. I can still see Peskov standing there, hands on hips, viewing that mess. Finally he barked out something in Russian and walked away disgustedly. The interpreter looked at me, grinned, and explained, "Mr. Peskov just said two things in Russian which in English translate out to 'Bastard' and 'Son-of-a-bitch!'"

FIREWOOD

A second aspect of the trail ethics code relates to fire and firewood. Keep cooking fires small. Also keep after-dinner, companionship-type fires small. This conserves wood and reduces the chance of a fire getting out of control. In private property areas, landowners become uneasy when hikers build unnecessarily large

Two unusual shelters on the Appalachian Trail. (Top) David Lesser shelter. (Bottom) Fontana Dam shelter, with Chan Chandler, Charles (Santa Claus) Ellis, and Mead Parce.

fires. When the woods are tinder-dry, do not build any fires. Use gasoline stoves, or eat food that requires no cooking. At shelters, always try to leave a supply of firewood for the next party. Be certain that in the supply you leave there is an ample amount of small twigs and tinder to get a fire started. You should follow this rule even if you are using nothing but a gasoline stove for your own cooking; this ensures that firewood is always available in case of emergency.

MISCELLANEOUS POINTS OF ETIQUETTE

The following are a few other concerns on Trail manners that both managers and hikers have suggested I include.

As described in Chapter 9, the lug soles and cleats of the heavy hiking boots damage both the trail and the vegetative cover. Upon reaching your destination for the day, whether it be shelter or campsite, you are urged to remove hiking boots and wear some type of soft-soled footwear around camp. This will give your feet a much-needed rest, and will lessen damage to the camp area.

The old-time practice of cutting balsam boughs for a bed is now verboten—just as is the former practice of digging trenches to divert water from your tent. One reader took me to task for cutting balsam boughs—a practice which I do not condone and in which I do not engage.

The long-distance backpacker, hiking from Georgia to Maine, has a heavy responsibility for exemplary conduct. The example he or she sets in meeting others along the Trail—especially young hikers—has a tremendous effect. Some of the long-distance hikers, upon reaching the AMC huts in New Hampshire, seem to expect certain privileges that they have no right to expect. Granted, hiking from Georgia to Maine for 2,000-plus miles is a significant feat, but the hut workers and hut managers have seen scores of 2,000-Milers and they are not inclined to get down on their knees and pay homage to each would-be 2,000-Miler who enters the doors of the hut. So act accordingly, and do not expect to receive privileges not accorded to other guests. Most long-distance backpackers reach the White Mountains during August, which is the busiest time of the year for the huts. Be sure to make reservations through AMC's Pinkham Notch Hut (by mail: Gorham, NH 03581; by phone: Reservations (603) 466-2727; other business (603) 466-2721).

Another aspect of the trail code relates to leaving instructions at trailside shelters and other points for fellow hikers. If you have located a difficult-to-find water source near a shelter, leave a note in the shelter as to the exact location of the water source. If there is a gap in the shelter chain and you have been fortunate in finding satisfactory lodging elsewhere, leave a note at the next shelter to inform fellow hikers of the place where you obtained lodging. If you have passed a home with a particularly vicious dog, leave a note so that fellow hikers will be forewarned. A number of the shelters are located at some distance from the Trail, and a few of these are marked with neither a sign nor blue blazes to indicate their presence. If you encounter situations like this, leave a note on a tree beside the Trail so that ensuing hikers will be alerted to the existence of, and directions to, the unsigned shelter. A quantity of 3 x 5 inch white cards and a few thumb tacks will serve admirably for this purpose. If your notes are to be left in spots exposed to the weather, do your writing with a soft lead pencil rather than with a pen.

One of the notes I left on my 1970 hike certainly bore fruit, as witnessed by the following letter I received just before Christmas in 1970:

December 15, 1970
Mr. Edward B. Garvey
c/o Appalachian Trail Conference
1718 N Street, NW
Washington, D.C. 20036

Mr. Garvey,

I've put off writing this letter of thanks long enough.

Last summer I and one of my friends started out hiking across Iron Mountain, beginning at Watauga Dam (near Elizabethton, Tenn.). We found the water scarce, or polluted, or almost dry. We had no maps of the trail. We simply put on our packs and took off, rather blindly, with one canteen of water each. The temperature was 93 F. We had walked about 6 miles, having a rough walk because the trail was overgrown (around June 15). (We aren't exactly used to hiking so far). We were getting desperate for water as we had used up our 1-quart canteens in a hurry because of the heat. At one of the shelters about halfway between Watauga Dam and Shady Valley, Tenn., we discovered one of your cards with directions to water about 700 yards below the shelter. Your card saved us a great hardship. It was nearly 10 miles out of there and that water hole carried us through.

The enclosed card came from one of the other shelters. I left your card and directions on the shelter for someone else. Once again I thank you and wish you a Merry Christmas.

Wallace G. Wright
Route 10 Kodak Heights
Kingsport, Tennessee 37664

The above letter expresses, more eloquently than anything I have said or written, the need for clear identification of all sources along the Trail. Secondly, I was pleased that the simple directional information I had written on one of my 3 x 5 cards had proved so helpful to a fellow hiker.

Finally, a few words about conduct at the shelters—your "home away from home" for five or six months. If you are the first one to enter the shelter or the last to leave, please take a few minutes to sweep out the shelter and the privy. Your fellow hikers will definitely appreciate your efforts. The shelters are one of the most distinctive aspects of life on the Trail, and one of the things that impressed me greatly when I saw my first shelter some 40 years ago. Treat them kindly!

12

Trail Acquisition and Management

In writing this book, I considered several possible names to give it. One such title would logically have been *Appalachian Hiker III*. However, when I began examining the changes we have made in the Trail, I realized the name of the book would have to be *The New Appalachian Trail*. The trail I hiked in 1970 and again in 1990 was completely different from the trail that was first completed on August 14, 1937.

In this chapter, I explore the progress made in acquiring the Appalachian Trail right-of-way, and some of the "sweet victories" of this acquisition. I have been involved in land acquisition since the first Trail bill was signed into law in 1968, and have a copy of every monthly report on land acquisition that has ever been issued. The progress we have made is almost unbelievable. Occasionally I hear a comment that we are not moving fast enough on the land acquisition and my reaction is something like this, "Friend, we are so far ahead of where I thought we'd be at this time that we could stop all land acquisition right now and we'd still be winners!"

Any project of the scope of the 2,000-mile Trail needs dreamers and doers. The first dreamer was Benton MacKaye, who, in 1921, was persuaded to write in the *Journal of the American Institute of Architects* an article entitled "An Appalachian Trail: A Project in Regional Planning." MacKaye had been talking about such a project for years, but it was not until 1921 that his peers cajoled him into actually writing the article. MacKaye's goal was to complete a trail reaching from Mount Washington, New Hampshire, to Mount Mitchell, North Carolina, that would include shelters, community camps, and food/farm camps.

A year later, in the Palisades Interstate Park in New York, the first mile of what was to become the Appalachian Trail was identified and marked. In retrospect, it was a tremendous example of faith and hope. One wonders if any of that first group of trail workers had any idea when or if the proposed long-distance trail would ever be completed. At the time, there was no Appalachian Trail Conference or other organization to direct their efforts. The group was operating solely under the stimulus of Benton MacKaye's article. The remarkable thing is that a mere 16 years later, on August 14, 1937, the Trail was completed near Sugarloaf Mountain in Maine.

If MacKaye was the dreamer, then Myron Avery was the doer. Avery, who came from Lubec, Maine, became interested in the Appalachian Trail movement early in the game. He knew that organized groups of people would be needed to mark and build the Trail. Avery was the one largely responsible for establishing trail clubs from Maine to Georgia and prodding them into completing the entire Trail.

In March of 1925, a group of hiking enthusiasts, including Benton MacKaye, interested in establishing a formal organization met in Washington, D.C. This resulted in the birth of the Appalachian Trail Conference (ATC). Major William A. Welch of the Palisades International Park Commission became the first chairman of the new organization.

In laying out the route of the original Trail, the individuals and clubs selecting the route had no money for land acquisition. They, therefore, chose a route that would take the trail through such public land organizations as the U.S. Forest Service, the National Park Service, and other state and public bodies. Where there were no public lands available, it was necessary to seek permission from private landowners. Where permission could not be obtained, the recourse was to utilize existing public roads. Because of some difficulty in gaining right of way, one 13-mile stretch of the Trail in northern Virginia was moved from a wooded area onto a public highway. On my 1970 hike of the Trail, I was forced to walk the entire distance on a hardtop highway in the sun. Not fun!

The practice of routing the Trail over private land posed problems. Land ownership occasionally would change; furthermore, as our population increased so did the demand for these lands in remote areas. Landowners became increasingly concerned about creating a cloud on their title as a result of having a permanent trail on their properties. It wasn't long before the ATC began attempts to obtain public ownership of the trail route. One congressman, Daniel K. Hoch, president of the Blue Mountain Eagle Climbing Club in Pennsylvania, had introduced a bill in 1945 in the U.S. Congress, but the bill died in committee.

It would be nearly 20 years before the issue of public ownership would get another hearing.

In 1963, at a party in Washington, D.C., Senator Gaylord Nelson was approached by a member of the Potomac Appalachian Trail Club—Dr. Cecil Cullander. Cullander was a trail maintainer who was well aware of the problems facing the Trail where it ran over private property. He found a sympathetic listener in Senator Nelson, who shortly thereafter assigned one of his staff members to draft a bill to protect the Trail. The staff member, Fred Madison, worked with a number of us in the Trail community, seeking suggestions as to what items should be included in the bill. Eventually, the bill, Senate Bill 2862, was introduced by Senator Nelson. Hearings were held, but the Nelson bill never became law.

Later, through the Bureau of Outdoor Recreation, the Johnson Administration introduced a new and stronger bill that passed in both houses of Congress and was signed into law by President Johnson on October 2, 1968. It became Public Law 90-543, the National Trails System Act. Within hours after the bill became law, I walked into the downtown office of the ATC, where someone had posted a huge sign: "TRAIL BILL PASSED—PUBLIC LAW 90-543!" What a welcome sight!

This new law enjoined two agencies of the government, the National Park Service and the U.S. Forest Service, to acquire lands from Georgia to Maine to protect the Trail. The 14 states through which the Trail passed also had an interest in acquiring land to protect the Trail. The law provided that once the official route of the Trail had been identified, the National Park Service, the U.S. Forest Service, and the states would have a period of two years to acquire land without interference from the federal government.

The U.S. Forest Service promptly began acquiring lands within the boundaries of the eight national forests. The National Park Service, which had been assigned primary responsibility for Trail acquisition, took no action to engage in a land purchase program. The National Park Service did not even identify the names of property owners who owned land over which the Trail passed. At the general membership meeting in Boone, North Carolina, in 1975, I introduced a resolution that bitterly criticized the National Park Service for failing to abide by the legislation to acquire the Trail right-of-way. The resolution passed, and a few days later it was published in the Congressional Record. Still the National Park Service took no action.

After seven years of Park Service inaction, three of us in the Washington, D.C., area—Grant Conway, John Oliphant, and I—visited the office of the Subcommittee on National Parks and Recreation of the House of Representatives. Our mission was to obtain oversight hearings on the National Trails System Act. Briefly stated, oversight hearings require a government agency to report to the committee the progress it has made in fulfilling the requirements of a particular piece of legislation. Oversight hearings also permit critics of the agency involved to voice their criticisms before members of the House committee. Our efforts were successful, and on March 11 and 12, 1976, the oversight hearings were held. In my own testimony I stated, among other things, that "the National Park Service, the agency charged with primary responsibility for administration of the Trail, had acquired not one acre of land or obtained a single easement for protection of the Trail."

In spite of the disclosures at the oversight hearings as to the Park Service's failure, the National Park Service remained inactive in Trail acquisition. It was not until Jimmy Carter became president and installed a new cast of characters in the Department of the Interior that good things began to happen. In May, 1977, at the biennial meeting of the ATC in Shepherdstown, West Virginia, the new Assistant Secretary of the Interior, Mr. Robert L. Herbst, declared in ringing tones that the Park Service would henceforth actively engage in a policy of land acquisition to protect the Trail. It was a much-welcomed speech and there were some moist eyes among the ATC members who heard Herbst's words.

Mr. Herbst was as good as his word—even better! In the ensuing months, he obtained new and stronger legislation for the funding of land acquisition activities. For instance, he and his staff drafted amendments to the Trail bill to increase the width of the right-of-way to 1,000 feet instead of the 200 in the original law. (Actually, neither the original law nor the amendments prescribed any limitation on the width of the corridor. The language did set a maximum on the acreage when condemnation was involved. There are many situations where the right-of-way exceeds the 1,000-foot figure.) The amendments also included a provision that $90 million would be authorized for the land purchase program. The proposed amendments became law on March 21, 1978. The pen used in signing the legislation into law was given by President Jimmy Carter to Congressman Goodloe E. Byron of Maryland, who had been an active supporter of the legislation, which came to be known as the Appalachian Trail Bill.

If the Department of the Interior was slow in establishing a trail purchase program, under the direction of Robert Herbst, it made up for lost time. Still, it took a while to get the land acquisition machinery in place, and it was not until January 29, 1979, that the National Park Service made its first purchase of 35 acres in Dutchess County, New York.

Since then, the agencies involved have been very busy. The November 1996 monthly land acquisition report shows that the Park Service had acquired 2,338 tracts of land, for a total of 99,709 acres and 598.3 miles. How do those 99,709 acres stack up with some of the other National Park properties? Here are a few: Acadia National Park in Maine, 39,000 acres; Shenandoah National Park in Virginia, 191,000; Harpers Ferry Historical Park in West Virginia, 2,000; Guadalupe Mountain National Park in Texas, 76,000; Redwood National Park in California, 62,000 acres. (Figures taken from a National Park Service book issued in 1977). The point—this piece of land that we call the Appalachian Trail is NOT a mere footpath. It is a multistate national park, a multistate national forest, a multistate national recreation area, or a little bit of all three.

While the National Park Service was acquiring 99,709 acres (598.3 miles), the Forest Service was acquiring 45,573 acres (142.1 miles), and the states were acquiring 20,206 acres (146.1 miles).

LAND ACQUISITION

What were the steps necessary to purchase these various tracts from Maine to Georgia? To obtain this information, I visited the Appalachian Trail Project Office in Harpers Ferry, West Virginia, and had a long discussion with the genial and very knowledgeable Don King. The Appalachian Trail Project Office is a branch of the National Park Service that coordinates with the ATC in land acquisition for the Trail corridor. At the time of my visit in 1995, Don was the Acting Project Manager. He had been in the Park Service's Trail purchase program since November 1979, just shortly after its inception.

To start the land acquisition project, Don had the mapping staff prepare detailed property maps for the entire Trail. These maps, called segment maps, were prepared to a scale of 1 inch for every 600 feet (except for Maine, where the scale was 1 inch for every 2,000 feet). To develop these maps, it was necessary to examine land ownership records, including deeds, surveys, tax maps, aerial photographs, etc., in each county's tax assessor's office and in the county office for the Recorder of Deeds. Some counties possessed no such records, in which case, the segment maps had to be developed from other sources of information. These segment maps are serially numbered—410 in all—and the segment number is a key component in retrieving information from the data bank maintained in the ATC office in Harpers Ferry.

After adequate maps had been prepared and the names and addresses of the landowners obtained, a letter was written to each landowner informing him of the need to protect the Trail. (Remember, we are trying to obtain a 1,000-foot strip of land to protect a four-foot trail.) After the landowner had had sufficient time to consider the issue, a phone call was made and a date set for the initial meeting. For that first meeting, the National Park Service realty specialist frequently found it expedient and helpful to be accompanied by a member of the local Trail club.

After the visit to the landowner came the preparation of a legal description, and possibly a survey of the property, this latter function performed either by a National Park Service employee or by a contractor. This could be a very difficult job where no accurate surveys had ever been done. After the legal description, there was an appraisal of the value of the property to be acquired, a function almost always performed by a contractor. A title search was also performed. After all of the above steps had been taken, a letter was sent to landowners informing them of the cash value appraisal and the amount to be offered by the government for purchase of the property. The offer would be in the same amount as the appraisal. Then followed a period in which negotiations would take place, and eventually an agreement was reached between the two parties. The final step was the conveyance of title to the property. Essentially, all of the above steps were taken for each tract of land purchased, regardless of its size.

Trail blazed across boulders on the way up Katahdin, Maine.

To accomplish the ambitious land purchase program desired by the Assistant Secretary of the Interior, the National Park Service established three land acquisition offices in different localities. Eventually, these offices were reduced to one, now located in Martinsburg, West Virginia. A longtime acquisition manager, Mr. Charles R. Rinaldi, was placed in charge of that office, while David Richie was appointed project manager for the Appalachian Trail Project Office, which was established in Harpers Ferry, West Virginia. Under Rinaldi's driving leadership, acquisition of Trail land progressed rapidly. In August, 1979, Rinaldi reported that 75 tracts of land had already been acquired from willing sellers.

The progress of the land acquisition would henceforth depend upon two things: (1) the number of land acquisition specialists Rinaldi could hire; and (2) the amount of money appropriated by Congress each year for land acquisition purposes. The amount of money appropriated varied somewhat from year to year, but, on the average, the Park Service received approximately $7 million a year for the purchase of private property outside the limits of any federal or state lands. The U.S. Forest Service received, on the average, some $1.5 million per year for acquisition of Trail land within the boundaries of the eight national forests.

The progress made in land acquisition since the establishment of the office in Martinsburg in 1979 has been phenomenal. In the midst of the energetic effort to acquire the Trail right-of-way, Rinaldi became concerned—concerned that in the rush to acquire the various tracts of land, there might be important pieces of the right-of-way that were being overlooked, tracts of land that, if later acquired and developed by private interests, might seriously affect the quality of the hiking experience. He therefore arranged to borrow the services of one David M. Sherman, who was employed by the National Park Service in the Washington, D.C., area, to engage in a corridor review program and to make recommendations for additional land purchases.

For a six-month period in 1984, Sherman drove and walked for hundreds of miles from the Tennessee line north to Katahdin. He was armed with the pertinent segment maps of the areas involved, a small camera, and a notebook. He made many recommendations for additional purchases along the route of the Trail, and the recommendations were promptly acted upon by Rinaldi and his staff. Sherman had hiked the entire Trail in bits and pieces over the years during his annual vacations. He was intensely interested in Trail protection and in those areas bordering the Trail that would provide beautiful vistas of the Appalachians. In checking with him, I found he had made a recommendation for additional protection on a section of the Trail in Maine that is very dear to me—Lake Nahmakanta and the area surrounding it.

This lake is in the 100-Mile Wilderness area north of Monson, Maine. I had hiked through it in 1969, in 1970 on my thru-hike that year, and again in 1990,

NATIONAL PARK SERVICE - APPALACHIAN NATIONAL SCENIC TRAIL
PROTECTION PROGRESS REPORT

As of November 1996

STATE	TOTAL MILES	MILES PROTECTED THRU FEB. OF 1978 N.P.S.	STATE	U.S. FOREST SVC.	TRAIL TO REMAIN ON RDS.	PROTECTED 3/78 TO PRESENT — NATIONAL PARK SERVICE MILES	ACRES	TRACTS	STATE MILES	ACRES	TRACTS	U.S. FOREST SERVICE MILES	ACRES	TRACTS	PROTECTION PENDING — NATIONAL PARK SERVICE MILES	ACRES	TRACTS	STATE MILES	ACRES	TRACTS	U.S. FOREST SERVICE MILES	ACRES	TRACTS
ME	263.3	0.0	21.0	0.0	0.0	169.9	28,645	110	68.2	9,731	17	0.0	0	0	2.8	923	5	1.4	128	2	0.0	0	0
NH	142.9	0.0	8.8	78.6	2.5	45.0	8,393	118	0.5	68	1	7.4	6,806	11	0.0	86	3	0.0	0	0	0.1	4	3
VT	131.6	0.0	4.3	52.1	2.8	49.2	8,982	197	3.1	384	2	18.3	8,799	29	1.8	3,507	17	0.0	0	0	0.0	41	3
MA	83.0	0.0	31.1	0.0	3.3	31.2	5,305	156	17.3	2,746	39	0.0	0	0	0.1	453	7	0.0	0	0	0.0	0	0
CT	45.2	0.0	2.5	0.0	1.7	32.2	6,220	125	6.0	550	3	0.0	0	0	2.8	624	12	0.0	0	0	0.0	0	0
NY	92.9	0.0	29.2	0.0	2.0	57.0	7,919	227	4.4	551	4	0.0	0	0	0.1	463	33	0.2	16	2	0.0	0	0
NJ	67.7	25.4	18.2	0.0	0.0	0.0	777	58	24.1	3,031	103	0.0	0	0	0.0	755	10	0.0	0	0	0.0	0	0
PA	228.8	3.1	110.1	0.0	4.9	97.0	13,062	573	10.3	1,447	29	0.0	0	0	3.4	257	26	0.0	0	0	0.0	0	0
MD	39.7	2.5	19.0	0.0	0.1	3.5	1,019	100	8.9	1,360	106	0.0	0	0	3.9	979	39	1.8	196	14	0.0	0	0
VA	557.6	114.8	15.2	289.0	3.9	87.7	16,033	541	3.3	371	8	32.0	12,890	159	5.7	1,896	51	0.2	1	1	5.8	2,386	33
WV/VA	25.6	0.0	0.0	0.0	0.0	25.6	3,355	133	0.0	0	0	0.0	0	0	0.0	16	2	0.0	0	0	0.0	4	1
NC/TN	361.8	68.7	0.0	202.5	0.0	0.0	0	0	0.0	0	0	83.2	16,633	341	0.0	0	0	0.0	0	0	7.4	2,734	113
GA	78.2	0.0	0.0	77.0	0.0	0.0	0	0	0.0	0	0	1.2	446	18	0.0	0	0	0.0	0	0	0.0	29	1
TOTAL	2,118.3	214.5	259.4	699.2	21.2	598.3	99,709	2,338	146.1	20,239	312	142.1	45,573	558	20.6	9,960	205	3.6	341	19	13.3	5198	154
					0.0	0.0	0	0	0.0	0	0	0.0	0	0									

NOTE: Figures in parenthesis represent monthly progress.

*) Includes 1.7 miles, 708 acres and 37 tracts in Pending Condemnation Actions.

Protection Progress Report.

on my 1,400-mile hike. The lake is some four miles in length, and lies in a north-south orientation. The Trail runs along the south and west sides of the lake. Part of the Trail is directly beside the lake, but further south it rises high above. A short path leads out from the southern end of the lake to a vantage point that permits an excellent view of the entire lake. On my 1990 hike, I stood for a long time at that vantage point, drinking in the beauty of the scene and thinking what a disaster it would be if private interests acquired possession of that eastern shore and began building docks, houses, fast food enterprises, etc. Not to worry! Sherman, in his 1984 review, had come to the same conclusion, and had recommended that the National Park Service acquire a 250-foot strip of land all along that eastern shore. Rinaldi's people acted promptly to acquire the needed 250-foot protective strip. Then, in 1994, the state of Maine purchased an additional 30,000 acres surrounding Lake Nahmakanta. Hikers of the future will enjoy this beautiful lake to the same degree that I did. This is just one of the scores and scores of recommendations that were promptly acted upon. Each such land acquisition resulted in a trail that is safer, prettier, or more protected from unwanted commercial development.

Each month, the Land Acquisition Office in Martinsburg, West Virginia, prepares and distributes a Protection Progress Report showing by state the total land acquisitions to date and identifying how much of that total figure was acquired during the one-month period involved. I have included a recent report in this book. It may take you a bit of study to decipher the information, but I urge you to study it. You will be mildly amazed at the figures shown.

THE TEN SWEETEST VICTORIES

As stated above, the National Park Service made its first purchase of land to protect the Trail on January 9, 1979. As of November 30, 1996, the NPS had acquired 598.3 miles of the Trail, involving 2,338 individual tract purchases. Most of these purchases were made rather routinely, but there were a significant number that were finalized only after years of negotiations; some of them were made in the nick of time, just as the landowner was about to sell to another party.

For several years, I have been trying to sell a "Ten Sweetest Victories" theme that would highlight the drama of the Trail purchase program. On one occasion, at a Trail gathering of some sort, Dave Sherman (now of the U.S. Forest Service) and Karen Wade (currently superintendent of the Great Smoky Mountains National Park, but at the time one of the people engaged in purchasing Trail land) and I began discussing the matter. Karen spoke with glee of her successful effort to acquire the parcels of land surrounding the famous McAfee Knob, an area in southwest Virginia near the city of Roanoke. Her story was fascinating, and I was convinced that there were others just as exciting. On another occasion, while driving with Dave Sherman, I asked him to recite what he thought might comprise the 10 sweetest victories. He began recollecting and I began writing—on the back of an envelope. A good start, but I managed to misplace the envelope!

With time getting short, I went back to Don King. Don was with the Appalachian Trail Project Office in 1995, and although he has since changed jobs (he is now chief of the New England and Capital Area Land Acquisition Field Office for the National Park Service), he still oversees all park service acquisitions for Trail lands. The following list is his, and while no two people would have selected the same examples, they would probably agree on most of them.

July 17, 1995

Mr. Garvey:

I had the opportunity to give a little thought to the "Ten sweetest victories" in dealing with land protection along the Appalachian Trail during my ride back from Lexington, Virginia, yesterday with my daughter, Robin. It is somewhat surprising to think of where time has gone; when I first came to the Trail in November 1979, Robin was in kindergarten. In the Fall, she will start her senior year at Washington and Lee.

I have been here quite a long time (some say too long) so it is a little difficult to give justice to all the acquisitions. Chuck Rinaldi was really the master organizer of our program in terms of land protection so it was quite easy when I took over that part of the program. Chuck also looked out for his employees and was quite helpful to me—always giving friendly advice. There are many more than "10" but I will give you my best shot by year.

1983

While I was not directly involved, the office was buzzing when the Wintergreen property in Virginia along the Blue Ridge Parkway was acquired. This was one of the few properties where direction came in our appropriations bill to encourage this purchase. The acquisiton was facilitated by the Appalachian Trail Conference. Acreage—2,729.3

1985

Another "sweet victory" by Chuck Rinaldi with the purchase of the Stanley Works property in Connecticut. Besides pulling together the deal which protected five miles of the Appalachian Trail along the Housatonic River. I recall Chuck turning the deal over to me after it was signed and saying to get this multi-million dollar deal closed in three days. Impossible, but, we closed in three days. Acreage—1,777 (4.9 miles)

1986

The trail route along Catawba Mountain was completed with the settlement on the Dr. Harry Johnson property in Virginia. This property included McAfee Knob. The Knob, itself, had a long history in terms of title. I was first introduced to the Knob by R.S. Kime, a respected Salem attorney who at the time, was retired. Mr. Kime shared with me photographs of the Knob and how he in his younger days drove a model-T up to the Knob. The black and white photo showed a young Mr. Kime hanging off the rock ledge—his initials are carved in the Devil's Kitchen area. In any event, the Knob was claimed by two owners and we finally ended up with three parties claiming ownership. The problem was created by Patrick Henry, who while governor of Virginia, provided a warrant for the same property to two different parties. It may have taken more than 175 years to straighten out, but we did with the settlement in the case. Acreage—369.3

1987

On October 7, we received a decision in the court case to acquire 8.7 acres from Herbert Bergdahl. While on the surface this was not a large piece of land, the acquisiton allowed us to complete the 14 mile "western route" in Connecticut. In addition to finalizing the route, the court reaffirmed the method in which the government went about acquiring the land, and concluded the government representatives were "extraordinarily patient" in dealing with Mr. Bergdahl. Acreage—8.7

1987

The purchase of 91 acres from the Estate of Samuel Sunday outside of Boiling Springs, Pennsylvania, appeared on the surface to be rather routine. However, this vital property in the heart of the Cumberland Valley 16-mile off-road route was a key purchase in locking the trail route. Clearly, it may have been one of the most important purchases in the Cumberland Valley relocation and helped us turn the corner in securing the most difficult trail relocation. Acreage—91

1988

In Maine, we were able to put vast sections of trail into the purchase column with each agreement. One highlight was the acquisition of 4,887 acres from the Scott Paper Company's subsidiary, S.D. Warren Company. Nine different properties from White Cap Mountain to Spaulding Mountain were purchased, including the summits of White Cap Mountain, Moxie Bald Mountain, North and South Crocker Mountains and two miles of shoreline along three remote and spectacular ponds, including Bald Mountain Pond, Moxie Pond and Pierce Pond. Acreage—4,887 acres (31.6 miles)

1990

Here we are again in Maine with an agreement to protect 27 miles of the Appalachian Trail with the purchase of 4,023 acres from Diamond Occidental Forest, Inc. Significant features included Nahmakanta Lake, a 1,024-acre, deep-water lake. Nahmakanta Lake has a diverse fish population, outstanding scenic and shore characteristics, and from the lookout on Nesuntabunt Mountain views of Nahmakanta Lake and Katahdin Mountain. Other sections of trail included the 3,644-foot summit of White Cap Mountain and part of Gulf Hagas as well as the longest river walk in Maine with five miles along the banks of the West Branch of the Piscataquis River. Acreage—4,023 (27 miles)

1990

In a different role, we negotiated to obtain a donated easement to the State of Maine from Great Northern Paper. This easement provides for the protection of nearly 4,500 acres of land including 29 miles of the Appalachian Trail. In 1985, Great Northern Paper contributed to the State an easement for the Trail across 3,300 acres. Prior to this transfer, the National Park Service raised its objection to the easement, citing the fact that the 1985 easement was considered inadequate long-term protection for the Trail. The lands involved in the easement included three miles along the West Branch of the Penobscot River, one of the finest river-walks along the entire Appalachian Trail. Acreage—4,500 (29 miles)

1991

In 1974, the Commonwealth of Massachusetts initiated negotiations for the purchase of a trail corridor through the Hollenback property near the Town of Dalton. We completed settlement for the protection of 149 acres, which vastly improved the trail route and provided a corridor that we are quite proud of. Acreage—149

1992

In striving to consider landowner's concerns in planning and locating the trail, we sometimes negotiate for years and years. That was the case with the planned trail route over Schaticoke Mountain in Connecticut involving the property of William Ray. After years of negotiations, including discussions with Director Mott and the Assistant Secretary's office, we were able to move forward with the decision of what land to acquire along this scenic trail section. The overall settlement finalized the trail location and brought into protection 118 acres, in the States of New York and Connecticut. Words cannot easily express the effort of the many individuals who worked on this acquisition. Acreage—118

THE CORRIDOR MANAGEMENT PROGRAM

During the period between 1978 and 1996, the U.S. Forest Service acquired 45,573 acres of land to protect the Trail. These lands are managed by the eight national forests through which the Trail passes. Eleven of the 14 states through which the Trail passes acquired 20,239 acres, and these lands will be managed by an agency of the state government. During the same period of time, the National Park Service acquired 99,709 acres of land outside the boundaries of any national forest or park. What agency would manage these lands?

Beginning in the 1920s, when the first miles of the Trail were laid out, the ATC and its member clubs established an enviable record of maintaining the Trail and the trailside shelters. Apparently, the Department of the Interior felt the ATC and its member clubs would be able to manage the corridor surrounding the actual footpath. So, in a very moving ceremony on January, 1984, in the presence of the Secretary of the Interior, William P. Clark, the delegation of management authority for these lands was made to the ATC by the Director of the National Park Service, Russell E. Dickenson. The ATC Chair at the time, Raymond F. Hunt, signed the document accepting the responsibility. My wife and I had been invited to attend the ceremony and it was most impressive. As I watched Ray Hunt sign the document, I could not help but think of the time 20 years earlier when I first became secretary of the ATC. At that time, the ATC was an organization with fewer than a thousand members, and the board, which had very little input in the operation of the conference, met only once every three years for about two hours after the general membership meetings. The ATC was kept alive by the generosity of the PATC, which rented the conference office space at a very nominal rate in the top floor of the PATC downtown office building in Washington, D.C. And yet there we were in 1984, entrusted by a major department of the government to manage a piece of real estate as large as a major national park. Incredible!

By 1984, the conference had changed dramatically. It no longer rented space from PATC, but owned its own office building in Harpers Ferry, West Virginia. It boasted an executive director and 24 employees, plus four regional offices with staffs to man them. The ATC had come a long way in 20 years. All signs indicated that the conference, and the 32 hiking clubs, were capable of the management responsibilities assigned to them.

PATC
Club

Appalachian Trail
Corridor Monitoring Report
(See instructions on reverse)

Please check the box if you found:

Unsightly garbage or litter on the property.	Evidence of trespass or other misuse of the property.	Violations of the special restrictions and terms of the deed. (If any restrictions apply)	Evidence of development on or near the property that could have an adverse effect on the Trail.	Evidence of damage to the property from natural causes such as insects, disease or fire.	Tracts Inspected Tract Number (List in numerical sequence. Note if easement.)	Acreage
☐	☐	☐	☐	☐ Trees down	419-02	11.08
☐	☐	☐	☐	☒	419-03	64.94
☐	☐	☐	☐	☐	419-16	34.65
☐	☐	☐	☐	☐	419-20	26.35
☐	☐	☐	☐	☐	419-21 (part)	1.33
☐	☐	☐	☐	☒	419-23 "	33.50
☐	☐	☐	☐	☐	419-25 "	23.02
☐	☐	☐	☐	☐	419-35 "	52.10

For each box that has been checked, please describe, using additional sheets, photos, xerox maps or sketches if necessary. Please specify tract number: _____

1. On March 30, 1995, Marie Grenan and I inspected our corridor boundaries counter-clockwise, from Survey Marker 12, on VA Route 725, around the external perimeters of Tracts 419-25, 419-23, 419-03, 419-02 and 419-16, to Survey Marker 27

2. Our progress was very slow between Markers 6 and 4, and between Marker 3 and 1, because of numerous major deadfalls and tangled vines that now totally block the boundaries.

3. There are no blazes between Survey Markers 52 and 53, on the north boundary of Tract 419-20

Follow-up needed (recommendations for clean-up/survey/road closure/structures removal, etc.):

4. Items 2 and 3 have both been reported to Don King, Appalachian Trail Land Aquisition Office.

5. No encroachments were observed. We will complete our inspection of Tracts 419-20, 419-23 and 419-25 later in April 1996, in connection with spring maintenance of this section of the Appalachian Trail.

Recommend follow-up action by: ☒ Corridor Monitor Coordinator ☐ Club ☐ ATC ☐ Other _____

Date(s) of Inspection: 3/30/95

Name and Address of Monitor: Phil Barringer, 4609 38th St NW, Washington DC 20016

Telephone: (703) 695-6386 (W)

Signature of Monitor: Phil Barringer   Date: 4/5/96

Please list the total number of hours spent monitoring: 5 x 2 persons = 10
3 x 2 persons = 6 driving hours

PLEASE SEND TO.........
BOB BUTT, SUPERVISOR OF CORRIDOR MANAGEMENT
POTOMAC APPALACHIAN TRAIL CLUB
118 PARK STREET S.E.
VIENNA, VA 22180

Corridor Monitoring Report.

In order to get a handle on this formidable bit of real estate, the ATC developed a computer-based program called TREAD (Trail and REsource Applied Database). A computer was purchased for the specific purpose of land management, and a computer specialist employed. One of the computer specialists, Peter Sucsy, wrote an article published in the *AT Register,* December, 1992, informing the readers of the 11 types of information to be included for each tract of land for which the ATC had assumed responsibility. In the preceding chapter, there is a printed monthly report on land acquisitions. If those acquisitions are completed as planned, the ATC will eventually monitor some 110,000 acres of land involving 2,495 tracts of land. (As of June, 1996, the level of Congressional appropriations for land acquisition would indicate that the land acquisition work required to complete the Trail project will not be finished in the foreseeable future.)

CORRIDOR MONITORS

For years, the exploits of the Trail maintainers have been written about, and that is as it should be. However, precious little has been written about a new army of Trail workers, the corridor monitors. Trail maintainers work along a cleared, marked trail. The corridor monitors work with maps, compass, and legal descriptions. Their route is indeed identified by paint blazes, which they have painted and are expected to renew as needed, but there is no cleared trail as such and undergrowth grows rapidly between inspections. In their inspections, the corridor monitors must look for improper uses of the Trail land—dumping of garbage, logging, and similar items.

In 1990 and again in 1993, I stopped in New York to visit a friend, Neil Santos, living in Hopewell Junction, New York, not too far north of New York City. We discussed his job as a corridor monitor at some length, and he showed me one of his reports. Copies of these reports are routed to the ATC in Harpers Ferry and the information is recorded in the database. The Protection Progress Report described previously shows that the National Park Service has purchased 2,338 tracts of land, and there should be a computer record of each of those tracts in the Harpers Ferry office.

Neil makes two trips each year to cover the boundaries of the 1,000-foot Trail corridor in his area. In 1990, he was repainting the original red boundary markers with yellow paint, an extremely demanding job. Whereas the Trail maintainers are only responsible for blazing and clearing a four-foot-wide swath, the corridor monitors must tend to the other 996 feet in the 1000-foot corridor. Corridor monitors have no trail to follow, but must use a map and compass to go from one boundary marker to another, checking for timber theft, trash dumping, and even the presence of squatters along the way.

In order to get a little better feel for the corridor management program as a whole, I also visited Robert Butt of Purcellville, Virginia, some 20 miles from the ATC headquarters at Harpers Ferry. Bob is the corridor manager for the PATC and he is responsible for monitoring activities over a 140-mile stretch of the Trail, extending north from the northern boundary of Shenandoah National Park in Virginia, through a small area of West Virginia, and ending in southern Pennsylvania. He deals with some 25 to 40 corridor monitors who patrol some 5,600 acres of land purchased by the National Park Service. He emphasizes to his corridor monitors the importance of establishing good relationships with our neighbors—those people whose properties border those acquired by the National Park Service. He informed me that in some cases these neighbors of ours have telephoned the corridor monitors to tell them of improper activities observed in the government-acquired land. An excellent example of good public relations.

The corridor management work performed by the corridor monitors has proven satisfactory. I draw this conclusion because, in February, 1994, Bruce Babbitt, the Secretary of the Interior, renewed the delegation of land management for another 10-year period. The agreement was signed this time by Margaret Drummond, then chair of the ATC.

13

Miscellany and Concluding Thoughts

These last few pages are devoted to items or activities that do not readily fit within the preceding chapters. I start out with a short biography of Benton MacKaye, the person who dreamed about an Appalachian Trail, wrote an article about it, then crusaded for it the rest of his life. Among other things, I discuss the origins of the Trail Conference, and the ATC today, some 70 years later; and I finish with a description of the general membership meeting of 1,003 people at Harrisonburg, Virginia, July 1–7, 1995.

BENTON MACKAYE

Benton MacKaye was born March 6, 1879, and died December 11, 1975, at the age of 96. He was a fabulous gentleman who had a wide circle of friends from many walks of life with whom he kept in constant touch by mail and phone. I had begun corresponding with him in 1967, and in May 1969 my wife and I drove to Shirley Center, Massachusetts, to pay him a visit. This, the first of several meetings I would have with him over the next few years, was an occasion to get acquainted. We spoke generally about the history and development of the Trail and quickly established a strong rapport.

When my retirement was imminent, I wrote Ben, telling him of my plans to hike the trail he helped bring about:

Nov. 26, 1969

Mr. Benton MacKaye
Shirley Center, Mass.

Dear Ben:

I am getting poor on my correspondence. Received your letter of July 18 from Windsor. Hope you saw the Francises during the summer. I haven't seen Harry Francis lately but have plans to do so soon. I heard from a couple of sources that you were quite ill during the summer but that you were O.K. now and back at Shirley Center.

My life has changed rather drastically during the past six weeks. On Oct. 22 Pres. Nixon signed a liberalized and very attractive retirement bill for Federal Employees. That action coupled with a few other considerations prompted me to take advantage of the new law. Among other things the law provided a 5% bonus to those who retired on or before Oct. 31. Thus it happened that Oct. 31 became my last day of duty. That was on Fri. Then the next two days I attended the annual meeting of the . . . ATC Board of Managers here in Washington . . . and the following day . . . Nov. 3 I attended the first meeting of the National Scenic Trails Appalachian Advisory Comm. held in the Interior penthouse and chaired by Bob Moore of Interior. Stan Murray was named vice chairman and an executive comm. was appointed of which I was fortunate to be selected.

I am now slowly grinding away on about 35–40 home projects and getting ready for some adventure that I had not planned at this stage of my life. In late Feb. or early March my wife and I plan to drive to Mobile, Ala. to see the famous Bellingrath Gardens . . . return in leisurely fashion thru Florida. This trip to take about 2 weeks. We will also probably take an Easter week trip to Fla. with our 11 year old Kevin. Then on March 30 or 31 I will leave for Springer Mtn. Georgia, to begin a 5 month hike of the AT from Ga. to Katahdin! I think I am in shape to do it right now. On Mon. morning of this week I drove to the Old Rag area of Shen. Nat. Park . . . hiked up by various trails to StoneyMan and Hawksbill, slept overnight at Hawksbill lean-to and hiked back by other trails on Tues. Carried a 33 lb. pack and hiked 30 miles in 2 days. Felt fine.

I journeyed up to Maine in late Aug. and early Sept. . . . hiked with party of 6 the last 60 miles of the AT in Maine, then climbed Katahdin over the KnifeEdge and down the other side. Had delightful weather and excellent swimming in those beautiful Maine lakes.

Oh yes . . . my 5 month hike on the AT will be interrupted for a week in late May to attend the tri-annual ATC conference meeting at Shippensburg Pa. State College. We are expecting as many as 600 people at this one. It is centrally located...the meeting dates coincide with a 3 day holiday (Memorial Day) and we now have over 4000 Class D (Individual) members of the Conference.

I am enclosing 3 prints taken when Mary and I were at your place in May . . . prints never seem to be as good as the slides. Lucy is very photogenic.

So much for now . . . our best to you and Lucy.

Ed Garvey

Here was his response:

Shirley Center, Mass. 01465
December 3, 1969

Dear Ed:

Your letter of Nov. 26 has come and glad I am to hear from you after a somewhat upset summer. My visit in Cornish N.H. was spent in bed followed by some weeks in a nursing home; but now I'm "back to normalcy" once more in Lucy's precious care. Thanks for the photos of herself and of me. While at Cornish I received a good visit from Sharon and Harry Francis and their young Christopher. As you must know, they have a farm in Charlestown, N.H., only a few miles south of Cornish.

I note that you say that your life has changed "drastically" and that October 1 was "your last day on duty." I gather from this that you have retired from official chores, and so here's to you with three rousing cheers and a welcome to the Elder Statesmen's Club!

I note too your recent and prospective activities. Especially with the A.T. Advisory Council. I'm glad indeed that you are on its "executive comm." and that Stan Murray is Vice Chairman.

Your prospective travels sound interesting, especially your A.T. jaunt next spring and summer, with the A.T.C. meeting in the middle.

Meanwhile I'll be staying "put," either here or in Cornish. I'm busy following various projects, especially two: a Range and a River—a path on the Appalachian Range and a cleanup on the Nashua River. I am one of the incorporators of the newly formed N.R.W.A (Nashua River Watershed Association).

So much for now. Kind remembrances to your nice Lady.

Yours—

Ben

Our letter writing and consequent friendship came about in the following way. Early in 1966, the Department of the Interior announced its highest departmental awards to nine individuals and two organizations for efforts in the conservation of natural resources. Benton MacKaye was one of those named. Shortly after this, I realized the ATC had never bestowed an honorary lifetime membership upon the very man who, 40 years earlier, had been responsible for creating the Trail and the organization itself. I proposed his name to the Conference Board of Managers, and its Executive Committee promptly approved.

Author and Benton MacKaye at Shirley Center, Massachusetts.

The announcement of Honorary Lifetime Membership was made in *Trailway News*, September, 1966. At the 1967 general meeting of the Conference, I was asked to prepare, and then to read to the membership, a citation for Benton MacKaye. At one time I thought the citation had been lost but I later found it— handwritten on the back of the hotel stationery where the Conference was held. It reads as follows:

> In recognition of his foresight in conceiving, writing, and planning for an extensive foot trail which would follow, generally, the crest of our eastern mountain range from Maine to Georgia; for his contributions in other fields such as participation in formation of the Wilderness Society; for his conception and writing on 'townless highways,' the forerunners of our interstate highway system; for these and many other accomplishments, the Appalachian Trail Conference confers honorary membership upon Benton MacKaye of Shirley Center, Massachusetts.

On June 4, 1967, Mr. MacKaye wrote me acknowledging the award and extending his thanks to the conference for the honor bestowed. He also furnished "A MEMORANDUM to the Appalachian Trail Conference," in which he provided many priceless details of the "prenatal" years of the conference.

At the time of his death, the Wilderness Society, another organization he helped to organize in 1935, devoted almost an entire issue of its quarterly magazine (*The Living Wilderness*, January-March, 1976) to MacKaye's life and his accomplishments. The ATC was much more modest in its *Trailway News*. The Trail was especially dear to his heart, and yet it seemed that the ATC was less appreciative of his contribution and held him in less esteem than did the Wilderness Society.

No description of MacKaye's final years would be complete without mentioning his next door neighbors, the Johnson family, who took ever-increasing care of him. Almost totally blind in his last years, he gratefully accepted the services of a battery of neighbors to perform his secretarial chores. In the very last years, it was Mrs. Lucy Johnson who acted not only as housekeeper, cook, and guardian, but also as his eyes, reading mail and publications for him, and frequently, along with other neighbors, writing letters for him. It came to be that visitors to Shirley Center looked forward to visiting not just one person but two: Benton MacKaye and Lucy Johnson, two wonderful people.

THE GOOD SAMARITANS OF THE APPALACHIAN TRAIL

Over the years there have been hundreds of people up and down the Trail who have performed heartwarming acts for those hiking the Trail, expecting nothing in return. The following list is a mere sample of a much larger group of people from Georgia to Maine who have lent a helping hand to Trail hikers. Many of them provide transportation, while others provide lodging. Here are just a few of the many:

Sam Waddle, Chuckey, Tennessee

Sam has more or less adopted Jerry Cabin. He acts as trail maintainer in the shelter area and has made the shelter a homey place by installing a "telephone" (there is no telephone line in the vicinity), and by bringing in food and sweets to the shelter occupants. One hiker, the recipient of Sam's largess, installed a hardwood, stained, and polished toilet seat in the open air, outside toilet.

The Methodist Church, Damascus, Virginia

In 1976, the church made available for hikers' use a large two-story frame building at the rear of the church property. During Appalachian Trail Days in May of each year, the church and surrounding lawn area are occupied by as many as 50 to 60 people sleeping inside or outside in tents. The now popular name for the building is simply, The Place. Since its opening, 35,000 hikers have stayed there.

Charles and Alice Trivett, Damascus, Virginia

From the day of the opening of The Place, Charlie Trivett has been the conscientious custodian. During the first year of operation, Mrs. Trivett prepared a dinner for each hiker. Charlie collected all monies deposited in the collection box, and after a dozen years of operation, $6,000 had been collected—enough to make major renovations.

Tillie Wood, Roswell, Georgia

For years, Tillie and her late husband, Roy, lived in a spacious old home near Pearisburg, Virginia, which they called Woodshole. Tillie now lives in Roswell, but each summer she returns to Woodshole to open up both the residence and the large building close by, which she runs as a hostel for Trail hikers. She charges a nominal sum for both sleeping quarters and breakfast and all proceeds are donated to the ATC.

Dorothy Mauldin, Marietta, Georgia

Badly injured in an accident years ago, Dorothy is forced to use two crutches to navigate, but she is able to drive, and drive she does, up and down the Trail giving help to anyone needing it. In 1993, and again in 1995, she set up shop in the Daicey Pond Campground area, just seven miles south of the northern terminus of the Trail at Katahdin. For a 10-day period in late summer, she cooked meals for those preparing to hike the last leg of their long journey from Georgia.

The Graymoor Monastery

Beginning in about 1975, the monastery, situated near NY 9 in southern New York, provided a night's lodging, hot showers, dinner, and breakfast for those hiking the Trail. Graymoor informed the ATC in 1995 that, due to shortage of personnel, the monastery was being forced to discontinue the arrangement; but thanks to help from ALDHA and the NY-NJ Trail Conference, Graymoor has reopened its doors to thru-hikers. During its first 20-year span, several thousand hikers received the benefit of the gracious Graymoor hospitality.

Clara Cassidy, Harpers Ferry, West Virginia

In the early 70s, Clara, who was born in 1902, began a 20-year period of helping long-distance hikers. She offered lodging in her house and made her yard available for tent camping, and she provided breakfasts featuring silver dollar gooseberry pancakes with fresh currants. Still living in Harpers Ferry at age 95, she maintains her interest in the Trail and often hears from those hikers she helped out years ago.

OTHER 2,000-MILERS

As of 1995, there were approximately 3,000 people who had hiked the entire Trail. For each of these 3,000 hikers, there were some special days or experiences that would make for interesting reading. In condensed form, I will describe a few of them that intrigued me.

Amy Robbins of Tulsa, Oklahoma
1993

I first met Amy in mid-October of 1993, at the annual meeting of ALDHA, the Appalachian Long Distance Hikers Association, held at the Pipestem State Park in West Virginia. Amy had finished her Trail hike on September 30, seven months after she began in Georgia, and she and her husband, Steve, were headed home, with a two day detour for the ALDHA meeting. I had a chance to talk to them briefly before they returned to their motel, and we agreed to get together for a talk the next day. Our meeting never took place; upon reaching their motel, they called home to Tulsa only to learn that Amy's brother had died rather suddenly. They quickly left for home. Later she wrote me at length about her hike and the situation at home that resulted in the hike.

Amy had experienced a familiar life—high school, college, marriage, childbearing (two boys)—but during her high school days, she had visited in the east and had hiked a bit on the Trail in the Shenandoah National Park. The 2,000-mile dream was born!

As the years passed, a string of setbacks, serious illnesses, and tragic deaths in her family had caused a great deal of stress and sadness in Amy's life—so much so that by 1993 Amy was becoming ill. Among other things, she had gained 50 pounds. Her husband was aware of her situation and he remembered that long-held dream of hers to hike the Trail. He drove her down to the southern terminus of the Trail, put her on the Trail, kissed her goodbye with a "go get healthy" piece of advice and she was on her way. He met her seven times during the long hike, frequently bringing the two boys with him.

In addition to the physical enjoyment of hiking in God's great outdoors, the hike gave Amy the opportunity to shake off the strain and stress of life. I quote one of her paragraphs near the end of her letter:

"If the Trail teaches anything, it is to take each day a step at a time. Do what needs to be done to meet the challenge at hand and enjoy whatever is given to you for that moment. Thru-hikers are often described as having a 'hardened' look, but I tend to think of it more as a sereneness and an accepting attitude. Just as the Trail went on, so does life—on this earth and beyond."

Dale MacMillan
1973–1975

In the spring of 1973, Dale, a young man of 18 years, accompanied by his mother, Elizabeth, visited my home to obtain counseling on his planned hike of the Trail. He had read my book, *Appalachian Hiker*, and had questions on certain items. Dale was planning to hike the Trail in the summer of 1973 and hoped to complete it by Christmas.

Owing to high school graduation exercises, he got a late start and did not begin hiking until July 26. He made good time and reached Damascus, Virginia, on Labor Day. As he was leaving the town, he was attacked by a dog, causing him to fall down. Unknown to him, he had cracked three bones in his arm; he thought he had merely sprained his elbow and continued hiking. The pain never went away, so in Pearisburg, Virginia, some 163 miles further north, he left the Trail for home. He was back on the Trail by early October.

On November 10, his mother met him in Shenandoah National Park, where he exchanged his summer clothes for winter items, including long pants, double sleeping bag, down jacket, snow shoes, crampons. His pack, with all of the winter gear included, weighed about 80 pounds, and he could average only about seven miles per day. He usually wore snow shoes, switching to crampons in icy areas.

He reached Greymoor Monastery in New York a few days before Christmas. He hitched a ride south to spend the holidays at home, then returned to Greymoor Monastery the first week in January, 1974. He would meet only seven backpackers in the next 700 miles! His coldest night was minus 31 degrees at Rangeley, Maine. His one big worry in Maine was the Kennebec River (no bridge). Fortunately, he met some weekenders who happened to know two canoe-racing brothers; schedules were worked out and when he reached the Kennebec (with eight feet of snow on the banks), he found the two brothers there right on time!

Most of his drinking water was snow, which he scooped up in the basket of his ski pole as he walked along the Trail, but he had to be very careful or his tongue would get stuck on the metal pole. To rest, he would sit down where there was a rock behind him to support the pack. He was careful to put his gloves down on the seat for insulation. On one occasion, he forgot to put his gloves down first. The result was that his body heat caused melting, then refreezing, so that it took him five minutes to free himself. He left a perfect pattern of green corduroy nap still attached to the rock.

The days were getting longer by the first week in April and there was some snow melt. He approached a steep ravine and judged that he could cross it without putting on the crampons. Wrong! He slid down the embankment, snapping off the lower one-third of his pack. Attempts to repair it proved futile.

About that time, he met a Maine warden who told him that Baxter State Park was closed until May, no exceptions. At that point, he had hiked 1,900 miles, but the sign said "Go Home," which he did. In late August, 1975, he returned to Maine, beginning his hike some 200 miles from Katahdin. He rehiked 100 miles of the Trail because "I wanted to see what had been under some of that snow and ice that I had walked over." He met a fellow Georgia-to-Maine hiker at Katahdin Stream campground whose nickname was Chip, which naturally resulted in "Chip and Dale!" The overcast skies cleared as they approached Baxter Peak, and they spent an hour drinking in the various views and eating all sort of odds-n-ends trail food, then headed back to the campground.

For Dale, the hike led to a career. In the ensuing years he accepted a number of jobs, both volunteer and temporary, eventually landing a full time job with the Natchez Trace Parkway. He now works at the Buffalo National River.

Elizabeth MacMillan
1979–1980, Entire Trail
1991, 1,800 miles of the Trail

Having assisted her son Dale in his successful hike of the entire Trail, Elizabeth MacMillan decided that when she retired she, too, would make the attempt. She had never done any serious hiking, and found it difficult to hike even one mile when she began her training. On April 23, 1979, she started her hike at Springer Mountain when she was 63 years old. The hike went well, but as she neared Erwin, Tennessee, she had a serious fall and required 10 stitches on her face. When she reached Greylock, Massachusetts, on September 15, she was met by her son Dale, and they drove to Baxter State Park in Maine to climb Katahdin together. Her son left her then and she kept hiking south until reaching Rangeley, Maine. At that point, there was an eight-day delay caused by a bad snowstorm. She and a fellow hiker tried to continue their hike, but the snow was too deep for them. Her son drove to Gorham, New Hampshire, picked her up, and drove her home to northern Virginia.

In July 1980, she returned to Rangeley, Maine, and continued her hike south to finish the entire Trail on September 5, 1980. She had hiked alone most of the time and had lost 20 pounds. She firmly maintained that it was the people she met along the Trail that made the hike so special. She was a 2,000-Miler, but she was not through hiking just yet.

In 1991, at the age of 75, she and a friend began hiking at Springer Mountain in Georgia. Her friend had to drop out for health reasons, so Elizabeth continued on alone. She got as far north as Boiling Springs in Pennsylvania, where she left the Trail to join her son and daughter-in-law to climb Katahdin. Afterwards she continued south by herself. Hurricane Bob and heavy rains forced her to skip parts of Maine, and she wound up at Boiling Springs. She had hiked 1800 miles at age 75, much of it alone. So ends the impressive tale of the Trail hikes by the MacMillans—mother and son!

Edna W. Williams
1979–1987

Edna began her hike at Katahdin Stream Campground on June 15, 1979. Eight years and three broken bones later, she finished at age 71 at Fulling Mill Mountain in Maine on August 30, 1987.

A widow and mother of a crippled daughter, Edna owned and operated a floral shop in the Melrose, Florida, area. The daughter died in 1982, and Edna began to spread her wings a bit, becoming active in both hiking and biking. Hiking seemed to present the greater challenge, and on June 14, 1979, she spent the night at Katahdin Stream Campground in Maine, ready to hike the 2,000-mile Appalachian Trail. The next day, she hiked from the campground to Baxter Peak, the northernmost point of the Trail. The next day, she began hiking south. She hiked steadily, and on August 19, she had gone some 272 miles. Within six miles of the Maine-New Hampshire border, on Fulling Mill Mountain, she fell and broke her leg in two places. There was not much she could do but crawl into her sleeping bag. The next morning, a couple hiking south found her. The wife stayed with Edna while the man walked 14 miles down the mountain for help. A rescue team of some 15 people was able to get her to a hospital. Eventually she returned to her home in Florida to recuperate.

One year later, she was back in Maine. It was the month of May, the day after Mother's Day, and on her first day of hiking, she suffered another fall and broke the same leg. Back to Florida for more months of recuperation.

Having had enough of Fulling Mill Mountain, Edna began her 1981 hiking at the southern terminus at Springer Mountain, Georgia. Her abbreviated itinerary for the next seven years follows:

1981—Springer Mountain, Georgia, to Clingmans Dome on the North Carolina-Tennessee border, the highest point on the Trail at 6,643 feet.

1982—Clingmans Dome to Unaka Mountain, Tennessee (Broke leg a third time!)

1983—Unaka Mountain to Damascus, Virginia
1984—Damascus to Troutville, Virginia
1985—Troutville to Loft Mountain, Shenandoah National Park
1986—Loft Mountain to Culver Gap, New Jersey
1987—Culver Gap to Fulling Mill Mountain, Maine

On August 30, 1987, Edna completed her seven-year quest to hike the entire Trail. She exited from the Trail via the Mahoosuc Notch Trail and on to Gorham, New Hampshire, and then home. The medical expenses involved in the three leg-breaking episodes came to approximately $19,000. No, she did not have medical insurance of any kind.

So much for the characterization of women as "the weaker sex!"

Jean W. Feldman
1988–1995

What started out as a thru-hike on March 30, 1988, ended eight years later at the Katahdin Stream Campground. Ms. Feldman was age 76 when she finished the hike on August 25, 1995. What happened during those eight years has been described in a five-page, single space, narrow margin, typewritten story that boggles the mind. Whereas Edna Williams coped with broken legs, Ms. Feldman seemed to have troubles with ankles—right and left ankles, no favorite, sometimes sprained, sometimes broken. She finished up with two plates and seven pins in her right ankle. The important thing, she writes, "is that the ankle works as well as ever!"

In 1989, she hiked only two days before breaking her ankle. On another occasion she and her husband were to rendezvous at a certain Pittsfield Road in Massachusetts. For four hours each of them waited in vain for the other to appear. Turned out that there were two roads by that name; Jean and her husband had been waiting for each other 10 miles apart. A local Trail Angel known as the Cookie Lady entered the picture and straightened things out. They were told that they would understand the situation much better if they lived there!

On another occasion, Jean set up her tent near a seldom-used road. After she was bedded down for the night, three carloads of noisy and apparently drunken people arrived and caroused until almost daybreak. Jean huddled in her tent hoping that no one would discover her. They didn't.

Ms. Feldman finishes her five-page recital with the following message:

"My Trail name is Jeannie Appleseed. I am a native of Ohio and grew up on the stories of Johnnie Appleseed. I feel he was the first hiker, first botanist, first environmentalist, and first individualist."

TRIALS AND TRIBULATIONS OF WRITING THIS BOOK

Most of the writing of this book was done in the year following my 1990 hike. The fairly easy part was Chapter 2— the day-to-day experiences which I could take almost directly from my diary. By the way, I highly recommend to those planning to hike the entire Trail, or even lengthy parts of it, that they keep a diary. It allows one to relive some very pleasant experiences, and even some that were not so pleasant, such as bad falls, getting soaked to the skin in a sudden rain, or, as happened to me, sleeping out covered only by leaves when I became separated from my pack and the Trail shelter on one occasion. Still, with or without a diary, book writing is hard work, a type of work that can easily be put off until another day. In addition to my laziness on the writing, my health began to fail. Here is an excerpt from a letter I wrote on August 24, 1992, to a young thru-hiking couple I met in 1990:

"My hiking days are over—really hurts me as I had great hopes to return to that lake country of Maine one more time. In November, 1991, my heart began acting up. I get out of breath within a hundred yards and get a tightness in the chest. I must walk slowly and take nitroglycerine pills! A heluva situation for a person who loves to walk briskly and for long distances! I quote a close friend who said, 'Ed, we've reached the point in life where we must be content with our memories, and I must say you've had more than your share!'"

Less than three months later, I was admitted to the emergency room of the hospital at 3 A.M. Tests showed I had a 96-percent blockage in my coronary arteries. I had heart surgery on November 21, 1992. The heart recovered satisfactorily, but the long period of being under anesthetic raised hob with my short term memory—a fairly common result.

But now it is 1995 and, with much help from my daughter Sharon, I plan to finish the manuscript and get it into the hands of Victoria Logue, the editor for the publisher—Menasha Ridge Press.

Thanks to the heart surgery, I've been granted a reprieve from the sedentary life I had foreseen. Within a couple months after the surgery, I was back walking and, nearly three years later, I continue to walk an average of five miles a day on the nearby Washington & Old Dominion Hiker-Biker Trail. This summer I plan to do some walking and hiking in Slovenia, despite the fact that my right knee, injured in a fall on Hay Mountain in Maine during my 1990 hike has continued to trouble me. My orthopedist has given me two choices: (1) live with the knee I have, or (2) have a new knee installed, which will involve five days in a hospital and three months of rehabilitation! My present inclination is to live with the knee I have unless the pain becomes more intense. Other than the knee and memory problems, I suffer from some of the same inconveniences that other 80-year-olds experience—hearing loss, occasional dizzy spells, and a reluctance to drive automobiles at night. I am certain that older readers of this book will recognize and sympathize with these problems.

Regular walking has become a way of life for me, both before and after the heart surgery. Within reason, I perform all errands by foot rather than by car. One man who finished hiking the Trail in 1963 was Dr. Frederick W. Luehring, who was 82 years old when he finished. Dr. Luehring had a tremendous career as an athlete, and later as director of athletic institutions. He played on the football teams of the famous years of the University of Chicago back in the 1915-1916 era when the forward pass was just being introduced. He was athletic director at the University of Minnesota in the '20s and '30s, when Bronko Nagurski was charging up and down the gridiron. And, he was on the Olympic swimming committee that developed rules for international competition in that activity. I was flattered when he and two companions drove down from Pennsylvania and New Jersey to attend my slide show in Washington, D.C. on my 1970 hike of the Trail. Conversing with me on another occasion, Dr. Luehring emphasized the value of daily walking, and, speaking of himself, he said, "Ed, I walk to live; I walk to live." He followed his own advice and lived to be 99$^1/_2$ years old.

CONCLUSION

The Appalachian Trail as it exists in 1997, and, hopefully, will always exist, consists of 2,100-plus miles of a beautiful, forested and flowered mountain area. Its beauty is accentuated in the spring and autumn, but it has its charms in any season of the year. It is within a day's drive of some 60 million people, and the Trail can be entered and exited from a myriad of points either by car or common carrier.

General administration of the Trail is performed by a non-profit organization, the Appalachian Trail Conference, Box 525, Harpers Ferry, West Virginia, 25425. The conference has some 26 paid employees at Harpers Ferry and a few additional employees at four regional offices at various towns along the Trail. The ATC will provide information as to maps and publications. Anyone interested in the Trail may join the conference. Annual dues in 1996 were $25. The actual work of maintaining the Trail and monitoring the 100-foot-wide corridor is the responsibility of 33 hiking clubs located from Maine to Georgia. The ATC will provide the names and addresses of these clubs upon request. The conference also publishes five times per year a magazine named *Appalachian Trailway News,* which is full of interesting and helpful information for those hiking the Trail. ATC members receive the magazine free of charge. Those wishing to obtain just the magazine may do so at a cost of $15 per year. Those contemplating a long hike on the Trail are advised to read the magazine to get a feel for this 2,100-mile Trail.

Every two years, the ATC conducts a general membership meeting at one of the 14 states through which the Trail runs. In recent years, attendance at these meetings has ranged from 1,200 to 1,500 people, making it the largest assembly of hikers in the country. In 1995, the meeting was held at James Madison University in Harrisonburg, Virginia, and hosted by the PATC of Washington,

ATC in Harpers Ferry, WV.

D.C. The meeting was held during the first week of July and the attendance was 1,292. In essence, these meetings provide a forum for the 27 members of the Board of Managers to report to the membership the progress made during the two-year period that just ended, and to discuss plans for the future. I have attended each of these meetings since 1961. All of them are good, and this one, along with a number of others I have attended, was outstanding. I came away from the meeting with the strong feeling that the affairs of the hiking public were in excellent hands and that, with just a little help from the U.S. Congress, we can acquire the remaining 40 miles of the Trail.

Edward Bohan Garvey
1914–1999

Ed Garvey died on September 20, 1999. He remained active right up until the end of his life, continuing to garden, chop wood for his evening fires, and care for his home. Always gregarious, he enjoyed his family, friends and neighbors, managing to stay in touch with old friends even while he continued to make new ones. He kept abreast of developments concerning the trail, especially land acquisition, and maintained a wide correspondence. Although he had had to give up mountain hiking, he daily walked to Mass and did a three-mile course along a local paved trail. On September 19, he went for his usual morning walk but took ill afterwards from what turned out to be congestive heart failure. He died the following day with his family around him.

A

Appendix

APPALACHIAN TRAIL MAINTAINING CLUBS
(In order of trail sections - South to North)

Georgia Appalachian Trail Club
P.O. Box 654
Atlanta Georgia 30301

Nantahala Hiking Club
173 Carl Slagle Road
Franklin, NC 28734

Smoky Mountains Hiking Club
P.O. Box 1454
Knoxville, TN 37901

Carolina Mountain Club
P.O. Box 68
Asheville, NC 28802

Tennessee Eastman Hiking Club
P.O. Box 511
Kingsport, TN 37662

**Mount Rogers
Appalachian Trail Club**
24198 Greenspring Road
Abingdon, VA 24211

**Piedmont
Appalachian Trail Hikers**
P.O. Box 4423
Greensboro, NC 27404

Virginia Tech Outing Club
P.O. Box 538
Blacksburg, VA 24060

Roanoke Appalachian Trail Club
P.O. Box 12282
Roanoke, VA 24024

**Natural Bridge
Appalachian Trail Club**
P.O. Box 3012
Lynchburg, VA 24503

Tidewater Appalachian Trail Club
P.O. Box 8246
Norfolk, VA 23503

**Old Dominion
Appalachian Trail Club**
P.O. Box 25283
Richmond, VA 23260

Potomac Appalachian Trail Club
118 Park Street SE
Vienna, VA 22180

Keystone Trails Association
Trail Care Chairman
P.O. Box 251
Cogan Station, PA 17728

The KTA is a blanket association representing the following clubs that help maintain the A.T. in Pennsylvania:
- Mountain Club of Maryland
- Cumberland Valley A.T. Management Association
- York Hiking Club
- Susquehanna Appalachian Trail Club
- Brandywine Valley Outing Club
- Allentown Hiking Club
- Blue Mountain Eagle Climbing Club
- Philadelphia Trail Club
- Appalachian Mountain Club, Delaware Valley Chapter
- Batona Hiking Club
- Wilmington Trail Club

New York-New Jersey Trail Conference
232 Madison Avenue, Room 401
New York, NY 10016

Appalachian Mountain Club-Berkshire Chapter
P.O. Box 9369
North Amherst, MA 01059

Appalachian Mountain Club, Connecticut Chapter
472 Burlington Avenue
Bristol, CT 06010

Green Mountain Club
4711 Waterbury-Stowe Road
Waterbury Center, VT 05677

Dartmouth Outing Club
c/o Outdoor Programs Office
119 Robinson Hall
Dartmouth College
Hanover, NH 03755

Appalachian Mountain Club
5 Joy Street
Boston, MA 02108

Maine Appalachian Trail Club
P.O. Box 283
Augusta, ME 04332

B

Appendix

HONORARY MEMBERS OF THE APPALACHIAN TRAIL CONFERENCE

Article 1, Sec. 3 of the ATC Constitution as revised provides for a special category of Honorary Members. The Constitutional language is: "Upon recommendation of the Executive Committee, honorary membership may be conferred by the Board of Managers at a regular meeting of the Conference on an individual who has made a distinguished contribution to the Appalachian Trail project." In the 70 year history of the Conference, only 41 memberships have been so awarded. The 41 members so honored can truly be considered as comprising the Appalachian Trail "Hall of Fame." Until the publication of my previous book, a list of the Hall of Famers had never been published; indeed, not until Lester L. Holmes, ATC Archivist, completed a several months search of old records in 1970, did we even know how many there were or who they were. At that time, both Col. Holmes and I felt that the list should be compiled and published; after that, it would be easy to maintain the list of future people selected for the honor.

The selection and awarding of the Honorary Memberships has proven to be a delicate operation. If the Conference waits too long to confer the honorary membership, intended recipients may either be dead or so advanced in years or in such poor health that they do not really appreciate the honor being bestowed. On the other hand, if the honor is conferred too early in life, the intended recipients may reason that the Conference is attempting to shove them out of the mainstream of Conference activity. On two occasions, the intended recipient has angrily refused to accept the honor for that very reason! My own feeling is that the Conference should award the honor whenever a member has met the criterion of having "made a distinguished contribution to the Appalachian Trail project," and that the conferring should take place regardless of whether the recipient is 50 years of age or 80.

I have met the recipients who received their awards in 1964 or later, and I have worked closely with many of them. The awards have been richly deserved. I would hope that the Conference would be able to locate or reconstruct these citations for each of the 41 recipients. Their "distinguished contributions to the Appalachian Trail project" have in many cases spanned periods of twenty to forty years. It would be a worthy addition to the Conference building at Harpers Ferry to have a Hall of Fame section where names, dates of award, pictures and citations of each of the Hall of Famers would be on display. (Readers will shortly discover that *my* name is among those on the list of honorary members! I wrote the above paragraph in 1971 for my book, *Appalachian Hiker*, at which time my name was *not* on the list. If I felt strongly about this issue then, you can imagine how I feel now!)

CRITERIA FOR HONORARY MEMBERSHIP
Approved by ATC Board of Managersat Poultney, Vermont
August 15, 1985

1. Nominee must have performed significant service independent of paid official duties.

2. The service performed shall have had an inspirational or exemplary effect because of its special quality/character or innovative aspects, rather than be service of conventional nature but performed in a superior manner.

3. There shall be no others having comparable qualifications who are not already honorary members or nominees themselves.

4. If the nominee's service has been mainly within a particular club, that must have had either regional implications or must bear upon the Trail as a whole, or upon the club's relationship to the Conference.

5. The service shall have been of considerable duration, demonstrating a long-term commitment to the Trail and Conference.

ATC HONORARY MEMBERS

1. Paul M. Fink
2. Frank Place
3. Harlean James
4. Marion Park
5. Frederick F. Schuetz
6. Rev. A. Rufus Morgan
7. Benton MacKaye
8. Max Sauter
9. Murray H. Stevens
10. George F. Blackburn
11. Walter Boardman
12. Sadye Giller
13. Seymour Smith
14. Thekla Stephan
15. Jean Stephenson
16. Thomas H. Campbell
17. Florence Nichol
18. Stanley A. Murray
19. Lois Shore
20. Richard Kimmel
21. Arch Nichols
22. Les Holmes
23. Robert Herbst
24. Elizabeth Levers
25. Henry Morris
26. Carl Newhall
27. Steve Clark
28. Edward B. Garvey
29. Charles Rinaldi
30. Norman A. Greist
31. David B. Field
32. Ruth E. Blackburn
33. David M. Sherman
34. Earl V. Shaffer
35. David A. Richie
36. James M. Denton
37. Thurston Griggs
38. Charles Sloan
39. Raymond Hunt
40. Dr. William Gordge
41. Collins Chew
42. Margaret Drummond

Myron H. Avery
— designated Honorary Chairman

C

Appendix

The list below shows the name of each hiker who completed the Trail from 1936 through 1970; and from 1971 through 1995 there is a recording by number of those who have performed the feat.

RECORDED APPALACHIAN TRAIL HIKERS THRU 1970

Myron H. Avery	1936	Mr. Edward N. Little	* 1959
Boy Scout Troup 256[†]	* 1936	Mr. Owen F. Allen	* 1960
Dr. George Outerbridge	1939	Mr. Lochlen L. Gregory	* 1960
Dr. Martin Kilpatrick	1939	D. Walter S. Boardman	1960
Dr. Mary Kilpatrick	1939	Mr. Herbert S. Hiler	1960
Mr. Orville Crowder	1939	Dr. Max Bende	1962
Mr. Charles Hazelhurst	1946	Dr. Frederick W. Luehring	1963
Mr. Earl V. Shaffer	* 1948	(Age 82)	
Dr. Robert Sosman	1948	Mr. James F. Fox, Jr.	1963
Mr. Carl E. Jones	1951	Mr. Paul Gehard	1963
Mr. Eugene Espy	* 1951	Mr. Chuck Ebersole	* 1964
Mr. Chester Dziengielewski	* 1951	Mr. John Ebersole	1964
Mr. Martin D. Papendick	* 1951	Mr. Ray Baker	* 1964
Mr. George F. Miller	* 1952	Mr. Garnett W. Martin	* 1964
Mr. Richard Lamb	* 1952	Mr. Richard Kuhl	* 1965
Mrs. Mildred Norman	* 1952	Mr. Norman Menger	1965
Mrs. Emma Gatewood	* 1955	Mr. Paul Macauley	* 1966
Miss Dorothy Laker	* 1957	Mr. Jim Shattuck	1966
Hon. William O. Douglas	1958	Mr. Michael Ebersole	1966
Mr. Murray S. Chism	* 1959	Mr. Leon L. Barkman	1967

[†]Troop 256 from the Bronx consisted of Mr. Max Gordon, Mr. Louis Zisk, Mr Seymour Dorfman and three other unidentified scouts.

Mr. Norman Menger	1967	Mr. Carlton B. Colquitt	1969
Mr. Clarence Boyer	1968	Mr. Edwin Bock	* 1969
Mr. Marc Boyer	1968	Mrs. Zillie Johnson	* 1969
(age13)		Mr. Branley Owen	* 1970
Mr. Howard E. Bassett	* 1968	(70 days)	
Mr. Elmer L. Onstott	* 1968	Mr. Richard A. Hudson	1970
Mrs. Nell Skinner	* 1968	Mr. Joseph Simpson	1970
Mr. Everett Skinner	* 1968	Mr. Charles Konopa	1970
Mr. Albert Field	1969	Mr. Thomas C. Herring	* 1970
Mr. Wm. O'Brien	* 1969	Mr. Edward B. Garvey	* 1970
Mr. Jeffrey Hancock	* 1969	Mrs. Margaret Smith	* 1970
Mr. Eric Ryback	* 1969	Mr. Clifford Smith	* 1970
(81 days)		Mr. Bradley Greuling	* 1970
Mr. Andrew J. Giger	1969	Mr. Paul Longway	1970

* Thru-hike

RECORDED LIST OF APPALACHIAN TRAIL HIKERS BY NUMBER
1971 through 1999[†]

1936-1970	69	1982	126	1994	236
1971	19	1983	115	1995	314
1972	35	1984	100	1996	404
1973	89	1985	124	1997	410
1974	76	1986	111	*Exceeded 4,000*	
1975	79	1987	147		
1976	103	1988	153	1998	388
1977	71	1989	203	1999	500
1978	97	*Exceeded 2,000*		*Exceeded 5,000*	
1979	129			(5,290)	
1980	161	1990	233		
1981	140	1991	204		
Exceeded 1,000		1992	222		
		1993	232		
		Exceeded 3,000			

It is interesting to note that whereas only 44 people were recorded as having hiked the entire Trail in the first 31 years of its existence as a complete Trail, another 16 people were recorded in the two years of 1969 and 1970. Beginning in 1971, the number completing the Trail each year began to increase dramatically. In 1971, the Conference appointed a committee to receive and evaluate the evidence of those who claimed to have hiked the entire Trail. But that procedure had to be discontinued in 1973 because of the tremendous increase in the number of 2,000-milers. At the present time, those who complete hiking the entire Trail are urged to notify the Conference of the year in which they complete it. In that letter of notification, the Conference would welcome a description of any unusual, out of the ordinary incident(s) that occurred during the hike. For those completing the hike, a cloth "2,000-Miler" rocker is available at a cost of $1 (members of ATC, $0.85) and a walnut plaque is available for $40 dollars (member price $35). The rocker is generally worn underneath the familiar round A..T. patch either on shirt, jacket, or pack. If you have spent four to six months and from $2,500 to $3,000 hiking the entire Trail, by all means order the patch and the plaque. Buy several of the patches and wear them. They are great conversation pieces and you may inspire others to try the long hike.

Membership Enrollment Form

To join the Appalachian Trail Conference, fill in the blanks and check the appropriate boxes below, and mail this panel with your check or credit-card information (for the amount in parentheses for your category) to the address at the bottom of the form.

Name

Address

City, State, ZIP Code

Annual Membership

❑ Individual ($25)
    ❑ Family ($30)
❑ Member of A.T. maintaining club–Individual ($18)
    ❑ Member of A.T. club–Family ($22)
Name of club: _____
❑ Senior Citizen (65 and older)–Individual ($18)
    ❑ Senior-Citizen Family ($22)
❑ Full-time Student–Individual ($18)
    ❑ Student–Family ($22)

Life Membership

   ❑ Individual ($500)   ❑ Couple ($750)

❑ I also wish to make a contribution of $ _____ .

Contributions and dues are tax-deductible in full.

Method of Payment

❑ Check or money order payable to "Appalachian Trail Conference"
❑ MasterCard ○ or Visa ○ number:

_____

Expires: ___ / ____

Signature: _____

Please send me more information on:
❑ A.T. guidebooks and maps *
❑ A.T. maintaining club nearest my address *
❑ The Trust for Appalachian Trail Lands
❑ Hiking the A.T ○ short-term ○ thru-hiking ○ this specific area:

_____

* Included in membership packet

Detach this panel and send with paymen. or charge information to: Appalachian Trail Conference, P.O. Box 807, Harpers Ferry, WV 25425-0807. Questions? Please call (304) 535-6331. The office is open 9 a.m. to 5 p.m., Eastern time, Monday–Friday, except most federal holidays.